THE RUST PROGRAMM **P** *TION*

T0073483

"*The Rust Programming Language* has always been, and continue, the first place I point anyone looking to learn Rust. It's referred to simply as "The Book," and with good reason . . . The 2nd edition is a reflection of the ongoing love for the book in the community, and ensures that it will remain a solid introduction to the best Rust has to offer for years to come."

—JON GJENGSET, AUTHOR OF *RUST FOR RUSTACEANS*

"*The Rust Programming Language*, 2nd Edition has been improved, refined, and still remains *the book* to get started with learning Rust. Whether an experienced or a new Rustacean it's an invaluable resource on how Rust works."

—MICHAEL GATTOZZI, SENIOR SOFTWARE ENGINEER AT FASTLY

"A great resource for mastering Rust's fundamentals. . . . If you're thinking about seriously learning Rust, this book is for you."

—ADAM VARTANIAN, ENGINEERING MANAGER AT CORD

"From a person who read the first edition front to back, the second edition of *The Rust Programming Language* met and exceeded my expectations! It's well-written and formatted to help introduce the reader to all the concepts of Rust. . . . [it's] an excellent addition to a programmer's personal library."

—JARED WOLFF, OWNER, CIRCUIT DOJO LLC

THE RUST PROGRAMMING LANGUAGE

2nd Edition

by Steve Klabnik and Carol Nichols,
with contributions from
the Rust Community

no starch
press®

San Francisco

Printed in the United States of America

Third printing

27 26 25 24 23   3 4 5 6 7

ISBN-13: 978-1-7185-0310-6 (print)
ISBN-13: 978-1-7185-0311-3 (ebook)

 Published by No Starch Press®, Inc.
245 8th Street, San Francisco, CA 94103
phone: +1.415.863.9900
www.nostarch.com; info@nostarch.com

Publisher: William Pollock
Managing Editor: Jill Franklin
Production Manager: Sabrina Plomitallo-González
Production Editors: Jennifer Kepler and Katrina Horlbeck Olsen
Developmental Editor: Liz Chadwick
Cover Illustration: Karen Rustad Tölva
Interior Design: Octopod Studios
Technical Reviewer: JT
Copyeditor: Audrey Doyle
Compositor: Jeff Lytle, Happenstance Type-O-Rama
Proofreader: Liz Wheeler

The Library of Congress has catalogued the first edition as follows:

Names: Klabnik, Steve, author. | Nichols, Carol, 1983- eauthor.
Title: The Rust programming language / by Steve Klabnik and Carol Nichols ; with contributions from
    the Rust Community.
Description: San Francisco : No Starch Press, Inc., 2018. | Includes index. Identifiers: LCCN
    2018014097 (print) | LCCN 2018019844 (ebook) | ISBN 9781593278519 (epub) | ISBN 1593278519 (epub)
    | ISBN 9781593278281 (paperback) | ISBN 1593278284 (paperback)
Subjects: LCSH: Rust (Computer programming language) | BISAC: COMPUTERS / Programming / Open Source.
    | COMPUTERS / Programming Languages / General. | COMPUTERS / Programming / General.
Classification: LCC QA76.73.R87 (ebook) | LCC QA76.73.R87 K53 2018 (print) | DDC 005.13/3--dc23
LC record available at https://lccn.loc.gov/2018014097

[S]

About the Authors

Steve Klabnik was the lead for the Rust documentation team and was one of Rust's core developers. A frequent speaker and a prolific open source contributor, he previously worked on projects such as Ruby and Ruby on Rails.

Carol Nichols is a member of the Rust Crates.io Team and a former member of the Rust Core Team. She's a co-founder of Integer 32, LLC, the world's first Rust-focused software consultancy. Nichols has also organized the Rust Belt Rust Conference.

About the Technical Reviewer

JT is a Rust core team member and the co-creator of the Rust error message format, Rust Language Server (RLS), and Nushell. They first started using Rust in 2011, and in 2016 joined Mozilla to work on Rust full-time, helping to shape its direction for widespread use. These days, they are a freelance Rust trainer and advocate for safe systems programming.

BRIEF CONTENTS

CONTENTS IN DETAIL

5
USING STRUCTS TO STRUCTURE RELATED DATA 85

6
ENUMS AND PATTERN MATCHING 103

7
MANAGING GROWING PROJECTS
WITH PACKAGES, CRATES, AND MODULES 119

8
COMMON COLLECTIONS

9
ERROR HANDLING

10
GENERIC TYPES, TRAITS, AND LIFETIMES

13
FUNCTIONAL LANGUAGE FEATURES: ITERATORS AND CLOSURES   273

14
MORE ABOUT CARGO AND CRATES.IO   295

15
SMART POINTERS   315

18
PATTERNS AND MATCHING
397

19
ADVANCED FEATURES
419

D
USEFUL DEVELOPMENT TOOLS

E
EDITIONS

INDEX

FOREWORD

It wasn't always so clear, but the Rust programming language is fundamentally about *empowerment*: no matter what kind of code you are writing now, Rust empowers you to reach further, to program with confidence in a wider variety of domains than you did before.

Take, for example, "systems-level" work that deals with low-level details of memory management, data representation, and concurrency. Traditionally, this realm of programming is seen as arcane, accessible to only a select few who have devoted the necessary years to learning it to avoid its infamous pitfalls. And even those who practice it do so with caution, lest their code be open to exploits, crashes, or corruption.

Rust breaks down these barriers by eliminating the old pitfalls and providing a friendly, polished set of tools to help you along the way. Programmers who need to "dip down" into lower-level control can do so with Rust, without taking on the customary risk of crashes or security holes and without having to learn the fine points of a fickle toolchain. Better yet, the language is designed to guide you naturally toward reliable code that is efficient in terms of speed and memory usage.

Programmers who are already working with low-level code can use Rust to raise their ambitions. For example, introducing parallelism in Rust is a relatively low-risk operation: the compiler will catch the classical mistakes for you. And you can tackle more aggressive optimizations in your code with the confidence that you won't accidentally introduce crashes or vulnerabilities.

But Rust isn't limited to low-level systems programming. It's expressive and ergonomic enough to make CLI apps, web servers, and many other kinds of code quite pleasant to write—you'll find simple examples later in the book. Working with Rust allows you to build skills that transfer from one domain to another; you can learn Rust by writing a web app, then apply those same skills to target your Raspberry Pi.

This book fully embraces the potential of Rust to empower its users. It's a friendly and approachable text intended to help you level up not just your knowledge of Rust, but also your reach and confidence as a programmer in general. So dive in, get ready to learn—and welcome to the Rust community!

Nicholas Matsakis and Aaron Turon

PREFACE

This version of the text assumes you're using Rust 1.62.0 (released 2022-06-30) or later with `edition="2021"` in the *Cargo.toml* file of all projects to configure them to use Rust 2021 edition idioms. See "Installation" on page 1 for instructions on installing or updating Rust, and see Appendix E for information on editions.

The 2021 edition of the Rust language includes a number of improvements that make Rust more ergonomic and that correct some inconsistencies. On top of a general update to reflect these improvements, this rendition of the book has a number of improvements to address specific feedback:

- Chapter 7 contains a new quick reference section on organizing your code into multiple files with modules.
- Chapter 13 has new and improved closure examples that more clearly illustrate captures, the `move` keyword, and the `Fn` traits.
- We fixed a number of small errors and imprecise wording throughout the book. Thank you to the readers who reported them!

Note that any code from earlier renditions of this book that compiled will continue to compile with the relevant edition in the project's *Cargo.toml*, even as you update the Rust compiler version you're using. That's Rust's backward-compatibility guarantees at work!

ACKNOWLEDGMENTS

We would like to thank everyone who has worked on the Rust language for creating an amazing language worth writing a book about. We're grateful to everyone in the Rust community for being welcoming and creating an environment worth welcoming more folks into.

We're especially thankful for everyone who read early versions of this book online and provided feedback, bug reports, and pull requests. Special thanks to Eduard-Mihai Burtescu, Alex Crichton, and JT for providing technical review, and to Karen Rustad Tölva for the cover art. Thank you to our team at No Starch, including Bill Pollock, Liz Chadwick, and Janelle Ludowise, for improving this book and bringing it to print.

Carol is grateful for the opportunity to work on this book. She thanks her family for their constant love and support, especially her husband, Jake Goulding, and her daughter, Vivian.

INTRODUCTION

 Welcome to *The Rust Programming Language,* an introductory book about Rust. The Rust programming language helps you write faster, more reliable software. High-level ergonomics and low-level control are often at odds in programming language design; Rust challenges that conflict. Through balancing powerful technical capacity and a great developer experience, Rust gives you the option to control low-level details (such as memory usage) without all the hassle traditionally associated with such control.

Who Rust Is For

Rust is ideal for many people for a variety of reasons. Let's look at a few of the most important groups.

Teams of Developers

Rust is proving to be a productive tool for collaborating among large teams of developers with varying levels of systems programming knowledge. Low-level code is prone to various subtle bugs, which in most other languages can only be caught through extensive testing and careful code review by experienced developers. In Rust, the compiler plays a gatekeeper role by refusing to compile code with these elusive bugs, including concurrency bugs. By working alongside the compiler, the team can spend their time focusing on the program's logic rather than chasing down bugs.

Rust also brings contemporary developer tools to the systems programming world:

- Cargo, the included dependency manager and build tool, makes adding, compiling, and managing dependencies painless and consistent across the Rust ecosystem.
- The rustfmt formatting tool ensures a consistent coding style across developers.
- The Rust Language Server powers integrated development environment (IDE) integration for code completion and inline error messages.

By using these and other tools in the Rust ecosystem, developers can be productive while writing systems-level code.

Students

Rust is for students and those who are interested in learning about systems concepts. Using Rust, many people have learned about topics like operating systems development. The community is very welcoming and happy to answer students' questions. Through efforts such as this book, the Rust teams want to make systems concepts more accessible to more people, especially those new to programming.

Companies

Hundreds of companies, large and small, use Rust in production for a variety of tasks, including command line tools, web services, DevOps tooling, embedded devices, audio and video analysis and transcoding, cryptocurrencies, bioinformatics, search engines, Internet of Things applications, machine learning, and even major parts of the Firefox web browser.

Open Source Developers

Rust is for people who want to build the Rust programming language, community, developer tools, and libraries. We'd love to have you contribute to the Rust language.

People Who Value Speed and Stability

Rust is for people who crave speed and stability in a language. By speed, we mean both how quickly Rust code can run and the speed at which Rust lets you write programs. The Rust compiler's checks ensure stability through feature additions and refactoring. This is in contrast to the brittle legacy code in languages without these checks, which developers are often afraid to modify. By striving for zero-cost abstractions—higher-level features that compile to lower-level code as fast as code written manually—Rust endeavors to make safe code be fast code as well.

The Rust language hopes to support many other users as well; those mentioned here are merely some of the biggest stakeholders. Overall, Rust's greatest ambition is to eliminate the trade-offs that programmers have accepted for decades by providing safety *and* productivity, speed *and* ergonomics. Give Rust a try and see if its choices work for you.

Who This Book Is For

This book assumes that you've written code in another programming language, but doesn't make any assumptions about which one. We've tried to make the material broadly accessible to those from a wide variety of programming backgrounds. We don't spend a lot of time talking about what programming *is* or how to think about it. If you're entirely new to programming, you would be better served by reading a book that specifically provides an introduction to programming.

How to Use This Book

In general, this book assumes that you're reading it in sequence from front to back. Later chapters build on concepts in earlier chapters, and earlier chapters might not delve into details on a particular topic but will revisit the topic in a later chapter.

You'll find two kinds of chapters in this book: concept chapters and project chapters. In concept chapters, you'll learn about an aspect of Rust. In project chapters, we'll build small programs together, applying what you've learned so far. Chapter 2, Chapter 12, and Chapter 20 are project chapters; the rest are concept chapters.

Chapter 1 explains how to install Rust, how to write a "Hello, world!" program, and how to use Cargo, Rust's package manager and build tool. **Chapter 2** is a hands-on introduction to writing a program in Rust, having you build up a number-guessing game. Here, we cover concepts at a high level, and later chapters will provide additional detail. If you want to get your hands dirty right away, Chapter 2 is the place for that. **Chapter 3** covers Rust features that are similar to those of other programming languages, and in **Chapter 4** you'll learn about Rust's ownership system. If you're a particularly meticulous learner who prefers to learn every detail before moving on to the next, you might want to skip Chapter 2 and go straight to Chapter 3, returning to Chapter 2 when you'd like to work on a project applying the details you've learned.

Chapter 5 discusses structs and methods, and **Chapter 6** covers enums, match expressions, and the if let control flow construct. You'll use structs and enums to make custom types in Rust.

In **Chapter 7**, you'll learn about Rust's module system and about privacy rules for organizing your code and its public application programming interface (API). **Chapter 8** discusses some common collection data structures that the standard library provides, such as vectors, strings, and hash maps. **Chapter 9** explores Rust's error-handling philosophy and techniques.

Chapter 10 digs into generics, traits, and lifetimes, which give you the power to define code that applies to multiple types. **Chapter 11** is all about testing, which even with Rust's safety guarantees is necessary to ensure your program's logic is correct. In **Chapter 12**, we'll build our own implementation of a subset of functionality from the grep command line tool that searches for text within files. For this, we'll use many of the concepts we discussed in the previous chapters.

Chapter 13 explores closures and iterators: features of Rust that come from functional programming languages. In **Chapter 14**, we'll examine Cargo in more depth and talk about best practices for sharing your libraries with others. **Chapter 15** discusses smart pointers that the standard library provides and the traits that enable their functionality.

In **Chapter 16**, we'll walk through different models of concurrent programming and talk about how Rust helps you program in multiple threads fearlessly. **Chapter 17** looks at how Rust idioms compare to object-oriented programming principles you might be familiar with.

Chapter 18 is a reference on patterns and pattern matching, which are powerful ways of expressing ideas throughout Rust programs. **Chapter 19** contains a smorgasbord of advanced topics of interest, including unsafe Rust, macros, and more about lifetimes, traits, types, functions, and closures.

In **Chapter 20**, we'll complete a project in which we'll implement a low-level multithreaded web server!

Finally, some appendixes contain useful information about the language in a more reference-like format. **Appendix A** covers Rust's keywords, **Appendix B** covers Rust's operators and symbols, **Appendix C** covers derivable traits provided by the standard library, **Appendix D** covers some useful development tools, and **Appendix E** explains Rust editions.

There is no wrong way to read this book: if you want to skip ahead, go for it! You might have to jump back to earlier chapters if you experience any confusion. But do whatever works for you.

An important part of the process of learning Rust is learning how to read the error messages the compiler displays: these will guide you toward working code. As such, we'll provide many examples that don't compile along with the error message the compiler will show you in each situation. Know that if you enter and run a random example, it may not compile! Make sure you read the surrounding text to see whether the example you're trying to run is meant to error. In most situations, we'll lead you to the correct version of any code that doesn't compile.

Resources and How to Contribute to This Book

This book is open source. If you find an error, please don't hesitate to file an issue or send a pull request on GitHub at *https://github.com/rust-lang/book*. Please see *CONTRIBUTING.md* at *https://github.com/rust-lang/book/blob/main/CONTRIBUTING.md* for more details.

The source code for the examples in this book, errata, and other information are available at *https://nostarch.com/rust-programming-language-2nd-edition*.

1

GETTING STARTED

Let's start your Rust journey! There's a lot to learn, but every journey starts somewhere. In this chapter, we'll discuss:

- Installing Rust on Linux, macOS, and Windows
- Writing a program that prints `Hello, world!`
- Using `cargo`, Rust's package manager and build system

Installation

The first step is to install Rust. We'll download Rust through rustup, a command line tool for managing Rust versions and associated tools. You'll need an internet connection for the download.

NOTE *If you prefer not to use* rustup *for some reason, please see the Other Rust Installation Methods page at* https://forge.rust-lang.org/infra/other-installation-methods .html *for more options.*

The following steps install the latest stable version of the Rust compiler. Rust's stability guarantees ensure that all the examples in the book that compile will continue to compile with newer Rust versions. The output might differ slightly between versions because Rust often improves error messages and warnings. In other words, any newer, stable version of Rust you install using these steps should work as expected with the content of this book.

COMMAND LINE NOTATION

In this chapter and throughout the book, we'll show some commands used in the terminal. Lines that you should enter in a terminal all start with $. You don't need to type the $ character; it's the command line prompt shown to indicate the start of each command. Lines that don't start with $ typically show the output of the previous command. Additionally, PowerShell-specific examples will use > rather than $.

Installing rustup on Linux or macOS

If you're using Linux or macOS, open a terminal and enter the following command:

```
$ curl --proto '=https' --tlsv1.3 https://sh.rustup.rs -sSf | sh
```

The command downloads a script and starts the installation of the rustup tool, which installs the latest stable version of Rust. You might be prompted for your password. If the install is successful, the following line will appear:

```
Rust is installed now. Great!
```

You will also need a *linker*, which is a program that Rust uses to join its compiled outputs into one file. It is likely you already have one. If you get linker errors, you should install a C compiler, which will typically include a linker. A C compiler is also useful because some common Rust packages depend on C code and will need a C compiler.

On macOS, you can get a C compiler by running:

```
$ xcode-select --install
```

Linux users should generally install GCC or Clang, according to their distribution's documentation. For example, if you use Ubuntu, you can install the build-essential package.

Installing rustup on Windows

On Windows, go to *https://www.rust-lang.org/tools/install* and follow the instructions for installing Rust. At some point in the installation, you'll receive a message explaining that you'll also need the MSVC build tools for Visual Studio 2013 or later.

To acquire the build tools, you'll need to install Visual Studio 2022 from *https://visualstudio.microsoft.com/downloads*. When asked which workloads to install, include:

- "Desktop Development with C++"
- The Windows 10 or 11 SDK
- The English language pack component, along with any other language pack of your choosing

The rest of this book uses commands that work in both *cmd.exe* and PowerShell. If there are specific differences, we'll explain which to use.

Troubleshooting

To check whether you have Rust installed correctly, open a shell and enter this line:

```
$ rustc --version
```

You should see the version number, commit hash, and commit date for the latest stable version that has been released, in the following format:

```
rustc x.y.z (abcabcabc yyyy-mm-dd)
```

If you see this information, you have installed Rust successfully! If you don't see this information, check that Rust is in your %PATH% system variable as follows.

In Windows CMD, use:

```
> echo %PATH%
```

In PowerShell, use:

```
> echo $env:Path
```

In Linux and macOS, use:

```
$ echo $PATH
```

If that's all correct and Rust still isn't working, there are a number of places you can get help. Find out how to get in touch with other Rustaceans (a silly nickname we call ourselves) on the community page at *https://www .rust-lang.org/community*.

Updating and Uninstalling

Once Rust is installed via rustup, updating to a newly released version is easy. From your shell, run the following update script:

```
$ rustup update
```

To uninstall Rust and rustup, run the following uninstall script from your shell:

```
$ rustup self uninstall
```

Local Documentation

The installation of Rust also includes a local copy of the documentation so that you can read it offline. Run rustup doc to open the local documentation in your browser.

Any time a type or function is provided by the standard library and you're not sure what it does or how to use it, use the application programming interface (API) documentation to find out!

Hello, World!

Now that you've installed Rust, it's time to write your first Rust program. It's traditional when learning a new language to write a little program that prints the text Hello, world! to the screen, so we'll do the same here!

NOTE   *This book assumes basic familiarity with the command line. Rust makes no specific demands about your editing or tooling or where your code lives, so if you prefer to use an integrated development environment (IDE) instead of the command line, feel free to use your favorite IDE. Many IDEs now have some degree of Rust support; check the IDE's documentation for details. The Rust team has been focusing on enabling great IDE support via* rust-analyzer. *See Appendix D for more details.*

Creating a Project Directory

You'll start by making a directory to store your Rust code. It doesn't matter to Rust where your code lives, but for the exercises and projects in this book, we suggest making a *projects* directory in your home directory and keeping all your projects there.

Open a terminal and enter the following commands to make a *projects* directory and a directory for the "Hello, world!" project within the *projects* directory.

For Linux, macOS, and PowerShell on Windows, enter this:

```
$ mkdir ~/projects
$ cd ~/projects
$ mkdir hello_world
$ cd hello_world
```

For Windows CMD, enter this:

```
> mkdir "%USERPROFILE%\projects"
> cd /d "%USERPROFILE%\projects"
> mkdir hello_world
> cd hello_world
```

Writing and Running a Rust Program

Next, make a new source file and call it *main.rs*. Rust files always end with the *.rs* extension. If you're using more than one word in your filename, the convention is to use an underscore to separate them. For example, use *hello_world.rs* rather than *helloworld.rs*.

Now open the *main.rs* file you just created and enter the code in Listing 1-1.

main.rs
```
fn main() {
    println!("Hello, world!");
}
```

Listing 1-1: A program that prints Hello, world!

Save the file and go back to your terminal window in the *~/projects/ hello_world* directory. On Linux or macOS, enter the following commands to compile and run the file:

```
$ rustc main.rs
$ ./main
Hello, world!
```

On Windows, enter the command .\main.exe instead of ./main:

```
> rustc main.rs
> .\main.exe
Hello, world!
```

Regardless of your operating system, the string Hello, world! should print to the terminal. If you don't see this output, refer back to "Troubleshooting" on page 3 for ways to get help.

If Hello, world! did print, congratulations! You've officially written a Rust program. That makes you a Rust programmer—welcome!

Anatomy of a Rust Program

Let's review this "Hello, world!" program in detail. Here's the first piece of the puzzle:

```
fn main() {

}
```

These lines define a function named main. The main function is special: it is always the first code that runs in every executable Rust program. Here, the first line declares a function named main that has no parameters and returns nothing. If there were parameters, they would go inside the parentheses ().

The function body is wrapped in {}. Rust requires curly brackets around all function bodies. It's good style to place the opening curly bracket on the same line as the function declaration, adding one space in between.

NOTE   *If you want to stick to a standard style across Rust projects, you can use an automatic formatter tool called rustfmt to format your code in a particular style (more on rustfmt in Appendix D). The Rust team has included this tool with the standard Rust distribution, as rustc is, so it should already be installed on your computer!*

The body of the main function holds the following code:

```
println!("Hello, world!");
```

This line does all the work in this little program: it prints text to the screen. There are four important details to notice here.

First, Rust style is to indent with four spaces, not a tab.

Second, println! calls a Rust macro. If it had called a function instead, it would be entered as println (without the !). We'll discuss Rust macros in more detail in Chapter 19. For now, you just need to know that using a ! means that you're calling a macro instead of a normal function and that macros don't always follow the same rules as functions.

Third, you see the "Hello, world!" string. We pass this string as an argument to println!, and the string is printed to the screen.

Fourth, we end the line with a semicolon (;), which indicates that this expression is over and the next one is ready to begin. Most lines of Rust code end with a semicolon.

Compiling and Running Are Separate Steps

You've just run a newly created program, so let's examine each step in the process.

Before running a Rust program, you must compile it using the Rust compiler by entering the rustc command and passing it the name of your source file, like this:

```
$ rustc main.rs
```

If you have a C or C++ background, you'll notice that this is similar to gcc or clang. After compiling successfully, Rust outputs a binary executable.

On Linux, macOS, and PowerShell on Windows, you can see the executable by entering the ls command in your shell:

```
$ ls
main  main.rs
```

On Linux and macOS, you'll see two files. With PowerShell on Windows, you'll see the same three files that you would see using CMD. With CMD on Windows, you would enter the following:

```
> dir /B %= the /B option says to only show the file names =%
main.exe
main.pdb
main.rs
```

This shows the source code file with the *.rs* extension, the executable file (*main.exe* on Windows, but *main* on all other platforms), and, when using Windows, a file containing debugging information with the *.pdb* extension. From here, you run the *main* or *main.exe* file, like this:

```
$ ./main # or .\main.exe on Windows
```

If your *main.rs* is your "Hello, world!" program, this line prints `Hello, world!` to your terminal.

If you're more familiar with a dynamic language, such as Ruby, Python, or JavaScript, you might not be used to compiling and running a program as separate steps. Rust is an *ahead-of-time compiled* language, meaning you can compile a program and give the executable to someone else, and they can run it even without having Rust installed. If you give someone a *.rb*, *.py*, or *.js* file, they need to have a Ruby, Python, or JavaScript implementation installed (respectively). But in those languages, you only need one command to compile and run your program. Everything is a trade-off in language design.

Just compiling with `rustc` is fine for simple programs, but as your project grows, you'll want to manage all the options and make it easy to share your code. Next, we'll introduce you to the Cargo tool, which will help you write real-world Rust programs.

Hello, Cargo!

Cargo is Rust's build system and package manager. Most Rustaceans use this tool to manage their Rust projects because Cargo handles a lot of tasks for you, such as building your code, downloading the libraries your code depends on, and building those libraries. (We call the libraries that your code needs *dependencies*.)

The simplest Rust programs, like the one we've written so far, don't have any dependencies. If we had built the "Hello, world!" project with Cargo, it would only use the part of Cargo that handles building your code. As you write more complex Rust programs, you'll add dependencies, and if you start a project using Cargo, adding dependencies will be much easier to do.

Because the vast majority of Rust projects use Cargo, the rest of this book assumes that you're using Cargo too. Cargo comes installed with Rust if you used the official installers discussed in "Installation" on page 1. If you installed Rust through some other means, check whether Cargo is installed by entering the following in your terminal:

```
$ cargo --version
```

If you see a version number, you have it! If you see an error, such as command not found, look at the documentation for your method of installation to determine how to install Cargo separately.

Creating a Project with Cargo

Let's create a new project using Cargo and look at how it differs from our original "Hello, world!" project. Navigate back to your *projects* directory (or wherever you decided to store your code). Then, on any operating system, run the following:

```
$ cargo new hello_cargo
$ cd hello_cargo
```

The first command creates a new directory and project called *hello_cargo*. We've named our project *hello_cargo*, and Cargo creates its files in a directory of the same name.

Go into the *hello_cargo* directory and list the files. You'll see that Cargo has generated two files and one directory for us: a *Cargo.toml* file and a *src* directory with a *main.rs* file inside.

It has also initialized a new Git repository along with a *.gitignore* file. Git files won't be generated if you run cargo new within an existing Git repository; you can override this behavior by using cargo new --vcs=git.

NOTE *Git is a common version control system. You can change* cargo new *to use a different version control system or no version control system by using the* --vcs *flag. Run* cargo new --help *to see the available options.*

Open *Cargo.toml* in your text editor of choice. It should look similar to the code in Listing 1-2.

Cargo.toml
```
[package]
name = "hello_cargo"
version = "0.1.0"
edition = "2021"

# See more keys and their definitions at https://doc.rust-lang.org/cargo
/reference/manifest.html

[dependencies]
```

Listing 1-2: Contents of Cargo.toml *generated by* cargo new

This file is in the *TOML* (*Tom's Obvious, Minimal Language*) format, which is Cargo's configuration format.

The first line, [package], is a section heading that indicates that the following statements are configuring a package. As we add more information to this file, we'll add other sections.

The next three lines set the configuration information Cargo needs to compile your program: the name, the version, and the edition of Rust to use. We'll talk about the edition key in Appendix E.

The last line, [dependencies], is the start of a section for you to list any of your project's dependencies. In Rust, packages of code are referred to as *crates*. We won't need any other crates for this project, but we will in the first project in Chapter 2, so we'll use this dependencies section then.

Now open *src/main.rs* and take a look:

src/main.rs
```
fn main() {
    println!("Hello, world!");
}
```

Cargo has generated a "Hello, world!" program for you, just like the one we wrote in Listing 1-1! So far, the differences between our project and the project Cargo generated are that Cargo placed the code in the *src* directory and we have a *Cargo.toml* configuration file in the top directory.

Cargo expects your source files to live inside the *src* directory. The top-level project directory is just for README files, license information, configuration files, and anything else not related to your code. Using Cargo helps you organize your projects. There's a place for everything, and everything is in its place.

If you started a project that doesn't use Cargo, as we did with the "Hello, world!" project, you can convert it to a project that does use Cargo. Move the project code into the *src* directory and create an appropriate *Cargo.toml* file.

Building and Running a Cargo Project

Now let's look at what's different when we build and run the "Hello, world!" program with Cargo! From your *hello_cargo* directory, build your project by entering the following command:

```
$ cargo build
   Compiling hello_cargo v0.1.0 (file:///projects/hello_cargo)
    Finished dev [unoptimized + debuginfo] target(s) in 2.85 secs
```

This command creates an executable file in *target/debug/hello_cargo* (or *target\debug\hello_cargo.exe* on Windows) rather than in your current directory. Because the default build is a debug build, Cargo puts the binary in a directory named *debug*. You can run the executable with this command:

```
$ ./target/debug/hello_cargo # or .\target\debug\hello_cargo.exe on Windows
Hello, world!
```

If all goes well, Hello, world! should print to the terminal. Running cargo build for the first time also causes Cargo to create a new file at the top level: *Cargo.lock*. This file keeps track of the exact versions of dependencies in your project. This project doesn't have dependencies, so the file is a bit sparse. You won't ever need to change this file manually; Cargo manages its contents for you.

We just built a project with `cargo build` and ran it with ./target/debug/ hello_cargo, but we can also use `cargo run` to compile the code and then run the resultant executable all in one command:

```
$ cargo run
    Finished dev [unoptimized + debuginfo] target(s) in 0.0 secs
     Running `target/debug/hello_cargo`
Hello, world!
```

Using `cargo run` is more convenient than having to remember to run `cargo build` and then use the whole path to the binary, so most developers use `cargo run`.

Notice that this time we didn't see output indicating that Cargo was compiling hello_cargo. Cargo figured out that the files hadn't changed, so it didn't rebuild but just ran the binary. If you had modified your source code, Cargo would have rebuilt the project before running it, and you would have seen this output:

```
$ cargo run
   Compiling hello_cargo v0.1.0 (file:///projects/hello_cargo)
    Finished dev [unoptimized + debuginfo] target(s) in 0.33 secs
     Running `target/debug/hello_cargo`
Hello, world!
```

Cargo also provides a command called `cargo check`. This command quickly checks your code to make sure it compiles but doesn't produce an executable:

```
$ cargo check
   Checking hello_cargo v0.1.0 (file:///projects/hello_cargo)
    Finished dev [unoptimized + debuginfo] target(s) in 0.32 secs
```

Why would you not want an executable? Often, `cargo check` is much faster than `cargo build` because it skips the step of producing an executable. If you're continually checking your work while writing the code, using `cargo check` will speed up the process of letting you know if your project is still compiling! As such, many Rustaccans run `cargo check` periodically as they write their program to make sure it compiles. Then they run `cargo build` when they're ready to use the executable.

Let's recap what we've learned so far about Cargo:

- We can create a project using `cargo new`.
- We can build a project using `cargo build`.
- We can build and run a project in one step using `cargo run`.
- We can build a project without producing a binary to check for errors using `cargo check`.
- Instead of saving the result of the build in the same directory as our code, Cargo stores it in the *target/debug* directory.

An additional advantage of using Cargo is that the commands are the same no matter which operating system you're working on. So, at this point, we'll no longer provide specific instructions for Linux and macOS versus Windows.

Building for Release

When your project is finally ready for release, you can use `cargo build --release` to compile it with optimizations. This command will create an executable in *target/release* instead of *target/debug*. The optimizations make your Rust code run faster, but turning them on lengthens the time it takes for your program to compile. This is why there are two different profiles: one for development, when you want to rebuild quickly and often, and another for building the final program you'll give to a user that won't be rebuilt repeatedly and that will run as fast as possible. If you're benchmarking your code's running time, be sure to run `cargo build --release` and benchmark with the executable in *target/release*.

Cargo as Convention

With simple projects, Cargo doesn't provide a lot of value over just using `rustc`, but it will prove its worth as your programs become more intricate. Once programs grow to multiple files or need a dependency, it's much easier to let Cargo coordinate the build.

Even though the `hello_cargo` project is simple, it now uses much of the real tooling you'll use in the rest of your Rust career. In fact, to work on any existing projects, you can use the following commands to check out the code using Git, change to that project's directory, and build:

```
$ git clone example.org/someproject
$ cd someproject
$ cargo build
```

For more information about Cargo, check out its documentation at *https://doc.rust-lang.org/cargo*.

Summary

You're already off to a great start on your Rust journey! In this chapter, you've learned how to:

- Install the latest stable version of Rust using `rustup`
- Update to a newer Rust version
- Open locally installed documentation
- Write and run a "Hello, world!" program using `rustc` directly
- Create and run a new project using the conventions of Cargo

This is a great time to build a more substantial program to get used to reading and writing Rust code. So, in Chapter 2, we'll build a guessing game program. If you would rather start by learning how common programming concepts work in Rust, see Chapter 3 and then return to Chapter 2.

2

PROGRAMMING A GUESSING GAME

Let's jump into Rust by working through a hands-on project together! This chapter introduces you to a few common Rust concepts by showing you how to use them in a real program. You'll learn about `let`, `match`, methods, associated functions, external crates, and more! In the following chapters, we'll explore these ideas in more detail. In this chapter, you'll just practice the fundamentals.

We'll implement a classic beginner programming problem: a guessing game. Here's how it works: the program will generate a random integer between 1 and 100. It will then prompt the player to enter a guess. After a guess is entered, the program will indicate whether the guess is too low or too high. If the guess is correct, the game will print a congratulatory message and exit.

Setting Up a New Project

To set up a new project, go to the *projects* directory that you created in Chapter 1 and make a new project using Cargo, like so:

```
$ cargo new guessing_game
$ cd guessing_game
```

The first command, cargo new, takes the name of the project (guessing _game) as the first argument. The second command changes to the new project's directory.

Look at the generated *Cargo.toml* file:

Cargo.toml
```
[package]
name = "guessing_game"
version = "0.1.0"
edition = "2021"

# See more keys and their definitions at https://doc.rust-lang.org/cargo
/reference/manifest.html

[dependencies]
```

As you saw in Chapter 1, cargo new generates a "Hello, world!" program for you. Check out the *src/main.rs* file:

src/main.rs
```
fn main() {
    println!("Hello, world!");
}
```

Now let's compile this "Hello, world!" program and run it in the same step using the cargo run command:

```
$ cargo run
   Compiling guessing_game v0.1.0 (file:///projects/guessing_game)
    Finished dev [unoptimized + debuginfo] target(s) in 1.50s
     Running `target/debug/guessing_game`
Hello, world!
```

The run command comes in handy when you need to rapidly iterate on a project, as we'll do in this game, quickly testing each iteration before moving on to the next one.

Reopen the *src/main.rs* file. You'll be writing all the code in this file.

Processing a Guess

The first part of the guessing game program will ask for user input, process that input, and check that the input is in the expected form. To start, we'll allow the player to input a guess. Enter the code in Listing 2-1 into *src/main.rs*.

src/main.rs

```rust
use std::io;

fn main() {
    println!("Guess the number!");

    println!("Please input your guess.");

    let mut guess = String::new();

    io::stdin()
        .read_line(&mut guess)
        .expect("Failed to read line");

    println!("You guessed: {guess}");
}
```

Listing 2-1: Code that gets a guess from the user and prints it

This code contains a lot of information, so let's go over it line by line. To obtain user input and then print the result as output, we need to bring the io input/output library into scope. The io library comes from the standard library, known as std:

```rust
use std::io;
```

By default, Rust has a set of items defined in the standard library that it brings into the scope of every program. This set is called the *prelude*, and you can see everything in it at *https://doc.rust-lang.org/std/prelude/index.html*.

If a type you want to use isn't in the prelude, you have to bring that type into scope explicitly with a use statement. Using the std::io library provides you with a number of useful features, including the ability to accept user input.

As you saw in Chapter 1, the main function is the entry point into the program:

```rust
fn main() {
```

The fn syntax declares a new function; the parentheses, (), indicate there are no parameters; and the curly bracket, {, starts the body of the function.

As you also learned in Chapter 1, println! is a macro that prints a string to the screen:

```rust
println!("Guess the number!");

println!("Please input your guess.");
```

This code is printing a prompt stating what the game is and requesting input from the user.

Storing Values with Variables

Next, we'll create a *variable* to store the user input, like this:

```
let mut guess = String::new();
```

Now the program is getting interesting! There's a lot going on in this little line. We use the `let` statement to create the variable. Here's another example:

```
let apples = 5;
```

This line creates a new variable named `apples` and binds it to the value 5. In Rust, variables are immutable by default, meaning once we give the variable a value, the value won't change. We'll be discussing this concept in detail in "Variables and Mutability" on page 32. To make a variable mutable, we add `mut` before the variable name:

```
let apples = 5; // immutable
let mut bananas = 5; // mutable
```

NOTE   *The `//` syntax starts a comment that continues until the end of the line. Rust ignores everything in comments. We'll discuss comments in more detail in Chapter 3.*

Returning to the guessing game program, you now know that `let mut guess` will introduce a mutable variable named guess. The equal sign (=) tells Rust we want to bind something to the variable now. On the right of the equal sign is the value that guess is bound to, which is the result of calling `String::new`, a function that returns a new instance of a `String`. `String` is a string type provided by the standard library that is a growable, UTF-8 encoded bit of text.

The `::` syntax in the `::new` line indicates that `new` is an associated function of the `String` type. An *associated function* is a function that's implemented on a type, in this case `String`. This `new` function creates a new, empty string. You'll find a `new` function on many types because it's a common name for a function that makes a new value of some kind.

In full, the `let mut guess = String::new();` line has created a mutable variable that is currently bound to a new, empty instance of a `String`. Whew!

Receiving User Input

Recall that we included the input/output functionality from the standard library with `use std::io;` on the first line of the program. Now we'll call the `stdin` function from the `io` module, which will allow us to handle user input:

```
io::stdin()
    .read_line(&mut guess)
```

If we hadn't imported the io library with use `std::io;` at the beginning of the program, we could still use the function by writing this function call as `std::io::stdin`. The `stdin` function returns an instance of `std::io::Stdin`, which is a type that represents a handle to the standard input for your terminal.

Next, the line `.read_line(&mut guess)` calls the `read_line` method on the standard input handle to get input from the user. We're also passing `&mut guess` as the argument to `read_line` to tell it what string to store the user input in. The full job of `read_line` is to take whatever the user types into standard input and append that into a string (without overwriting its contents), so we therefore pass that string as an argument. The string argument needs to be mutable so the method can change the string's content.

The `&` indicates that this argument is a *reference*, which gives you a way to let multiple parts of your code access one piece of data without needing to copy that data into memory multiple times. References are a complex feature, and one of Rust's major advantages is how safe and easy it is to use references. You don't need to know a lot of those details to finish this program. For now, all you need to know is that, like variables, references are immutable by default. Hence, you need to write `&mut guess` rather than `&guess` to make it mutable. (Chapter 4 will explain references more thoroughly.)

Handling Potential Failure with Result

We're still working on this line of code. We're now discussing a third line of text, but note that it's still part of a single logical line of code. The next part is this method:

```
.expect("Failed to read line");
```

We could have written this code as:

```
io::stdin().read_line(&mut guess).expect("Failed to read line");
```

However, one long line is difficult to read, so it's best to divide it. It's often wise to introduce a newline and other whitespace to help break up long lines when you call a method with the `.method_name()` syntax. Now let's discuss what this line does.

As mentioned earlier, `read_line` puts whatever the user enters into the string we pass to it, but it also returns a `Result` value. `Result` is an *enumeration*, often called an *enum*, which is a type that can be in one of multiple possible states. We call each possible state a *variant*.

Chapter 6 will cover enums in more detail. The purpose of these `Result` types is to encode error-handling information.

`Result`'s variants are `Ok` and `Err`. The `Ok` variant indicates the operation was successful, and inside `Ok` is the successfully generated value. The `Err` variant means the operation failed, and `Err` contains information about how or why the operation failed.

Values of the `Result` type, like values of any type, have methods defined on them. An instance of `Result` has an `expect` method that you can call. If this instance of Result is an Err value, expect will cause the program to crash and display the message that you passed as an argument to expect. If the read_line method returns an Err, it would likely be the result of an error coming from the underlying operating system. If this instance of Result is an Ok value, expect will take the return value that Ok is holding and return just that value to you so you can use it. In this case, that value is the number of bytes in the user's input.

If you don't call expect, the program will compile, but you'll get a warning:

```
$ cargo build
   Compiling guessing_game v0.1.0 (file:///projects/guessing_game)
warning: unused `Result` that must be used
  --> src/main.rs:10:5
   |
10 |     io::stdin().read_line(&mut guess);
   |     ^^^^^^^^^^^^^^^^^^^^^^^^^^^^^^^^^^
   |
   = note: `#[warn(unused_must_use)]` on by default
   = note: this `Result` may be an `Err` variant, which should be handled

warning: `guessing_game` (bin "guessing_game") generated 1 warning
    Finished dev [unoptimized + debuginfo] target(s) in 0.59s
```

Rust warns that you haven't used the Result value returned from read_line, indicating that the program hasn't handled a possible error.

The right way to suppress the warning is to actually write error-handling code, but in our case we just want to crash this program when a problem occurs, so we can use expect. You'll learn about recovering from errors in Chapter 9.

Printing Values with println! Placeholders

Aside from the closing curly bracket, there's only one more line to discuss in the code so far:

```
println!("You guessed: {guess}");
```

This line prints the string that now contains the user's input. The {} set of curly brackets is a placeholder: think of {} as little crab pincers that hold a value in place. When printing the value of a variable, the variable name can go inside the curly brackets. When printing the result of evaluating an expression, place empty curly brackets in the format string, then follow the format string with a comma-separated list of expressions to print in each empty curly bracket placeholder in the same order. Printing a variable and the result of an expression in one call to println! would look like this:

```
let x = 5;
let y = 10;

println!("x = {x} and y + 2 = {}", y + 2);
```

This code would print x = 5 and y + 2 = 12.

Testing the First Part

Let's test the first part of the guessing game. Run it using cargo run:

```
$ cargo run
   Compiling guessing_game v0.1.0 (file:///projects/guessing_game)
    Finished dev [unoptimized + debuginfo] target(s) in 6.44s
     Running `target/debug/guessing_game`
Guess the number!
Please input your guess.
6
You guessed: 6
```

At this point, the first part of the game is done: we're getting input from the keyboard and then printing it.

Generating a Secret Number

Next, we need to generate a secret number that the user will try to guess. The secret number should be different every time so the game is fun to play more than once. We'll use a random number between 1 and 100 so the game isn't too difficult. Rust doesn't yet include random number functionality in its standard library. However, the Rust team does provide a rand crate at *https://crates.io/crates/rand* with said functionality.

Using a Crate to Get More Functionality

Remember that a crate is a collection of Rust source code files. The project we've been building is a *binary crate*, which is an executable. The rand crate is a *library crate*, which contains code that is intended to be used in other programs and can't be executed on its own.

Cargo's coordination of external crates is where Cargo really shines. Before we can write code that uses rand, we need to modify the *Cargo.toml* file to include the rand crate as a dependency. Open that file now and add the following line to the bottom, beneath the [dependencies] section header that Cargo created for you. Be sure to specify rand exactly as we have here, with this version number, or the code examples in this tutorial may not work:

Cargo.toml
```
[dependencies]
rand = "0.8.5"
```

In the *Cargo.toml* file, everything that follows a header is part of that section that continues until another section starts. In [dependencies] you tell Cargo which external crates your project depends on and which versions of those crates you require. In this case, we specify the rand crate with the semantic version specifier 0.8.5. Cargo understands Semantic Versioning (sometimes called *SemVer*), which is a standard for writing version numbers.

The specifier 0.8.5 is actually shorthand for ^0.8.5, which means any version that is at least 0.8.5 but below 0.9.0.

Cargo considers these versions to have public APIs compatible with version 0.8.5, and this specification ensures you'll get the latest patch release that will still compile with the code in this chapter. Any version 0.9.0 or greater is not guaranteed to have the same API as what the following examples use.

Now, without changing any of the code, let's build the project, as shown in Listing 2-2.

```
$ cargo build
    Updating crates.io index
  Downloaded rand v0.8.5
  Downloaded libc v0.2.127
  Downloaded getrandom v0.2.7
  Downloaded cfg-if v1.0.0
  Downloaded ppv-lite86 v0.2.16
  Downloaded rand_chacha v0.3.1
  Downloaded rand_core v0.6.3
   Compiling rand_core v0.6.3
   Compiling libc v0.2.127
   Compiling getrandom v0.2.7
   Compiling cfg-if v1.0.0
   Compiling ppv-lite86 v0.2.16
   Compiling rand_chacha v0.3.1
   Compiling rand v0.8.5
   Compiling guessing_game v0.1.0 (file:///projects/guessing_game)
    Finished dev [unoptimized + debuginfo] target(s) in 2.53s
```

Listing 2-2: The output from running cargo build *after adding the* rand *crate as a dependency*

You may see different version numbers (but they will all be compatible with the code, thanks to SemVer!) and different lines (depending on the operating system), and the lines may be in a different order.

When we include an external dependency, Cargo fetches the latest versions of everything that dependency needs from the *registry*, which is a copy of data from Crates.io at *https://crates.io*. Crates.io is where people in the Rust ecosystem post their open source Rust projects for others to use.

After updating the registry, Cargo checks the [dependencies] section and downloads any crates listed that aren't already downloaded. In this case, although we only listed rand as a dependency, Cargo also grabbed other crates that rand depends on to work. After downloading the crates, Rust compiles them and then compiles the project with the dependencies available.

If you immediately run cargo build again without making any changes, you won't get any output aside from the Finished line. Cargo knows it has already downloaded and compiled the dependencies, and you haven't changed anything about them in your *Cargo.toml* file. Cargo also knows that you haven't changed anything about your code, so it doesn't recompile that either. With nothing to do, it simply exits.

If you open the *src/main.rs* file, make a trivial change, and then save it and build again, you'll only see two lines of output:

```
$ cargo build
   Compiling guessing_game v0.1.0 (file:///projects/guessing_game)
    Finished dev [unoptimized + debuginfo] target(s) in 2.53 secs
```

These lines show that Cargo only updates the build with your tiny change to the *src/main.rs* file. Your dependencies haven't changed, so Cargo knows it can reuse what it has already downloaded and compiled for those.

Ensuring Reproducible Builds with the Cargo.lock File

Cargo has a mechanism that ensures you can rebuild the same artifact every time you or anyone else builds your code: Cargo will use only the versions of the dependencies you specified until you indicate otherwise. For example, say that next week version 0.8.6 of the rand crate comes out, and that version contains an important bug fix, but it also contains a regression that will break your code. To handle this, Rust creates the *Cargo.lock* file the first time you run cargo build, so we now have this in the *guessing_game* directory.

When you build a project for the first time, Cargo figures out all the versions of the dependencies that fit the criteria and then writes them to the *Cargo.lock* file. When you build your project in the future, Cargo will see that the *Cargo.lock* file exists and will use the versions specified there rather than doing all the work of figuring out versions again. This lets you have a reproducible build automatically. In other words, your project will remain at 0.8.5 until you explicitly upgrade, thanks to the *Cargo.lock* file. Because the *Cargo.lock* file is important for reproducible builds, it's often checked into source control with the rest of the code in your project.

Updating a Crate to Get a New Version

When you *do* want to update a crate, Cargo provides the command update, which will ignore the *Cargo.lock* file and figure out all the latest versions that fit your specifications in *Cargo.toml*. Cargo will then write those versions to the *Cargo.lock* file. Otherwise, by default, Cargo will only look for versions greater than 0.8.5 and less than 0.9.0. If the rand crate has released the two new versions 0.8.6 and 0.9.0, you would see the following if you ran cargo update:

```
$ cargo update
    Updating crates.io index
    Updating rand v0.8.5 -> v0.8.6
```

Cargo ignores the 0.9.0 release. At this point, you would also notice a change in your *Cargo.lock* file noting that the version of the rand crate you are now using is 0.8.6. To use rand version 0.9.0 or any version in the 0.9.*x* series, you'd have to update the *Cargo.toml* file to look like this instead:

```
[dependencies]
rand = "0.9.0"
```

The next time you run `cargo build`, Cargo will update the registry of crates available and reevaluate your rand requirements according to the new version you have specified.

There's a lot more to say about Cargo and its ecosystem, which we'll discuss in Chapter 14, but for now, that's all you need to know. Cargo makes it very easy to reuse libraries, so Rustaceans are able to write smaller projects that are assembled from a number of packages.

Generating a Random Number

Let's start using rand to generate a number to guess. The next step is to update *src/main.rs*, as shown in Listing 2-3.

src/main.rs

```
use std::io;
❶ use rand::Rng;

fn main() {
    println!("Guess the number!");

❷   let secret_number = rand::thread_rng().gen_range(1..=100);

❸   println!("The secret number is: {secret_number}");

    println!("Please input your guess.");

    let mut guess = String::new();

    io::stdin()
        .read_line(&mut guess)
        .expect("Failed to read line");

    println!("You guessed: {guess}");
}
```

Listing 2-3: Adding code to generate a random number

First we add the line use `rand::Rng`; ❶. The Rng trait defines methods that random number generators implement, and this trait must be in scope for us to use those methods. Chapter 10 will cover traits in detail.

Next, we're adding two lines in the middle. In the first line ❷, we call the `rand::thread_rng` function that gives us the particular random number generator we're going to use: one that is local to the current thread of execution and is seeded by the operating system. Then we call the `gen_range` method on the random number generator. This method is defined by the Rng trait that we brought into scope with the use `rand::Rng`; statement. The `gen_range` method takes a range expression as an argument and generates a random number in the range. The kind of range expression we're using here takes the form start..=end and is inclusive on the lower and upper bounds, so we need to specify 1..=100 to request a number between 1 and 100.

You won't just know which traits to use and which methods and functions to call from a crate, so each crate has documentation with instructions for using it. Another neat feature of Cargo is that running the cargo doc --open *command will build documentation provided by all your dependencies locally and open it in your browser. If you're interested in other functionality in the* rand *crate, for example, run* cargo doc --open *and click* rand *in the sidebar on the left.*

The second new line ❸ prints the secret number. This is useful while we're developing the program to be able to test it, but we'll delete it from the final version. It's not much of a game if the program prints the answer as soon as it starts!

Try running the program a few times:

```
$ cargo run
   Compiling guessing_game v0.1.0 (file:///projects/guessing_game)
    Finished dev [unoptimized + debuginfo] target(s) in 2.53s
     Running `target/debug/guessing_game`
Guess the number!
The secret number is: 7
Please input your guess.
4
You guessed: 4

$ cargo run
    Finished dev [unoptimized + debuginfo] target(s) in 0.02s
     Running `target/debug/guessing_game`
Guess the number!
The secret number is: 83
Please input your guess.
5
You guessed: 5
```

You should get different random numbers, and they should all be numbers between 1 and 100. Great job!

Comparing the Guess to the Secret Number

Now that we have user input and a random number, we can compare them. That step is shown in Listing 2-4. Note that this code won't compile just yet, as we will explain.

src/main.rs
```
use rand::Rng;
❶ use std::cmp::Ordering;
use std::io;

fn main() {
    --snip--

    println!("You guessed: {guess}");
```

```
❷ match guess.❸cmp(&secret_number) {
        Ordering::Less => println!("Too small!"),
        Ordering::Greater => println!("Too big!"),
        Ordering::Equal => println!("You win!"),
    }
}
```

Listing 2-4: Handling the possible return values of comparing two numbers

First we add another use statement ❶, bringing a type called std::cmp
::Ordering into scope from the standard library. The Ordering type is another
enum and has the variants Less, Greater, and Equal. These are the three out-
comes that are possible when you compare two values.

Then we add five new lines at the bottom that use the Ordering type. The
cmp method ❸ compares two values and can be called on anything that can
be compared. It takes a reference to whatever you want to compare with:
here it's comparing guess to secret_number. Then it returns a variant of the
Ordering enum we brought into scope with the use statement. We use a match
expression ❷ to decide what to do next based on which variant of Ordering
was returned from the call to cmp with the values in guess and secret_number.

A match expression is made up of *arms*. An arm consists of a *pattern* to
match against, and the code that should be run if the value given to match
fits that arm's pattern. Rust takes the value given to match and looks through
each arm's pattern in turn. Patterns and the match construct are powerful
Rust features: they let you express a variety of situations your code might
encounter and they make sure you handle them all. These features will be
covered in detail in Chapter 6 and Chapter 18, respectively.

Let's walk through an example with the match expression we use here.
Say that the user has guessed 50 and the randomly generated secret number this time is 38.

When the code compares 50 to 38, the cmp method will return Ordering
::Greater because 50 is greater than 38. The match expression gets the
Ordering::Greater value and starts checking each arm's pattern. It looks at
the first arm's pattern, Ordering::Less, and sees that the value Ordering
::Greater does not match Ordering::Less, so it ignores the code in that arm
and moves to the next arm. The next arm's pattern is Ordering::Greater,
which *does* match Ordering::Greater! The associated code in that arm will
execute and print Too big! to the screen. The match expression ends after
the first successful match, so it won't look at the last arm in this scenario.

However, the code in Listing 2-4 won't compile yet. Let's try it:

```
$ cargo build
   Compiling guessing_game v0.1.0 (file:///projects/guessing_game)
error[E0308]: mismatched types
  --> src/main.rs:22:21
   |
22 |     match guess.cmp(&secret_number) {
   |                     ^^^^^^^^^^^^^^ expected struct `String`, found integer
   |
   = note: expected reference `&String`
              found reference `&{integer}`
```

The core of the error states that there are *mismatched types*. Rust has a strong, static type system. However, it also has type inference. When we wrote let mut guess = String::new(), Rust was able to infer that guess should be a String and didn't make us write the type. The secret_number, on the other hand, is a number type. A few of Rust's number types can have a value between 1 and 100: i32, a 32-bit number; u32, an unsigned 32-bit number; i64, a 64-bit number; as well as others. Unless otherwise specified, Rust defaults to an i32, which is the type of secret_number unless you add type information elsewhere that would cause Rust to infer a different numerical type. The reason for the error is that Rust cannot compare a string and a number type.

Ultimately, we want to convert the String the program reads as input into a real number type so we can compare it numerically to the secret number. We do so by adding this line to the main function body:

src/main.rs
```
--snip--

let mut guess = String::new();

io::stdin()
    .read_line(&mut guess)
    .expect("Failed to read line");

let guess: u32 = guess
    .trim()
    .parse()
    .expect("Please type a number!");

println!("You guessed: {guess}");

match guess.cmp(&secret_number) {
    Ordering::Less => println!("Too small!"),
    Ordering::Greater => println!("Too big!"),
    Ordering::Equal => println!("You win!"),
}
```

We create a variable named guess. But wait, doesn't the program already have a variable named guess? It does, but helpfully Rust allows us to shadow the previous value of guess with a new one. *Shadowing* lets us reuse the guess variable name rather than forcing us to create two unique variables, such as guess_str and guess, for example. We'll cover this in more detail in Chapter 3, but for now, know that this feature is often used when you want to convert a value from one type to another type.

We bind this new variable to the expression guess.trim().parse(). The guess in the expression refers to the original guess variable that contained the input as a string. The trim method on a String instance will eliminate any whitespace at the beginning and end, which we must do to be able to compare the string to the u32, which can only contain numerical data. The user must press ENTER to satisfy read_line and input their guess, which adds a newline character to the string. For example, if the user types 5 and presses ENTER, guess looks like this: 5\n. The \n represents "newline." (On Windows, pressing ENTER results in a carriage return and a newline, \r\n.) The trim method eliminates \n or \r\n, resulting in just 5.

The parse method on strings converts a string to another type. Here, we use it to convert from a string to a number. We need to tell Rust the exact number type we want by using let guess: u32. The colon (:) after guess tells Rust we'll annotate the variable's type. Rust has a few built-in number types; the u32 seen here is an unsigned, 32-bit integer. It's a good default choice for a small positive number. You'll learn about other number types in Chapter 3.

Additionally, the u32 annotation in this example program and the comparison with secret_number means Rust will infer that secret_number should be a u32 as well. So now the comparison will be between two values of the same type!

The parse method will only work on characters that can logically be converted into numbers and so can easily cause errors. If, for example, the string contained A👍 %, there would be no way to convert that to a number. Because it might fail, the parse method returns a Result type, much as the read_line method does (discussed earlier in "Handling Potential Failure with Result" on page 17). We'll treat this Result the same way by using the expect method again. If parse returns an Err Result variant because it couldn't create a number from the string, the expect call will crash the game and print the message we give it. If parse can successfully convert the string to a number, it will return the Ok variant of Result, and expect will return the number that we want from the Ok value.

Let's run the program now:

```
$ cargo run
   Compiling guessing_game v0.1.0 (file:///projects/guessing_game)
    Finished dev [unoptimized + debuginfo] target(s) in 0.43s
     Running `target/debug/guessing_game`
Guess the number!
The secret number is: 58
Please input your guess.
  76
You guessed: 76
Too big!
```

Nice! Even though spaces were added before the guess, the program still figured out that the user guessed 76. Run the program a few times to verify the different behavior with different kinds of input: guess the number correctly, guess a number that is too high, and guess a number that is too low.

We have most of the game working now, but the user can make only one guess. Let's change that by adding a loop!

Allowing Multiple Guesses with Looping

The loop keyword creates an infinite loop. We'll add a loop to give users more chances at guessing the number.

```
--snip--

println!("The secret number is: {secret_number}");

loop {
    println!("Please input your guess.");

    --snip--

    match guess.cmp(&secret_number) {
        Ordering::Less => println!("Too small!"),
        Ordering::Greater => println!("Too big!"),
        Ordering::Equal => println!("You win!"),
    }
}
```

As you can see, we've moved everything from the guess input prompt onward into a loop. Be sure to indent the lines inside the loop another four spaces each and run the program again. The program will now ask for another guess forever, which actually introduces a new problem. It doesn't seem like the user can quit!

The user could always interrupt the program by using the keyboard shortcut CTRL-C. But there's another way to escape this insatiable monster, as mentioned in the parse discussion in "Comparing the Guess to the Secret Number" on page 23: if the user enters a non-number answer, the program will crash. We can take advantage of that to allow the user to quit, as shown here:

```
$ cargo run
   Compiling guessing_game v0.1.0 (file:///projects/guessing_game)
    Finished dev [unoptimized + debuginfo] target(s) in 1.50s
     Running `target/debug/guessing_game`
Guess the number!
The secret number is: 59
Please input your guess.
45
You guessed: 45
Too small!
Please input your guess.
60
You guessed: 60
Too big!
Please input your guess.
59
You guessed: 59
You win!
Please input your guess.
quit
thread 'main' panicked at 'Please type a number!: ParseIntError
{ kind: InvalidDigit }', src/main.rs:28:47
note: run with `RUST_BACKTRACE=1` environment variable to display a backtrace
```

Typing quit will quit the game, but as you'll notice, so will entering any other non-number input. This is suboptimal, to say the least; we want the game to also stop when the correct number is guessed.

Quitting After a Correct Guess

Let's program the game to quit when the user wins by adding a break statement:

src/main.rs

```
--snip--

    match guess.cmp(&secret_number) {
        Ordering::Less => println!("Too small!"),
        Ordering::Greater => println!("Too big!"),
        Ordering::Equal => {
            println!("You win!");
            break;
        }
    }
}
```

Adding the break line after You win! makes the program exit the loop when the user guesses the secret number correctly. Exiting the loop also means exiting the program, because the loop is the last part of main.

Handling Invalid Input

To further refine the game's behavior, rather than crashing the program when the user inputs a non-number, let's make the game ignore a non-number so the user can continue guessing. We can do that by altering the line where guess is converted from a String to a u32, as shown in Listing 2-5.

src/main.rs

```
--snip--

    io::stdin()
        .read_line(&mut guess)
        .expect("Failed to read line");

    let guess: u32 = match guess.trim().parse() {
        Ok(num) => num,
        Err(_) => continue,
    };

    println!("You guessed: {guess}");

    --snip--
```

Listing 2-5: Ignoring a non-number guess and asking for another guess instead of crashing the program

We switch from an expect call to a match expression to move from crashing on an error to handling the error. Remember that parse returns a Result type and Result is an enum that has the variants Ok and Err. We're using a match expression here, as we did with the Ordering result of the cmp method.

If parse is able to successfully turn the string into a number, it will return an Ok value that contains the resultant number. That Ok value will match the first arm's pattern, and the match expression will just return the num value that parse produced and put inside the Ok value. That number will end up right where we want it in the new guess variable we're creating.

If parse is *not* able to turn the string into a number, it will return an Err value that contains more information about the error. The Err value does not match the Ok(num) pattern in the first match arm, but it does match the Err(_) pattern in the second arm. The underscore, _, is a catch-all value; in this example, we're saying we want to match all Err values, no matter what information they have inside them. So the program will execute the second arm's code, continue, which tells the program to go to the next iteration of the loop and ask for another guess. So, effectively, the program ignores all errors that parse might encounter!

Now everything in the program should work as expected. Let's try it:

```
$ cargo run
   Compiling guessing_game v0.1.0 (file:///projects/guessing_game)
    Finished dev [unoptimized + debuginfo] target(s) in 4.45s
     Running `target/debug/guessing_game`
Guess the number!
The secret number is: 61
Please input your guess.
10
You guessed: 10
Too small!
Please input your guess.
99
You guessed: 99
Too big!
Please input your guess.
foo
Please input your guess.
61
You guessed: 61
You win!
```

Awesome! With one tiny final tweak, we will finish the guessing game. Recall that the program is still printing the secret number. That worked well for testing, but it ruins the game. Let's delete the println! that outputs the secret number. Listing 2-6 shows the final code.

src/main.rs
```
use rand::Rng;
use std::cmp::Ordering;
use std::io;

fn main() {
    println!("Guess the number!");

    let secret_number = rand::thread_rng().gen_range(1..=100);
```

```
loop {
    println!("Please input your guess.");

    let mut guess = String::new();

    io::stdin()
        .read_line(&mut guess)
        .expect("Failed to read line");

    let guess: u32 = match guess.trim().parse() {
        Ok(num) => num,
        Err(_) => continue,
    };

    println!("You guessed: {guess}");

    match guess.cmp(&secret_number) {
        Ordering::Less => println!("Too small!"),
        Ordering::Greater => println!("Too big!"),
        Ordering::Equal => {
            println!("You win!");
            break;
        }
    }
}
}
```

Listing 2-6: Complete guessing game code

At this point, you've successfully built the guessing game. Congratulations!

Summary

This project was a hands-on way to introduce you to many new Rust concepts: let, match, functions, the use of external crates, and more. In the next few chapters, you'll learn about these concepts in more detail. Chapter 3 covers concepts that most programming languages have, such as variables, data types, and functions, and shows how to use them in Rust. Chapter 4 explores ownership, a feature that makes Rust different from other languages. Chapter 5 discusses structs and method syntax, and Chapter 6 explains how enums work.

3

COMMON PROGRAMMING CONCEPTS

 This chapter covers concepts that appear in almost every programming language and how they work in Rust. Many programming languages have much in common at their core. None of the concepts presented in this chapter are unique to Rust, but we'll discuss them in the context of Rust and explain the conventions around using these concepts.

Specifically, you'll learn about variables, basic types, functions, comments, and control flow. These foundations will be in every Rust program, and learning them early will give you a strong core to start from.

Variables and Mutability

As mentioned in "Storing Values with Variables" on page 16, by default, variables are immutable. This is one of many nudges Rust gives you to write your code in a way that takes advantage of the safety and easy concurrency that Rust offers. However, you still have the option to make your variables mutable. Let's explore how and why Rust encourages you to favor immutability and why sometimes you might want to opt out.

When a variable is immutable, once a value is bound to a name, you can't change that value. To illustrate this, generate a new project called *variables* in your *projects* directory by using cargo new variables.

Then, in your new *variables* directory, open *src/main.rs* and replace its code with the following code, which won't compile just yet:

src/main.rs
```
fn main() {
    let x = 5;
    println!("The value of x is: {x}");
    x = 6;
    println!("The value of x is: {x}");
}
```

Save and run the program using cargo run. You should receive an error message regarding an immutability error, as shown in this output:

```
$ cargo run
   Compiling variables v0.1.0 (file:///projects/variables)
error[E0384]: cannot assign twice to immutable variable `x`
 --> src/main.rs:4:5
  |
2 |     let x = 5;
  |         -
  |         |
  |         first assignment to `x`
  |         help: consider making this binding mutable: `mut x`
3 |     println!("The value of x is: {x}");
4 |     x = 6;
  |     ^^^^^ cannot assign twice to immutable variable
```

This example shows how the compiler helps you find errors in your programs. Compiler errors can be frustrating, but really they only mean your program isn't safely doing what you want it to do yet; they do *not* mean that you're not a good programmer! Experienced Rustaceans still get compiler errors.

You received the error message cannot assign twice to immutable variable `x` because you tried to assign a second value to the immutable x variable.

It's important that we get compile-time errors when we attempt to change a value that's designated as immutable because this very situation can lead to bugs. If one part of our code operates on the assumption that a value will never change and another part of our code changes that value, it's possible that the first part of the code won't do what it was designed to do. The cause of this kind of bug can be difficult to track down after the fact, especially when the second piece of code changes the value only *sometimes*. The Rust compiler guarantees that when you state that a value won't change, it really won't change, so you don't have to keep track of it yourself. Your code is thus easier to reason through.

But mutability can be very useful, and can make code more convenient to write. Although variables are immutable by default, you can make them mutable by adding mut in front of the variable name as you did in Chapter 2. Adding mut also conveys intent to future readers of the code by indicating that other parts of the code will be changing this variable's value.

For example, let's change *src/main.rs* to the following:

src/main.rs
```
fn main() {
    let mut x = 5;
    println!("The value of x is: {x}");
    x = 6;
    println!("The value of x is: {x}");
}
```

When we run the program now, we get this:

```
$ cargo run
   Compiling variables v0.1.0 (file:///projects/variables)
    Finished dev [unoptimized + debuginfo] target(s) in 0.30s
     Running `target/debug/variables`
The value of x is: 5
The value of x is: 6
```

We're allowed to change the value bound to x from 5 to 6 when mut is used. Ultimately, deciding whether to use mutability or not is up to you and depends on what you think is clearest in that particular situation.

Constants

Like immutable variables, *constants* are values that are bound to a name and are not allowed to change, but there are a few differences between constants and variables.

First, you aren't allowed to use mut with constants. Constants aren't just immutable by default—they're always immutable. You declare constants using the const keyword instead of the let keyword, and the type of the value *must* be annotated. We'll cover types and type annotations in "Data Types" on page 36, so don't worry about the details right now. Just know that you must always annotate the type.

Constants can be declared in any scope, including the global scope, which makes them useful for values that many parts of code need to know about.

The last difference is that constants may be set only to a constant expression, not the result of a value that could only be computed at runtime.

Here's an example of a constant declaration:

```
const THREE_HOURS_IN_SECONDS: u32 = 60 * 60 * 3;
```

The constant's name is THREE_HOURS_IN_SECONDS and its value is set to the result of multiplying 60 (the number of seconds in a minute) by 60 (the number of minutes in an hour) by 3 (the number of hours we want to count in this program). Rust's naming convention for constants is to use all upper-case with underscores between words. The compiler is able to evaluate a limited set of operations at compile time, which lets us choose to write out this value in a way that's easier to understand and verify, rather than setting this constant to the value 10,800. See the Rust Reference's section on constant evaluation at *https://doc.rust-lang.org/reference/const_eval.html* for more information on what operations can be used when declaring constants.

Constants are valid for the entire time a program runs, within the scope in which they were declared. This property makes constants useful for values in your application domain that multiple parts of the program might need to know about, such as the maximum number of points any player of a game is allowed to earn, or the speed of light.

Naming hardcoded values used throughout your program as constants is useful in conveying the meaning of that value to future maintainers of the code. It also helps to have only one place in your code you would need to change if the hardcoded value needed to be updated in the future.

Shadowing

As you saw in the guessing game tutorial in Chapter 2, you can declare a new variable with the same name as a previous variable. Rustaceans say that the first variable is *shadowed* by the second, which means that the second variable is what the compiler will see when you use the name of the variable. In effect, the second variable overshadows the first, taking any uses of the variable name to itself until either it itself is shadowed or the scope ends. We can shadow a variable by using the same variable's name and repeating the use of the let keyword as follows:

src/main.rs
```
fn main() {
    let x = 5;

    let x = x + 1;

    {
        let x = x * 2;
```

```
    println!("The value of x in the inner scope is: {x}");
}

println!("The value of x is: {x}");
}
```

This program first binds x to a value of 5. Then it creates a new variable x by repeating let x =, taking the original value and adding 1 so the value of x is then 6. Then, within an inner scope created with the curly brackets, the third let statement also shadows x and creates a new variable, multiplying the previous value by 2 to give x a value of 12. When that scope is over, the inner shadowing ends and x returns to being 6. When we run this program, it will output the following:

```
$ cargo run
   Compiling variables v0.1.0 (file:///projects/variables)
    Finished dev [unoptimized + debuginfo] target(s) in 0.31s
     Running `target/debug/variables`
The value of x in the inner scope is: 12
The value of x is: 6
```

Shadowing is different from marking a variable as mut because we'll get a compile-time error if we accidentally try to reassign to this variable without using the let keyword. By using let, we can perform a few transformations on a value but have the variable be immutable after those transformations have been completed.

The other difference between mut and shadowing is that because we're effectively creating a new variable when we use the let keyword again, we can change the type of the value but reuse the same name. For example, say our program asks a user to show how many spaces they want between some text by inputting space characters, and then we want to store that input as a number:

```
let spaces = "   ";
let spaces = spaces.len();
```

The first spaces variable is a string type and the second spaces variable is a number type. Shadowing thus spares us from having to come up with different names, such as spaces_str and spaces_num; instead, we can reuse the simpler spaces name. However, if we try to use mut for this, as shown here, we'll get a compile-time error:

```
let mut spaces = "   ";
spaces = spaces.len();
```

The error says we're not allowed to mutate a variable's type:

```
$ cargo run
   Compiling variables v0.1.0 (file:///projects/variables)
error[E0308]: mismatched types
 --> src/main.rs:3:14
```

```
  |
2 |     let mut spaces = "   ";
  |                      ----- expected due to this value
3 |     spaces = spaces.len();
  |              ^^^^^^^^^^^^ expected `&str`, found `usize`
```

Now that we've explored how variables work, let's look at more data types they can have.

Data Types

Every value in Rust is of a certain *data type*, which tells Rust what kind of data is being specified so it knows how to work with that data. We'll look at two data type subsets: scalar and compound.

Keep in mind that Rust is a *statically typed* language, which means that it must know the types of all variables at compile time. The compiler can usually infer what type we want to use based on the value and how we use it. In cases when many types are possible, such as when we converted a String to a numeric type using parse in "Comparing the Guess to the Secret Number" on page 23, we must add a type annotation, like this:

```
let guess: u32 = "42".parse().expect("Not a number!");
```

If we don't add the : u32 type annotation shown in the preceding code, Rust will display the following error, which means the compiler needs more information from us to know which type we want to use:

```
$ cargo build
   Compiling no_type_annotations v0.1.0 (file:///projects/no_type_annotations)
error[E0282]: type annotations needed
 --> src/main.rs:2:9
  |
2 |     let guess = "42".parse().expect("Not a number!");
  |         ^^^^^ consider giving `guess` a type
```

You'll see different type annotations for other data types.

Scalar Types

A *scalar* type represents a single value. Rust has four primary scalar types: integers, floating-point numbers, Booleans, and characters. You may recognize these from other programming languages. Let's jump into how they work in Rust.

Integer Types

An *integer* is a number without a fractional component. We used one integer type in Chapter 2, the u32 type. This type declaration indicates that the value it's associated with should be an unsigned integer (signed integer

```
```

types start with i instead of u) that takes up 32 bits of space. Table 3-1 shows the built-in integer types in Rust. We can use any of these variants to declare the type of an integer value.

Table 3-1: Integer Types in Rust

Length	Signed	Unsigned
8-bit	i8	u8
16-bit	i16	u16
32-bit	i32	u32
64-bit	i64	u64
128-bit	i128	u128
arch	isize	usize

Each variant can be either signed or unsigned and has an explicit size. *Signed* and *unsigned* refer to whether it's possible for the number to be negative—in other words, whether the number needs to have a sign with it (signed) or whether it will only ever be positive and can therefore be represented without a sign (unsigned). It's like writing numbers on paper: when the sign matters, a number is shown with a plus sign or a minus sign; however, when it's safe to assume the number is positive, it's shown with no sign. Signed numbers are stored using two's complement representation.

Each signed variant can store numbers from $-(2^{n-1})$ to $2^{n-1} - 1$ inclusive, where n is the number of bits that variant uses. So an i8 can store numbers from $-(2^7)$ to $2^7 - 1$, which equals −128 to 127. Unsigned variants can store numbers from 0 to $2^n - 1$, so a u8 can store numbers from 0 to $2^8 - 1$, which equals 0 to 255.

Additionally, the isize and usize types depend on the architecture of the computer your program is running on, which is denoted in the table as "arch": 64 bits if you're on a 64-bit architecture and 32 bits if you're on a 32-bit architecture.

You can write integer literals in any of the forms shown in Table 3-2. Note that number literals that can be multiple numeric types allow a type suffix, such as 57u8, to designate the type. Number literals can also use _ as a visual separator to make the number easier to read, such as 1_000, which will have the same value as if you had specified 1000.

Table 3-2: Integer Literals in Rust

Number literals	Example
Decimal	98_222
Hex	0xff
Octal	0o77
Binary	0b1111_0000
Byte (u8 only)	b'A'

So how do you know which type of integer to use? If you're unsure, Rust's defaults are generally good places to start: integer types default to i32. The primary situation in which you'd use isize or usize is when indexing some sort of collection.

INTEGER OVERFLOW

Let's say you have a variable of type u8 that can hold values between 0 and 255. If you try to change the variable to a value outside that range, such as 256, *integer overflow* will occur, which can result in one of two behaviors. When you're compiling in debug mode, Rust includes checks for integer overflow that cause your program to *panic* at runtime if this behavior occurs. Rust uses the term *panicking* when a program exits with an error; we'll discuss panics in more depth in "Unrecoverable Errors with panic!" on page 162.

When you're compiling in release mode with the --release flag, Rust does *not* include checks for integer overflow that cause panics. Instead, if overflow occurs, Rust performs *two's complement wrapping*. In short, values greater than the maximum value the type can hold "wrap around" to the minimum of the values the type can hold. In the case of a u8, the value 256 becomes 0, the value 257 becomes 1, and so on. The program won't panic, but the variable will have a value that probably isn't what you were expecting it to have. Relying on integer overflow's wrapping behavior is considered an error.

To explicitly handle the possibility of overflow, you can use these families of methods provided by the standard library for primitive numeric types:

- Wrap in all modes with the wrapping_* methods, such as wrapping_add.
- Return the None value if there is overflow with the checked_* methods.
- Return the value and a Boolean indicating whether there was overflow with the overflowing_* methods.
- Saturate at the value's minimum or maximum values with the saturating_* methods.

Floating-Point Types

Rust also has two primitive types for *floating-point numbers*, which are numbers with decimal points. Rust's floating-point types are f32 and f64, which are 32 bits and 64 bits in size, respectively. The default type is f64 because on modern CPUs, it's roughly the same speed as f32 but is capable of more precision. All floating-point types are signed.

Here's an example that shows floating-point numbers in action:

src/main.rs
```
fn main() {
    let x = 2.0; // f64

    let y: f32 = 3.0; // f32
}
```

Floating-point numbers are represented according to the IEEE-754 standard. The f32 type is a single-precision float, and f64 has double precision.

Numeric Operations

Rust supports the basic mathematical operations you'd expect for all the number types: addition, subtraction, multiplication, division, and remainder. Integer division truncates toward zero to the nearest integer. The following code shows how you'd use each numeric operation in a let statement:

src/main.rs
```
fn main() {
    // addition
    let sum = 5 + 10;

    // subtraction
    let difference = 95.5 - 4.3;

    // multiplication
    let product = 4 * 30;

    // division
    let quotient = 56.7 / 32.2;
    let truncated = -5 / 3; // Results in -1

    // remainder
    let remainder = 43 % 5;
}
```

Each expression in these statements uses a mathematical operator and evaluates to a single value, which is then bound to a variable. Appendix B contains a list of all operators that Rust provides.

The Boolean Type

As in most other programming languages, a Boolean type in Rust has two possible values: true and false. Booleans are one byte in size. The Boolean type in Rust is specified using bool. For example:

src/main.rs
```
fn main() {
    let t = true;

    let f: bool = false; // with explicit type annotation
}
```

The main way to use Boolean values is through conditionals, such as an if expression. We'll cover how if expressions work in Rust in "Control Flow" on page 50.

The Character Type

Rust's char type is the language's most primitive alphabetic type. Here are some examples of declaring char values:

src/main.rs

```
fn main() {
    let c = 'z';
    let z: char = 'Z'; // with explicit type annotation
    let heart_eyed_cat = '😻';
}
```

Note that we specify char literals with single quotes, as opposed to string literals, which use double quotes. Rust's char type is four bytes in size and represents a Unicode scalar value, which means it can represent a lot more than just ASCII. Accented letters; Chinese, Japanese, and Korean characters; emoji; and zero-width spaces are all valid char values in Rust. Unicode scalar values range from U+0000 to U+D7FF and U+E000 to U+10FFFF inclusive. However, a "character" isn't really a concept in Unicode, so your human intuition for what a "character" is may not match up with what a char is in Rust. We'll discuss this topic in detail in "Storing UTF-8 Encoded Text with Strings" on page 147.

Compound Types

Compound types can group multiple values into one type. Rust has two primitive compound types: tuples and arrays.

The Tuple Type

A *tuple* is a general way of grouping together a number of values with a variety of types into one compound type. Tuples have a fixed length: once declared, they cannot grow or shrink in size.

We create a tuple by writing a comma-separated list of values inside parentheses. Each position in the tuple has a type, and the types of the different values in the tuple don't have to be the same. We've added optional type annotations in this example:

src/main.rs

```
fn main() {
    let tup: (i32, f64, u8) = (500, 6.4, 1);
}
```

The variable tup binds to the entire tuple because a tuple is considered a single compound element. To get the individual values out of a tuple, we can use pattern matching to destructure a tuple value, like this:

src/main.rs

```
fn main() {
    let tup = (500, 6.4, 1);

    let (x, y, z) = tup;

    println!("The value of y is: {y}");
}
```

This program first creates a tuple and binds it to the variable tup. It then uses a pattern with let to take tup and turn it into three separate variables, x, y, and z. This is called *destructuring* because it breaks the single tuple into three parts. Finally, the program prints the value of y, which is 6.4.

We can also access a tuple element directly by using a period (.) followed by the index of the value we want to access. For example:

src/main.rs
```
fn main() {
    let x: (i32, f64, u8) = (500, 6.4, 1);

    let five_hundred = x.0;

    let six_point_four = x.1;

    let one = x.2;
}
```

This program creates the tuple x and then accesses each element of the tuple using their respective indices. As with most programming languages, the first index in a tuple is 0.

The tuple without any values has a special name, *unit*. This value and its corresponding type are both written () and represent an empty value or an empty return type. Expressions implicitly return the unit value if they don't return any other value.

The Array Type

Another way to have a collection of multiple values is with an *array*. Unlike a tuple, every element of an array must have the same type. Unlike arrays in some other languages, arrays in Rust have a fixed length.

We write the values in an array as a comma-separated list inside square brackets:

src/main.rs
```
fn main() {
    let a = [1, 2, 3, 4, 5];
}
```

Arrays are useful when you want your data allocated on the stack rather than the heap (we will discuss the stack and the heap more in Chapter 4) or when you want to ensure you always have a fixed number of elements. An array isn't as flexible as the vector type, though. A *vector* is a similar collection type provided by the standard library that *is* allowed to grow or shrink in size. If you're unsure whether to use an array or a vector, chances are you should use a vector. Chapter 8 discusses vectors in more detail.

However, arrays are more useful when you know the number of elements will not need to change. For example, if you were using the names of

the month in a program, you would probably use an array rather than a vector because you know it will always contain 12 elements:

```
let months = ["January", "February", "March", "April", "May", "June", "July",
              "August", "September", "October", "November", "December"];
```

You write an array's type using square brackets with the type of each
element, a semicolon, and then the number of elements in the array, like so:

```
let a: [i32; 5] = [1, 2, 3, 4, 5];
```

Here, i32 is the type of each element. After the semicolon, the number 5
indicates the array contains five elements.

You can also initialize an array to contain the same value for each element by specifying the initial value, followed by a semicolon, and then the
length of the array in square brackets, as shown here:

```
let a = [3; 5];
```

The array named a will contain 5 elements that will all be set to the
value 3 initially. This is the same as writing let a = [3, 3, 3, 3, 3]; but in a
more concise way.

Accessing Array Elements

An array is a single chunk of memory of a known, fixed size that can be
allocated on the stack. You can access elements of an array using indexing,
like this:

src/main.rs
```
fn main() {
    let a = [1, 2, 3, 4, 5];

    let first = a[0];
    let second = a[1];
}
```

In this example, the variable named first will get the value 1 because
that is the value at index [0] in the array. The variable named second will get
the value 2 from index [1] in the array.

Invalid Array Element Access

Let's see what happens if you try to access an element of an array that is past
the end of the array. Say you run this code, similar to the guessing game in
Chapter 2, to get an array index from the user:

src/main.rs
```
use std::io;

fn main() {
    let a = [1, 2, 3, 4, 5];
```

```
    println!("Please enter an array index.");

    let mut index = String::new();

    io::stdin()
        .read_line(&mut index)
        .expect("Failed to read line");

    let index: usize = index
        .trim()
        .parse()
        .expect("Index entered was not a number");

    let element = a[index];

    println!(
        "The value of the element at index {index} is: {element}"
    );
}
```

This code compiles successfully. If you run this code using `cargo run` and enter 0, 1, 2, 3, or 4, the program will print out the corresponding value at that index in the array. If you instead enter a number past the end of the array, such as 10, you'll see output like this:

```
thread 'main' panicked at 'index out of bounds: the len is 5 but the index is
10', src/main.rs:19:19
note: run with `RUST_BACKTRACE=1` environment variable to display a backtrace
```

The program resulted in a *runtime* error at the point of using an invalid value in the indexing operation. The program exited with an error message and didn't execute the final println! statement. When you attempt to access an element using indexing, Rust will check that the index you've specified is less than the array length. If the index is greater than or equal to the length, Rust will panic. This check has to happen at runtime, especially in this case, because the compiler can't possibly know what value a user will enter when they run the code later.

This is an example of Rust's memory safety principles in action. In many low-level languages, this kind of check is not done, and when you provide an incorrect index, invalid memory can be accessed. Rust protects you against this kind of error by immediately exiting instead of allowing the memory access and continuing. Chapter 9 discusses more of Rust's error handling and how you can write readable, safe code that neither panics nor allows invalid memory access.

Functions

Functions are prevalent in Rust code. You've already seen one of the most important functions in the language: the main function, which is the entry point of many programs. You've also seen the fn keyword, which allows you to declare new functions.

Rust code uses *snake case* as the conventional style for function and variable names, in which all letters are lowercase and underscores separate words. Here's a program that contains an example function definition:

```
fn main() {
    println!("Hello, world!");

    another_function();
}

fn another_function() {
    println!("Another function.");
}
```

We define a function in Rust by entering fn followed by a function name and a set of parentheses. The curly brackets tell the compiler where the function body begins and ends.

We can call any function we've defined by entering its name followed by a set of parentheses. Because another_function is defined in the program, it can be called from inside the main function. Note that we defined another _function *after* the main function in the source code; we could have defined it before as well. Rust doesn't care where you define your functions, only that they're defined somewhere in a scope that can be seen by the caller.

Let's start a new binary project named *functions* to explore functions further. Place the another_function example in *src/main.rs* and run it. You should see the following output:

```
$ cargo run
   Compiling functions v0.1.0 (file:///projects/functions)
    Finished dev [unoptimized + debuginfo] target(s) in 0.28s
     Running `target/debug/functions`
Hello, world!
Another function.
```

The lines execute in the order in which they appear in the main function. First the "Hello, world!" message prints, and then another_function is called and its message is printed.

Parameters

We can define functions to have *parameters*, which are special variables that are part of a function's signature. When a function has parameters, you can provide it with concrete values for those parameters. Technically, the concrete values are called *arguments*, but in casual conversation, people tend to use the words *parameter* and *argument* interchangeably for either the variables in a function's definition or the concrete values passed in when you call a function.

In this version of another_function we add a parameter:

src/main.rs
```
fn main() {
    another_function(5);
}

fn another function(x: i32) {
    println!("The value of x is: {x}");
}
```

Try running this program; you should get the following output:

```
$ cargo run
   Compiling functions v0.1.0 (file:///projects/functions)
    Finished dev [unoptimized + debuginfo] target(s) in 1.21s
     Running `target/debug/functions`
The value of x is: 5
```

The declaration of another_function has one parameter named x. The type of x is specified as i32. When we pass 5 in to another_function, the println! macro puts 5 where the pair of curly brackets containing x was in the format string.

In function signatures, you *must* declare the type of each parameter. This is a deliberate decision in Rust's design: requiring type annotations in function definitions means the compiler almost never needs you to use them elsewhere in the code to figure out what type you mean. The compiler is also able to give more helpful error messages if it knows what types the function expects.

When defining multiple parameters, separate the parameter declarations with commas, like this:

src/main.rs
```
fn main() {
    print_labeled_measurement(5, 'h');
}

fn print_labeled_measurement(value: i32, unit_label: char) {
    println!("The measurement is: {value}{unit_label}");
}
```

This example creates a function named print_labeled_measurement with two parameters. The first parameter is named value and is an i32. The second is named unit_label and is type char. The function then prints text containing both the value and the unit_label.

Let's try running this code. Replace the program currently in your *functions* project's *src/main.rs* file with the preceding example and run it using cargo run:

```
$ cargo run
   Compiling functions v0.1.0 (file:///projects/functions)
    Finished dev [unoptimized + debuginfo] target(s) in 0.31s
     Running `target/debug/functions`
The measurement is: 5h
```

Because we called the function with 5 as the value for value and 'h' as the value for unit_label, the program output contains those values.

Statements and Expressions

Function bodies are made up of a series of statements optionally ending in an expression. So far, the functions we've covered haven't included an ending expression, but you have seen an expression as part of a statement. Because Rust is an expression-based language, this is an important distinction to understand. Other languages don't have the same distinctions, so let's look at what statements and expressions are and how their differences affect the bodies of functions.

- Statements are instructions that perform some action and do not return a value.

- Expressions evaluate to a resultant value.

Let's look at some examples.

We've actually already used statements and expressions. Creating a variable and assigning a value to it with the let keyword is a statement. In Listing 3-1, let y = 6; is a statement.

src/main.rs
```
fn main() {
    let y = 6;
}
```

Listing 3-1: A main function declaration containing one statement

Function definitions are also statements; the entire preceding example is a statement in itself.

Statements do not return values. Therefore, you can't assign a let statement to another variable, as the following code tries to do; you'll get an error:

src/main.rs
```
fn main() {
    let x = (let y = 6);
}
```

When you run this program, the error you'll get looks like this:

```
$ cargo run
   Compiling functions v0.1.0 (file:///projects/functions)
error: expected expression, found statement (`let`)
 --> src/main.rs:2:14
  |
2 |     let x = (let y = 6);
  |              ^^^^^^^^^
  |
  = note: variable declaration using `let` is a statement

error[E0658]: `let` expressions in this position are unstable
 --> src/main.rs:2:14
```

```
2 |        let x = (let y = 6);
  |                ^^^^^^^^^
  |
  = note: see issue #53667 <https://github.com/rust-lang/rust/issues/53667> for
more information
```

The let y = 6 statement does not return a value, so there isn't anything for x to bind to. This is different from what happens in other languages, such as C and Ruby, where the assignment returns the value of the assignment. In those languages, you can write x = y = 6 and have both x and y have the value 6; that is not the case in Rust.

Expressions evaluate to a value and make up most of the rest of the code that you'll write in Rust. Consider a math operation, such as 5 + 6, which is an expression that evaluates to the value 11. Expressions can be part of statements: in Listing 3-1, the 6 in the statement let y = 6; is an expression that evaluates to the value 6. Calling a function is an expression. Calling a macro is an expression. A new scope block created with curly brackets is an expression, for example:

src/main.rs
```
fn main() {
  ❶ let y = {❷
        let x = 3;
      ❸ x + 1
    };

    println!("The value of y is: {y}");
}
```

The expression ❷ is a block that, in this case, evaluates to 4. That value gets bound to y as part of the let statement ❶. Note the line without a semicolon at the end ❸, which is unlike most of the lines you've seen so far. Expressions do not include ending semicolons. If you add a semicolon to the end of an expression, you turn it into a statement, and it will then not return a value. Keep this in mind as you explore function return values and expressions next.

Functions with Return Values

Functions can return values to the code that calls them. We don't name return values, but we must declare their type after an arrow (->). In Rust, the return value of the function is synonymous with the value of the final expression in the block of the body of a function. You can return early from a function by using the return keyword and specifying a value, but most functions return the last expression implicitly. Here's an example of a function that returns a value:

src/main.rs
```
fn five() -> i32 {
    5
}
```

```
fn main() {
    let x = five();

    println!("The value of x is: {x}");
}
```

There are no function calls, macros, or even let statements in the five function—just the number 5 by itself. That's a perfectly valid function in Rust. Note that the function's return type is specified too, as -> i32. Try running this code; the output should look like this:

```
$ cargo run
   Compiling functions v0.1.0 (file:///projects/functions)
    Finished dev [unoptimized + debuginfo] target(s) in 0.30s
     Running `target/debug/functions`
The value of x is: 5
```

The 5 in five is the function's return value, which is why the return type is i32. Let's examine this in more detail. There are two important bits: first, the line let x = five(); shows that we're using the return value of a function to initialize a variable. Because the function five returns a 5, that line is the same as the following:

```
let x = 5;
```

Second, the five function has no parameters and defines the type of the return value, but the body of the function is a lonely 5 with no semicolon because it's an expression whose value we want to return.

Let's look at another example:

src/main.rs
```
fn main() {
    let x = plus_one(5);

    println!("The value of x is: {x}");
}

fn plus_one(x: i32) -> i32 {
    x + 1
}
```

Running this code will print The value of x is: 6. But if we place a semicolon at the end of the line containing x + 1, changing it from an expression to a statement, we'll get an error:

src/main.rs
```
fn main() {
    let x = plus_one(5);

    println!("The value of x is: {x}");
}
```

```
fn plus_one(x: i32) -> i32 {
    x + 1;
}
```

Compiling this code produces an error, as follows:

```
$ cargo run
   Compiling functions v0.1.0 (file:///projects/functions)
error[E0308]: mismatched types
 --> src/main.rs:7:24
  |
7 | fn plus_one(x: i32) -> i32 {
  |    --------                ^^^ expected `i32`, found `()`
  |    |
  |    implicitly returns `()` as its body has no tail or `return` expression
8 |     x + 1;
  |          - help: remove this semicolon
  |
```

The main error message, mismatched types, reveals the core issue with this code. The definition of the function plus_one says that it will return an i32, but statements don't evaluate to a value, which is expressed by (), the unit type. Therefore, nothing is returned, which contradicts the function definition and results in an error. In this output, Rust provides a message to possibly help rectify this issue: it suggests removing the semicolon, which would fix the error.

Comments

All programmers strive to make their code easy to understand, but sometimes extra explanation is warranted. In these cases, programmers leave *comments* in their source code that the compiler will ignore but people reading the source code may find useful.

Here's a simple comment:

```
// hello, world
```

In Rust, the idiomatic comment style starts a comment with two slashes, and the comment continues until the end of the line. For comments that extend beyond a single line, you'll need to include // on each line, like this:

```
// So we're doing something complicated here, long enough that we need
// multiple lines of comments to do it! Whew! Hopefully, this comment will
// explain what's going on.
```

Comments can also be placed at the end of lines containing code:

src/main.rs
```
fn main() {
    let lucky_number = 7; // I'm feeling lucky today
}
```

But you'll more often see them used in this format, with the comment on a separate line above the code it's annotating:

```
src/main.rs    fn main() {
                   // I'm feeling lucky today
                   let lucky_number = 7;
               }
```

Rust also has another kind of comment, documentation comments, which we'll discuss in "Publishing a Crate to Crates.io" on page 297.

Control Flow

The ability to run some code depending on whether a condition is true and to run some code repeatedly while a condition is true are basic building blocks in most programming languages. The most common constructs that let you control the flow of execution of Rust code are if expressions and loops.

if Expressions

An if expression allows you to branch your code depending on conditions. You provide a condition and then state, "If this condition is met, run this block of code. If the condition is not met, do not run this block of code."

Create a new project called *branches* in your *projects* directory to explore the if expression. In the *src/main.rs* file, input the following:

```
src/main.rs    fn main() {
                   let number = 3;

                   if number < 5 {
                       println!("condition was true");
                   } else {
                       println!("condition was false");
                   }
               }
```

All if expressions start with the keyword if, followed by a condition. In this case, the condition checks whether or not the variable number has a value less than 5. We place the block of code to execute if the condition is true immediately after the condition inside curly brackets. Blocks of code associated with the conditions in if expressions are sometimes called *arms*, just like the arms in match expressions that we discussed in "Comparing the Guess to the Secret Number" on page 23.

Optionally, we can also include an else expression, which we chose to do here, to give the program an alternative block of code to execute should the condition evaluate to false. If you don't provide an else expression and the condition is false, the program will just skip the if block and move on to the next bit of code.

Try running this code; you should see the following output:

```
$ cargo run
   Compiling branches v0.1.0 (file:///projects/branches)
    Finished dev [unoptimized + debuginfo] target(s) in 0.31s
     Running `target/debug/branches`
condition was true
```

Let's try changing the value of number to a value that makes the condition false to see what happens:

```
let number = 7;
```

Run the program again, and look at the output:

```
$ cargo run
   Compiling branches v0.1.0 (file:///projects/branches)
    Finished dev [unoptimized + debuginfo] target(s) in 0.31s
     Running `target/debug/branches`
condition was false
```

It's also worth noting that the condition in this code *must* be a bool. If the condition isn't a bool, we'll get an error. For example, try running the following code:

src/main.rs
```
fn main() {
    let number = 3;

    if number {
        println!("number was three");
    }
}
```

The if condition evaluates to a value of 3 this time, and Rust throws an error:

```
$ cargo run
   Compiling branches v0.1.0 (file:///projects/branches)
error[E0308]: mismatched types
 --> src/main.rs:4:8
  |
4 |     if number {
  |        ^^^^^^ expected `bool`, found integer
```

The error indicates that Rust expected a bool but got an integer. Unlike languages such as Ruby and JavaScript, Rust will not automatically try to convert non-Boolean types to a Boolean. You must be explicit and always provide if with a Boolean as its condition. If we want the if code block to run only when a number is not equal to 0, for example, we can change the if expression to the following:

src/main.rs
```
fn main() {
    let number = 3;
```

```
    if number != 0 {
        println!("number was something other than zero");
    }
}
```

Running this code will print `number was something other than zero`.

Handling Multiple Conditions with else if

You can use multiple conditions by combining if and else in an else if expression. For example:

src/main.rs
```
fn main() {
    let number = 6;

    if number % 4 == 0 {
        println!("number is divisible by 4");
    } else if number % 3 == 0 {
        println!("number is divisible by 3");
    } else if number % 2 == 0 {
        println!("number is divisible by 2");
    } else {
        println!("number is not divisible by 4, 3, or 2");
    }
}
```

This program has four possible paths it can take. After running it, you should see the following output:

```
$ cargo run
   Compiling branches v0.1.0 (file:///projects/branches)
    Finished dev [unoptimized + debuginfo] target(s) in 0.31s
     Running `target/debug/branches`
number is divisible by 3
```

When this program executes, it checks each if expression in turn and executes the first body for which the condition evaluates to true. Note that even though 6 is divisible by 2, we don't see the output `number is divisible by 2`, nor do we see the `number is not divisible by 4, 3, or 2` text from the else block. That's because Rust only executes the block for the first true condition, and once it finds one, it doesn't even check the rest.

Using too many else if expressions can clutter your code, so if you have more than one, you might want to refactor your code. Chapter 6 describes a powerful Rust branching construct called match for these cases.

Using if in a let Statement

Because if is an expression, we can use it on the right side of a let statement to assign the outcome to a variable, as in Listing 3-2.

src/main.rs
```
fn main() {
    let condition = true;
```

```
    let number = if condition { 5 } else { 6 };

    println!("The value of number is: {number}");
}
```

Listing 3-2: Assigning the result of an if expression to a variable

The number variable will be bound to a value based on the outcome of
the if expression. Run this code to see what happens:

```
$ cargo run
   Compiling branches v0.1.0 (file:///projects/branches)
    Finished dev [unoptimized + debuginfo] target(s) in 0.30s
     Running `target/debug/branches`
The value of number is: 5
```

Remember that blocks of code evaluate to the last expression in them,
and numbers by themselves are also expressions. In this case, the value of
the whole if expression depends on which block of code executes. This
means the values that have the potential to be results from each arm of the
if must be the same type; in Listing 3-2, the results of both the if arm and
the else arm were i32 integers. If the types are mismatched, as in the following example, we'll get an error:

src/main.rs
```
fn main() {
    let condition = true;

    let number = if condition { 5 } else { "six" };

    println!("The value of number is: {number}");
}
```

When we try to compile this code, we'll get an error. The if and else
arms have value types that are incompatible, and Rust indicates exactly
where to find the problem in the program:

```
$ cargo run
   Compiling branches v0.1.0 (file:///projects/branches)
error[E0308]: `if` and `else` have incompatible types
 --> src/main.rs:4:44
  |
4 |     let number = if condition { 5 } else { "six" };
  |                                 -          ^^^^^ expected integer, found `&str`
  |                                 |
  |                                 expected because of this
```

The expression in the if block evaluates to an integer, and the expression in the else block evaluates to a string. This won't work because variables
must have a single type, and Rust needs to know at compile time what type
the number variable is, definitively. Knowing the type of number lets the compiler verify the type is valid everywhere we use number. Rust wouldn't be able

to do that if the type of number was only determined at runtime; the compiler would be more complex and would make fewer guarantees about the code if it had to keep track of multiple hypothetical types for any variable.

Repetition with Loops

It's often useful to execute a block of code more than once. For this task, Rust provides several *loops*, which will run through the code inside the loop body to the end and then start immediately back at the beginning. To experiment with loops, let's make a new project called *loops*.

Rust has three kinds of loops: loop, while, and for. Let's try each one.

Repeating Code with loop

The loop keyword tells Rust to execute a block of code over and over again forever or until you explicitly tell it to stop.

As an example, change the *src/main.rs* file in your *loops* directory to look like this:

src/main.rs
```
fn main() {
    loop {
        println!("again!");
    }
}
```

When we run this program, we'll see again! printed over and over continuously until we stop the program manually. Most terminals support the keyboard shortcut CTRL-C to interrupt a program that is stuck in a continual loop. Give it a try:

```
$ cargo run
   Compiling loops v0.1.0 (file:///projects/loops)
    Finished dev [unoptimized + debuginfo] target(s) in 0.29s
     Running `target/debug/loops`
again!
again!
again!
again!
^Cagain!
```

The symbol ^C represents where you pressed CTRL-C. You may or may not see the word again! printed after the ^C, depending on where the code was in the loop when it received the interrupt signal.

Fortunately, Rust also provides a way to break out of a loop using code. You can place the break keyword within the loop to tell the program when to stop executing the loop. Recall that we did this in the guessing game in "Quitting After a Correct Guess" on page 28 to exit the program when the user won the game by guessing the correct number.

We also used continue in the guessing game, which in a loop tells the program to skip over any remaining code in this iteration of the loop and go to the next iteration.

Returning Values from Loops

One of the uses of a `loop` is to retry an operation you know might fail, such as checking whether a thread has completed its job. You might also need to pass the result of that operation out of the loop to the rest of your code. To do this, you can add the value you want returned after the `break` expression you use to stop the loop; that value will be returned out of the loop so you can use it, as shown here:

```
fn main() {
    let mut counter = 0;

    let result = loop {
        counter += 1;

        if counter == 10 {
            break counter * 2;
        }
    };

    println!("The result is {result}");
}
```

Before the loop, we declare a variable named `counter` and initialize it to 0. Then we declare a variable named `result` to hold the value returned from the loop. On every iteration of the loop, we add 1 to the `counter` variable, and then check whether the `counter` is equal to 10. When it is, we use the `break` keyword with the value `counter * 2`. After the loop, we use a semicolon to end the statement that assigns the value to `result`. Finally, we print the value in `result`, which in this case is 20.

Loop Labels to Disambiguate Between Multiple Loops

If you have loops within loops, `break` and `continue` apply to the innermost loop at that point. You can optionally specify a *loop label* on a loop that you can then use with `break` or `continue` to specify that those keywords apply to the labeled loop instead of the innermost loop. Loop labels must begin with a single quote. Here's an example with two nested loops:

```
fn main() {
    let mut count = 0;
    'counting_up: loop {
        println!("count = {count}");
        let mut remaining = 10;

        loop {
            println!("remaining = {remaining}");
            if remaining == 9 {
                break;
            }
            if count == 2 {
                break 'counting_up;
            }
            remaining -= 1;
```

```
        }

            count += 1;
        }
        println!("End count = {count}");
    }
```

The outer loop has the label 'counting_up, and it will count up from 0 to 2. The inner loop without a label counts down from 10 to 9. The first break that doesn't specify a label will exit the inner loop only. The break 'counting _up; statement will exit the outer loop. This code prints:

```
   Compiling loops v0.1.0 (file:///projects/loops)
    Finished dev [unoptimized + debuginfo] target(s) in 0.58s
     Running `target/debug/loops`
count = 0
remaining = 10
remaining = 9
count = 1
remaining = 10
remaining = 9
count = 2
remaining = 10
End count = 2
```

Conditional Loops with while

A program will often need to evaluate a condition within a loop. While the condition is true, the loop runs. When the condition ceases to be true, the program calls break, stopping the loop. It's possible to implement behavior like this using a combination of loop, if, else, and break; you could try that now in a program, if you'd like. However, this pattern is so common that Rust has a built-in language construct for it, called a while loop. In Listing 3-3, we use while to loop the program three times, counting down each time, and then, after the loop, print a message and exit.

src/main.rs
```
fn main() {
    let mut number = 3;

    while number != 0 {
        println!("{number}!");

        number -= 1;
    }

    println!("LIFTOFF!!!");
}
```

Listing 3-3: Using a while loop to run code while a condition evaluates to true

This construct eliminates a lot of nesting that would be necessary if you used loop, if, else, and break, and it's clearer. While a condition evaluates to true, the code runs; otherwise, it exits the loop.

Looping Through a Collection with for

You can choose to use the while construct to loop over the elements of a collection, such as an array. For example, the loop in Listing 3-4 prints each element in the array a.

src/main.rs
```
fn main() {
    let a = [10, 20, 30, 40, 50];
    let mut index = 0;

    while index < 5 {
        println!("the value is: {}", a[index]);

        index += 1;
    }
}
```

Listing 3-4: Looping through each element of a collection using a while loop

Here, the code counts up through the elements in the array. It starts at index 0, and then loops until it reaches the final index in the array (that is, when index < 5 is no longer true). Running this code will print every element in the array:

```
$ cargo run
   Compiling loops v0.1.0 (file:///projects/loops)
    Finished dev [unoptimized + debuginfo] target(s) in 0.32s
     Running `target/debug/loops`
the value is: 10
the value is: 20
the value is: 30
the value is: 40
the value is: 50
```

All five array values appear in the terminal, as expected. Even though index will reach a value of 5 at some point, the loop stops executing before trying to fetch a sixth value from the array.

However, this approach is error prone; we could cause the program to panic if the index value or test condition is incorrect. For example, if you changed the definition of the a array to have four elements but forgot to update the condition to while index < 4, the code would panic. It's also slow, because the compiler adds runtime code to perform the conditional check of whether the index is within the bounds of the array on every iteration through the loop.

As a more concise alternative, you can use a for loop and execute some code for each item in a collection. A for loop looks like the code in Listing 3-5.

src/main.rs
```
fn main() {
    let a = [10, 20, 30, 40, 50];

    for element in a {
```

```
        println!("the value is: {element}");
    }
}
```

Listing 3-5: Looping through each element of a collection using a for loop

When we run this code, we'll see the same output as in Listing 3-4. More importantly, we've now increased the safety of the code and eliminated the chance of bugs that might result from going beyond the end of the array or not going far enough and missing some items.

Using the for loop, you wouldn't need to remember to change any other code if you changed the number of values in the array, as you would with the method used in Listing 3-4.

The safety and conciseness of for loops make them the most commonly used loop construct in Rust. Even in situations in which you want to run some code a certain number of times, as in the countdown example that used a while loop in Listing 3-3, most Rustaceans would use a for loop. The way to do that would be to use a Range, provided by the standard library, which generates all numbers in sequence starting from one number and ending before another number.

Here's what the countdown would look like using a for loop and another method we've not yet talked about, rev, to reverse the range:

src/main.rs
```
fn main() {
    for number in (1..4).rev() {
        println!("{number}!");
    }
    println!("LIFTOFF!!!");
}
```

This code is a bit nicer, isn't it?

Summary

You made it! This was a sizable chapter: you learned about variables, scalar and compound data types, functions, comments, if expressions, and loops! To practice with the concepts discussed in this chapter, try building programs to do the following:

- Convert temperatures between Fahrenheit and Celsius.
- Generate the *n*th Fibonacci number.
- Print the lyrics to the Christmas carol "The Twelve Days of Christmas," taking advantage of the repetition in the song.

When you're ready to move on, we'll talk about a concept in Rust that *doesn't* commonly exist in other programming languages: ownership.

4

UNDERSTANDING OWNERSHIP

Ownership is Rust's most unique feature and has deep implications for the rest of the language. It enables Rust to make memory safety guarantees without needing a garbage collector, so it's important to understand how ownership works. In this chapter, we'll talk about ownership as well as several related features: borrowing, slices, and how Rust lays data out in memory.

What Is Ownership?

Ownership is a set of rules that govern how a Rust program manages memory. All programs have to manage the way they use a computer's memory while running. Some languages have garbage collection that regularly looks for no-longer-used memory as the program runs; in other languages, the programmer must explicitly allocate and free the memory. Rust uses a third approach: memory is managed through a system of ownership with a set of rules that the compiler checks. If any of the rules are violated, the program won't compile. None of the features of ownership will slow down your program while it's running.

Because ownership is a new concept for many programmers, it does take some time to get used to. The good news is that the more experienced you become with Rust and the rules of the ownership system, the easier you'll find it to naturally develop code that is safe and efficient. Keep at it!

When you understand ownership, you'll have a solid foundation for understanding the features that make Rust unique. In this chapter, you'll learn ownership by working through some examples that focus on a very common data structure: strings.

THE STACK AND THE HEAP

Many programming languages don't require you to think about the stack and the heap very often. But in a systems programming language like Rust, whether a value is on the stack or the heap affects how the language behaves and why you have to make certain decisions. Parts of ownership will be described in relation to the stack and the heap later in this chapter, so here is a brief explanation in preparation.

Both the stack and the heap are parts of memory available to your code to use at runtime, but they are structured in different ways. The stack stores values in the order it gets them and removes the values in the opposite order. This is referred to as *last in, first out*. Think of a stack of plates: when you add more plates, you put them on top of the pile, and when you need a plate, you take one off the top. Adding or removing plates from the middle or bottom wouldn't work as well! Adding data is called *pushing onto the stack*, and removing data is called *popping off the stack*. All data stored on the stack must have a known, fixed size. Data with an unknown size at compile time or a size that might change must be stored on the heap instead.

The heap is less organized: when you put data on the heap, you request a certain amount of space. The memory allocator finds an empty spot in the heap that is big enough, marks it as being in use, and returns a *pointer*, which is the address of that location. This process is called *allocating on the heap* and is sometimes abbreviated as just *allocating* (pushing values onto the stack is not considered allocating). Because the pointer to the heap is a known, fixed size, you can store the pointer on the stack, but when you want the actual data, you must follow the pointer. Think of being seated at a restaurant. When you enter, you state the number of people in your group, and the host finds an empty table that fits everyone and leads you there. If someone in your group comes late, they can ask where you've been seated to find you.

Pushing to the stack is faster than allocating on the heap because the allocator never has to search for a place to store new data; that location is always at the top of the stack. Comparatively, allocating space on the heap requires more work because the allocator must first find a big enough space to hold the data and then perform bookkeeping to prepare for the next allocation.

Accessing data in the heap is slower than accessing data on the stack because you have to follow a pointer to get there. Contemporary processors are faster if they jump around less in memory. Continuing the analogy, consider a server at a restaurant taking orders from many tables. It's most efficient to get all the orders at one table before moving on to the next table. Taking an order from table A, then an order from table B, then one from A again, and then one from B again would be a much slower process. By the same token, a processor can do its job better if it works on data that's close to other data (as it is on the stack) rather than farther away (as it can be on the heap).

When your code calls a function, the values passed into the function (including, potentially, pointers to data on the heap) and the function's local variables get pushed onto the stack. When the function is over, those values get popped off the stack.

Keeping track of what parts of code are using what data on the heap, minimizing the amount of duplicate data on the heap, and cleaning up unused data on the heap so you don't run out of space are all problems that ownership addresses. Once you understand ownership, you won't need to think about the stack and the heap very often, but knowing that the main purpose of ownership is to manage heap data can help explain why it works the way it does.

Ownership Rules

First, let's take a look at the ownership rules. Keep these rules in mind as we work through the examples that illustrate them:

- Each value in Rust has an *owner*.
- There can only be one owner at a time.
- When the owner goes out of scope, the value will be dropped.

Variable Scope

Now that we're past basic Rust syntax, we won't include all the `fn main() {` code in examples, so if you're following along, make sure to put the following examples inside a `main` function manually. As a result, our examples will be a bit more concise, letting us focus on the actual details rather than boilerplate code.

As a first example of ownership, we'll look at the *scope* of some variables. A scope is the range within a program for which an item is valid. Take the following variable:

```
let s = "hello";
```

The variable s refers to a string literal, where the value of the string is hardcoded into the text of our program. The variable is valid from the point at which it's declared until the end of the current *scope*. Listing 4-1 shows a program with comments annotating where the variable s would be valid.

```
{                       // s is not valid here, since it's not yet declared
    let s = "hello";    // s is valid from this point forward

    // do stuff with s
}                       // this scope is now over, and s is no longer valid
```

Listing 4-1: A variable and the scope in which it is valid

In other words, there are two important points in time here:

- When s comes *into* scope, it is valid.
- It remains valid until it goes *out of* scope.

At this point, the relationship between scopes and when variables are valid is similar to that in other programming languages. Now we'll build on top of this understanding by introducing the String type.

The String Type

To illustrate the rules of ownership, we need a data type that is more complex than those we covered in "Data Types" on page 36. The types covered previously are of a known size, can be stored on the stack and popped off the stack when their scope is over, and can be quickly and trivially copied to make a new, independent instance if another part of code needs to use the same value in a different scope. But we want to look at data that is stored on the heap and explore how Rust knows when to clean up that data, and the String type is a great example.

We'll concentrate on the parts of String that relate to ownership. These aspects also apply to other complex data types, whether they are provided by the standard library or created by you. We'll discuss String in more depth in Chapter 8.

We've already seen string literals, where a string value is hardcoded into our program. String literals are convenient, but they aren't suitable for every situation in which we may want to use text. One reason is that they're immutable. Another is that not every string value can be known when we write our code: for example, what if we want to take user input and store it? For these situations, Rust has a second string type, String. This type manages data allocated on the heap and as such is able to store an amount of text that is unknown to us at compile time. You can create a String from a string literal using the from function, like so:

```
let s = String::from("hello");
```

The double colon :: operator allows us to namespace this particular from function under the String type rather than using some sort of name like string_from. We'll discuss this syntax more in "Method Syntax" on page 97, and when we talk about namespacing with modules in "Paths for Referring to an Item in the Module Tree" on page 125.

This kind of string *can* be mutated:

```
let mut s = String::from("hello");

s.push_str(", world!"); // push_str() appends a literal to a String

println!("{s}"); // this will print `hello, world!`
```

So, what's the difference here? Why can String be mutated but literals cannot? The difference is in how these two types deal with memory.

Memory and Allocation

In the case of a string literal, we know the contents at compile time, so the text is hardcoded directly into the final executable. This is why string literals are fast and efficient. But these properties only come from the string literal's immutability. Unfortunately, we can't put a blob of memory into the binary for each piece of text whose size is unknown at compile time and whose size might change while running the program.

With the String type, in order to support a mutable, growable piece of text, we need to allocate an amount of memory on the heap, unknown at compile time, to hold the contents. This means:

- The memory must be requested from the memory allocator at runtime.
- We need a way of returning this memory to the allocator when we're done with our String.

That first part is done by us: when we call String::from, its implementation requests the memory it needs. This is pretty much universal in programming languages.

However, the second part is different. In languages with a *garbage collector (GC)*, the GC keeps track of and cleans up memory that isn't being used anymore, and we don't need to think about it. In most languages without a GC, it's our responsibility to identify when memory is no longer being used and to call code to explicitly free it, just as we did to request it. Doing this correctly has historically been a difficult programming problem. If we forget, we'll waste memory. If we do it too early, we'll have an invalid variable. If we do it twice, that's a bug too. We need to pair exactly one allocate with exactly one free.

Rust takes a different path: the memory is automatically returned once the variable that owns it goes out of scope. Here's a version of our scope example from Listing 4-1 using a String instead of a string literal:

```
{
    let s = String::from("hello"); // s is valid from this point forward

    // do stuff with s
}                                   // this scope is now over, and s is no
                                    // longer valid
```

There is a natural point at which we can return the memory our String needs to the allocator: when s goes out of scope. When a variable goes out of scope, Rust calls a special function for us. This function is called drop, and it's where the author of String can put the code to return the memory. Rust calls drop automatically at the closing curly bracket.

NOTE   *In C++, this pattern of deallocating resources at the end of an item's lifetime is sometimes called* Resource Acquisition Is Initialization (RAII). *The drop function in Rust will be familiar to you if you've used RAII patterns.*

This pattern has a profound impact on the way Rust code is written. It may seem simple right now, but the behavior of code can be unexpected in more complicated situations when we want to have multiple variables use the data we've allocated on the heap. Let's explore some of those situations now.

Variables and Data Interacting with Move

Multiple variables can interact with the same data in different ways in Rust. Let's look at an example using an integer in Listing 4-2.

```
let x = 5;
let y = x;
```

Listing 4-2: Assigning the integer value of variable x to y

We can probably guess what this is doing: "bind the value 5 to x; then make a copy of the value in x and bind it to y." We now have two variables, x and y, and both equal 5. This is indeed what is happening, because integers are simple values with a known, fixed size, and these two 5 values are pushed onto the stack.

Now let's look at the String version:

```
let s1 = String::from("hello");
let s2 = s1;
```

This looks very similar, so we might assume that the way it works would be the same: that is, the second line would make a copy of the value in s1 and bind it to s2. But this isn't quite what happens.

Take a look at Figure 4-1 to see what is happening to String under the covers. A String is made up of three parts, shown on the left: a pointer to the memory that holds the contents of the string, a length, and a capacity. This group of data is stored on the stack. On the right is the memory on the heap that holds the contents.

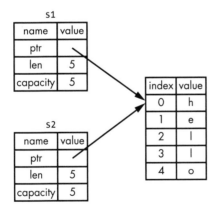

s1			index	value
name	value		0	h
ptr	→		1	e
len	5		2	l
capacity	5		3	l
			4	o

Figure 4-1: Representation in memory of a String holding the value "hello" bound to s1

The length is how much memory, in bytes, the contents of the String are currently using. The capacity is the total amount of memory, in bytes, that the String has received from the allocator. The difference between length and capacity matters, but not in this context, so for now, it's fine to ignore the capacity.

When we assign s1 to s2, the String data is copied, meaning we copy the pointer, the length, and the capacity that are on the stack. We do not copy the data on the heap that the pointer refers to. In other words, the data representation in memory looks like Figure 4-2.

s1			index	value
name	value		0	h
ptr			1	e
len	5		2	l
capacity	5		3	l
			4	o

s2		
name	value	
ptr		
len	5	
capacity	5	

Figure 4-2: Representation in memory of the variable s2 that has a copy of the pointer, length, and capacity of s1

The representation does *not* look like Figure 4-3, which is what memory would look like if Rust instead copied the heap data as well. If Rust did this, the operation s2 = s1 could be very expensive in terms of runtime performance if the data on the heap were large.

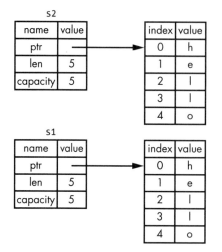

Figure 4-3: Another possibility for what
s2 = s1 might do if Rust copied the heap
data as well

Earlier, we said that when a variable goes out of scope, Rust automatically calls the drop function and cleans up the heap memory for that variable. But Figure 4-2 shows both data pointers pointing to the same location. This is a problem: when s2 and s1 go out of scope, they will both try to free the same memory. This is known as a *double free* error and is one of the memory safety bugs we mentioned previously. Freeing memory twice can lead to memory corruption, which can potentially lead to security vulnerabilities.

To ensure memory safety, after the line let s2 = s1;, Rust considers s1 as no longer valid. Therefore, Rust doesn't need to free anything when s1 goes out of scope. Check out what happens when you try to use s1 after s2 is created; it won't work:

```
let s1 = String::from("hello");
let s2 = s1;

println!("{s1}, world!");
```

You'll get an error like this because Rust prevents you from using the invalidated reference:

```
error[E0382]: borrow of moved value: `s1`
 --> src/main.rs:5:28
  |
2 |     let s1 = String::from("hello");
  |         -- move occurs because `s1` has type `String`, which
does not implement the `Copy` trait
3 |     let s2 = s1;
  |              -- value moved here
4 |
5 |     println!("{s1}, world!");
  |               ^^ value borrowed here after move
```

If you've heard the terms *shallow copy* and *deep copy* while working with other languages, the concept of copying the pointer, length, and capacity without copying the data probably sounds like making a shallow copy. But because Rust also invalidates the first variable, instead of being called a shallow copy, it's known as a *move*. In this example, we would say that s1 was *moved* into s2. So, what actually happens is shown in Figure 4-4.

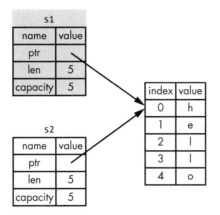

Figure 4-4: Representation in memory after s1 has been invalidated

That solves our problem! With only s2 valid, when it goes out of scope it alone will free the memory, and we're done.

In addition, there's a design choice that's implied by this: Rust will never automatically create "deep" copies of your data. Therefore, any *automatic* copying can be assumed to be inexpensive in terms of runtime performance.

Variables and Data Interacting with Clone

If we *do* want to deeply copy the heap data of the String, not just the stack data, we can use a common method called clone. We'll discuss method syntax in Chapter 5, but because methods are a common feature in many programming languages, you've probably seen them before.

Here's an example of the clone method in action:

```
let s1 = String::from("hello");
let s2 = s1.clone();

println!("s1 = {s1}, s2 = {s2}");
```

This works just fine and explicitly produces the behavior shown in Figure 4-3, where the heap data *does* get copied.

When you see a call to clone, you know that some arbitrary code is being executed and that code may be expensive. It's a visual indicator that something different is going on.

Stack-Only Data: Copy

There's another wrinkle we haven't talked about yet. This code using integers—part of which was shown in Listing 4-2—works and is valid:

```
let x = 5;
let y = x;

println!("x = {x}, y = {y}");
```

But this code seems to contradict what we just learned: we don't have a call to clone, but x is still valid and wasn't moved into y.

The reason is that types such as integers that have a known size at compile time are stored entirely on the stack, so copies of the actual values are quick to make. That means there's no reason we would want to prevent x from being valid after we create the variable y. In other words, there's no difference between deep and shallow copying here, so calling clone wouldn't do anything different from the usual shallow copying, and we can leave it out.

Rust has a special annotation called the Copy trait that we can place on types that are stored on the stack, as integers are (we'll talk more about traits in Chapter 10). If a type implements the Copy trait, variables that use it do not move, but rather are trivially copied, making them still valid after assignment to another variable.

Rust won't let us annotate a type with Copy if the type, or any of its parts, has implemented the Drop trait. If the type needs something special to happen when the value goes out of scope and we add the Copy annotation to that type, we'll get a compile-time error. To learn about how to add the Copy annotation to your type to implement the trait, see Appendix C.

So, what types implement the Copy trait? You can check the documentation for the given type to be sure, but as a general rule, any group of simple scalar values can implement Copy, and nothing that requires allocation or is some form of resource can implement Copy. Here are some of the types that implement Copy:

- All the integer types, such as u32.
- The Boolean type, bool, with values true and false.
- All the floating-point types, such as f64.
- The character type, char.
- Tuples, if they only contain types that also implement Copy. For example, (i32, i32) implements Copy, but (i32, String) does not.

Ownership and Functions

The mechanics of passing a value to a function are similar to those when assigning a value to a variable. Passing a variable to a function will move or copy, just as assignment does. Listing 4-3 has an example with some annotations showing where variables go into and out of scope.

```rust
fn main() {
    let s = String::from("hello");  // s comes into scope

    takes_ownership(s);             // s's value moves into the function...
                                    // ... and so is no longer valid here

    let x = 5;                      // x comes into scope

    makes_copy(x);                  // x would move into the function,
                                    // but i32 is Copy, so it's okay to still
                                    // use x afterward

} // Here, x goes out of scope, then s. However, because s's value was moved,
  // nothing special happens.

fn takes_ownership(some_string: String) { // some_string comes into scope
    println!("{some_string}");
} // Here, some_string goes out of scope and `drop` is called. The backing
  // memory is freed.

fn makes_copy(some_integer: i32) { // some_integer comes into scope
    println!("{some_integer}");
} // Here, some_integer goes out of scope. Nothing special happens.
```

Listing 4-3: Functions with ownership and scope annotated

If we tried to use s after the call to takes_ownership, Rust would throw a compile-time error. These static checks protect us from mistakes. Try adding code to main that uses s and x to see where you can use them and where the ownership rules prevent you from doing so.

Return Values and Scope

Returning values can also transfer ownership. Listing 4-4 shows an example of a function that returns some value, with similar annotations as those in Listing 4-3.

```rust
fn main() {
    let s1 = gives_ownership();         // gives_ownership moves its return
                                        // value into s1

    let s2 = String::from("hello");     // s2 comes into scope

    let s3 = takes_and_gives_back(s2);  // s2 is moved into
                                        // takes_and_gives_back, which also
                                        // moves its return value into s3
} // Here, s3 goes out of scope and is dropped. s2 was moved, so nothing
  // happens. s1 goes out of scope and is dropped.

fn gives_ownership() -> String {        // gives_ownership will move its
                                        // return value into the function
                                        // that calls it
```

```
    let some_string = String::from("yours"); // some_string comes into scope

    some_string                              // some_string is returned and
                                             // moves out to the calling
                                             // function
}

// This function takes a String and returns a String.
fn takes_and_gives_back(a_string: String) -> String { // a_string comes into
                                                      // scope

    a_string  // a_string is returned and moves out to the calling function
}
```

Listing 4-4: Transferring ownership of return values

The ownership of a variable follows the same pattern every time: assigning a value to another variable moves it. When a variable that includes data on the heap goes out of scope, the value will be cleaned up by drop unless ownership of the data has been moved to another variable.

While this works, taking ownership and then returning ownership with every function is a bit tedious. What if we want to let a function use a value but not take ownership? It's quite annoying that anything we pass in also needs to be passed back if we want to use it again, in addition to any data resulting from the body of the function that we might want to return as well.

Rust does let us return multiple values using a tuple, as shown in Listing 4-5.

src/main.rs
```
fn main() {
    let s1 = String::from("hello");

    let (s2, len) = calculate_length(s1);

    println!("The length of '{s2}' is {len}.");
}

fn calculate_length(s: String) -> (String, usize) {
    let length = s.len(); // len() returns the length of a String

    (s, length)
}
```

Listing 4-5: Returning ownership of parameters

But this is too much ceremony and a lot of work for a concept that should be common. Luckily for us, Rust has a feature for using a value without transferring ownership, called *references*.

References and Borrowing

The issue with the tuple code in Listing 4-5 is that we have to return the String to the calling function so we can still use the String after the call to calculate_length, because the String was moved into calculate_length. Instead, we can provide a reference to the String value. A *reference* is like a pointer in that it's an address we can follow to access the data stored at that address; that data is owned by some other variable. Unlike a pointer, a reference is guaranteed to point to a valid value of a particular type for the life of that reference.

Here is how you would define and use a calculate_length function that has a reference to an object as a parameter instead of taking ownership of the value:

src/main.rs
```
fn main() {
    let s1 = String::from("hello");

    let len = calculate_length(&s1);

    println!("The length of '{s1}' is {len}.");
}

fn calculate_length(s: &String) -> usize {
    s.len()
}
```

First, notice that all the tuple code in the variable declaration and the function return value is gone. Second, note that we pass &s1 into calculate _length and, in its definition, we take &String rather than String. These ampersands represent *references*, and they allow you to refer to some value without taking ownership of it. Figure 4-5 depicts this concept.

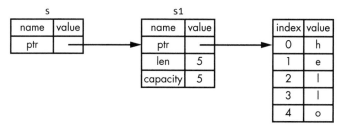

Figure 4-5: A diagram of &String s pointing at String s1

NOTE   *The opposite of referencing by using & is dereferencing, which is accomplished with the dereference operator, *. We'll see some uses of the dereference operator in Chapter 8 and discuss details of dereferencing in Chapter 15.*

Let's take a closer look at the function call here:

```
let s1 = String::from("hello");

let len = calculate_length(&s1);
```

The &s1 syntax lets us create a reference that *refers* to the value of s1 but does not own it. Because it does not own it, the value it points to will not be dropped when the reference stops being used.

Likewise, the signature of the function uses & to indicate that the type of the parameter s is a reference. Let's add some explanatory annotations:

```
fn calculate_length(s: &String) -> usize { // s is a reference to a String
    s.len()
} // Here, s goes out of scope. But because it does not have ownership of what
  // it refers to, the String is not dropped.
```

The scope in which the variable s is valid is the same as any function parameter's scope, but the value pointed to by the reference is not dropped when s stops being used, because s doesn't have ownership. When functions have references as parameters instead of the actual values, we won't need to return the values in order to give back ownership, because we never had ownership.

We call the action of creating a reference *borrowing*. As in real life, if a person owns something, you can borrow it from them. When you're done, you have to give it back. You don't own it.

So, what happens if we try to modify something we're borrowing? Try the code in Listing 4-6. Spoiler alert: it doesn't work!

src/main.rs
```
fn main() {
    let s = String::from("hello");

    change(&s);
}

fn change(some_string: &String) {
    some_string.push_str(", world");
}
```

Listing 4-6: Attempting to modify a borrowed value

Here's the error:

```
error[E0596]: cannot borrow `*some_string` as mutable, as it is behind a `&` reference
 --> src/main.rs:8:5
  |
7 | fn change(some_string: &String) {
  |                        ------- help: consider changing this to be a mutable
reference: `&mut String`
8 |     some_string.push_str(", world");
  |     ^^^^^^^^^^^^^^^^^^^^^^^^^^^^^^^^ `some_string` is a `&` reference, so
the data it refers to cannot be borrowed as mutable
```

Just as variables are immutable by default, so are references. We're not allowed to modify something we have a reference to.

Mutable References

We can fix the code from Listing 4-6 to allow us to modify a borrowed value with just a few small tweaks that use, instead, a *mutable reference*:

```
fn main() {
    let mut s = String::from("hello");

    change(&mut s);
}

fn change(some_string: &mut String) {
    some_string.push_str(", world");
}
```
src/main.rs

First we change s to be `mut`. Then we create a mutable reference with `&mut s` where we call the `change` function, and update the function signature to accept a mutable reference with `some_string: &mut String`. This makes it very clear that the `change` function will mutate the value it borrows.

Mutable references have one big restriction: if you have a mutable reference to a value, you can have no other references to that value. This code that attempts to create two mutable references to s will fail:

```
let mut s = String::from("hello");

let r1 = &mut s;
let r2 = &mut s;

println!("{r1}, {r2}");
```
src/main.rs

Here's the error:

```
error[E0499]: cannot borrow `s` as mutable more than once at a time
 --> src/main.rs:5:14
  |
4 |     let r1 = &mut s;
  |              ------ first mutable borrow occurs here
5 |     let r2 = &mut s;
  |              ^^^^^^ second mutable borrow occurs here
6 |
7 |     println!("{r1}, {r2}");
  |               -- first borrow later used here
```

This error says that this code is invalid because we cannot borrow s as mutable more than once at a time. The first mutable borrow is in r1 and must last until it's used in the `println!`, but between the creation of that mutable reference and its usage, we tried to create another mutable reference in r2 that borrows the same data as r1.

The restriction preventing multiple mutable references to the same data at the same time allows for mutation but in a very controlled fashion.

It's something that new Rustaceans struggle with because most languages let you mutate whenever you'd like. The benefit of having this restriction is that Rust can prevent data races at compile time. A *data race* is similar to a race condition and happens when these three behaviors occur:

- Two or more pointers access the same data at the same time.
- At least one of the pointers is being used to write to the data.
- There's no mechanism being used to synchronize access to the data.

Data races cause undefined behavior and can be difficult to diagnose and fix when you're trying to track them down at runtime; Rust prevents this problem by refusing to compile code with data races!

As always, we can use curly brackets to create a new scope, allowing for multiple mutable references, just not *simultaneous* ones:

```
let mut s = String::from("hello");

{
    let r1 = &mut s;
} // r1 goes out of scope here, so we can make a new reference with no problems

let r2 = &mut s;
```

Rust enforces a similar rule for combining mutable and immutable references. This code results in an error:

```
let mut s = String::from("hello");

let r1 = &s; // no problem
let r2 = &s; // no problem
let r3 = &mut s; // BIG PROBLEM

println!("{r1}, {r2}, and {r3}");
```

Here's the error:

```
error[E0502]: cannot borrow `s` as mutable because it is also borrowed as immutable
 --> src/main.rs:6:14
  |
4 |     let r1 = &s; // no problem
  |              -- immutable borrow occurs here
5 |     let r2 = &s; // no problem
6 |     let r3 = &mut s; // BIG PROBLEM
  |              ^^^^^^ mutable borrow occurs here
7 |
8 |     println!("{r1}, {r2}, and {r3}");
  |               -- immutable borrow later used here
```

Whew! We *also* cannot have a mutable reference while we have an immutable one to the same value.

Users of an immutable reference don't expect the value to suddenly change out from under them! However, multiple immutable references are allowed because no one who is just reading the data has the ability to affect anyone else's reading of the data.

Note that a reference's scope starts from where it is introduced and continues through the last time that reference is used. For instance, this code will compile because the last usage of the immutable references, the println!, occurs before the mutable reference is introduced:

```
let mut s = String::from("hello");

let r1 = &s; // no problem
let r2 = &s; // no problem
println!("{r1} and {r2}");
// Variables r1 and r2 will not be used after this point.

let r3 = &mut s; // no problem
println!("{r3}");
```

The scopes of the immutable references r1 and r2 end after the println! where they are last used, which is before the mutable reference r3 is created. These scopes don't overlap, so this code is allowed: the compiler can tell that the reference is no longer being used at a point before the end of the scope.

Even though borrowing errors may be frustrating at times, remember that it's the Rust compiler pointing out a potential bug early (at compile time rather than at runtime) and showing you exactly where the problem is. Then you don't have to track down why your data isn't what you thought it was.

Dangling References

In languages with pointers, it's easy to erroneously create a *dangling pointer*—a pointer that references a location in memory that may have been given to someone else—by freeing some memory while preserving a pointer to that memory. In Rust, by contrast, the compiler guarantees that references will never be dangling references: if you have a reference to some data, the compiler will ensure that the data will not go out of scope before the reference to the data does.

Let's try to create a dangling reference to see how Rust prevents them with a compile-time error:

src/main.rs
```
fn main() {
    let reference_to_nothing = dangle();
}

fn dangle() -> &String {
    let s = String::from("hello");

    &s
}
```

Here's the error:

```
error[E0106]: missing lifetime specifier
 --> src/main.rs:5:16
  |
5 | fn dangle() -> &String {
  |                ^ expected named lifetime parameter
  |
  = help: this function's return type contains a borrowed value,
but there is no value for it to be borrowed from
help: consider using the `'static` lifetime
  |
5 | fn dangle() -> &'static String {
  |                 ~~~~~~~~
```

This error message refers to a feature we haven't covered yet: lifetimes. We'll discuss lifetimes in detail in Chapter 10. But, if you disregard the parts about lifetimes, the message does contain the key to why this code is a problem:

```
this function's return type contains a borrowed value, but there
is no value for it to be borrowed from
```

Let's take a closer look at exactly what's happening at each stage of our dangle code:

```
// src/main.rs
fn dangle() -> &String { // dangle returns a reference to a String

    let s = String::from("hello"); // s is a new String

    &s // we return a reference to the String, s
} // Here, s goes out of scope and is dropped, so its memory goes away.
  // Danger!
```

Because s is created inside dangle, when the code of dangle is finished, s will be deallocated. But we tried to return a reference to it. That means this reference would be pointing to an invalid String. That's no good! Rust won't let us do this.

The solution here is to return the String directly:

```
fn no_dangle() -> String {
    let s = String::from("hello");

    s
}
```

This works without any problems. Ownership is moved out, and nothing is deallocated.

The Rules of References

Let's recap what we've discussed about references:

- At any given time, you can have *either* one mutable reference *or* any number of immutable references.
- References must always be valid.

Next, we'll look at a different kind of reference: slices.

The Slice Type

Slices let you reference a contiguous sequence of elements in a collection rather than the whole collection. A slice is a kind of reference, so it does not have ownership.

Here's a small programming problem: write a function that takes a string of words separated by spaces and returns the first word it finds in that string. If the function doesn't find a space in the string, the whole string must be one word, so the entire string should be returned.

Let's work through how we'd write the signature of this function without using slices, to understand the problem that slices will solve:

```
fn first_word(s: &String) -> ?
```

The first_word function has a parameter of type &String. We don't want ownership, so this is fine. But what should we return? We don't really have a way to talk about *part* of a string. However, we could return the index of the end of the word, indicated by a space. Let's try that, as shown in Listing 4-7.

```
src/main.rs   fn first_word(s: &String) -> usize {
            ❶ let bytes = s.as_bytes();

              for (❷i, &item) in ❸ bytes.iter().enumerate() {
                ❹ if item == b' ' {
                    return i;
                }
              }

            ❺ s.len()
            }
```

Listing 4-7: The first_word function that returns a byte index value into the String parameter

Because we need to go through the String element by element and check whether a value is a space, we'll convert our String to an array of bytes using the as_bytes method ❶.

Next, we create an iterator over the array of bytes using the iter method ❸. We'll discuss iterators in more detail in Chapter 13. For now, know that iter is a method that returns each element in a collection and that enumerate wraps the result of iter and returns each element as part of a tuple instead. The first element of the tuple returned from enumerate is the index, and the second element is a reference to the element. This is a bit more convenient than calculating the index ourselves.

Because the enumerate method returns a tuple, we can use patterns to destructure that tuple. We'll be discussing patterns more in Chapter 6. In the for loop, we specify a pattern that has i for the index in the tuple and &item for the single byte in the tuple ❷. Because we get a reference to the element from .iter().enumerate(), we use & in the pattern.

Inside the for loop, we search for the byte that represents the space by using the byte literal syntax ❹. If we find a space, we return the position. Otherwise, we return the length of the string by using s.len() ❺.

We now have a way to find out the index of the end of the first word in the string, but there's a problem. We're returning a usize on its own, but it's only a meaningful number in the context of the &String. In other words, because it's a separate value from the String, there's no guarantee that it will still be valid in the future. Consider the program in Listing 4-8 that uses the first_word function from Listing 4-7.

```
// src/main.rs
fn main() {
    let mut s = String::from("hello world");

    let word = first_word(&s); // word will get the value 5

    s.clear(); // this empties the String, making it equal to ""

    // word still has the value 5 here, but there's no more string that
    // we could meaningfully use the value 5 with. word is now totally invalid!
}
```

Listing 4-8: Storing the result from calling the first_word function and then changing the String contents

This program compiles without any errors and would also do so if we used word after calling s.clear(). Because word isn't connected to the state of s at all, word still contains the value 5. We could use that value 5 with the variable s to try to extract the first word out, but this would be a bug because the contents of s have changed since we saved 5 in word.

Having to worry about the index in word getting out of sync with the data in s is tedious and error prone! Managing these indices is even more brittle if we write a second_word function. Its signature would have to look like this:

```
fn second_word(s: &String) -> (usize, usize) {
```

Now we're tracking a starting *and* an ending index, and we have even more values that were calculated from data in a particular state but aren't tied to that state at all. We have three unrelated variables floating around that need to be kept in sync.

Luckily, Rust has a solution to this problem: string slices.

String Slices

A *string slice* is a reference to part of a String, and it looks like this:

```
let s = String::from("hello world");

let hello = &s[0..5];
let world = &s[6..11];
```

Rather than a reference to the entire String, hello is a reference to a portion of the String, specified in the extra [0..5] bit. We create slices using a range within brackets by specifying [*starting_index..ending_index*], where *starting_index* is the first position in the slice and *ending_index* is one more than the last position in the slice. Internally, the slice data structure stores the starting position and the length of the slice, which corresponds to *ending_index* minus *starting_index*. So, in the case of let world = &s[6..11];, world would be a slice that contains a pointer to the byte at index 6 of s with a length value of 5.

Figure 4-6 shows this in a diagram.

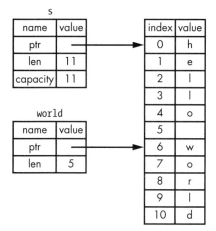

Figure 4-6: String slice referring to part of a String

With Rust's .. range syntax, if you want to start at index 0, you can drop the value before the two periods. In other words, these are equal:

```
let s = String::from("hello");

let slice = &s[0..2];
let slice = &s[..2];
```

By the same token, if your slice includes the last byte of the String, you can drop the trailing number. That means these are equal:

```
let s = String::from("hello");

let len = s.len();
```

```
let slice = &s[3..len];
let slice = &s[3..];
```

You can also drop both values to take a slice of the entire string. So these are equal:

```
let s = String::from("hello");

let len = s.len();

let slice = &s[0..len];
let slice = &s[..];
```

NOTE *String slice range indices must occur at valid UTF-8 character boundaries. If you attempt to create a string slice in the middle of a multibyte character, your program will exit with an error. For the purposes of introducing string slices, we are assuming ASCII only in this section; a more thorough discussion of UTF-8 handling is in "Storing UTF-8 Encoded Text with Strings" on page 147.*

With all this information in mind, let's rewrite first_word to return a slice. The type that signifies "string slice" is written as &str:

src/main.rs
```
fn first_word(s: &String) -> &str {
    let bytes = s.as_bytes();

    for (i, &item) in bytes.iter().enumerate() {
        if item == b' ' {
            return &s[0..i];
        }
    }

    &s[..]
}
```

We get the index for the end of the word the same way we did in Listing 4-7, by looking for the first occurrence of a space. When we find a space, we return a string slice using the start of the string and the index of the space as the starting and ending indices.

Now when we call first_word, we get back a single value that is tied to the underlying data. The value is made up of a reference to the starting point of the slice and the number of elements in the slice.

Returning a slice would also work for a second_word function:

```
fn second_word(s: &String) -> &str {
```

We now have a straightforward API that's much harder to mess up because the compiler will ensure the references into the String remain valid. Remember the bug in the program in Listing 4-8, when we got the index to the end of the first word but then cleared the string so our index was invalid? That code was logically incorrect but didn't show any immediate errors. The problems would show up later if we kept trying to use the first word index with an emptied string. Slices make this bug impossible and let us know we have a problem with our code much sooner. Using the slice version of first_word will throw a compile-time error:

src/main.rs
```
fn main() {
    let mut s = String::from("hello world");

    let word = first_word(&s);

    s.clear(); // error!

    println!("the first word is: {word}");
}
```

Here's the compiler error:

```
error[E0502]: cannot borrow `s` as mutable because it is also borrowed as immutable
  --> src/main.rs:18:5
   |
16 |     let word = first_word(&s);
   |                           -- immutable borrow occurs here
17 |
18 |     s.clear(); // error!
   |     ^^^^^^^^^ mutable borrow occurs here
19 |
20 |     println!("the first word is: {word}");
   |                                   ---- immutable borrow later used here
```

Recall from the borrowing rules that if we have an immutable reference to something, we cannot also take a mutable reference. Because clear needs to truncate the String, it needs to get a mutable reference. The println! after the call to clear uses the reference in word, so the immutable reference must still be active at that point. Rust disallows the mutable reference in clear and the immutable reference in word from existing at the same time, and compilation fails. Not only has Rust made our API easier to use, but it has also eliminated an entire class of errors at compile time!

String Literals as Slices

Recall that we talked about string literals being stored inside the binary. Now that we know about slices, we can properly understand string literals:

```
let s = "Hello, world!";
```

The type of s here is &str: it's a slice pointing to that specific point of the binary. This is also why string literals are immutable; &str is an immutable reference.

String Slices as Parameters

Knowing that you can take slices of literals and String values leads us to one more improvement on first_word, and that's its signature:

```
fn first_word(s: &String) -> &str {
```

A more experienced Rustacean would write the signature shown in Listing 4-9 instead because it allows us to use the same function on both &String values and &str values.

```
fn first_word(s: &str) -> &str {
```

Listing 4-9: Improving the first_word function by using a string slice for the type of the s parameter

If we have a string slice, we can pass that directly. If we have a String, we can pass a slice of the String or a reference to the String. This flexibility takes advantage of *deref coercions*, a feature we will cover in "Implicit Deref Coercions with Functions and Methods" on page 325.

Defining a function to take a string slice instead of a reference to a String makes our API more general and useful without losing any functionality:

src/main.rs
```
fn main() {
    let my_string = String::from("hello world");

    // `first_word` works on slices of `String`s, whether partial
    // or whole.
    let word = first_word(&my_string[0..6]);
    let word = first_word(&my_string[..]);
    // `first_word` also works on references to `String`s, which
    // are equivalent to whole slices of `String`s.
    let word = first_word(&my_string);

    let my_string_literal = "hello world";

    // `first_word` works on slices of string literals,
    // whether partial or whole.
    let word = first_word(&my_string_literal[0..6]);
    let word = first_word(&my_string_literal[..]);

    // Because string literals *are* string slices already,
    // this works too, without the slice syntax!
    let word = first_word(my_string_literal);
}
```

Other Slices

String slices, as you might imagine, are specific to strings. But there's a more general slice type too. Consider this array:

```
let a = [1, 2, 3, 4, 5];
```

Just as we might want to refer to part of a string, we might want to refer to part of an array. We'd do so like this:

```
let a = [1, 2, 3, 4, 5];

let slice = &a[1..3];

assert_eq!(slice, &[2, 3]);
```

This slice has the type &[i32]. It works the same way as string slices do, by storing a reference to the first element and a length. You'll use this kind of slice for all sorts of other collections. We'll discuss these collections in detail when we talk about vectors in Chapter 8.

Summary

The concepts of ownership, borrowing, and slices ensure memory safety in Rust programs at compile time. The Rust language gives you control over your memory usage in the same way as other systems' programming languages, but having the owner of data automatically clean up that data when the owner goes out of scope means you don't have to write and debug extra code to get this control.

Ownership affects how lots of other parts of Rust work, so we'll talk about these concepts further throughout the rest of the book. Let's move on to Chapter 5 and look at grouping pieces of data together in a struct.

5

USING STRUCTS TO STRUCTURE RELATED DATA

 A *struct*, or *structure*, is a custom data type that lets you package together and name multiple related values that make up a meaningful group. If you're familiar with an object-oriented language, a *struct* is like an object's data attributes. In this chapter, we'll compare and contrast tuples with structs to build on what you already know and demonstrate when structs are a better way to group data.

We'll demonstrate how to define and instantiate structs. We'll discuss how to define associated functions, especially the kind of associated functions called *methods*, to specify behavior associated with a struct type. Structs and enums (discussed in Chapter 6) are the building blocks for creating new types in your program's domain to take full advantage of Rust's compile-time type checking.

Defining and Instantiating Structs

Structs are similar to tuples, discussed in "The Tuple Type" on page 40, in that both hold multiple related values. Like tuples, the pieces of a struct can be different types. Unlike with tuples, in a struct you'll name each piece of data so it's clear what the values mean. Adding these names means that structs are more flexible than tuples: you don't have to rely on the order of the data to specify or access the values of an instance.

To define a struct, we enter the keyword struct and name the entire struct. A struct's name should describe the significance of the pieces of data being grouped together. Then, inside curly brackets, we define the names and types of the pieces of data, which we call *fields*. For example, Listing 5-1 shows a struct that stores information about a user account.

src/main.rs
```
struct User {
    active: bool,
    username: String,
    email: String,
    sign_in_count: u64,
}
```

Listing 5-1: A User struct definition

To use a struct after we've defined it, we create an *instance* of that struct by specifying concrete values for each of the fields. We create an instance by stating the name of the struct and then add curly brackets containing *key: value* pairs, where the keys are the names of the fields and the values are the data we want to store in those fields. We don't have to specify the fields in the same order in which we declared them in the struct. In other words, the struct definition is like a general template for the type, and instances fill in that template with particular data to create values of the type. For example, we can declare a particular user as shown in Listing 5-2.

src/main.rs
```
fn main() {
    let user1 = User {
        active: true,
        username: String::from("someusername123"),
        email: String::from("someone@example.com"),
        sign_in_count: 1,
    };
}
```

Listing 5-2: Creating an instance of the User struct

To get a specific value from a struct, we use dot notation. For example, to access this user's email address, we use user1.email. If the instance is mutable, we can change a value by using the dot notation and assigning into a particular field. Listing 5-3 shows how to change the value in the email field of a mutable User instance.

src/main.rs
```
fn main() {
    let mut user1 = User {
```

```
        active: true,
        username: String::from("someusername123"),
        email: String::from("someone@example.com"),
        sign_in_count: 1,
    };

    user1.email = String::from("anotheremail@example.com");
}
```

Listing 5-3: Changing the value in the email field of a User instance

Note that the entire instance must be mutable; Rust doesn't allow us to mark only certain fields as mutable. As with any expression, we can construct a new instance of the struct as the last expression in the function body to implicitly return that new instance.

Listing 5-4 shows a build_user function that returns a User instance with the given email and username. The active field gets the value of true, and the sign_in_count gets a value of 1.

```
fn build_user(email: String, username: String) -> User {
    User {
        active: true,
        username: username,
        email: email,
        sign_in_count: 1,
    }
}
```

Listing 5-4: A build_user function that takes an email and username and returns a User instance

It makes sense to name the function parameters with the same name as the struct fields, but having to repeat the email and username field names and variables is a bit tedious. If the struct had more fields, repeating each name would get even more annoying. Luckily, there's a convenient shorthand!

Using the Field Init Shorthand

Because the parameter names and the struct field names are exactly the same in Listing 5-4, we can use the *field init shorthand* syntax to rewrite build_user so it behaves exactly the same but doesn't have the repetition of username and email, as shown in Listing 5-5.

```
fn build_user(email: String, username: String) -> User {
    User {
        active: true,
        username,
        email,
        sign_in_count: 1,
    }
}
```

Listing 5-5: A build_user function that uses field init shorthand because the username and email parameters have the same name as struct fields

Here, we're creating a new instance of the User struct, which has a field named email. We want to set the email field's value to the value in the email parameter of the build_user function. Because the email field and the email parameter have the same name, we only need to write email rather than email: email.

Creating Instances from Other Instances with Struct Update Syntax

It's often useful to create a new instance of a struct that includes most of the values from another instance, but changes some. You can do this using *struct update syntax.*

First, in Listing 5-6 we show how to create a new User instance in user2 regularly, without the update syntax. We set a new value for email but otherwise use the same values from user1 that we created in Listing 5-2.

src/main.rs
```
fn main() {
    --snip--

    let user2 = User {
        active: user1.active,
        username: user1.username,
        email: String::from("another@example.com"),
        sign_in_count: user1.sign_in_count,
    };
}
```

Listing 5-6: Creating a new User instance using one of the values from user1

Using struct update syntax, we can achieve the same effect with less code, as shown in Listing 5-7. The syntax .. specifies that the remaining fields not explicitly set should have the same value as the fields in the given instance.

src/main.rs
```
fn main() {
    --snip--

    let user2 = User {
        email: String::from("another@example.com"),
        ..user1
    };
}
```

Listing 5-7: Using struct update syntax to set a new email value for a User instance but to use the rest of the values from user1

The code in Listing 5-7 also creates an instance in user2 that has a different value for email but has the same values for the username, active, and sign_in_count fields from user1. The ..user1 must come last to specify that any remaining fields should get their values from the corresponding fields in user1, but we can choose to specify values for as many fields as we want in any order, regardless of the order of the fields in the struct's definition.

Note that the struct update syntax uses = like an assignment; this is because it moves the data, just as we saw in "Variables and Data Interacting with Move" on page 64. In this example, we can no longer use user1 after creating user2 because the String in the username field of user1 was moved into user2. If we had given user2 new String values for both email and username, and thus only used the active and sign_in_count values from user1, then user1 would still be valid after creating user2. Both active and sign_in_count are types that implement the Copy trait, so the behavior we discussed in "Stack-Only Data: Copy" on page 68 would apply.

Using Tuple Structs Without Named Fields to Create Different Types

Rust also supports structs that look similar to tuples, called *tuple structs*. Tuple structs have the added meaning the struct name provides but don't have names associated with their fields; rather, they just have the types of the fields. Tuple structs are useful when you want to give the whole tuple a name and make the tuple a different type from other tuples, and when naming each field as in a regular struct would be verbose or redundant.

To define a tuple struct, start with the struct keyword and the struct name followed by the types in the tuple. For example, here we define and use two tuple structs named Color and Point:

src/main.rs
```
struct Color(i32, i32, i32);
struct Point(i32, i32, i32);

fn main() {
    let black = Color(0, 0, 0);
    let origin = Point(0, 0, 0);
}
```

Note that the black and origin values are different types because they're instances of different tuple structs. Each struct you define is its own type, even though the fields within the struct might have the same types. For example, a function that takes a parameter of type Color cannot take a Point as an argument, even though both types are made up of three i32 values. Otherwise, tuple struct instances are similar to tuples in that you can destructure them into their individual pieces, and you can use a . followed by the index to access an individual value.

Unit-Like Structs Without Any Fields

You can also define structs that don't have any fields! These are called *unit-like structs* because they behave similarly to (), the unit type that we mentioned in "The Tuple Type" on page 40. Unit-like structs can be useful when you need to implement a trait on some type but don't have any data that you want to store in the type itself. We'll discuss traits in Chapter 10.

Here's an example of declaring and instantiating a unit struct named AlwaysEqual:

```rust
struct AlwaysEqual;

fn main() {
    let subject = AlwaysEqual;
}
```

To define AlwaysEqual, we use the struct keyword, the name we want, and then a semicolon. No need for curly brackets or parentheses! Then we can get an instance of AlwaysEqual in the subject variable in a similar way: using the name we defined, without any curly brackets or parentheses. Imagine that later we'll implement behavior for this type such that every instance of AlwaysEqual is always equal to every instance of any other type, perhaps to have a known result for testing purposes. We wouldn't need any data to implement that behavior! You'll see in Chapter 10 how to define traits and implement them on any type, including unit-like structs.

OWNERSHIP OF STRUCT DATA

In the User struct definition in Listing 5-1, we used the owned String type rather than the &str string slice type. This is a deliberate choice because we want each instance of this struct to own all of its data and for that data to be valid for as long as the entire struct is valid.

It's also possible for structs to store references to data owned by something else, but to do so requires the use of *lifetimes*, a Rust feature that we'll discuss in Chapter 10. Lifetimes ensure that the data referenced by a struct is valid for as long as the struct is. Let's say you try to store a reference in a struct without specifying lifetimes, like the following in *src/main.rs*; this won't work:

```rust
struct User {
    active: bool,
    username: &str,
    email: &str,
    sign_in_count: u64,
}

fn main() {
    let user1 = User {
        active: true,
        username: "someusername123",
        email: "someone@example.com",
        sign_in_count: 1,
    };
}
```

The compiler will complain that it needs lifetime specifiers:

```
$ cargo run
   Compiling structs v0.1.0 (file:///projects/structs)
error[E0106]: missing lifetime specifier
 --> src/main.rs:3:15
  |
3 |     username: &str,
  |               ^ expected named lifetime parameter
  |
help: consider introducing a named lifetime parameter
  |
1 ~ struct User<'a> {
2 |     active: bool,
3 ~     username: &'a str,
  |

error[E0106]: missing lifetime specifier
 --> src/main.rs:4:12
  |
4 |     email: &str,
  |            ^ expected named lifetime parameter
  |
help: consider introducing a named lifetime parameter
  |
1 ~ struct User<'a> {
2 |     active: bool,
3 |     username: &str,
4 ~     email: &'a str,
  |
```

In Chapter 10, we'll discuss how to fix these errors so you can store references in structs, but for now, we'll fix errors like these using owned types like String instead of references like &str.

An Example Program Using Structs

To understand when we might want to use structs, let's write a program that calculates the area of a rectangle. We'll start by using single variables, and then refactor the program until we're using structs instead.

Let's make a new binary project with Cargo called *rectangles* that will take the width and height of a rectangle specified in pixels and calculate the area of the rectangle. Listing 5-8 shows a short program with one way of doing exactly that in our project's *src/main.rs*.

src/main.rs
```
fn main() {
    let width1 = 30;
    let height1 = 50;
```

```
    println!(
        "The area of the rectangle is {} square pixels.",
        area(width1, height1)
    );
}

fn area(width: u32, height: u32) -> u32 {
    width * height
}
```

Listing 5-8: Calculating the area of a rectangle specified by separate width and height variables

Now, run this program using cargo run:

```
The area of the rectangle is 1500 square pixels.
```

This code succeeds in figuring out the area of the rectangle by calling the area function with each dimension, but we can do more to make this code clear and readable.

The issue with this code is evident in the signature of area:

```
fn area(width: u32, height: u32) -> u32 {
```

The area function is supposed to calculate the area of one rectangle, but the function we wrote has two parameters, and it's not clear anywhere in our program that the parameters are related. It would be more readable and more manageable to group width and height together. We've already discussed one way we might do that in "The Tuple Type" on page 40: by using tuples.

Refactoring with Tuples

Listing 5-9 shows another version of our program that uses tuples.

src/main.rs
```
fn main() {
    let rect1 = (30, 50);

    println!(
        "The area of the rectangle is {} square pixels.",
      ❶ area(rect1)
    );
}

fn area(dimensions: (u32, u32)) -> u32 {
  ❷ dimensions.0 * dimensions.1
}
```

Listing 5-9: Specifying the width and height of the rectangle with a tuple

In one way, this program is better. Tuples let us add a bit of structure, and we're now passing just one argument ❶. But in another way, this version is less clear: tuples don't name their elements, so we have to index into the parts of the tuple ❷, making our calculation less obvious.

Mixing up the width and height wouldn't matter for the area calculation, but if we want to draw the rectangle on the screen, it would matter! We would have to keep in mind that `width` is the tuple index 0 and `height` is the tuple index 1. This would be even harder for someone else to figure out and keep in mind if they were to use our code. Because we haven't conveyed the meaning of our data in our code, it's now easier to introduce errors.

Refactoring with Structs: Adding More Meaning

We use structs to add meaning by labeling the data. We can transform the tuple we're using into a struct with a name for the whole as well as names for the parts, as shown in Listing 5-10.

```
src/main.rs  ❶ struct Rectangle {
                ❷ width: u32,
                   height: u32,
               }

               fn main() {
                ❸ let rect1 = Rectangle {
                       width: 30,
                       height: 50,
                   };

                   println!(
                       "The area of the rectangle is {} square pixels.",
                       area(&rect1)
                   );
               }

             ❹ fn area(rectangle: &Rectangle) -> u32 {
                ❺ rectangle.width * rectangle.height
               }
```

Listing 5-10: Defining a Rectangle struct

Here, we've defined a struct and named it `Rectangle` ❶. Inside the curly brackets, we defined the fields as `width` and `height`, both of which have type `u32` ❷. Then, in main, we created a particular instance of `Rectangle` that has a width of 30 and a height of 50 ❸.

Our area function is now defined with one parameter, which we've named rectangle, whose type is an immutable borrow of a struct `Rectangle` instance ❹. As mentioned in Chapter 4, we want to borrow the struct rather than take ownership of it. This way, main retains its ownership and can continue using rect1, which is the reason we use the `&` in the function signature and where we call the function.

The area function accesses the `width` and `height` fields of the `Rectangle` instance ❺ (note that accessing fields of a borrowed struct instance does not move the field values, which is why you often see borrows of structs). Our function signature for area now says exactly what we mean: calculate the area of `Rectangle`, using its `width` and `height` fields. This conveys that the width and height are related to each other, and it gives descriptive names to the values rather than using the tuple index values of 0 and 1. This is a win for clarity.

Adding Useful Functionality with Derived Traits

It'd be useful to be able to print an instance of Rectangle while we're debugging our program and see the values for all its fields. Listing 5-11 tries using the println! macro as we have used in previous chapters. This won't work, however.

src/main.rs
```
struct Rectangle {
    width: u32,
    height: u32,
}

fn main() {
    let rect1 = Rectangle {
        width: 30,
        height: 50,
    };

    println!("rect1 is {}", rect1);
}
```

Listing 5-11: Attempting to print a Rectangle instance

When we compile this code, we get an error with this core message:

```
error[E0277]: `Rectangle` doesn't implement `std::fmt::Display`
```

The println! macro can do many kinds of formatting, and by default, the curly brackets tell println! to use formatting known as Display: output intended for direct end user consumption. The primitive types we've seen so far implement Display by default because there's only one way you'd want to show a 1 or any other primitive type to a user. But with structs, the way println! should format the output is less clear because there are more display possibilities: Do you want commas or not? Do you want to print the curly brackets? Should all the fields be shown? Due to this ambiguity, Rust doesn't try to guess what we want, and structs don't have a provided implementation of Display to use with println! and the {} placeholder.

If we continue reading the errors, we'll find this helpful note:

```
= help: the trait `std::fmt::Display` is not implemented for `Rectangle`
= note: in format strings you may be able to use `{:?}` (or {:#?} for pretty-print) instead
```

Let's try it! The println! macro call will now look like println!("rect1 is {:?}", rect1);. Putting the specifier :? inside the curly brackets tells println! we want to use an output format called Debug. The Debug trait enables us to print our struct in a way that is useful for developers so we can see its value while we're debugging our code.

Compile the code with this change. Drat! We still get an error:

```
error[E0277]: `Rectangle` doesn't implement `Debug`
```

But again, the compiler gives us a helpful note:

```
= help: the trait `Debug` is not implemented for `Rectangle`
= note: add `#[derive(Debug)]` or manually implement `Debug`
```

Rust *does* include functionality to print out debugging information, but we have to explicitly opt in to make that functionality available for our struct. To do that, we add the outer attribute #[derive(Debug)] just before the struct definition, as shown in Listing 5-12.

src/main.rs
```
#[derive(Debug)]
struct Rectangle {
    width: u32,
    height: u32,
}

fn main() {
    let rect1 = Rectangle {
        width: 30,
        height: 50,
    };

    println!("rect1 is {:?}", rect1);
}
```

Listing 5-12: Adding the attribute to derive the Debug trait and printing the Rectangle instance using debug formatting

Now when we run the program, we won't get any errors, and we'll see the following output:

```
rect1 is Rectangle { width: 30, height: 50 }
```

Nice! It's not the prettiest output, but it shows the values of all the fields for this instance, which would definitely help during debugging. When we have larger structs, it's useful to have output that's a bit easier to read; in those cases, we can use {:#?} instead of {:?} in the println! string. In this example, using the {:#?} style will output the following:

```
rect1 is Rectangle {
    width: 30,
    height: 50,
}
```

Another way to print out a value using the Debug format is to use the dbg! macro, which takes ownership of an expression (as opposed to println!, which takes a reference), prints the file and line number of where that dbg! macro call occurs in your code along with the resultant value of that expression, and returns ownership of the value.

NOTE *Calling the dbg! macro prints to the standard error console stream (stderr), as opposed to println!, which prints to the standard output console stream (stdout). We'll talk more about stderr and stdout in "Writing Error Messages to Standard Error Instead of Standard Output" on page 270.*

Here's an example where we're interested in the value that gets assigned to the width field, as well as the value of the whole struct in rect1:

src/main.rs
```
#[derive(Debug)]
struct Rectangle {
    width: u32,
    height: u32,
}

fn main() {
    let scale = 2;
    let rect1 = Rectangle {
      ❶ width: dbg!(30 * scale),
        height: 50,
    };

  ❷ dbg!(&rect1);
}
```

We can put dbg! around the expression 30 * scale ❶ and, because dbg! returns ownership of the expression's value, the width field will get the same value as if we didn't have the dbg! call there. We don't want dbg! to take ownership of rect1, so we use a reference to rect1 in the next call ❷. Here's what the output of this example looks like:

```
[src/main.rs:10] 30 * scale = 60
[src/main.rs:14] &rect1 = Rectangle {
    width: 60,
    height: 50,
}
```

We can see the first bit of output came from ❶ where we're debugging the expression 30 * scale, and its resultant value is 60 (the Debug formatting implemented for integers is to print only their value). The dbg! call at ❷ outputs the value of &rect1, which is the Rectangle struct. This output uses the pretty Debug formatting of the Rectangle type. The dbg! macro can be really helpful when you're trying to figure out what your code is doing!

In addition to the Debug trait, Rust has provided a number of traits for us to use with the derive attribute that can add useful behavior to our custom types. Those traits and their behaviors are listed in Appendix C. We'll cover how to implement these traits with custom behavior as well as how to create your own traits in Chapter 10. There are also many attributes other than derive; for more information, see the "Attributes" section of the Rust Reference at *https://doc.rust-lang.org/reference/attributes.html*.

Our area function is very specific: it only computes the area of rectangles. It would be helpful to tie this behavior more closely to our Rectangle struct because it won't work with any other type. Let's look at how we can continue to refactor this code by turning the area function into an area *method* defined on our Rectangle type.

Method Syntax

Methods are similar to functions: we declare them with the `fn` keyword and a name, they can have parameters and a return value, and they contain some code that's run when the method is called from somewhere else. Unlike functions, methods are defined within the context of a struct (or an enum or a trait object, which we cover in Chapter 6 and Chapter 17, respectively), and their first parameter is always `self`, which represents the instance of the struct the method is being called on.

Defining Methods

Let's change the area function that has a Rectangle instance as a parameter and instead make an area method defined on the Rectangle struct, as shown in Listing 5-13.

src/main.rs
```
#[derive(Debug)]
struct Rectangle {
    width: u32,
    height: u32,
}

❶ impl Rectangle {
    ❷ fn area(&self) -> u32 {
        self.width * self.height
    }
}

fn main() {
    let rect1 = Rectangle {
        width: 30,
        height: 50,
    };

    println!(
        "The area of the rectangle is {} square pixels.",
      ❸ rect1.area()
    );
}
```

Listing 5-13: Defining an area method on the Rectangle struct

To define the function within the context of Rectangle, we start an `impl` (implementation) block for Rectangle ❶. Everything within this `impl` block will be associated with the Rectangle type. Then we move the area function within the `impl` curly brackets ❷ and change the first (and in this case, only) parameter to be `self` in the signature and everywhere within the body. In main, where we called the area function and passed rect1 as an argument, we can instead use *method syntax* to call the area method on our Rectangle instance ❸. The method syntax goes after an instance: we add a dot followed by the method name, parentheses, and any arguments.

In the signature for area, we use &self instead of rectangle: &Rectangle. The &self is actually short for self: &Self. Within an impl block, the type Self is an alias for the type that the impl block is for. Methods must have a parameter named self of type Self for their first parameter, so Rust lets you abbreviate this with only the name self in the first parameter spot. Note that we still need to use the & in front of the self shorthand to indicate that this method borrows the Self instance, just as we did in rectangle: &Rectangle. Methods can take ownership of self, borrow self immutably, as we've done here, or borrow self mutably, just as they can any other parameter.

We chose &self here for the same reason we used &Rectangle in the function version: we don't want to take ownership, and we just want to read the data in the struct, not write to it. If we wanted to change the instance that we've called the method on as part of what the method does, we'd use &mut self as the first parameter. Having a method that takes ownership of the instance by using just self as the first parameter is rare; this technique is usually used when the method transforms self into something else and you want to prevent the caller from using the original instance after the transformation.

The main reason for using methods instead of functions, in addition to providing method syntax and not having to repeat the type of self in every method's signature, is for organization. We've put all the things we can do with an instance of a type in one impl block rather than making future users of our code search for capabilities of Rectangle in various places in the library we provide.

Note that we can choose to give a method the same name as one of the struct's fields. For example, we can define a method on Rectangle that is also named width:

src/main.rs
```rust
impl Rectangle {
    fn width(&self) -> bool {
        self.width > 0
    }
}

fn main() {
    let rect1 = Rectangle {
        width: 30,
        height: 50,
    };

    if rect1.width() {
        println!(
            "The rectangle has a nonzero width; it is {}",
            rect1.width
        );
    }
}
```

Here, we're choosing to make the `width` method return `true` if the value in the instance's `width` field is greater than `0` and `false` if the value is `0`: we can use a field within a method of the same name for any purpose. In `main`, when we follow `rect1.width` with parentheses, Rust knows we mean the method `width`. When we don't use parentheses, Rust knows we mean the field `width`.

Often, but not always, when we give methods with the same name as a field we want it to only return the value in the field and do nothing else. Methods like this are called *getters*, and Rust does not implement them automatically for struct fields as some other languages do. Getters are useful because you can make the field private but the method public, and thus enable read-only access to that field as part of the type's public API. We will discuss what public and private are and how to designate a field or method as public or private in Chapter 7.

WHERE'S THE -> OPERATOR?

In C and C++, two different operators are used for calling methods: you use `.` if you're calling a method on the object directly and `->` if you're calling the method on a pointer to the object and need to dereference the pointer first. In other words, if `object` is a pointer, `object-> something()` is similar to `(*object). something()`.

Rust doesn't have an equivalent to the `->` operator; instead, Rust has a feature called *automatic referencing and dereferencing*. Calling methods is one of the few places in Rust that has this behavior.

Here's how it works: when you call a method with `object. something()`, Rust automatically adds in `&`, `&mut`, or `*` so `object` matches the signature of the method. In other words, the following are the same:

```
p1.distance(&p2);
(&p1).distance(&p2);
```

The first one looks much cleaner. This automatic referencing behavior works because methods have a clear receiver—the type of `self`. Given the receiver and name of a method, Rust can figure out definitively whether the method is reading (`&self`), mutating (`&mut self`), or consuming (`self`). The fact that Rust makes borrowing implicit for method receivers is a big part of making ownership ergonomic in practice.

Methods with More Parameters

Let's practice using methods by implementing a second method on the `Rectangle` struct. This time we want an instance of `Rectangle` to take another instance of `Rectangle` and return `true` if the second `Rectangle` can fit completely within self (the first Rectangle); otherwise, it should return false. That is, once we've defined the can_hold method, we want to be able to write the program shown in Listing 5-14.

src/main.rs
```
fn main() {
    let rect1 = Rectangle {
        width: 30,
        height: 50,
    };
    let rect2 = Rectangle {
        width: 10,
        height: 40,
    };
    let rect3 = Rectangle {
        width: 60,
        height: 45,
    };

    println!("Can rect1 hold rect2? {}", rect1.can_hold(&rect2));
    println!("Can rect1 hold rect3? {}", rect1.can_hold(&rect3));
}
```

Listing 5-14: Using the as-yet-unwritten can_hold method

The expected output would look like the following because both dimensions of rect2 are smaller than the dimensions of rect1, but rect3 is wider than rect1:

```
Can rect1 hold rect2? true
Can rect1 hold rect3? false
```

We know we want to define a method, so it will be within the impl Rectangle block. The method name will be can_hold, and it will take an immutable borrow of another Rectangle as a parameter. We can tell what the type of the parameter will be by looking at the code that calls the method: rect1.can_hold(&rect2) passes in &rect2, which is an immutable borrow to rect2, an instance of Rectangle. This makes sense because we only need to read rect2 (rather than write, which would mean we'd need a mutable borrow), and we want main to retain ownership of rect2 so we can use it again after calling the can_hold method. The return value of can_hold will be a Boolean, and the implementation will check whether the width and height of self are greater than the width and height of the other Rectangle, respectively. Let's add the new can_hold method to the impl block from Listing 5-13, shown in Listing 5-15.

src/main.rs
```
impl Rectangle {
    fn area(&self) -> u32 {
        self.width * self.height
    }
```

```
    fn can_hold(&self, other: &Rectangle) -> bool {
        self.width > other.width && self.height > other.height
    }
}
```

Listing 5-15: Implementing the can_hold method on Rectangle that takes another Rectangle instance as a parameter

When we run this code with the `main` function in Listing 5-14, we'll get our desired output. Methods can take multiple parameters that we add to the signature after the `self` parameter, and those parameters work just like parameters in functions.

Associated Functions

All functions defined within an `impl` block are called *associated functions* because they're associated with the type named after the `impl`. We can define associated functions that don't have `self` as their first parameter (and thus are not methods) because they don't need an instance of the type to work with. We've already used one function like this: the `String::from` function that's defined on the `String` type.

Associated functions that aren't methods are often used for constructors that will return a new instance of the struct. These are often called `new`, but `new` isn't a special name and isn't built into the language. For example, we could choose to provide an associated function named `square` that would have one dimension parameter and use that as both width and height, thus making it easier to create a square `Rectangle` rather than having to specify the same value twice:

src/main.rs
```
impl Rectangle {
    fn square(size: u32) -> ❶ Self {
        ❷ Self {
            width: size,
            height: size,
        }
    }
}
```

The `Self` keywords in the return type ❶ and in the body of the function ❷ are aliases for the type that appears after the `impl` keyword, which in this case is `Rectangle`.

To call this associated function, we use the `::` syntax with the struct name; `let sq = Rectangle::square(3);` is an example. This function is namespaced by the struct: the `::` syntax is used for both associated functions and namespaces created by modules. We'll discuss modules in Chapter 7.

Multiple impl Blocks

Each struct is allowed to have multiple `impl` blocks. For example, Listing 5-15 is equivalent to the code shown in Listing 5-16, which has each method in its own `impl` block.

```
impl Rectangle {
    fn area(&self) -> u32 {
        self.width * self.height
    }
}

impl Rectangle {
    fn can_hold(&self, other: &Rectangle) -> bool {
        self.width > other.width && self.height > other.height
    }
}
```

Listing 5-16: Rewriting Listing 5-15 using multiple `impl` blocks

There's no reason to separate these methods into multiple `impl` blocks here, but this is valid syntax. We'll see a case in which multiple `impl` blocks are useful in Chapter 10, where we discuss generic types and traits.

Summary

Structs let you create custom types that are meaningful for your domain. By using structs, you can keep associated pieces of data connected to each other and name each piece to make your code clear. In `impl` blocks, you can define functions that are associated with your type, and methods are a kind of associated function that let you specify the behavior that instances of your structs have.

But structs aren't the only way you can create custom types: let's turn to Rust's enum feature to add another tool to your toolbox.

6

ENUMS AND PATTERN MATCHING

 In this chapter, we'll look at *enumerations*, also referred to as *enums*. Enums allow you to define a type by enumerating its possible *variants*. First we'll define and use an enum to show how an enum can encode meaning along with data. Next, we'll explore a particularly useful enum, called Option, which expresses that a value can be either something or nothing. Then we'll look at how pattern matching in the match expression makes it easy to run different code for different values of an enum. Finally, we'll cover how the if let construct is another convenient and concise idiom available to handle enums in your code.

Defining an Enum

Where structs give you a way of grouping together related fields and data, like a Rectangle with its width and height, enums give you a way of saying a value is one of a possible set of values. For example, we may want to say that Rectangle is one of a set of possible shapes that also includes Circle and Triangle. To do this, Rust allows us to encode these possibilities as an enum.

Let's look at a situation we might want to express in code and see why enums are useful and more appropriate than structs in this case. Say we need to work with IP addresses. Currently, two major standards are used for IP addresses: version four and version six. Because these are the only possibilities for an IP address that our program will come across, we can *enumerate* all possible variants, which is where enumeration gets its name.

Any IP address can be either a version four or a version six address, but not both at the same time. That property of IP addresses makes the enum data structure appropriate because an enum value can only be one of its variants. Both version four and version six addresses are still fundamentally IP addresses, so they should be treated as the same type when the code is handling situations that apply to any kind of IP address.

We can express this concept in code by defining an IpAddrKind enumeration and listing the possible kinds an IP address can be, V4 and V6. These are the variants of the enum:

```
enum IpAddrKind {
    V4,
    V6,
}
```

IpAddrKind is now a custom data type that we can use elsewhere in our code.

Enum Values

We can create instances of each of the two variants of IpAddrKind like this:

```
let four = IpAddrKind::V4;
let six = IpAddrKind::V6;
```

Note that the variants of the enum are namespaced under its identifier, and we use a double colon to separate the two. This is useful because now both values IpAddrKind::V4 and IpAddrKind::V6 are of the same type: IpAddrKind. We can then, for instance, define a function that takes any IpAddrKind:

```
fn route(ip_kind: IpAddrKind) {}
```

And we can call this function with either variant:

```
route(IpAddrKind::V4);
route(IpAddrKind::V6);
```

Using enums has even more advantages. Thinking more about our IP address type, at the moment we don't have a way to store the actual IP address *data*; we only know what *kind* it is. Given that you just learned about structs in Chapter 5, you might be tempted to tackle this problem with structs as shown in Listing 6-1.

```
❶ enum IpAddrKind {
      V4,
      V6,
  }

❷ struct IpAddr {
    ❸ kind: IpAddrKind,
    ❹ address: String,
  }

❺ let home = IpAddr {
      kind: IpAddrKind::V4,
      address: String::from("127.0.0.1"),
  };

❻ let loopback = IpAddr {
      kind: IpAddrKind::V6,
      address: String::from("::1"),
  };
```

Listing 6-1: Storing the data and IpAddrKind variant of an IP address using a struct

Here, we've defined a struct IpAddr ❷ that has two fields: a kind field ❸ that is of type IpAddrKind (the enum we defined previously ❶) and an address field ❹ of type String. We have two instances of this struct. The first is home ❺, and it has the value IpAddrKind::V4 as its kind with associated address data of 127.0.0.1. The second instance is loopback ❻. It has the other variant of IpAddrKind as its kind value, V6, and has address ::1 associated with it. We've used a struct to bundle the kind and address values together, so now the variant is associated with the value.

However, representing the same concept using just an enum is more concise: rather than an enum inside a struct, we can put data directly into each enum variant. This new definition of the IpAddr enum says that both V4 and V6 variants will have associated String values:

```
enum IpAddr {
    V4(String),
    V6(String),
}

let home = IpAddr::V4(String::from("127.0.0.1"));

let loopback = IpAddr::V6(String::from("::1"));
```

We attach data to each variant of the enum directly, so there is no need for an extra struct. Here, it's also easier to see another detail of how enums work: the name of each enum variant that we define also becomes a function that constructs an instance of the enum. That is, IpAddr::V4() is a function call that takes a String argument and returns an instance of the IpAddr type. We automatically get this constructor function defined as a result of defining the enum.

There's another advantage to using an enum rather than a struct: each variant can have different types and amounts of associated data. Version four IP addresses will always have four numeric components that will have values between 0 and 255. If we wanted to store V4 addresses as four u8 values but still express V6 addresses as one String value, we wouldn't be able to with a struct. Enums handle this case with ease:

```
enum IpAddr {
    V4(u8, u8, u8, u8),
    V6(String),
}

let home = IpAddr::V4(127, 0, 0, 1);

let loopback = IpAddr::V6(String::from("::1"));
```

We've shown several different ways to define data structures to store version four and version six IP addresses. However, as it turns out, wanting to store IP addresses and encode which kind they are is so common that the standard library has a definition we can use! Let's look at how the standard library defines IpAddr: it has the exact enum and variants that we've defined and used, but it embeds the address data inside the variants in the form of two different structs, which are defined differently for each variant:

```
struct Ipv4Addr {
    --snip--
}

struct Ipv6Addr {
    --snip--
}

enum IpAddr {
    V4(Ipv4Addr),
    V6(Ipv6Addr),
}
```

This code illustrates that you can put any kind of data inside an enum variant: strings, numeric types, or structs, for example. You can even include another enum! Also, standard library types are often not much more complicated than what you might come up with.

Note that even though the standard library contains a definition for IpAddr, we can still create and use our own definition without conflict because we haven't brought the standard library's definition into our scope. We'll talk more about bringing types into scope in Chapter 7.

Let's look at another example of an enum in Listing 6-2: this one has a wide variety of types embedded in its variants.

```
enum Message {
    Quit,
    Move { x: i32, y: i32 },
```

```
    Write(String),
    ChangeColor(i32, i32, i32),
}
```

Listing 6-2: A Message enum whose variants each store different amounts and types of values

This enum has four variants with different types:

Quit   Has no data associated with it at all

Move   Has named fields, like a struct does

Write   Includes a single String

ChangeColor   Includes three i32 values

Defining an enum with variants such as the ones in Listing 6-2 is similar to defining different kinds of struct definitions, except the enum doesn't use the struct keyword and all the variants are grouped together under the Message type. The following structs could hold the same data that the preceding enum variants hold:

```
struct QuitMessage; // unit struct
struct MoveMessage {
    x: i32,
    y: i32,
}
struct WriteMessage(String); // tuple struct
struct ChangeColorMessage(i32, i32, i32); // tuple struct
```

But if we used the different structs, each of which has its own type, we couldn't as easily define a function to take any of these kinds of messages as we could with the Message enum defined in Listing 6-2, which is a single type.

There is one more similarity between enums and structs: just as we're able to define methods on structs using impl, we're also able to define methods on enums. Here's a method named call that we could define on our Message enum:

```
impl Message {
    fn call(&self) {
      ❶ // method body would be defined here
    }
}
```

```
❷ let m = Message::Write(String::from("hello"));
  m.call();
```

The body of the method would use self to get the value that we called the method on. In this example, we've created a variable m ❷ that has the value Message::Write(String::from("hello")), and that is what self will be in the body of the call method ❶ when m.call() runs.

Let's look at another enum in the standard library that is very common and useful: Option.

The Option Enum and Its Advantages Over Null Values

This section explores a case study of Option, which is another enum defined by the standard library. The Option type encodes the very common scenario in which a value could be something or it could be nothing.

For example, if you request the first item in a list containing multiple items, you would get a value. If you request the first item in an empty list, you would get nothing. Expressing this concept in terms of the type system means the compiler can check whether you've handled all the cases you should be handling; this functionality can prevent bugs that are extremely common in other programming languages.

Programming language design is often thought of in terms of which features you include, but the features you exclude are important too. Rust doesn't have the null feature that many other languages have. *Null* is a value that means there is no value there. In languages with null, variables can always be in one of two states: null or not-null.

In his 2009 presentation "Null References: The Billion Dollar Mistake," Tony Hoare, the inventor of null, had this to say:

> I call it my billion-dollar mistake. At that time, I was designing the first comprehensive type system for references in an object-oriented language. My goal was to ensure that all use of references should be absolutely safe, with checking performed automatically by the compiler. But I couldn't resist the temptation to put in a null reference, simply because it was so easy to implement. This has led to innumerable errors, vulnerabilities, and system crashes, which have probably caused a billion dollars of pain and damage in the last forty years.

The problem with null values is that if you try to use a null value as a not-null value, you'll get an error of some kind. Because this null or not-null property is pervasive, it's extremely easy to make this kind of error.

However, the concept that null is trying to express is still a useful one: a null is a value that is currently invalid or absent for some reason.

The problem isn't really with the concept but with the particular implementation. As such, Rust does not have nulls, but it does have an enum that can encode the concept of a value being present or absent. This enum is Option<T>, and it is defined by the standard library as follows:

```
enum Option<T> {
    None,
    Some(T),
}
```

The Option<T> enum is so useful that it's even included in the prelude; you don't need to bring it into scope explicitly. Its variants are also included in the prelude: you can use Some and None directly without the Option:: prefix. The Option<T> enum is still just a regular enum, and Some(T) and None are still variants of type Option<T>.

The <T> syntax is a feature of Rust we haven't talked about yet. It's a generic type parameter, and we'll cover generics in more detail in Chapter 10. For now, all you need to know is that <T> means that the Some variant of the Option enum can hold one piece of data of any type, and that each concrete type that gets used in place of T makes the overall Option<T> type a different type. Here are some examples of using Option values to hold number types and string types:

```
let some_number = Some(5);
let some_char = Some('e');

let absent_number: Option<i32> = None;
```

The type of some_number is Option<i32>. The type of some_char is Option<char>, which is a different type. Rust can infer these types because we've specified a value inside the Some variant. For absent_number, Rust requires us to annotate the overall Option type: the compiler can't infer the type that the corresponding Some variant will hold by looking only at a None value. Here, we tell Rust that we mean for absent_number to be of type Option<i32>.

When we have a Some value, we know that a value is present and the value is held within the Some. When we have a None value, in some sense it means the same thing as null: we don't have a valid value. So why is having Option<T> any better than having null?

In short, because Option<T> and T (where T can be any type) are different types, the compiler won't let us use an Option<T> value as if it were definitely a valid value. For example, this code won't compile, because it's trying to add an i8 to an Option<i8>:

```
let x: i8 = 5;
let y: Option<i8> = Some(5);

let sum = x + y;
```

If we run this code, we get an error message like this one:

```
error[E0277]: cannot add `Option<i8>` to `i8`
 --> src/main.rs:5:17
  |
5 |     let sum = x + y;
  |                 ^ no implementation for `i8 + Option<i8>`
  |
  = help: the trait `Add<Option<i8>>` is not implemented for `i8`
```

Intense! In effect, this error message means that Rust doesn't understand how to add an i8 and an Option<i8>, because they're different types. When we have a value of a type like i8 in Rust, the compiler will ensure that we always have a valid value. We can proceed confidently without having to check for null before using that value. Only when we have an Option<i8> (or whatever type of value we're working with) do we have to worry about possibly not having a value, and the compiler will make sure we handle that case before using the value.

In other words, you have to convert an Option<T> to a T before you can perform T operations with it. Generally, this helps catch one of the most common issues with null: assuming that something isn't null when it actually is.

Eliminating the risk of incorrectly assuming a not-null value helps you to be more confident in your code. In order to have a value that can possibly be null, you must explicitly opt in by making the type of that value Option<T>. Then, when you use that value, you are required to explicitly handle the case when the value is null. Everywhere that a value has a type that isn't an Option<T>, you *can* safely assume that the value isn't null. This was a deliberate design decision for Rust to limit null's pervasiveness and increase the safety of Rust code.

So how do you get the T value out of a Some variant when you have a value of type Option<T> so that you can use that value? The Option<T> enum has a large number of methods that are useful in a variety of situations; you can check them out in its documentation. Becoming familiar with the methods on Option<T> will be extremely useful in your journey with Rust.

In general, in order to use an Option<T> value, you want to have code that will handle each variant. You want some code that will run only when you have a Some(T) value, and this code is allowed to use the inner T. You want some other code to run only if you have a None value, and that code doesn't have a T value available. The match expression is a control flow construct that does just this when used with enums: it will run different code depending on which variant of the enum it has, and that code can use the data inside the matching value.

The match Control Flow Construct

Rust has an extremely powerful control flow construct called match that allows you to compare a value against a series of patterns and then execute code based on which pattern matches. Patterns can be made up of literal values, variable names, wildcards, and many other things; Chapter 18 covers all the different kinds of patterns and what they do. The power of match comes from the expressiveness of the patterns and the fact that the compiler confirms that all possible cases are handled.

Think of a match expression as being like a coin-sorting machine: coins slide down a track with variously sized holes along it, and each coin falls through the first hole it encounters that it fits into. In the same way, values go through each pattern in a match, and at the first pattern the value "fits," the value falls into the associated code block to be used during execution.

Speaking of coins, let's use them as an example using match! We can write a function that takes an unknown US coin and, in a similar way as the counting machine, determines which coin it is and returns its value in cents, as shown in Listing 6-3.

```
❶ enum Coin {
    Penny,
    Nickel,
    Dime,
    Quarter,
}

fn value_in_cents(coin: Coin) -> u8 {
  ❷ match coin {
      ❸ Coin::Penny => 1,
        Coin::Nickel => 5,
        Coin::Dime => 10,
        Coin::Quarter => 25,
    }
}
```

Listing 6-3: An enum and a match expression that has the variants of the enum as its patterns

Let's break down the match in the value_in_cents function. First we list the match keyword followed by an expression, which in this case is the value coin ❷. This seems very similar to a conditional expression used with if, but there's a big difference: with if, the condition needs to evaluate to a Boolean value, but here it can be any type. The type of coin in this example is the Coin enum that we defined at ❶.

Next are the match arms. An arm has two parts: a pattern and some code. The first arm here has a pattern that is the value Coin::Penny and then the => operator that separates the pattern and the code to run ❸. The code in this case is just the value 1. Each arm is separated from the next with a comma.

When the match expression executes, it compares the resultant value against the pattern of each arm, in order. If a pattern matches the value, the code associated with that pattern is executed. If that pattern doesn't match the value, execution continues to the next arm, much as in a coin-sorting machine. We can have as many arms as we need: in Listing 6-3, our match has four arms.

The code associated with each arm is an expression, and the resultant value of the expression in the matching arm is the value that gets returned for the entire match expression.

We don't typically use curly brackets if the match arm code is short, as it is in Listing 6-3 where each arm just returns a value. If you want to run multiple lines of code in a match arm, you must use curly brackets, and the comma following the arm is then optional. For example, the following code prints "Lucky penny!" every time the method is called with a Coin::Penny, but still returns the last value of the block, 1:

```
fn value_in_cents(coin: Coin) -> u8 {
    match coin {
        Coin::Penny => {
            println!("Lucky penny!");
            1
```

```
        }
        Coin::Nickel => 5,
        Coin::Dime => 10,
        Coin::Quarter => 25,
    }
}
```

Patterns That Bind to Values

Another useful feature of match arms is that they can bind to the parts of the values that match the pattern. This is how we can extract values out of enum variants.

As an example, let's change one of our enum variants to hold data inside it. From 1999 through 2008, the United States minted quarters with different designs for each of the 50 states on one side. No other coins got state designs, so only quarters have this extra value. We can add this information to our enum by changing the Quarter variant to include a UsState value stored inside it, which we've done in Listing 6-4.

```
#[derive(Debug)] // so we can inspect the state in a minute
enum UsState {
    Alabama,
    Alaska,
    --snip--
}

enum Coin {
    Penny,
    Nickel,
    Dime,
    Quarter(UsState),
}
```

Listing 6-4: A Coin enum in which the Quarter variant also holds a UsState value

Let's imagine that a friend is trying to collect all 50 state quarters. While we sort our loose change by coin type, we'll also call out the name of the state associated with each quarter so that if it's one our friend doesn't have, they can add it to their collection.

In the match expression for this code, we add a variable called state to the pattern that matches values of the variant Coin::Quarter. When a Coin::Quarter matches, the state variable will bind to the value of that quarter's state. Then we can use state in the code for that arm, like so:

```
fn value_in_cents(coin: Coin) -> u8 {
    match coin {
        Coin::Penny => 1,
        Coin::Nickel => 5,
        Coin::Dime => 10,
        Coin::Quarter(state) => {
            println!("State quarter from {:?}!", state);
            25
```

```
          }
       }
    }
```

If we were to call value_in_cents(Coin::Quarter(UsState::Alaska)), coin would be Coin::Quarter(UsState::Alaska). When we compare that value with each of the match arms, none of them match until we reach Coin::Quarter(state). At that point, the binding for state will be the value UsState::Alaska. We can then use that binding in the println! expression, thus getting the inner state value out of the Coin enum variant for Quarter.

Matching with Option<T>

In the previous section, we wanted to get the inner T value out of the Some case when using Option<T>; we can also handle Option<T> using match, as we did with the Coin enum! Instead of comparing coins, we'll compare the variants of Option<T>, but the way the match expression works remains the same.

Let's say we want to write a function that takes an Option<i32> and, if there's a value inside, adds 1 to that value. If there isn't a value inside, the function should return the None value and not attempt to perform any operations.

This function is very easy to write, thanks to match, and will look like Listing 6-5.

```
fn plus_one(x: Option<i32>) -> Option<i32> {
    match x {
      ❶ None => None,
      ❷ Some(i) => Some(i + 1),
    }
}

let five = Some(5);
let six = plus_one(five); ❸
let none = plus_one(None); ❹
```

Listing 6-5: A function that uses a match expression on an Option<i32>

Let's examine the first execution of plus_one in more detail. When we call plus_one(five) ❸, the variable x in the body of plus_one will have the value Some(5). We then compare that against each match arm:

```
None => None,
```

The Some(5) value doesn't match the pattern None ❶, so we continue to the next arm:

```
Some(i) => Some(i + 1),
```

Does Some(5) match Some(i) ❷? Why yes, it does! We have the same variant. The i binds to the value contained in Some, so i takes the value 5. The code in the match arm is then executed, so we add 1 to the value of i and create a new Some value with our total 6 inside.

Now let's consider the second call of plus_one in Listing 6-5, where x is None ❹. We enter the match and compare to the first arm ❶.

It matches! There's no value to add to, so the program stops and returns the None value on the right side of =>. Because the first arm matched, no other arms are compared.

Combining match and enums is useful in many situations. You'll see this pattern a lot in Rust code: match against an enum, bind a variable to the data inside, and then execute code based on it. It's a bit tricky at first, but once you get used to it, you'll wish you had it in all languages. It's consistently a user favorite.

Matches Are Exhaustive

There's one other aspect of match we need to discuss: the arms' patterns must cover all possibilities. Consider this version of our plus_one function, which has a bug and won't compile:

```
fn plus_one(x: Option<i32>) -> Option<i32> {
    match x {
        Some(i) => Some(i + 1),
    }
}
```

We didn't handle the None case, so this code will cause a bug. Luckily, it's a bug Rust knows how to catch. If we try to compile this code, we'll get this error:

```
error[E0004]: non-exhaustive patterns: `None` not covered
 --> src/main.rs:3:15
  |
3 |          match x {
  |                ^ pattern `None` not covered
  |
  note: `Option<i32>` defined here
      = note: the matched value is of type `Option<i32>`
help: ensure that all possible cases are being handled by adding
a match arm with a wildcard pattern or an explicit pattern as
shown
  |
4 ~              Some(i) => Some(i + 1),
5 ~              None => todo!(),
  |
```

Rust knows that we didn't cover every possible case, and even knows which pattern we forgot! Matches in Rust are *exhaustive*: we must exhaust every last possibility in order for the code to be valid. Especially in the case of Option<T>, when Rust prevents us from forgetting to explicitly handle the None case, it protects us from assuming that we have a value when we might have null, thus making the billion-dollar mistake discussed earlier impossible.

Catch-All Patterns and the _ Placeholder

Using enums, we can also take special actions for a few particular values, but for all other values take one default action. Imagine we're implementing a game where, if you roll a 3 on a dice roll, your player doesn't move, but instead gets a new fancy hat. If you roll a 7, your player loses a fancy hat. For all other values, your player moves that number of spaces on the game board. Here's a `match` that implements that logic, with the result of the dice roll hardcoded rather than a random value, and all other logic represented by functions without bodies because actually implementing them is out of scope for this example:

```
let dice_roll = 9;
match dice_roll {
    3 => add_fancy_hat(),
    7 => remove_fancy_hat(),
  ❶ other => move_player(other),
}

fn add_fancy_hat() {}
fn remove_fancy_hat() {}
fn move_player(num_spaces: u8) {}
```

For the first two arms, the patterns are the literal values 3 and 7. For the last arm that covers every other possible value, the pattern is the variable we've chosen to name other ❶. The code that runs for the `other` arm uses the variable by passing it to the `move_player` function.

This code compiles, even though we haven't listed all the possible values a u8 can have, because the last pattern will match all values not specifically listed. This catch-all pattern meets the requirement that `match` must be exhaustive. Note that we have to put the catch-all arm last because the patterns are evaluated in order. If we put the catch-all arm earlier, the other arms would never run, so Rust will warn us if we add arms after a catch-all!

Rust also has a pattern we can use when we want a catch-all but don't want to *use* the value in the catch-all pattern: _ is a special pattern that matches any value and does not bind to that value. This tells Rust we aren't going to use the value, so Rust won't warn us about an unused variable.

Let's change the rules of the game: now, if you roll anything other than a 3 or a 7, you must roll again. We no longer need to use the catch-all value, so we can change our code to use _ instead of the variable named other:

```
let dice_roll = 9;
match dice_roll {
    3 => add_fancy_hat(),
    7 => remove_fancy_hat(),
    _ => reroll(),
}

fn add_fancy_hat() {}
fn remove_fancy_hat() {}
fn reroll() {}
```

This example also meets the exhaustiveness requirement because we're explicitly ignoring all other values in the last arm; we haven't forgotten anything.

Finally, we'll change the rules of the game one more time so that nothing else happens on your turn if you roll anything other than a 3 or a 7. We can express that by using the unit value (the empty tuple type we mentioned in "The Tuple Type" on page 40) as the code that goes with the _ arm:

```
let dice_roll = 9;
match dice_roll {
    3 => add_fancy_hat(),
    7 => remove_fancy_hat(),
    _ => (),
}

fn add_fancy_hat() {}
fn remove_fancy_hat() {}
```

Here, we're telling Rust explicitly that we aren't going to use any other value that doesn't match a pattern in an earlier arm, and we don't want to run any code in this case.

There's more about patterns and matching that we'll cover in Chapter 18. For now, we're going to move on to the if let syntax, which can be useful in situations where the match expression is a bit wordy.

Concise Control Flow with if let

The if let syntax lets you combine if and let into a less verbose way to handle values that match one pattern while ignoring the rest. Consider the program in Listing 6-6 that matches on an Option<u8> value in the config_max variable but only wants to execute code if the value is the Some variant.

```
let config_max = Some(3u8);
match config_max {
    Some(max) => println!("The maximum is configured to be {max}"),
    _ => (),
}
```

Listing 6-6: A match that only cares about executing code when the value is Some

If the value is Some, we print out the value in the Some variant by binding the value to the variable max in the pattern. We don't want to do anything with the None value. To satisfy the match expression, we have to add _ => () after processing just one variant, which is annoying boilerplate code to add.

Instead, we could write this in a shorter way using if let. The following code behaves the same as the match in Listing 6-6:

```
let config_max = Some(3u8);
if let Some(max) = config_max {
    println!("The maximum is configured to be {max}");
}
```

The syntax if let takes a pattern and an expression separated by an equal sign. It works the same way as a match, where the expression is given to the match and the pattern is its first arm. In this case, the pattern is Some(max), and the max binds to the value inside the Some. We can then use max in the body of the if let block in the same way we used max in the corresponding match arm. The code in the if let block isn't run if the value doesn't match the pattern.

Using if let means less typing, less indentation, and less boilerplate code. However, you lose the exhaustive checking that match enforces. Choosing between match and if let depends on what you're doing in your particular situation and whether gaining conciseness is an appropriate trade-off for losing exhaustive checking.

In other words, you can think of if let as syntax sugar for a match that runs code when the value matches one pattern and then ignores all other values.

We can include an else with an if let. The block of code that goes with the else is the same as the block of code that would go with the _ case in the match expression that is equivalent to the if let and else. Recall the Coin enum definition in Listing 6-4, where the Quarter variant also held a UsState value. If we wanted to count all non-quarter coins we see while also announcing the state of the quarters, we could do that with a match expression, like this:

```
let mut count = 0;
match coin {
    Coin::Quarter(state) => println!("State quarter from {:?}!", state),
    _ => count += 1,
}
```

Or we could use an if let and else expression, like this:

```
let mut count = 0;
if let Coin::Quarter(state) = coin {
    println!("State quarter from {:?}!", state);
} else {
    count += 1;
}
```

If you have a situation in which your program has logic that is too verbose to express using a match, remember that if let is in your Rust toolbox as well.

Summary

We've now covered how to use enums to create custom types that can be one of a set of enumerated values. We've shown how the standard library's Option<T> type helps you use the type system to prevent errors. When enum values have data inside them, you can use match or if let to extract and use those values, depending on how many cases you need to handle.

Your Rust programs can now express concepts in your domain using structs and enums. Creating custom types to use in your API ensures type safety: the compiler will make certain your functions only get values of the type each function expects.

In order to provide a well-organized API to your users that is straightforward to use and only exposes exactly what your users will need, let's now turn to Rust's modules.

7

MANAGING GROWING PROJECTS WITH PACKAGES, CRATES, AND MODULES

As you write large programs, organizing your code will become increasingly important. By grouping related functionality and separating code with distinct features, you'll clarify where to find code that implements a particular feature and where to go to change how a feature works.

The programs we've written so far have been in one module in one file. As a project grows, you should organize code by splitting it into multiple modules and then multiple files. A package can contain multiple binary crates and optionally one library crate. As a package grows, you can extract parts into separate crates that become external dependencies. This chapter covers all these techniques. For very large projects comprising a set of interrelated packages that evolve together, Cargo provides *workspaces*, which we'll cover in "Cargo Workspaces" on page 307.

We'll also discuss encapsulating implementation details, which lets you reuse code at a higher level: once you've implemented an operation, other code can call your code via its public interface without having to know how the implementation works. The way you write code defines which parts are public for other code to use and which parts are private implementation details that you reserve the right to change. This is another way to limit the amount of detail you have to keep in your head.

A related concept is scope: the nested context in which code is written has a set of names that are defined as "in scope." When reading, writing, and compiling code, programmers and compilers need to know whether a particular name at a particular spot refers to a variable, function, struct, enum, module, constant, or other item and what that item means. You can create scopes and change which names are in or out of scope. You can't have two items with the same name in the same scope; tools are available to resolve name conflicts.

Rust has a number of features that allow you to manage your code's organization, including which details are exposed, which details are private, and what names are in each scope in your programs. These features, sometimes collectively referred to as the *module system*, include:

Packages   A Cargo feature that lets you build, test, and share crates

Crates   A tree of modules that produces a library or executable

Modules and use   Let you control the organization, scope, and privacy of paths

Paths   A way of naming an item, such as a struct, function, or module

In this chapter, we'll cover all these features, discuss how they interact, and explain how to use them to manage scope. By the end, you should have a solid understanding of the module system and be able to work with scopes like a pro!

Packages and Crates

The first parts of the module system we'll cover are packages and crates.

A *crate* is the smallest amount of code that the Rust compiler considers at a time. Even if you run rustc rather than cargo and pass a single source code file (as we did all the way back in "Writing and Running a Rust Program" on page 5), the compiler considers that file to be a crate. Crates can contain modules, and the modules may be defined in other files that get compiled with the crate, as we'll see in the coming sections.

A crate can come in one of two forms: a binary crate or a library crate. *Binary crates* are programs you can compile to an executable that you can run, such as a command line program or a server. Each must have a function called main that defines what happens when the executable runs. All the crates we've created so far have been binary crates.

Library crates don't have a main function, and they don't compile to an executable. Instead, they define functionality intended to be shared with multiple projects. For example, the rand crate we used in Chapter 2 provides functionality that generates random numbers. Most of the time when Rustaceans say "crate," they mean library crate, and they use "crate" interchangeably with the general programming concept of a "library."

The *crate root* is a source file that the Rust compiler starts from and makes up the root module of your crate (we'll explain modules in depth in "Defining Modules to Control Scope and Privacy" on page 123).

A *package* is a bundle of one or more crates that provides a set of functionality. A package contains a *Cargo.toml* file that describes how to build those crates. Cargo is actually a package that contains the binary crate for the command line tool you've been using to build your code. The Cargo package also contains a library crate that the binary crate depends on. Other projects can depend on the Cargo library crate to use the same logic the Cargo command line tool uses.

A crate can come in one of two forms: a binary crate or a library crate. A package can contain as many binary crates as you like, but at most only one library crate. A package must contain at least one crate, whether that's a library or binary crate.

Let's walk through what happens when we create a package. First we enter the command `cargo new my-project`:

```
$ cargo new my-project
    Created binary (application) `my-project` package
$ ls my-project
Cargo.toml
src
$ ls my-project/src
main.rs
```

After we run `cargo new my-project`, we use `ls` to see what Cargo creates. In the project directory, there's a *Cargo.toml* file, giving us a package. There's also a *src* directory that contains *main.rs*. Open *Cargo.toml* in your text editor, and note there's no mention of *src/main.rs*. Cargo follows a convention that *src/main.rs* is the crate root of a binary crate with the same name as the package. Likewise, Cargo knows that if the package directory contains *src/lib.rs*, the package contains a library crate with the same name as the package, and *src/lib.rs* is its crate root. Cargo passes the crate root files to rustc to build the library or binary.

Here, we have a package that only contains *src/main.rs*, meaning it only contains a binary crate named my-project. If a package contains *src/main.rs* and *src/lib.rs*, it has two crates: a binary and a library, both with the same name as the package. A package can have multiple binary crates by placing files in the *src/bin* directory: each file will be a separate binary crate.

MODULES CHEAT SHEET

Before we get to the details of modules and paths, here we provide a quick reference on how modules, paths, the use keyword, and the pub keyword work in the compiler, and how most developers organize their code. We'll be going

(continued)

---

through examples of each of these rules throughout this chapter, but this is a great place to refer to as a reminder of how modules work.

Start from the crate root When compiling a crate, the compiler first looks in the crate root file (usually *src/lib.rs* for a library crate or *src/main.rs* for a binary crate) for code to compile.

Declaring modules In the crate root file, you can declare new modules; say you declare a "garden" module with `mod garden;`. The compiler will look for the module's code in these places:

- Inline, within curly brackets that replace the semicolon following `mod garden`
- In the file *src/garden.rs*
- In the file *src/garden/mod.rs*

Declaring submodules In any file other than the crate root, you can declare submodules. For example, you might declare `mod vegetables;` in *src/garden.rs*. The compiler will look for the submodule's code within the directory named for the parent module in these places:

- Inline, directly following `mod vegetables`, within curly brackets instead of the semicolon
- In the file *src/garden/vegetables.rs*
- In the file *src/garden/vegetables/mod.rs*

Paths to code in modules Once a module is part of your crate, you can refer to code in that module from anywhere else in that same crate, as long as the privacy rules allow, using the path to the code. For example, an Asparagus type in the garden vegetables module would be found at `crate::garden::vegetables::Asparagus`.

Private vs. public Code within a module is private from its parent modules by default. To make a module public, declare it with `pub mod` instead of `mod`. To make items within a public module public as well, use `pub` before their declarations.

The use keyword Within a scope, the use keyword creates shortcuts to items to reduce repetition of long paths. In any scope that can refer to `crate::garden::vegetables::Asparagus`, you can create a shortcut with `use crate::garden::vegetables::Asparagus;` and from then on you only need to write Asparagus to make use of that type in the scope.

Here, we create a binary crate named backyard that illustrates these rules. The crate's directory, also named backyard, contains these files and directories:

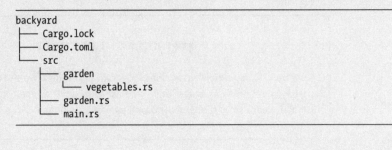

```
backyard
├── Cargo.lock
├── Cargo.toml
└── src
    ├── garden
    │   └── vegetables.rs
    ├── garden.rs
    └── main.rs
```

The crate root file in this case is *src/main.rs*, and it contains:

```
use crate::garden::vegetables::Asparagus;

pub mod garden;

fn main() {
    let plant = Asparagus {};
    println!("I'm growing {:?}!", plant);
}
```

The pub mod garden; line tells the compiler to include the code it finds in *src/garden.rs*, which is:

```
pub mod vegetables;
```

Here, pub mod vegetables; means the code in *src/garden/vegetables.rs* is included too. That code is:

```
#[derive(Debug)]
pub struct Asparagus {}
```

Now let's get into the details of these rules and demonstrate them in action!

Defining Modules to Control Scope and Privacy

In this section, we'll talk about modules and other parts of the module system, namely *paths*, which allow you to name items; the use keyword that brings a path into scope; and the pub keyword to make items public. We'll also discuss the as keyword, external packages, and the glob operator.

Modules let us organize code within a crate for readability and easy reuse. Modules also allow us to control the *privacy* of items because code within a module is private by default. Private items are internal implementation details not available for outside use. We can choose to make modules and the items within them public, which exposes them to allow external code to use and depend on them.

As an example, let's write a library crate that provides the functionality of a restaurant. We'll define the signatures of functions but leave their bodies empty to concentrate on the organization of the code rather than the implementation of a restaurant.

In the restaurant industry, some parts of a restaurant are referred to as *front of house* and others as *back of house*. Front of house is where customers are; this encompasses where the hosts seat customers, servers take orders and payment, and bartenders make drinks. Back of house is where the chefs and cooks work in the kitchen, dishwashers clean up, and managers do administrative work.

To structure our crate in this way, we can organize its functions into nested modules. Create a new library named restaurant by running cargo new restaurant --lib. Then enter the code in Listing 7-1 into *src/lib.rs* to define some modules and function signatures; this code is the front of house section.

```
src/lib.rs    mod front_of_house {
                  mod hosting {
                      fn add_to_waitlist() {}

                      fn seat_at_table() {}
                  }

                  mod serving {
                      fn take_order() {}

                      fn serve_order() {}

                      fn take_payment() {}
                  }
              }
```

Listing 7-1: A front_of_house module containing other modules that then contain functions

We define a module with the mod keyword followed by the name of the module (in this case, front_of_house). The body of the module then goes inside curly brackets. Inside modules, we can place other modules, as in this case with the modules hosting and serving. Modules can also hold definitions for other items, such as structs, enums, constants, traits, and as in Listing 7-1, functions.

By using modules, we can group related definitions together and name why they're related. Programmers using this code can navigate the code based on the groups rather than having to read through all the definitions, making it easier to find the definitions relevant to them. Programmers adding new functionality to this code would know where to place the code to keep the program organized.

Earlier, we mentioned that *src/main.rs* and *src/lib.rs* are called crate roots. The reason for their name is that the contents of either of these two files form a module named crate at the root of the crate's module structure, known as the *module tree.*

Listing 7-2 shows the module tree for the structure in Listing 7-1.

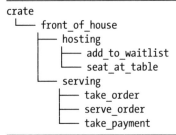

```
crate
 └── front_of_house
      ├── hosting
      │    ├── add_to_waitlist
      │    └── seat_at_table
      └── serving
           ├── take_order
           ├── serve_order
           └── take_payment
```

Listing 7-2: The module tree for the code in Listing 7-1

This tree shows how some of the modules nest inside other modules; for example, hosting nests inside front_of_house. The tree also shows that some modules are *siblings*, meaning they're defined in the same module; hosting and serving are siblings defined within front_of_house. If module A is contained inside module B, we say that module A is the *child* of module B and that module B is the *parent* of module A. Notice that the entire module tree is rooted under the implicit module named crate.

The module tree might remind you of the filesystem's directory tree on your computer; this is a very apt comparison! Just like directories in a filesystem, you use modules to organize your code. And just like files in a directory, we need a way to find our modules.

Paths for Referring to an Item in the Module Tree

To show Rust where to find an item in a module tree, we use a path in the same way we use a path when navigating a filesystem. To call a function, we need to know its path.

A path can take two forms:

- An *absolute path* is the full path starting from a crate root; for code from an external crate, the absolute path begins with the crate name, and for code from the current crate, it starts with the literal crate.

- A *relative path* starts from the current module and uses self, super, or an identifier in the current module.

Both absolute and relative paths are followed by one or more identifiers separated by double colons (::).

Returning to Listing 7-1, say we want to call the add_to_waitlist function. This is the same as asking: what's the path of the add_to_waitlist function? Listing 7-3 contains Listing 7-1 with some of the modules and functions removed.

We'll show two ways to call the add_to_waitlist function from a new function, eat_at_restaurant, defined in the crate root. These paths are correct, but there's another problem remaining that will prevent this example from compiling as is. We'll explain why in a bit.

The eat_at_restaurant function is part of our library crate's public API, so we mark it with the pub keyword. In "Exposing Paths with the pub Keyword" on page 127, we'll go into more detail about pub.

src/lib.rs
```
mod front_of_house {
    mod hosting {
        fn add_to_waitlist() {}
    }
}

pub fn eat_at_restaurant() {
    // Absolute path
    crate::front_of_house::hosting::add_to_waitlist();
```

```
    // Relative path
    front_of_house::hosting::add_to_waitlist();
}
```

Listing 7-3: Calling the add_to_waitlist function using absolute and relative paths

The first time we call the add_to_waitlist function in eat_at_restaurant, we use an absolute path. The add_to_waitlist function is defined in the same crate as eat_at_restaurant, which means we can use the crate keyword to start an absolute path. We then include each of the successive modules until we make our way to add_to_waitlist. You can imagine a filesystem with the same structure: we'd specify the path /front_of_house/hosting/add_to_waitlist to run the add_to_waitlist program; using the crate name to start from the crate root is like using / to start from the filesystem root in your shell.

The second time we call add_to_waitlist in eat_at_restaurant, we use a relative path. The path starts with front_of_house, the name of the module defined at the same level of the module tree as eat_at_restaurant. Here the filesystem equivalent would be using the path front_of_house/hosting/add_to _waitlist. Starting with a module name means that the path is relative.

Choosing whether to use a relative or absolute path is a decision you'll make based on your project, and it depends on whether you're more likely to move item definition code separately from or together with the code that uses the item. For example, if we moved the front_of_house module and the eat_at_restaurant function into a module named customer_experience, we'd need to update the absolute path to add_to_waitlist, but the relative path would still be valid. However, if we moved the eat_at_restaurant function separately into a module named dining, the absolute path to the add_to_waitlist call would stay the same, but the relative path would need to be updated. Our preference in general is to specify absolute paths because it's more likely we'll want to move code definitions and item calls independently of each other.

Let's try to compile Listing 7-3 and find out why it won't compile yet! The errors we get are shown in Listing 7-4.

```
$ cargo build
   Compiling restaurant v0.1.0 (file:///projects/restaurant)
error[E0603]: module `hosting` is private
  --> src/lib.rs:9:28
   |
9  |     crate::front_of_house::hosting::add_to_waitlist();
   |                            ^^^^^^^ private module
   |
note: the module `hosting` is defined here
  --> src/lib.rs:2:5
   |
2  |     mod hosting {
   |     ^^^^^^^^^^^

error[E0603]: module `hosting` is private
  --> src/lib.rs:12:21
```

```
12 |         front_of_house::hosting::add_to_waitlist();
   |                          ^^^^^^^ private module
   |
note: the module `hosting` is defined here
  --> src/lib.rs:2:5
   |
 2 |     mod hosting {
   |     ^^^^^^^^^^^
```

Listing 7-4: Compiler errors from building the code in Listing 7-3

The error messages say that module hosting is private. In other words, we have the correct paths for the hosting module and the add_to_waitlist function, but Rust won't let us use them because it doesn't have access to the private sections. In Rust, all items (functions, methods, structs, enums, modules, and constants) are private to parent modules by default. If you want to make an item like a function or struct private, you put it in a module.

Items in a parent module can't use the private items inside child modules, but items in child modules can use the items in their ancestor modules. This is because child modules wrap and hide their implementation details, but the child modules can see the context in which they're defined. To continue with our metaphor, think of the privacy rules as being like the back office of a restaurant: what goes on in there is private to restaurant customers, but office managers can see and do everything in the restaurant they operate.

Rust chose to have the module system function this way so that hiding inner implementation details is the default. That way, you know which parts of the inner code you can change without breaking outer code. However, Rust does give you the option to expose inner parts of child modules' code to outer ancestor modules by using the pub keyword to make an item public.

Exposing Paths with the pub Keyword

Let's return to the error in Listing 7-4 that told us the hosting module is private. We want the eat_at_restaurant function in the parent module to have access to the add_to_waitlist function in the child module, so we mark the hosting module with the pub keyword, as shown in Listing 7-5.

src/lib.rs
```
mod front_of_house {
    pub mod hosting {
        fn add_to_waitlist() {}
    }
}

--snip--
```

Listing 7-5: Declaring the hosting module as pub to use it from eat_at_restaurant

Unfortunately, the code in Listing 7-5 still results in compiler errors, as shown in Listing 7-6.

```
$ cargo build
   Compiling restaurant v0.1.0 (file:///projects/restaurant)
error[E0603]: function `add_to_waitlist` is private
  --> src/lib.rs:9:37
   |
9  |     crate::front_of_house::hosting::add_to_waitlist();
   |                                     ^^^^^^^^^^^^^^^ private function
   |
note: the function `add_to_waitlist` is defined here
  --> src/lib.rs:3:9
   |
3  |         fn add_to_waitlist() {}
   |         ^^^^^^^^^^^^^^^^^^^^^^^^

error[E0603]: function `add_to_waitlist` is private
  --> src/lib.rs:12:30
   |
12 |     front_of_house::hosting::add_to_waitlist();
   |                              ^^^^^^^^^^^^^^^ private function
   |
note: the function `add_to_waitlist` is defined here
  --> src/lib.rs:3:9
   |
3  |         fn add_to_waitlist() {}
   |         ^^^^^^^^^^^^^^^^^^^^^^^^
```

Listing 7-6: Compiler errors from building the code in Listing 7-5

What happened? Adding the pub keyword in front of mod hosting makes the module public. With this change, if we can access front_of_house, we can access hosting. But the *contents* of hosting are still private; making the module public doesn't make its contents public. The pub keyword on a module only lets code in its ancestor modules refer to it, not access its inner code. Because modules are containers, there's not much we can do by only making the module public; we need to go further and choose to make one or more of the items within the module public as well.

The errors in Listing 7-6 say that the add_to_waitlist function is private. The privacy rules apply to structs, enums, functions, and methods as well as modules.

Let's also make the add_to_waitlist function public by adding the pub keyword before its definition, as in Listing 7-7.

src/lib.rs
```
mod front_of_house {
    pub mod hosting {
        pub fn add_to_waitlist() {}
    }
}

--snip--
```

Listing 7-7: Adding the pub keyword to mod hosting and fn add_to_waitlist lets us call the function from eat_at_restaurant.

Now the code will compile! To see why adding the pub keyword lets us use these paths in add_to_waitlist with respect to the privacy rules, let's look at the absolute and the relative paths.

In the absolute path, we start with crate, the root of our crate's module tree. The front_of_house module is defined in the crate root. While front_of_house isn't public, because the eat_at_restaurant function is defined in the same module as front_of_house (that is, eat_at_restaurant and front_of_house are siblings), we can refer to front_of_house from eat_at_restaurant. Next is the hosting module marked with pub. We can access the parent module of hosting, so we can access hosting. Finally, the add_to_waitlist function is marked with pub and we can access its parent module, so this function call works!

In the relative path, the logic is the same as the absolute path except for the first step: rather than starting from the crate root, the path starts from front_of_house. The front_of_house module is defined within the same module as eat_at_restaurant, so the relative path starting from the module in which eat_at_restaurant is defined works. Then, because hosting and add_to_waitlist are marked with pub, the rest of the path works, and this function call is valid!

If you plan on sharing your library crate so other projects can use your code, your public API is your contract with users of your crate that determines how they can interact with your code. There are many considerations around managing changes to your public API to make it easier for people to depend on your crate. These considerations are beyond the scope of this book; if you're interested in this topic, see the Rust API Guidelines at *https://rust-lang.github.io/api-guidelines*.

**BEST PRACTICES FOR PACKAGES WITH
A BINARY AND A LIBRARY**

We mentioned that a package can contain both a *src/main.rs* binary crate root as well as a *src/lib.rs* library crate root, and both crates will have the package name by default. Typically, packages with this pattern of containing both a library and a binary crate will have just enough code in the binary crate to start an executable that calls code with the library crate. This lets other projects benefit from the most functionality that the package provides because the library crate's code can be shared.

The module tree should be defined in *src/lib.rs*. Then, any public items can be used in the binary crate by starting paths with the name of the package. The binary crate becomes a user of the library crate just like a completely external crate would use the library crate: it can only use the public API. This helps you design a good API; not only are you the author, you're also a client!

In Chapter 12, we'll demonstrate this organizational practice with a command line program that will contain both a binary crate and a library crate.

Starting Relative Paths with super

We can construct relative paths that begin in the parent module, rather than the current module or the crate root, by using super at the start of the path. This is like starting a filesystem path with the .. syntax. Using super allows us to reference an item that we know is in the parent module, which can make rearranging the module tree easier when the module is closely related to the parent but the parent might be moved elsewhere in the module tree someday.

Consider the code in Listing 7-8 that models the situation in which a chef fixes an incorrect order and personally brings it out to the customer. The function fix_incorrect_order defined in the back_of_house module calls the function deliver_order defined in the parent module by specifying the path to deliver_order, starting with super.

src/lib.rs

```
fn deliver_order() {}

mod back_of_house {
    fn fix_incorrect_order() {
        cook_order();
        super::deliver_order();
    }

    fn cook_order() {}
}
```

Listing 7-8: Calling a function using a relative path starting with super

The fix_incorrect_order function is in the back_of_house module, so we can use super to go to the parent module of back_of_house, which in this case is crate, the root. From there, we look for deliver_order and find it. Success! We think the back_of_house module and the deliver_order function are likely to stay in the same relationship to each other and get moved together should we decide to reorganize the crate's module tree. Therefore, we used super so we'll have fewer places to update code in the future if this code gets moved to a different module.

Making Structs and Enums Public

We can also use pub to designate structs and enums as public, but there are a few extra details to the usage of pub with structs and enums. If we use pub before a struct definition, we make the struct public, but the struct's fields will still be private. We can make each field public or not on a case-by-case basis. In Listing 7-9, we've defined a public back_of_house::Breakfast struct with a public toast field but a private seasonal_fruit field. This models the case in a restaurant where the customer can pick the type of bread that comes with a meal, but the chef decides which fruit accompanies the meal based on what's in season and in stock. The available fruit changes quickly, so customers can't choose the fruit or even see which fruit they'll get.

```
src/lib.rs    mod back_of_house {
                  pub struct Breakfast {
                      pub toast: String,
                      seasonal_fruit: String,
                  }

                  impl Breakfast {
                      pub fn summer(toast: &str) -> Breakfast {
                          Breakfast {
                              toast: String::from(toast),
                              seasonal_fruit: String::from("peaches"),
                          }
                      }
                  }
              }

              pub fn eat_at_restaurant() {
                  // Order a breakfast in the summer with Rye toast.
                  let mut meal = back_of_house::Breakfast::summer("Rye");
                  // Change our mind about what bread we'd like.
                  meal.toast = String::from("Wheat");
                  println!("I'd like {} toast please", meal.toast);

                  // The next line won't compile if we uncomment it; we're not
                  // allowed to see or modify the seasonal fruit that comes
                  // with the meal.
                  // meal.seasonal_fruit = String::from("blueberries");
              }
```

Listing 7-9: A struct with some public fields and some private fields

Because the toast field in the back_of_house::Breakfast struct is public, in eat_at_restaurant we can write and read to the toast field using dot notation. Notice that we can't use the seasonal_fruit field in eat_at_restaurant, because seasonal_fruit is private. Try uncommenting the line modifying the seasonal _fruit field value to see what error you get!

Also, note that because back_of_house::Breakfast has a private field, the struct needs to provide a public associated function that constructs an instance of Breakfast (we've named it summer here). If Breakfast didn't have such a function, we couldn't create an instance of Breakfast in eat_at_restaurant because we couldn't set the value of the private seasonal_fruit field in eat_at _restaurant.

In contrast, if we make an enum public, all of its variants are then public. We only need the pub before the enum keyword, as shown in Listing 7-10.

```
src/lib.rs    mod back_of_house {
                  pub enum Appetizer {
                      Soup,
                      Salad,
                  }
              }
```

```
pub fn eat_at_restaurant() {
    let order1 = back_of_house::Appetizer::Soup;
    let order2 = back_of_house::Appetizer::Salad;
}
```

Listing 7-10: Designating an enum as public makes all its variants public.

Because we made the Appetizer enum public, we can use the Soup and
Salad variants in eat_at_restaurant.

Enums aren't very useful unless their variants are public; it would be
annoying to have to annotate all enum variants with pub in every case, so
the default for enum variants is to be public. Structs are often useful
without their fields being public, so struct fields follow the general rule of
everything being private by default unless annotated with pub.

There's one more situation involving pub that we haven't covered, and
that is our last module system feature: the use keyword. We'll cover use by
itself first, and then we'll show how to combine pub and use.

Bringing Paths into Scope with the use Keyword

Having to write out the paths to call functions can feel inconvenient and
repetitive. In Listing 7-7, whether we chose the absolute or relative path to
the add_to_waitlist function, every time we wanted to call add_to_waitlist
we had to specify front_of_house and hosting too. Fortunately, there's a way
to simplify this process: we can create a shortcut to a path with the use keyword once, and then use the shorter name everywhere else in the scope.

In Listing 7-11, we bring the crate::front_of_house::hosting module
into the scope of the eat_at_restaurant function so we only have to specify
hosting::add_to_waitlist to call the add_to_waitlist function in eat_at
_restaurant.

src/lib.rs
```
mod front_of_house {
    pub mod hosting {
        pub fn add_to_waitlist() {}
    }
}

use crate::front_of_house::hosting;

pub fn eat_at_restaurant() {
    hosting::add_to_waitlist();
}
```

Listing 7-11: Bringing a module into scope with use

Adding use and a path in a scope is similar to creating a symbolic link
in the filesystem. By adding use crate::front_of_house::hosting in the crate
root, hosting is now a valid name in that scope, just as though the hosting
module had been defined in the crate root. Paths brought into scope with
use also check privacy, like any other paths.

Note that use only creates the shortcut for the particular scope in which the use occurs. Listing 7-12 moves the eat_at_restaurant function into a new child module named customer, which is then a different scope than the use statement, so the function body won't compile.

src/lib.rs
```
mod front_of_house {
    pub mod hosting {
        pub fn add_to_waitlist() {}
    }
}

use crate::front_of_house::hosting;

mod customer {
    pub fn eat_at_restaurant() {
        hosting::add_to_waitlist();
    }
}
```

Listing 7-12: A use statement only applies in the scope it's in.

The compiler error shows that the shortcut no longer applies within the customer module:

```
error[E0433]: failed to resolve: use of undeclared crate or module `hosting`
  --> src/lib.rs:11:9
   |
11 |         hosting::add_to_waitlist();
   |         ^^^^^^^ use of undeclared crate or module `hosting`

warning: unused import: `crate::front_of_house::hosting`
  --> src/lib.rs:7:5
   |
7  | use crate::front_of_house::hosting;
   |     ^^^^^^^^^^^^^^^^^^^^^^^^^^^^^^^
   |
   = note: `#[warn(unused_imports)]` on by default
```

Notice there's also a warning that the use is no longer used in its scope! To fix this problem, move the use within the customer module too, or reference the shortcut in the parent module with super::hosting within the child customer module.

Creating Idiomatic use Paths

In Listing 7-11, you might have wondered why we specified use crate::front _of_house::hosting and then called hosting::add_to_waitlist in eat_at_restaurant, rather than specifying the use path all the way out to the add_to_waitlist function to achieve the same result, as in Listing 7-13.

src/lib.rs
```
mod front_of_house {
    pub mod hosting {
        pub fn add_to_waitlist() {}
```

```
        }
    }

    use crate::front_of_house::hosting::add_to_waitlist;

    pub fn eat_at_restaurant() {
        add_to_waitlist();
    }
```

Listing 7-13: Bringing the add_to_waitlist function into scope with use, which is unidiomatic

Although both Listing 7-11 and Listing 7-13 accomplish the same task, Listing 7-11 is the idiomatic way to bring a function into scope with use. Bringing the function's parent module into scope with use means we have to specify the parent module when calling the function. Specifying the parent module when calling the function makes it clear that the function isn't locally defined while still minimizing repetition of the full path. The code in Listing 7-13 is unclear as to where add_to_waitlist is defined.

On the other hand, when bringing in structs, enums, and other items with use, it's idiomatic to specify the full path. Listing 7-14 shows the idiomatic way to bring the standard library's HashMap struct into the scope of a binary crate.

src/main.rs
```
use std::collections::HashMap;

fn main() {
    let mut map = HashMap::new();
    map.insert(1, 2);
}
```

Listing 7-14: Bringing HashMap into scope in an idiomatic way

There's no strong reason behind this idiom: it's just the convention that has emerged, and folks have gotten used to reading and writing Rust code this way.

The exception to this idiom is if we're bringing two items with the same name into scope with use statements, because Rust doesn't allow that. Listing 7-15 shows how to bring two Result types into scope that have the same name but different parent modules, and how to refer to them.

src/lib.rs
```
use std::fmt;
use std::io;

fn function1() -> fmt::Result {
    --snip--
}

fn function2() -> io::Result<()> {
    --snip--
}
```

Listing 7-15: Bringing two types with the same name into the same scope requires using their parent modules.

As you can see, using the parent modules distinguishes the two `Result` types. If instead we specified use `std::fmt::Result` and use `std::io::Result`, we'd have two `Result` types in the same scope, and Rust wouldn't know which one we meant when we used `Result`.

Providing New Names with the as Keyword

There's another solution to the problem of bringing two types of the same name into the same scope with use: after the path, we can specify as and a new local name, or *alias*, for the type. Listing 7-16 shows another way to write the code in Listing 7-15 by renaming one of the two `Result` types using as.

src/lib.rs

```
use std::fmt::Result;
use std::io::Result as IoResult;

fn function1() -> Result {
    --snip--
}

fn function2() -> IoResult<()> {
    --snip--
}
```

Listing 7-16: Renaming a type when it's brought into scope with the as keyword

In the second use statement, we chose the new name IoResult for the `std::io::Result` type, which won't conflict with the `Result` from `std::fmt` that we've also brought into scope. Listing 7-15 and Listing 7-16 are considered idiomatic, so the choice is up to you!

Re-exporting Names with pub use

When we bring a name into scope with the use keyword, the name available in the new scope is private. To enable the code that calls our code to refer to that name as if it had been defined in that code's scope, we can combine pub and use. This technique is called *re-exporting* because we're bringing an item into scope but also making that item available for others to bring into their scope.

Listing 7-17 shows the code in Listing 7-11 with use in the root module changed to pub use.

src/lib.rs

```
mod front_of_house {
    pub mod hosting {
        pub fn add_to_waitlist() {}
    }
}

pub use crate::front_of_house::hosting;

pub fn eat_at_restaurant() {
    hosting::add_to_waitlist();
}
```

Listing 7-17: Making a name available for any code to use from a new scope with pub use

Before this change, external code would have to call the `add_to_waitlist` function by using the path `restaurant::front_of_house::hosting::add_to_waitlist()`. Now that this `pub use` has re-exported the `hosting` module from the root module, external code can use the path `restaurant::hosting::add_to_waitlist()` instead.

Re-exporting is useful when the internal structure of your code is different from how programmers calling your code would think about the domain. For example, in this restaurant metaphor, the people running the restaurant think about "front of house" and "back of house." But customers visiting a restaurant probably won't think about the parts of the restaurant in those terms. With `pub use`, we can write our code with one structure but expose a different structure. Doing so makes our library well organized for programmers working on the library and programmers calling the library. We'll look at another example of `pub use` and how it affects your crate's documentation in "Exporting a Convenient Public API with pub use" on page 300.

Using External Packages

In Chapter 2, we programmed a guessing game project that used an external package called `rand` to get random numbers. To use `rand` in our project, we added this line to *Cargo.toml*:

Cargo.toml
```
rand = "0.8.5"
```

Adding `rand` as a dependency in *Cargo.toml* tells Cargo to download the `rand` package and any dependencies from *https://crates.io*, and make `rand` available to our project.

Then, to bring `rand` definitions into the scope of our package, we added a use line starting with the name of the crate, `rand`, and listed the items we wanted to bring into scope. Recall that in "Generating a Random Number" on page 22, we brought the `Rng` trait into scope and called the `rand::thread_rng` function:

```
use rand::Rng;

fn main() {
    let secret_number = rand::thread_rng().gen_range(1..=100);
}
```

Members of the Rust community have made many packages available at *https://crates.io*, and pulling any of them into your package involves these same steps: listing them in your package's *Cargo.toml* file and using use to bring items from their crates into scope.

Note that the standard `std` library is also a crate that's external to our package. Because the standard library is shipped with the Rust language, we don't need to change *Cargo.toml* to include `std`. But we do need to refer to it with use to bring items from there into our package's scope. For example, with `HashMap` we would use this line:

```
use std::collections::HashMap;
```

This is an absolute path starting with std, the name of the standard library crate.

Using Nested Paths to Clean Up Large use Lists

If we're using multiple items defined in the same crate or same module, listing each item on its own line can take up a lot of vertical space in our files. For example, these two use statements we had in the guessing game in Listing 2-4 bring items from std into scope:

src/main.rs
```
--snip--
use std::cmp::Ordering;
use std::io;
--snip--
```

Instead, we can use nested paths to bring the same items into scope in one line. We do this by specifying the common part of the path, followed by two colons, and then curly brackets around a list of the parts of the paths that differ, as shown in Listing 7-18.

src/main.rs
```
--snip--
use std::{cmp::Ordering, io};
--snip--
```

Listing 7-18: Specifying a nested path to bring multiple items with the same prefix into scope

In bigger programs, bringing many items into scope from the same crate or module using nested paths can reduce the number of separate use statements needed by a lot!

We can use a nested path at any level in a path, which is useful when combining two use statements that share a subpath. For example, Listing 7-19 shows two use statements: one that brings std::io into scope and one that brings std::io::Write into scope.

src/lib.rs
```
use std::io;
use std::io::Write;
```

Listing 7-19: Two use statements where one is a subpath of the other

The common part of these two paths is std::io, and that's the complete first path. To merge these two paths into one use statement, we can use self in the nested path, as shown in Listing 7-20.

src/lib.rs
```
use std::io::{self, Write};
```

Listing 7-20: Combining the paths in Listing 7-19 into one use statement

This line brings std::io and std::io::Write into scope.

The Glob Operator

If we want to bring *all* public items defined in a path into scope, we can specify that path followed by the * glob operator:

```
use std::collections::*;
```

This use statement brings all public items defined in std::collections into the current scope. Be careful when using the glob operator! Glob can make it harder to tell what names are in scope and where a name used in your program was defined.

The glob operator is often used when testing to bring everything under test into the tests module; we'll talk about that in "How to Write Tests" on page 216. The glob operator is also sometimes used as part of the prelude pattern: see the standard library documentation for more information on that pattern.

Separating Modules into Different Files

So far, all the examples in this chapter defined multiple modules in one file. When modules get large, you might want to move their definitions to a separate file to make the code easier to navigate.

For example, let's start from the code in Listing 7-17 that had multiple restaurant modules. We'll extract modules into files instead of having all the modules defined in the crate root file. In this case, the crate root file is *src/lib.rs*, but this procedure also works with binary crates whose crate root file is *src/main.rs*.

First we'll extract the front_of_house module to its own file. Remove the code inside the curly brackets for the front_of_house module, leaving only the mod front_of_house; declaration, so that *src/lib.rs* contains the code shown in Listing 7-21. Note that this won't compile until we create the *src/front_of _house.rs* file in Listing 7-22.

src/lib.rs
```
mod front_of_house;

pub use crate::front_of_house::hosting;

pub fn eat_at_restaurant() {
    hosting::add_to_waitlist();
}
```

Listing 7-21: Declaring the front_of_house module whose body will be in src/front_of _house.rs

Next, place the code that was in the curly brackets into a new file named *src/front_of_house.rs*, as shown in Listing 7-22. The compiler knows to look in this file because it came across the module declaration in the crate root with the name front_of_house.

```
src/front_of_house.rs   pub mod hosting {
                            pub fn add_to_waitlist() {}
                        }
```

Listing 7-22: Definitions inside the front_of_house *module in* src/front_of_house.rs

Note that you only need to load a file using a mod declaration *once* in your module tree. Once the compiler knows the file is part of the project (and knows where in the module tree the code resides because of where you've put the mod statement), other files in your project should refer to the loaded file's code using a path to where it was declared, as covered in "Paths for Referring to an Item in the Module Tree" on page 125. In other words, mod is *not* an "include" operation that you may have seen in other programming languages.

Next, we'll extract the hosting module to its own file. The process is a bit different because hosting is a child module of front_of_house, not of the root module. We'll place the file for hosting in a new directory that will be named for its ancestors in the module tree, in this case *src/front_of_house*.

To start moving hosting, we change *src/front_of_house.rs* to contain only the declaration of the hosting module:

```
src/front_of_house.rs   pub mod hosting;
```

Then we create a *src/front_of_house* directory and a *hosting.rs* file to contain the definitions made in the hosting module:

```
src/front_of        pub fn add_to_waitlist() {}
_house/hosting.rs
```

If we instead put *hosting.rs* in the *src* directory, the compiler would expect the *hosting.rs* code to be in a hosting module declared in the crate root, and not declared as a child of the front_of_house module. The compiler's rules for which files to check for which modules' code mean the directories and files more closely match the module tree.

ALTERNATE FILE PATHS

So far we've covered the most idiomatic file paths the Rust compiler uses, but Rust also supports an older style of file path. For a module named front_of _house declared in the crate root, the compiler will look for the module's code in:

- *src/front_of_house.rs* (what we covered)
- *src/front_of_house/mod.rs* (older style, still supported path)

For a module named hosting that is a submodule of front_of_house, the compiler will look for the module's code in:

- *src/front_of_house/hosting.rs* (what we covered)
- *src/front_of_house/hosting/mod.rs* (older style, still supported path)

(continued)

If you use both styles for the same module, you'll get a compiler error. Using a mix of both styles for different modules in the same project is allowed, but might be confusing for people navigating your project.

The main downside to the style that uses files named *mod.rs* is that your project can end up with many files named *mod.rs*, which can get confusing when you have them open in your editor at the same time.

We've moved each module's code to a separate file, and the module tree remains the same. The function calls in eat_at_restaurant will work without any modification, even though the definitions live in different files. This technique lets you move modules to new files as they grow in size.

Note that the pub use crate::front_of_house::hosting statement in *src/lib.rs* also hasn't changed, nor does use have any impact on what files are compiled as part of the crate. The mod keyword declares modules, and Rust looks in a file with the same name as the module for the code that goes into that module.

Summary

Rust lets you split a package into multiple crates and a crate into modules so you can refer to items defined in one module from another module. You can do this by specifying absolute or relative paths. These paths can be brought into scope with a use statement so you can use a shorter path for multiple uses of the item in that scope. Module code is private by default, but you can make definitions public by adding the pub keyword.

In the next chapter, we'll look at some collection data structures in the standard library that you can use in your neatly organized code.

8

COMMON COLLECTIONS

 Rust's standard library includes a number of very useful data structures called *collections*. Most other data types represent one specific value, but collections can contain multiple values. Unlike the built-in array and tuple types, the data that these collections point to is stored on the heap, which means the amount of data does not need to be known at compile time and can grow or shrink as the program runs. Each kind of collection has different capabilities and costs, and choosing an appropriate one for your current situation is a skill you'll develop over time. In this chapter, we'll discuss three collections that are used very often in Rust programs:

- A *vector* allows you to store a variable number of values next to each other.
- A *string* is a collection of characters. We've mentioned the String type previously, but in this chapter we'll talk about it in depth.
- A *hash map* allows you to associate a value with a specific key. It's a particular implementation of the more general data structure called a *map*.

To learn about the other kinds of collections provided by the standard library, see the documentation at *https://doc.rust-lang.org/std/collections/index.html.*

We'll discuss how to create and update vectors, strings, and hash maps, as well as what makes each special.

Storing Lists of Values with Vectors

The first collection type we'll look at is Vec<T>, also known as a *vector*. Vectors allow you to store more than one value in a single data structure that puts all the values next to each other in memory. Vectors can only store values of the same type. They are useful when you have a list of items, such as the lines of text in a file or the prices of items in a shopping cart.

Creating a New Vector

To create a new empty vector, we call the Vec::new function, as shown in Listing 8-1.

```
let v: Vec<i32> = Vec::new();
```

Listing 8-1: Creating a new, empty vector to hold values of type i32

Note that we added a type annotation here. Because we aren't inserting any values into this vector, Rust doesn't know what kind of elements we intend to store. This is an important point. Vectors are implemented using generics; we'll cover how to use generics with your own types in Chapter 10. For now, know that the Vec<T> type provided by the standard library can hold any type. When we create a vector to hold a specific type, we can specify the type within angle brackets. In Listing 8-1, we've told Rust that the Vec<T> in v will hold elements of the i32 type.

More often, you'll create a Vec<T> with initial values and Rust will infer the type of value you want to store, so you rarely need to do this type annotation. Rust conveniently provides the vec! macro, which will create a new vector that holds the values you give it. Listing 8-2 creates a new Vec<i32> that holds the values 1, 2, and 3. The integer type is i32 because that's the default integer type, as we discussed in "Data Types" on page 36.

```
let v = vec![1, 2, 3];
```

Listing 8-2: Creating a new vector containing values

Because we've given initial i32 values, Rust can infer that the type of v is Vec<i32>, and the type annotation isn't necessary. Next, we'll look at how to modify a vector.

Updating a Vector

To create a vector and then add elements to it, we can use the push method, as shown in Listing 8-3.

```
let mut v = Vec::new();

v.push(5);
v.push(6);
v.push(7);
v.push(8);
```

Listing 8-3: Using the push method to add values to a vector

As with any variable, if we want to be able to change its value, we need to make it mutable using the mut keyword, as discussed in Chapter 3. The numbers we place inside are all of type i32, and Rust infers this from the data, so we don't need the Vec<i32> annotation.

Reading Elements of Vectors

There are two ways to reference a value stored in a vector: via indexing or by using the get method. In the following examples, we've annotated the types of the values that are returned from these functions for extra clarity.

Listing 8-4 shows both methods of accessing a value in a vector, with indexing syntax and the get method.

```
let v = vec![1, 2, 3, 4, 5];

❶ let third: &i32 = &v[2];
  println!("The third element is {third}");

❷ let third: Option<&i32> = v.get(2);
  match third {
      Some(third) => println!("The third element is {third}"),
      None => println!("There is no third element."),
  }
```

Listing 8-4: Using indexing syntax and using the get method to access an item in a vector

Note a few details here. We use the index value of 2 to get the third element ❶ because vectors are indexed by number, starting at zero. Using & and [] gives us a reference to the element at the index value. When we use the get method with the index passed as an argument ❷, we get an Option<&T> that we can use with match.

Rust provides these two ways to reference an element so you can choose how the program behaves when you try to use an index value outside the range of existing elements. As an example, let's see what happens when we have a vector of five elements and then we try to access an element at index 100 with each technique, as shown in Listing 8-5.

```
let v = vec![1, 2, 3, 4, 5];

let does_not_exist = &v[100];
let does_not_exist = v.get(100);
```

Listing 8-5: Attempting to access the element at index 100 in a vector containing five elements

When we run this code, the first [] method will cause the program to panic because it references a nonexistent element. This method is best used when you want your program to crash if there's an attempt to access an element past the end of the vector.

When the get method is passed an index that is outside the vector, it returns None without panicking. You would use this method if accessing an element beyond the range of the vector may happen occasionally under normal circumstances. Your code will then have logic to handle having either Some(&element) or None, as discussed in Chapter 6. For example, the index could be coming from a person entering a number. If they accidentally enter a number that's too large and the program gets a None value, you could tell the user how many items are in the current vector and give them another chance to enter a valid value. That would be more user-friendly than crashing the program due to a typo!

When the program has a valid reference, the borrow checker enforces the ownership and borrowing rules (covered in Chapter 4) to ensure this reference and any other references to the contents of the vector remain valid. Recall the rule that states you can't have mutable and immutable references in the same scope. That rule applies in Listing 8-6, where we hold an immutable reference to the first element in a vector and try to add an element to the end. This program won't work if we also try to refer to that element later in the function.

```
let mut v = vec![1, 2, 3, 4, 5];

let first = &v[0];

v.push(6);

println!("The first element is: {first}");
```

Listing 8-6: Attempting to add an element to a vector while holding a reference to an item

Compiling this code will result in this error:

```
error[E0502]: cannot borrow `v` as mutable because it is also borrowed as
immutable
 --> src/main.rs:6:5
  |
4 |     let first = &v[0];
  |                  - immutable borrow occurs here
5 |
6 |     v.push(6);
  |     ^^^^^^^^^ mutable borrow occurs here
7 |
8 |     println!("The first element is: {first}");
  |                                      ----- immutable borrow later used here
```

The code in Listing 8-6 might look like it should work: why should a reference to the first element care about changes at the end of the vector? This error is due to the way vectors work: because vectors put the values next to each other in memory, adding a new element onto the end of the vector might require allocating new memory and copying the old elements to the new space, if there isn't enough room to put all the elements next to each other where the vector is currently stored. In that case, the reference to the first element would be pointing to deallocated memory. The borrowing rules prevent programs from ending up in that situation.

NOTE *For more on the implementation details of the Vec<T> type, see "The Rustonomicon" at https://doc.rust-lang.org/nomicon/vec/vec.html.*

Iterating Over the Values in a Vector

To access each element in a vector in turn, we would iterate through all of the elements rather than use indices to access one at a time. Listing 8-7 shows how to use a for loop to get immutable references to each element in a vector of i32 values and print them.

```
let v = vec![100, 32, 57];
for i in &v {
    println!("{i}");
}
```

Listing 8-7: Printing each element in a vector by iterating over the elements using a for loop

We can also iterate over mutable references to each element in a mutable vector in order to make changes to all the elements. The for loop in Listing 8-8 will add 50 to each element.

```
let mut v = vec![100, 32, 57];
for i in &mut v {
    *i += 50;
}
```

Listing 8-8: Iterating over mutable references to elements in a vector

To change the value that the mutable reference refers to, we have to use the * dereference operator to get to the value in i before we can use the += operator. We'll talk more about the dereference operator in "Following the Pointer to the Value" on page 322.

Iterating over a vector, whether immutably or mutably, is safe because of the borrow checker's rules. If we attempted to insert or remove items in the for loop bodies in Listing 8-7 and Listing 8-8, we would get a compiler error similar to the one we got with the code in Listing 8-6. The reference to the vector that the for loop holds prevents simultaneous modification of the whole vector.

Using an Enum to Store Multiple Types

Vectors can only store values that are of the same type. This can be inconvenient; there are definitely use cases for needing to store a list of items of different types. Fortunately, the variants of an enum are defined under the same enum type, so when we need one type to represent elements of different types, we can define and use an enum!

For example, say we want to get values from a row in a spreadsheet in which some of the columns in the row contain integers, some floating-point numbers, and some strings. We can define an enum whose variants will hold the different value types, and all the enum variants will be considered the same type: that of the enum. Then we can create a vector to hold that enum and so, ultimately, hold different types. We've demonstrated this in Listing 8-9.

```
enum SpreadsheetCell {
    Int(i32),
    Float(f64),
    Text(String),
}

let row = vec![
    SpreadsheetCell::Int(3),
    SpreadsheetCell::Text(String::from("blue")),
    SpreadsheetCell::Float(10.12),
];
```

Listing 8-9: Defining an enum to store values of different types in one vector

Rust needs to know what types will be in the vector at compile time so it knows exactly how much memory on the heap will be needed to store each element. We must also be explicit about what types are allowed in this vector. If Rust allowed a vector to hold any type, there would be a chance that one or more of the types would cause errors with the operations performed on the elements of the vector. Using an enum plus a match expression means that Rust will ensure at compile time that every possible case is handled, as discussed in Chapter 6.

If you don't know the exhaustive set of types a program will get at runtime to store in a vector, the enum technique won't work. Instead, you can use a trait object, which we'll cover in Chapter 17.

Now that we've discussed some of the most common ways to use vectors, be sure to review the API documentation for all of the many useful methods defined on Vec<T> by the standard library. For example, in addition to push, a pop method removes and returns the last element.

Dropping a Vector Drops Its Elements

Like any other struct, a vector is freed when it goes out of scope, as annotated in Listing 8-10.

```
{
    let v = vec![1, 2, 3, 4];

    // do stuff with v
} // <- v goes out of scope and is freed here
```

Listing 8-10: Showing where the vector and its elements are dropped

When the vector gets dropped, all of its contents are also dropped, meaning the integers it holds will be cleaned up. The borrow checker ensures that any references to contents of a vector are only used while the vector itself is valid.

Let's move on to the next collection type: String!

Storing UTF-8 Encoded Text with Strings

We talked about strings in Chapter 4, but we'll look at them in more depth now. New Rustaceans commonly get stuck on strings for a combination of three reasons: Rust's propensity for exposing possible errors, strings being a more complicated data structure than many programmers give them credit for, and UTF-8. These factors combine in a way that can seem difficult when you're coming from other programming languages.

We discuss strings in the context of collections because strings are implemented as a collection of bytes, plus some methods to provide useful functionality when those bytes are interpreted as text. In this section, we'll talk about the operations on String that every collection type has, such as creating, updating, and reading. We'll also discuss the ways in which String is different from the other collections, namely how indexing into a String is complicated by the differences between how people and computers interpret String data.

What Is a String?

We'll first define what we mean by the term *string*. Rust has only one string type in the core language, which is the string slice str that is usually seen in its borrowed form &str. In Chapter 4, we talked about *string slices*, which are references to some UTF-8 encoded string data stored elsewhere. String literals, for example, are stored in the program's binary and are therefore string slices.

The String type, which is provided by Rust's standard library rather than coded into the core language, is a growable, mutable, owned, UTF-8 encoded string type. When Rustaceans refer to "strings" in Rust, they might be referring to either the String or the string slice &str types, not just one of those types. Although this section is largely about String, both types are used heavily in Rust's standard library, and both String and string slices are UTF-8 encoded.

Creating a New String

Many of the same operations available with Vec<T> are available with String as well because String is actually implemented as a wrapper around a vector of bytes with some extra guarantees, restrictions, and capabilities. An example of a function that works the same way with Vec<T> and String is the new function to create an instance, shown in Listing 8-11.

```
let mut s = String::new();
```

Listing 8-11: Creating a new, empty String

This line creates a new, empty string called s, into which we can then load data. Often, we'll have some initial data with which we want to start the string. For that, we use the to_string method, which is available on any type that implements the Display trait, as string literals do. Listing 8-12 shows two examples.

```
let data = "initial contents";

let s = data.to_string();

// The method also works on a literal directly:
let s = "initial contents".to_string();
```

Listing 8-12: Using the to_string method to create a String from a string literal

This code creates a string containing initial contents.

We can also use the function String::from to create a String from a string literal. The code in Listing 8-13 is equivalent to the code in Listing 8-12 that uses to_string.

```
let s = String::from("initial contents");
```

Listing 8-13: Using the String::from function to create a String from a string literal

Because strings are used for so many things, we can use many different generic APIs for strings, providing us with a lot of options. Some of them can seem redundant, but they all have their place! In this case, String::from and to_string do the same thing, so which one you choose is a matter of style and readability.

Remember that strings are UTF-8 encoded, so we can include any properly encoded data in them, as shown in Listing 8-14.

```
let hello = String::from("السلام عليكم");
let hello = String::from("Dobrý den");
let hello = String::from("Hello");
let hello = String::from("שלום");
let hello = String::from("नमस्ते");
let hello = String::from("こんにちは");
let hello = String::from("안녕하세요");
let hello = String::from("你好");
let hello = String::from("Olá");
let hello = String::from("Здравствуйте");
let hello = String::from("Hola");
```

Listing 8-14: Storing greetings in different languages in strings

All of these are valid String values.

Updating a String

A String can grow in size and its contents can change, just like the contents of a Vec<T>, if you push more data into it. In addition, you can conveniently use the + operator or the format! macro to concatenate String values.

Appending to a String with push_str and push

We can grow a String by using the push_str method to append a string slice, as shown in Listing 8-15.

```
let mut s = String::from("foo");
s.push_str("bar");
```

Listing 8-15: Appending a string slice to a String using the push_str method

After these two lines, s will contain foobar. The push_str method takes a string slice because we don't necessarily want to take ownership of the parameter. For example, in the code in Listing 8-16, we want to be able to use s2 after appending its contents to s1.

```
let mut s1 = String::from("foo");
let s2 = "bar";
s1.push_str(s2);
println!("s2 is {s2}");
```

Listing 8-16: Using a string slice after appending its contents to a String

If the push_str method took ownership of s2, we wouldn't be able to print its value on the last line. However, this code works as we'd expect!

The push method takes a single character as a parameter and adds it to the String. Listing 8-17 adds the letter *l* to a String using the push method.

```
let mut s = String::from("lo");
s.push('l');
```

Listing 8-17: Adding one character to a String value using push

As a result, s will contain lol.

Concatenation with the + Operator or the format! Macro

Often, you'll want to combine two existing strings. One way to do so is to use the + operator, as shown in Listing 8-18.

```
let s1 = String::from("Hello, ");
let s2 = String::from("world!");
let s3 = s1 + &s2; // note s1 has been moved here and can no longer be used
```

Listing 8-18: Using the + operator to combine two String values into a new String value

The string s3 will contain Hello, world!. The reason s1 is no longer valid after the addition, and the reason we used a reference to s2, has to do with the signature of the method that's called when we use the + operator. The + operator uses the add method, whose signature looks something like this:

```
fn add(self, s: &str) -> String {
```

In the standard library, you'll see add defined using generics and associated types. Here, we've substituted in concrete types, which is what happens when we call this method with String values. We'll discuss generics in Chapter 10. This signature gives us the clues we need in order to understand the tricky bits of the + operator.

First, s2 has an &, meaning that we're adding a *reference* of the second string to the first string. This is because of the s parameter in the add function: we can only add a &str to a String; we can't add two String values together. But wait—the type of &s2 is &String, not &str, as specified in the second parameter to add. So why does Listing 8-18 compile?

The reason we're able to use &s2 in the call to add is that the compiler can *coerce* the &String argument into a &str. When we call the add method, Rust uses a *deref coercion*, which here turns &s2 into &s2[..]. We'll discuss deref coercion in more depth in Chapter 15. Because add does not take ownership of the s parameter, s2 will still be a valid String after this operation.

Second, we can see in the signature that add takes ownership of self because self does *not* have an &. This means s1 in Listing 8-18 will be moved into the add call and will no longer be valid after that. So, although let s3 = s1 + &s2; looks like it will copy both strings and create a new one, this statement actually takes ownership of s1, appends a copy of the contents of s2, and then returns ownership of the result. In other words, it looks like it's making a lot of copies, but it isn't; the implementation is more efficient than copying.

If we need to concatenate multiple strings, the behavior of the + operator gets unwieldy:

```
let s1 = String::from("tic");
let s2 = String::from("tac");
let s3 = String::from("toe");

let s = s1 + "-" + &s2 + "-" + &s3;
```

At this point, s will be tic-tac-toe. With all of the + and " characters, it's difficult to see what's going on. For combining strings in more complicated ways, we can instead use the format! macro:

```
let s1 = String::from("tic");
let s2 = String::from("tac");
let s3 = String::from("toe");

let s = format!("{s1}-{s2}-{s3}");
```

This code also sets s to tic-tac-toe. The format! macro works like println!, but instead of printing the output to the screen, it returns a String with the contents. The version of the code using format! is much easier to read, and the code generated by the format! macro uses references so that this call doesn't take ownership of any of its parameters.

Indexing into Strings

In many other programming languages, accessing individual characters in a string by referencing them by index is a valid and common operation. However, if you try to access parts of a `String` using indexing syntax in Rust, you'll get an error. Consider the invalid code in Listing 8-19.

```
let s1 = String::from("hello");
let h = s1[0];
```

Listing 8-19: Attempting to use indexing syntax with a `String`

This code will result in the following error:

```
error[E0277]: the type `String` cannot be indexed by `{integer}`
 --> src/main.rs:3:13
  |
3 |     let h = s1[0];
  |             ^^^^^ `String` cannot be indexed by `{integer}`
  |
  = help: the trait `Index<{integer}>` is not implemented for
`String`
```

The error and the note tell the story: Rust strings don't support indexing. But why not? To answer that question, we need to discuss how Rust stores strings in memory.

Internal Representation

A `String` is a wrapper over a `Vec<u8>`. Let's look at some of our properly encoded UTF-8 example strings from Listing 8-14. First, this one:

```
let hello = String::from("Hola");
```

In this case, `len` will be 4, which means the vector storing the string `"Hola"` is 4 bytes long. Each of these letters takes one byte when encoded in UTF-8. The following line, however, may surprise you (note that this string begins with the capital Cyrillic letter *Ze*, not the number 3):

```
let hello = String::from("Здравствуйте");
```

If you were asked how long the string is, you might say 12. In fact, Rust's answer is 24: that's the number of bytes it takes to encode "Здравствуйте" in UTF-8, because each Unicode scalar value in that string takes 2 bytes of storage. Therefore, an index into the string's bytes will not always correlate to a valid Unicode scalar value. To demonstrate, consider this invalid Rust code:

```
let hello = "Здравствуйте";
let answer = &hello[0];
```

You already know that `answer` will not be 3, the first letter. When encoded in UTF-8, the first byte of 3 is 208 and the second is 151, so it would seem that answer should in fact be 208, but 208 is not a valid character on its own. Returning 208 is likely not what a user would want if they asked for the first letter of this string; however, that's the only data that Rust has at byte index 0. Users generally don't want the byte value returned, even if the string contains only Latin letters: if &"hello"[0] were valid code that returned the byte value, it would return 104, not h.

The answer, then, is that to avoid returning an unexpected value and causing bugs that might not be discovered immediately, Rust doesn't compile this code at all and prevents misunderstandings early in the development process.

Bytes and Scalar Values and Grapheme Clusters! Oh My!

Another point about UTF-8 is that there are actually three relevant ways to look at strings from Rust's perspective: as bytes, scalar values, and grapheme clusters (the closest thing to what we would call *letters*).

If we look at the Hindi word नमस्ते written in the Devanagari script, it is stored as a vector of u8 values that looks like this:

```
[224, 164, 168, 224, 164, 174, 224, 164, 184, 224, 165, 141, 224,
164, 164, 224, 165, 135]
```

That's 18 bytes and is how computers ultimately store this data. If we look at them as Unicode scalar values, which are what Rust's char type is, those bytes look like this:

```
['न', 'म', 'स', '्', 'त', 'े']
```

There are six char values here, but the fourth and sixth are not letters: they're diacritics that don't make sense on their own. Finally, if we look at them as grapheme clusters, we'd get what a person would call the four letters that make up the Hindi word:

```
["न", "म", "स्", "ते"]
```

Rust provides different ways of interpreting the raw string data that computers store so that each program can choose the interpretation it needs, no matter what human language the data is in.

A final reason Rust doesn't allow us to index into a String to get a character is that indexing operations are expected to always take constant time (O(1)). But it isn't possible to guarantee that performance with a String, because Rust would have to walk through the contents from the beginning to the index to determine how many valid characters there were.

Slicing Strings

Indexing into a string is often a bad idea because it's not clear what the return type of the string-indexing operation should be: a byte value, a character, a grapheme cluster, or a string slice. If you really need to use indices to create string slices, therefore, Rust asks you to be more specific.

Rather than indexing using [] with a single number, you can use []
with a range to create a string slice containing particular bytes:

```
let hello = "Здравствуйте";

let s = &hello[0..4];
```

Here, s will be a &str that contains the first four bytes of the string.
Earlier, we mentioned that each of these characters was two bytes, which
means s will be Зд.

If we were to try to slice only part of a character's bytes with something
like &hello[0..1], Rust would panic at runtime in the same way as if an
invalid index were accessed in a vector:

```
thread 'main' panicked at 'byte index 1 is not a char boundary;
it is inside 'З' (bytes 0..2) of `Здравствуйте`', src/main.rs:4:14
```

You should use caution when creating string slices with ranges, because
doing so can crash your program.

Methods for Iterating Over Strings

The best way to operate on pieces of strings is to be explicit about whether
you want characters or bytes. For individual Unicode scalar values, use the
chars method. Calling chars on "Зд" separates out and returns two values of
type char, and you can iterate over the result to access each element:

```
for c in "Зд".chars() {
    println!("{c}");
}
```

This code will print the following:

```
З
д
```

Alternatively, the bytes method returns each raw byte, which might be
appropriate for your domain:

```
for b in "Зд".bytes() {
    println!("{b}");
}
```

This code will print the four bytes that make up this string:

```
208
151
208
180
```

But be sure to remember that valid Unicode scalar values may be made
up of more than one byte.

Getting grapheme clusters from strings, as with the Devanagari script, is complex, so this functionality is not provided by the standard library. Crates are available at *https://crates.io* if this is the functionality you need.

Strings Are Not So Simple

To summarize, strings are complicated. Different programming languages make different choices about how to present this complexity to the programmer. Rust has chosen to make the correct handling of String data the default behavior for all Rust programs, which means programmers have to put more thought into handling UTF-8 data up front. This trade-off exposes more of the complexity of strings than is apparent in other programming languages, but it prevents you from having to handle errors involving non-ASCII characters later in your development life cycle.

The good news is that the standard library offers a lot of functionality built off the String and &str types to help handle these complex situations correctly. Be sure to check out the documentation for useful methods like contains for searching in a string and replace for substituting parts of a string with another string.

Let's switch to something a bit less complex: hash maps!

Storing Keys with Associated Values in Hash Maps

The last of our common collections is the *hash map*. The type HashMap<K, V> stores a mapping of keys of type K to values of type V using a *hashing function*, which determines how it places these keys and values into memory. Many programming languages support this kind of data structure, but they often use a different name, such as *hash, map, object, hash table, dictionary,* or *associative array,* just to name a few.

Hash maps are useful when you want to look up data not by using an index, as you can with vectors, but by using a key that can be of any type. For example, in a game, you could keep track of each team's score in a hash map in which each key is a team's name and the values are each team's score. Given a team name, you can retrieve its score.

We'll go over the basic API of hash maps in this section, but many more goodies are hiding in the functions defined on HashMap<K, V> by the standard library. As always, check the standard library documentation for more information.

Creating a New Hash Map

One way to create an empty hash map is to use new and to add elements with insert. In Listing 8-20, we're keeping track of the scores of two teams whose names are *Blue* and *Yellow*. The Blue team starts with 10 points, and the Yellow team starts with 50.

```
use std::collections::HashMap;

let mut scores = HashMap::new();
```

```
scores.insert(String::from("Blue"), 10);
scores.insert(String::from("Yellow"), 50);
```

Listing 8-20: Creating a new hash map and inserting some keys and values

Note that we need to first use the HashMap from the collections portion of the standard library. Of our three common collections, this one is the least often used, so it's not included in the features brought into scope automatically in the prelude. Hash maps also have less support from the standard library; there's no built-in macro to construct them, for example.

Just like vectors, hash maps store their data on the heap. This HashMap has keys of type String and values of type i32. Like vectors, hash maps are homogeneous: all of the keys must have the same type, and all of the values must have the same type.

Accessing Values in a Hash Map

We can get a value out of the hash map by providing its key to the get method, as shown in Listing 8-21.

```
use std::collections::HashMap;

let mut scores = HashMap::new();

scores.insert(String::from("Blue"), 10);
scores.insert(String::from("Yellow"), 50);

let team_name = String::from("Blue");
let score = scores.get(&team_name).copied().unwrap_or(0);
```

Listing 8-21: Accessing the score for the Blue team stored in the hash map

Here, score will have the value that's associated with the Blue team, and the result will be 10. The get method returns an Option<&V>; if there's no value for that key in the hash map, get will return None. This program handles the Option by calling copied to get an Option<i32> rather than an Option<&i32>, then unwrap_or to set score to zero if scores doesn't have an entry for the key.

We can iterate over each key-value pair in a hash map in a similar manner as we do with vectors, using a for loop:

```
use std::collections::HashMap;

let mut scores = HashMap::new();

scores.insert(String::from("Blue"), 10);
scores.insert(String::from("Yellow"), 50);

for (key, value) in &scores {
    println!("{key}: {value}");
}
```

This code will print each pair in an arbitrary order:

```
Yellow: 50
Blue: 10
```

Hash Maps and Ownership

For types that implement the Copy trait, like i32, the values are copied into the hash map. For owned values like String, the values will be moved and the hash map will be the owner of those values, as demonstrated in Listing 8-22.

```
use std::collections::HashMap;

let field_name = String::from("Favorite color");
let field_value = String::from("Blue");

let mut map = HashMap::new();
map.insert(field_name, field_value);
// field_name and field_value are invalid at this point, try
// using them and see what compiler error you get!
```

Listing 8-22: Showing that keys and values are owned by the hash map once they're inserted

We aren't able to use the variables field_name and field_value after they've been moved into the hash map with the call to insert.

If we insert references to values into the hash map, the values won't be moved into the hash map. The values that the references point to must be valid for at least as long as the hash map is valid. We'll talk more about these issues in "Validating References with Lifetimes" on page 201.

Updating a Hash Map

Although the number of key and value pairs is growable, each unique key can only have one value associated with it at a time (but not vice versa: for example, both the Blue team and the Yellow team could have the value 10 stored in the scores hash map).

When you want to change the data in a hash map, you have to decide how to handle the case when a key already has a value assigned. You could replace the old value with the new value, completely disregarding the old value. You could keep the old value and ignore the new value, only adding the new value if the key *doesn't* already have a value. Or you could combine the old value and the new value. Let's look at how to do each of these!

Overwriting a Value

If we insert a key and a value into a hash map and then insert that same key with a different value, the value associated with that key will be replaced. Even though the code in Listing 8-23 calls insert twice, the hash map will only contain one key-value pair because we're inserting the value for the Blue team's key both times.

```
use std::collections::HashMap;

let mut scores = HashMap::new();

scores.insert(String::from("Blue"), 10);
scores.insert(String::from("Blue"), 25);

println!("{:?}", scores);
```

Listing 8-23: Replacing a value stored with a particular key

This code will print {"Blue": 25}. The original value of 10 has been overwritten.

Adding a Key and Value Only If a Key Isn't Present

It's common to check whether a particular key already exists in the hash map with a value and then to take the following actions: if the key does exist in the hash map, the existing value should remain the way it is; if the key doesn't exist, insert it and a value for it.

Hash maps have a special API for this called entry that takes the key you want to check as a parameter. The return value of the entry method is an enum called Entry that represents a value that might or might not exist. Let's say we want to check whether the key for the Yellow team has a value associated with it. If it doesn't, we want to insert the value 50, and the same for the Blue team. Using the entry API, the code looks like Listing 8-24.

```
use std::collections::HashMap;

let mut scores = HashMap::new();
scores.insert(String::from("Blue"), 10);

scores.entry(String::from("Yellow")).or_insert(50);
scores.entry(String::from("Blue")).or_insert(50);

println!("{:?}", scores);
```

Listing 8-24: Using the entry method to only insert if the key does not already have a value

The or_insert method on Entry is defined to return a mutable reference to the value for the corresponding Entry key if that key exists, and if not, it inserts the parameter as the new value for this key and returns a mutable reference to the new value. This technique is much cleaner than writing the logic ourselves and, in addition, plays more nicely with the borrow checker.

Running the code in Listing 8-24 will print {"Yellow": 50, "Blue": 10}. The first call to entry will insert the key for the Yellow team with the value 50 because the Yellow team doesn't have a value already. The second call to entry will not change the hash map because the Blue team already has the value 10.

Updating a Value Based on the Old Value

Another common use case for hash maps is to look up a key's value and then update it based on the old value. For instance, Listing 8-25 shows code that counts how many times each word appears in some text. We use a hash map with the words as keys and increment the value to keep track of how many times we've seen that word. If it's the first time we've seen a word, we'll first insert the value 0.

```
use std::collections::HashMap;

let text = "hello world wonderful world";

let mut map = HashMap::new();

for word in text.split_whitespace() {
    let count = map.entry(word).or_insert(0);
    *count += 1;
}

println!("{:?}", map);
```

Listing 8-25: Counting occurrences of words using a hash map that stores words and counts

This code will print {"world": 2, "hello": 1, "wonderful": 1}. You might see the same key-value pairs printed in a different order: recall from "Accessing Values in a Hash Map" on page 155 that iterating over a hash map happens in an arbitrary order.

The split_whitespace method returns an iterator over subslices, separated by whitespace, of the value in text. The or_insert method returns a mutable reference (&mut V) to the value for the specified key. Here, we store that mutable reference in the count variable, so in order to assign to that value, we must first dereference count using the asterisk (*). The mutable reference goes out of scope at the end of the for loop, so all of these changes are safe and allowed by the borrowing rules.

Hashing Functions

By default, HashMap uses a hashing function called *SipHash* that can provide resistance to denial-of-service (DoS) attacks involving hash tables. This is not the fastest hashing algorithm available, but the trade-off for better security that comes with the drop in performance is worth it. If you profile your code and find that the default hash function is too slow for your purposes, you can switch to another function by specifying a different hasher. A *hasher* is a type that implements the BuildHasher trait. We'll talk about traits and how to implement them in Chapter 10. You don't necessarily have to implement your own hasher from scratch; *https://crates.io* has libraries shared by other Rust users that provide hashers implementing many common hashing algorithms.

Summary

Vectors, strings, and hash maps will provide a large amount of functionality necessary in programs when you need to store, access, and modify data. Here are some exercises you should now be equipped to solve:

1. Given a list of integers, use a vector and return the median (when sorted, the value in the middle position) and mode (the value that occurs most often; a hash map will be helpful here) of the list.

2. Convert strings to pig latin. The first consonant of each word is moved to the end of the word and *ay* is added, so *first* becomes *irst-fay*. Words that start with a vowel have *hay* added to the end instead (*apple* becomes *apple-hay*). Keep in mind the details about UTF-8 encoding!

3. Using a hash map and vectors, create a text interface to allow a user to add employee names to a department in a company; for example, "Add Sally to Engineering" or "Add Amir to Sales." Then let the user retrieve a list of all people in a department or all people in the company by department, sorted alphabetically.

The standard library API documentation describes methods that vectors, strings, and hash maps have that will be helpful for these exercises!

We're getting into more complex programs in which operations can fail, so it's a perfect time to discuss error handling. We'll do that next!

9

ERROR HANDLING

Errors are a fact of life in software, so Rust has a number of features for handling situations in which something goes wrong. In many cases, Rust requires you to acknowledge the possibility of an error and take some action before your code will compile. This requirement makes your program more robust by ensuring that you'll discover errors and handle them appropriately before deploying your code to production!

Rust groups errors into two major categories: *recoverable* and *unrecoverable* errors. For a recoverable error, such as a *file not found* error, we most likely just want to report the problem to the user and retry the operation. Unrecoverable errors are always symptoms of bugs, such as trying to access a location beyond the end of an array, and so we want to immediately stop the program.

Most languages don't distinguish between these two kinds of errors and handle both in the same way, using mechanisms such as exceptions. Rust doesn't have exceptions. Instead, it has the type Result<T, E> for recoverable errors and the panic! macro that stops execution when the program encounters an unrecoverable error. This chapter covers calling panic! first and then talks about returning Result<T, E> values. Additionally, we'll explore considerations when deciding whether to try to recover from an error or to stop execution.

Unrecoverable Errors with panic!

Sometimes bad things happen in your code, and there's nothing you can do about it. In these cases, Rust has the panic! macro. There are two ways to cause a panic in practice: by taking an action that causes our code to panic (such as accessing an array past the end) or by explicitly calling the panic! macro. In both cases, we cause a panic in our program. By default, these panics will print a failure message, unwind, clean up the stack, and quit. Via an environment variable, you can also have Rust display the call stack when a panic occurs to make it easier to track down the source of the panic.

UNWINDING THE STACK OR ABORTING
IN RESPONSE TO A PANIC

By default, when a panic occurs the program starts *unwinding*, which means Rust walks back up the stack and cleans up the data from each function it encounters. However, walking back and cleaning up is a lot of work. Rust, therefore, allows you to choose the alternative of immediately *aborting*, which ends the program without cleaning up.

Memory that the program was using will then need to be cleaned up by the operating system. If in your project you need to make the resultant binary as small as possible, you can switch from unwinding to aborting upon a panic by adding panic = 'abort' to the appropriate [profile] sections in your *Cargo.toml* file. For example, if you want to abort on panic in release mode, add this:

```
[profile.release]
panic = 'abort'
```

Let's try calling panic! in a simple program:

src/main.rs
```
fn main() {
    panic!("crash and burn");
}
```

When you run the program, you'll see something like this:

```
thread 'main' panicked at 'crash and burn', src/main.rs:2:5
note: run with `RUST_BACKTRACE=1` environment variable to display
a backtrace
```

The call to panic! causes the error message contained in the last two lines. The first line shows our panic message and the place in our source code where the panic occurred: *src/main.rs:2:5* indicates that it's the second line, fifth character of our *src/main.rs* file.

In this case, the line indicated is part of our code, and if we go to that line, we see the panic! macro call. In other cases, the panic! call might be in code that our code calls, and the filename and line number reported by the error message will be someone else's code where the panic! macro is called, not the line of our code that eventually led to the panic! call.

We can use the backtrace of the functions the panic! call came from to figure out the part of our code that is causing the problem. To understand how to use a panic! backtrace, let's look at another example and see what it's like when a panic! call comes from a library because of a bug in our code instead of from our code calling the macro directly. Listing 9-1 has some code that attempts to access an index in a vector beyond the range of valid indexes.

src/main.rs
```
fn main() {
    let v = vec![1, 2, 3];

    v[99];
}
```

Listing 9-1: Attempting to access an element beyond the end of a vector, which will cause a call to panic!

Here, we're attempting to access the 100th element of our vector (which is at index 99 because indexing starts at zero), but the vector has only three elements. In this situation, Rust will panic. Using [] is supposed to return an element, but if you pass an invalid index, there's no element that Rust could return here that would be correct.

In C, attempting to read beyond the end of a data structure is undefined behavior. You might get whatever is at the location in memory that would correspond to that element in the data structure, even though the memory doesn't belong to that structure. This is called a *buffer overread* and can lead to security vulnerabilities if an attacker is able to manipulate the index in such a way as to read data they shouldn't be allowed to that is stored after the data structure.

To protect your program from this sort of vulnerability, if you try to read an element at an index that doesn't exist, Rust will stop execution and refuse to continue. Let's try it and see:

```
thread 'main' panicked at 'index out of bounds: the len is 3 but the index is
99', src/main.rs:4:5
note: run with `RUST_BACKTRACE=1` environment variable to display a backtrace
```

This error points at line 4 of our *main.rs* where we attempt to access index. The note: line tells us that we can set the RUST_BACKTRACE environment variable to get a backtrace of exactly what happened to cause the error. A *backtrace* is a list of all the functions that have been called to get to this point. Backtraces in Rust work as they do in other languages: the key to reading the backtrace is to start from the top and read until you see files you wrote. That's the spot where the problem originated. The lines above that spot are code that your code has called; the lines below are code that called your code. These before-and-after lines might include core Rust code, standard library code, or crates that you're using. Let's try getting a backtrace by setting the RUST_BACKTRACE environment variable to any value except 0. Listing 9-2 shows output similar to what you'll see.

```
$ RUST_BACKTRACE=1 cargo run
thread 'main' panicked at 'index out of bounds: the len is 3 but the index is
99', src/main.rs:4:5
stack backtrace:
   0: rust_begin_unwind
             at /rustc/e092d0b6b43f2de967af0887873151bb1c0b18d3/library/std
/src/panicking.rs:584:5
   1: core::panicking::panic_fmt
             at /rustc/e092d0b6b43f2de967af0887873151bb1c0b18d3/library/core
/src/panicking.rs:142:14
   2: core::panicking::panic_bounds_check
             at /rustc/e092d0b6b43f2de967af0887873151bb1c0b18d3/library/core
/src/panicking.rs:84:5
   3: <usize as core::slice::index::SliceIndex<[T]>>::index
             at /rustc/e092d0b6b43f2de967af0887873151bb1c0b18d3/library/core
/src/slice/index.rs:242:10
   4: core::slice::index::<impl core::ops::index::Index<I> for [T]>::index
             at /rustc/e092d0b6b43f2de967af0887873151bb1c0b18d3/library/core
/src/slice/index.rs:18:9
   5: <alloc::vec::Vec<T,A> as core::ops::index::Index<I>>::index
             at /rustc/e092d0b6b43f2de967af0887873151bb1c0b18d3/library/alloc
/src/vec/mod.rs:2591:9
   6: panic::main
             at ./src/main.rs:4:5
   7: core::ops::function::FnOnce::call_once
             at /rustc/e092d0b6b43f2de967af0887873151bb1c0b18d3/library/core
/src/ops/function.rs:248:5
note: Some details are omitted, run with `RUST_BACKTRACE=full` for a verbose backtrace.
```

Listing 9-2: The backtrace generated by a call to panic! displayed when the environment variable RUST_BACKTRACE is set

That's a lot of output! The exact output you see might be different depending on your operating system and Rust version. In order to get backtraces with this information, debug symbols must be enabled. Debug symbols are enabled by default when using cargo build or cargo run without the --release flag, as we have here.

In the output in Listing 9-2, line 6 of the backtrace points to the line in our project that's causing the problem: line 4 of *src/main.rs*. If we don't want our program to panic, we should start our investigation at the location pointed to by the first line mentioning a file we wrote. In Listing 9-1, where we deliberately wrote code that would panic, the way to fix the panic is to not request an element beyond the range of the vector indexes. When your code panics in the future, you'll need to figure out what action the code is taking with what values to cause the panic and what the code should do instead.

We'll come back to panic! and when we should and should not use panic! to handle error conditions in "To panic! or Not to panic!" on page 175. Next, we'll look at how to recover from an error using Result.

Recoverable Errors with Result

Most errors aren't serious enough to require the program to stop entirely. Sometimes when a function fails it's for a reason that you can easily interpret and respond to. For example, if you try to open a file and that operation fails because the file doesn't exist, you might want to create the file instead of terminating the process.

Recall from "Handling Potential Failure with Result" on page 17 that the Result enum is defined as having two variants, Ok and Err, as follows:

```
enum Result<T, E> {
    Ok(T),
    Err(E),
}
```

The T and E are generic type parameters: we'll discuss generics in more detail in Chapter 10. What you need to know right now is that T represents the type of the value that will be returned in a success case within the Ok variant, and E represents the type of the error that will be returned in a failure case within the Err variant. Because Result has these generic type parameters, we can use the Result type and the functions defined on it in many different situations where the success value and error value we want to return may differ.

Let's call a function that returns a Result value because the function could fail. In Listing 9-3 we try to open a file.

src/main.rs
```
use std::fs::File;

fn main() {
    let greeting_file_result = File::open("hello.txt");
}
```

Listing 9-3: Opening a file

The return type of File::open is a Result<T, E>. The generic parameter T has been filled in by the implementation of File::open with the type of the success value, std::fs::File, which is a file handle. The type of E used in the error value is std::io::Error. This return type means the call to File::open might succeed and return a file handle that we can read from or write to.

The function call also might fail: for example, the file might not exist, or we might not have permission to access the file. The File::open function needs to have a way to tell us whether it succeeded or failed and at the same time give us either the file handle or error information. This information is exactly what the Result enum conveys.

In the case where File::open succeeds, the value in the variable greeting _file_result will be an instance of Ok that contains a file handle. In the case where it fails, the value in greeting_file_result will be an instance of Err that contains more information about the kind of error that occurred.

We need to add to the code in Listing 9-3 to take different actions depending on the value File::open returns. Listing 9-4 shows one way to handle the Result using a basic tool, the match expression that we discussed in Chapter 6.

src/main.rs

```
use std::fs::File;

fn main() {
    let greeting_file_result = File::open("hello.txt");

    let greeting_file = match greeting_file_result {
        Ok(file) => file,
        Err(error) => {
            panic!("Problem opening the file: {:?}", error);
        }
    };
}
```

Listing 9-4: Using a match expression to handle the Result variants that might be returned

Note that, like the Option enum, the Result enum and its variants have been brought into scope by the prelude, so we don't need to specify Result:: before the Ok and Err variants in the match arms.

When the result is Ok, this code will return the inner file value out of the Ok variant, and we then assign that file handle value to the variable greeting_file. After the match, we can use the file handle for reading or writing.

The other arm of the match handles the case where we get an Err value from File::open. In this example, we've chosen to call the panic! macro. If there's no file named *hello.txt* in our current directory and we run this code, we'll see the following output from the panic! macro:

```
thread 'main' panicked at 'Problem opening the file: Os { code:
 2, kind: NotFound, message: "No such file or directory" }',
src/main.rs:8:23
```

As usual, this output tells us exactly what has gone wrong.

Matching on Different Errors

The code in Listing 9-4 will panic! no matter why File::open failed. However, we want to take different actions for different failure reasons. If File::open failed because the file doesn't exist, we want to create the file and return the handle to the new file. If File::open failed for any other reason—for example, because we didn't have permission to open the file—we still want the code to panic! in the same way it did in Listing 9-4. For this, we add an inner match expression, shown in Listing 9-5.

src/main.rs

```
use std::fs::File;
use std::io::ErrorKind;

fn main() {
    let greeting_file_result = File::open("hello.txt");

    let greeting_file = match greeting_file_result {
        Ok(file) => file,
        Err(error) => match error.kind() {
            ErrorKind::NotFound => {
                match File::create("hello.txt") {
                    Ok(fc) => fc,
                    Err(e) => panic!(
                        "Problem creating the file: {:?}",
                        e
                    ),
                }
            }
            other_error => {
                panic!(
                    "Problem opening the file: {:?}",
                    other_error
                );
            }
        },
    };
}
```

Listing 9-5: Handling different kinds of errors in different ways

The type of the value that File::open returns inside the Err variant is io::Error, which is a struct provided by the standard library. This struct has a method kind that we can call to get an io::ErrorKind value. The enum io::ErrorKind is provided by the standard library and has variants representing the different kinds of errors that might result from an io operation. The variant we want to use is ErrorKind::NotFound, which indicates the file we're trying to open doesn't exist yet. So we match on greeting_file_result, but we also have an inner match on error.kind().

The condition we want to check in the inner match is whether the value returned by error.kind() is the NotFound variant of the ErrorKind enum. If it is, we try to create the file with File::create. However, because File::create could also fail, we need a second arm in the inner match expression. When the file can't be created, a different error message is printed. The second arm of the outer match stays the same, so the program panics on any error besides the missing file error.

Alternatives to Using match with Result<T, E>

That's a lot of match! The match expression is very useful but also very much a primitive. In Chapter 13, you'll learn about closures, which are used with many of the methods defined on Result<T, E>. These methods can be more concise than using match when handling Result<T, E> values in your code.

For example, here's another way to write the same logic as shown in Listing 9-5, this time using closures and the unwrap_or_else method:

src/main.rs
```
use std::fs::File;
use std::io::ErrorKind;

fn main() {
    let greeting_file = File::open("hello.txt").unwrap_or_else(|error| {
        if error.kind() == ErrorKind::NotFound {
            File::create("hello.txt").unwrap_or_else(|error| {
                panic!("Problem creating the file: {:?}", error);
            })
        } else {
            panic!("Problem opening the file: {:?}", error);
        }
    });
}
```

Although this code has the same behavior as Listing 9-5, it doesn't contain any match expressions and is cleaner to read. Come back to this example after you've read Chapter 13, and look up the unwrap_or_else method in the standard library documentation. Many more of these methods can clean up huge nested match expressions when you're dealing with errors.

Shortcuts for Panic on Error: unwrap and expect

Using match works well enough, but it can be a bit verbose and doesn't always communicate intent well. The Result<T, E> type has many helper methods defined on it to do various, more specific tasks. The unwrap method is a shortcut method implemented just like the match expression we wrote in Listing 9-4. If the Result value is the Ok variant, unwrap will return the value inside the Ok. If the Result is the Err variant, unwrap will call the panic! macro for us. Here is an example of unwrap in action:

src/main.rs
```
use std::fs::File;

fn main() {
    let greeting_file = File::open("hello.txt").unwrap();
}
```

If we run this code without a *hello.txt* file, we'll see an error message from the panic! call that the unwrap method makes:

```
thread 'main' panicked at 'called `Result::unwrap()` on an `Err` value: Os {
code: 2, kind: NotFound, message: "No such file or directory" }',
src/main.rs:4:49
```

Similarly, the expect method lets us also choose the panic! error message. Using expect instead of unwrap and providing good error messages can convey your intent and make tracking down the source of a panic easier. The syntax of expect looks like this:

src/main.rs
```
use std::fs::File;

fn main() {
    let greeting_file = File::open("hello.txt")
        .expect("hello.txt should be included in this project");
}
```

We use expect in the same way as unwrap: to return the file handle or call the panic! macro. The error message used by expect in its call to panic! will be the parameter that we pass to expect, rather than the default panic! message that unwrap uses. Here's what it looks like:

```
thread 'main' panicked at 'hello.txt should be included in this project: Os {
code: 2, kind: NotFound, message: "No such file or directory" }',
src/main.rs:5:10
```

In production-quality code, most Rustaceans choose expect rather than unwrap and give more context about why the operation is expected to always succeed. That way, if your assumptions are ever proven wrong, you have more information to use in debugging.

Propagating Errors

When a function's implementation calls something that might fail, instead of handling the error within the function itself, you can return the error to the calling code so that it can decide what to do. This is known as *propagating* the error and gives more control to the calling code, where there might be more information or logic that dictates how the error should be handled than what you have available in the context of your code.

For example, Listing 9-6 shows a function that reads a username from a file. If the file doesn't exist or can't be read, this function will return those errors to the code that called the function.

src/main.rs
```
use std::fs::File;
use std::io::{self, Read};

❶ fn read_username_from_file() -> Result<String, io::Error> {
    ❷ let username_file_result = File::open("hello.txt");

    ❸ let mut username_file = match username_file_result {
        ❹ Ok(file) => file,
        ❺ Err(e) => return Err(e),
    };

    ❻ let mut username = String::new();

    ❼ match username_file.read_to_string(&mut username) {
```

```
        ❽ Ok(_) => Ok(username),
        ❾ Err(e) => Err(e),
        }
    }
}
```

Listing 9-6: A function that returns errors to the calling code using match

This function can be written in a much shorter way, but we're going to
start by doing a lot of it manually in order to explore error handling; at the
end, we'll show the shorter way. Let's look at the return type of the function
first: Result<String, io::Error> ❶. This means the function is returning a
value of the type Result<T, E>, where the generic parameter T has been filled
in with the concrete type String and the generic type E has been filled in
with the concrete type io::Error.

If this function succeeds without any problems, the code that calls this
function will receive an Ok value that holds a String—the username that
this function read from the file ❽. If this function encounters any problems,
the calling code will receive an Err value that holds an instance of io::
Error that contains more information about what the problems were. We
chose io::Error as the return type of this function because that happens to
be the type of the error value returned from both of the operations we're
calling in this function's body that might fail: the File::open function ❷
and the read_to_string method ❼.

The body of the function starts by calling the File::open function ❷.
Then we handle the Result value with a match similar to the match in Listing 9-4.
If File::open succeeds, the file handle in the pattern variable file ❹ becomes
the value in the mutable variable username_file ❸ and the function continues.
In the Err case, instead of calling panic!, we use the return keyword to return
early out of the function entirely and pass the error value from File::open,
now in the pattern variable e, back to the calling code as this function's error
value ❺.

So, if we have a file handle in username_file, the function then creates a
new String in variable username ❻ and calls the read_to_string method on the
file handle in username_file to read the contents of the file into username ❼.
The read_to_string method also returns a Result because it might fail, even
though File::open succeeded. So we need another match to handle that Result:
if read_to_string succeeds, then our function has succeeded, and we return
the username from the file that's now in username wrapped in an Ok. If read
_to_string fails, we return the error value in the same way that we returned
the error value in the match that handled the return value of File::open.
However, we don't need to explicitly say return, because this is the last
expression in the function ❾.

The code that calls this code will then handle getting either an Ok value
that contains a username or an Err value that contains an io::Error. It's up
to the calling code to decide what to do with those values. If the calling
code gets an Err value, it could call panic! and crash the program, use a
default username, or look up the username from somewhere other than a
file, for example. We don't have enough information on what the calling

code is actually trying to do, so we propagate all the success or error information upward for it to handle appropriately.

This pattern of propagating errors is so common in Rust that Rust provides the question mark operator ? to make this easier.

A Shortcut for Propagating Errors: The ? Operator

Listing 9-7 shows an implementation of read_username_from_file that has the same functionality as in Listing 9-6, but this implementation uses the ? operator.

src/main.rs
```
use std::fs::File;
use std::io::{self, Read};

fn read_username_from_file() -> Result<String, io::Error> {
    let mut username_file = File::open("hello.txt")?;
    let mut username = String::new();
    username_file.read_to_string(&mut username)?;
    Ok(username)
}
```

Listing 9-7: A function that returns errors to the calling code using the ? operator

The ? placed after a Result value is defined to work in almost the same way as the match expressions we defined to handle the Result values in Listing 9-6. If the value of the Result is an Ok, the value inside the Ok will get returned from this expression, and the program will continue. If the value is an Err, the Err will be returned from the whole function as if we had used the return keyword so the error value gets propagated to the calling code.

There is a difference between what the match expression from Listing 9-6 does and what the ? operator does: error values that have the ? operator called on them go through the from function, defined in the From trait in the standard library, which is used to convert values from one type into another. When the ? operator calls the from function, the error type received is converted into the error type defined in the return type of the current function. This is useful when a function returns one error type to represent all the ways a function might fail, even if parts might fail for many different reasons.

For example, we could change the read_username_from_file function in Listing 9-7 to return a custom error type named OurError that we define. If we also define impl From<io::Error> for OurError to construct an instance of OurError from an io::Error, then the ? operator calls in the body of read _username_from_file will call from and convert the error types without needing to add any more code to the function.

In the context of Listing 9-7, the ? at the end of the File::open call will return the value inside an Ok to the variable username_file. If an error occurs, the ? operator will return early out of the whole function and give any Err value to the calling code. The same thing applies to the ? at the end of the read_to_string call.

The ? operator eliminates a lot of boilerplate and makes this function's implementation simpler. We could even shorten this code further by chaining method calls immediately after the ?, as shown in Listing 9-8.

src/main.rs

```
use std::fs::File;
use std::io::{self, Read};

fn read_username_from_file() -> Result<String, io::Error> {
    let mut username = String::new();

    File::open("hello.txt")?.read_to_string(&mut username)?;

    Ok(username)
}
```

Listing 9-8: Chaining method calls after the ? operator

We've moved the creation of the new String in username to the beginning of the function; that part hasn't changed. Instead of creating a variable username_file, we've chained the call to read_to_string directly onto the result of File::open("hello.txt")?. We still have a ? at the end of the read_to_string call, and we still return an Ok value containing username when both File::open and read_to_string succeed rather than returning errors. The functionality is again the same as in Listing 9-6 and Listing 9-7; this is just a different, more ergonomic way to write it.

Listing 9-9 shows a way to make this even shorter using fs::read_to_string.

src/main.rs

```
use std::fs;
use std::io;

fn read_username_from_file() -> Result<String, io::Error> {
    fs::read_to_string("hello.txt")
}
```

Listing 9-9: Using fs::read_to_string instead of opening and then reading the file

Reading a file into a string is a fairly common operation, so the standard library provides the convenient fs::read_to_string function that opens the file, creates a new String, reads the contents of the file, puts the contents into that String, and returns it. Of course, using fs::read_to_string doesn't give us the opportunity to explain all the error handling, so we did it the longer way first.

Where the ? Operator Can Be Used

The ? operator can only be used in functions whose return type is compatible with the value the ? is used on. This is because the ? operator is defined to perform an early return of a value out of the function, in the same manner as the match expression we defined in Listing 9-6. In Listing 9-6, the match was using a Result value, and the early return arm returned an Err(e) value. The return type of the function has to be a Result so that it's compatible with this return.

In Listing 9-10, let's look at the error we'll get if we use the ? operator in a main function with a return type that is incompatible with the type of the value we use ? on.

```
use std::fs::File;

fn main() {
    let greeting_file = File::open("hello.txt")?;
}
```

Listing 9-10: Attempting to use the ? in the main function that returns () won't compile.

This code opens a file, which might fail. The ? operator follows the Result value returned by File::open, but this main function has the return type of (), not Result. When we compile this code, we get the following error message:

```
error[E0277]: the `?` operator can only be used in a function that returns
`Result` or `Option` (or another type that implements `FromResidual`)
 --> src/main.rs:4:48
  |
3 | / fn main() {
4 | |     let greeting_file = File::open("hello.txt")?;
  | |                                                ^ cannot use the `?`
operator in a function that returns `()`
5 | | }
  | |_- this function should return `Result` or `Option` to accept `?`
  |
  = help: the trait `FromResidual<Result<Infallible, std::io::Error>>` is not
implemented for `()`
```

This error points out that we're only allowed to use the ? operator in a function that returns Result, Option, or another type that implements FromResidual.

To fix the error, you have two choices. One choice is to change the return type of your function to be compatible with the value you're using the ? operator on as long as you have no restrictions preventing that. The other choice is to use a match or one of the Result<T, E> methods to handle the Result<T, E> in whatever way is appropriate.

The error message also mentioned that ? can be used with Option<T> values as well. As with using ? on Result, you can only use ? on Option in a function that returns an Option. The behavior of the ? operator when called on an Option<T> is similar to its behavior when called on a Result<T, E>: if the value is None, the None will be returned early from the function at that point. If the value is Some, the value inside the Some is the resultant value of the expression, and the function continues. Listing 9-11 has an example of a function that finds the last character of the first line in the given text.

```
fn last_char_of_first_line(text: &str) -> Option<char> {
    text.lines().next()?.chars().last()
}
```

Listing 9-11: Using the ? operator on an Option<T> value

This function returns Option<char> because it's possible that there is a character there, but it's also possible that there isn't. This code takes the text string slice argument and calls the lines method on it, which returns an iterator over the lines in the string. Because this function wants to examine the first line, it calls next on the iterator to get the first value from the iterator. If text is the empty string, this call to next will return None, in which case we use ? to stop and return None from last_char_of_first_line. If text is not the empty string, next will return a Some value containing a string slice of the first line in text.

The ? extracts the string slice, and we can call chars on that string slice to get an iterator of its characters. We're interested in the last character in this first line, so we call last to return the last item in the iterator. This is an Option because it's possible that the first line is the empty string; for example, if text starts with a blank line but has characters on other lines, as in "\nhi". However, if there is a last character on the first line, it will be returned in the Some variant. The ? operator in the middle gives us a concise way to express this logic, allowing us to implement the function in one line. If we couldn't use the ? operator on Option, we'd have to implement this logic using more method calls or a match expression.

Note that you can use the ? operator on a Result in a function that returns Result, and you can use the ? operator on an Option in a function that returns Option, but you can't mix and match. The ? operator won't automatically convert a Result to an Option or vice versa; in those cases, you can use methods like the ok method on Result or the ok_or method on Option to do the conversion explicitly.

So far, all the main functions we've used return (). The main function is special because it's the entry point and exit point of an executable program, and there are restrictions on what its return type can be for the program to behave as expected.

Luckily, main can also return a Result<(), E>. Listing 9-12 has the code from Listing 9-10, but we've changed the return type of main to be Result<(), Box<dyn Error>> and added a return value Ok(()) to the end. This code will now compile.

src/main.rs
```
use std::error::Error;
use std::fs::File;

fn main() -> Result<(), Box<dyn Error>> {
    let greeting_file = File::open("hello.txt")?;

    Ok(())
}
```

Listing 9-12: Changing main to return Result<(), E> allows the use of the ? operator on Result values.

The Box<dyn Error> type is a *trait object*, which we'll talk about in "Using Trait Objects That Allow for Values of Different Types" on page 379. For now, you can read Box<dyn Error> to mean "any kind of error." Using ? on a Result value in a main function with the error type Box<dyn Error> is allowed because it allows any `Err` value to be returned early. Even though the body of this `main` function will only ever return errors of type `std::io::Error`, by specifying `Box<dyn Error>`, this signature will continue to be correct even if more code that returns other errors is added to the body of `main`.

When a `main` function returns a `Result<(), E>`, the executable will exit with a value of `0` if `main` returns `Ok(())` and will exit with a nonzero value if `main` returns an `Err` value. Executables written in C return integers when they exit: programs that exit successfully return the integer `0`, and programs that error return some integer other than `0`. Rust also returns integers from executables to be compatible with this convention.

The `main` function may return any types that implement the `std::process::Termination` trait, which contains a function `report` that returns an `ExitCode`. Consult the standard library documentation for more information on implementing the `Termination` trait for your own types.

Now that we've discussed the details of calling `panic!` or returning `Result`, let's return to the topic of how to decide which is appropriate to use in which cases.

To panic! or Not to panic!

So how do you decide when you should call `panic!` and when you should return `Result`? When code panics, there's no way to recover. You could call `panic!` for any error situation, whether there's a possible way to recover or not, but then you're making the decision that a situation is unrecoverable on behalf of the calling code. When you choose to return a `Result` value, you give the calling code options. The calling code could choose to attempt to recover in a way that's appropriate for its situation, or it could decide that an `Err` value in this case is unrecoverable, so it can call `panic!` and turn your recoverable error into an unrecoverable one. Therefore, returning `Result` is a good default choice when you're defining a function that might fail.

In situations such as examples, prototype code, and tests, it's more appropriate to write code that panics instead of returning a `Result`. Let's explore why, then discuss situations in which the compiler can't tell that failure is impossible, but you as a human can. The chapter will conclude with some general guidelines on how to decide whether to panic in library code.

Examples, Prototype Code, and Tests

When you're writing an example to illustrate some concept, also including robust error-handling code can make the example less clear. In examples, it's understood that a call to a method like `unwrap` that could panic is meant as a placeholder for the way you'd want your application to handle errors, which can differ based on what the rest of your code is doing.

Similarly, the `unwrap` and `expect` methods are very handy when prototyping, before you're ready to decide how to handle errors. They leave clear markers in your code for when you're ready to make your program more robust.

If a method call fails in a test, you'd want the whole test to fail, even if that method isn't the functionality under test. Because `panic!` is how a test is marked as a failure, calling `unwrap` or `expect` is exactly what should happen.

Cases in Which You Have More Information Than the Compiler

It would also be appropriate to call unwrap or expect when you have some other logic that ensures the Result will have an Ok value, but the logic isn't something the compiler understands. You'll still have a Result value that you need to handle: whatever operation you're calling still has the possibility of failing in general, even though it's logically impossible in your particular situation. If you can ensure by manually inspecting the code that you'll never have an Err variant, it's perfectly acceptable to call unwrap, and even better to document the reason you think you'll never have an Err variant in the expect text. Here's an example:

```
use std::net::IpAddr;

let home: IpAddr = "127.0.0.1"
    .parse()
    .expect("Hardcoded IP address should be valid");
```

We're creating an IpAddr instance by parsing a hardcoded string. We can see that 127.0.0.1 is a valid IP address, so it's acceptable to use expect here. However, having a hardcoded, valid string doesn't change the return type of the parse method: we still get a Result value, and the compiler will still make us handle the Result as if the Err variant is a possibility because the compiler isn't smart enough to see that this string is always a valid IP address. If the IP address string came from a user rather than being hard-coded into the program and therefore *did* have a possibility of failure, we'd definitely want to handle the Result in a more robust way instead. Mentioning the assumption that this IP address is hardcoded will prompt us to change expect to better error-handling code if, in the future, we need to get the IP address from some other source instead.

Guidelines for Error Handling

It's advisable to have your code panic when it's possible that your code could end up in a bad state. In this context, a *bad state* is when some assumption, guarantee, contract, or invariant has been broken, such as when invalid values, contradictory values, or missing values are passed to your code—plus one or more of the following:

- The bad state is something that is unexpected, as opposed to something that will likely happen occasionally, like a user entering data in the wrong format.
- Your code after this point needs to rely on not being in this bad state, rather than checking for the problem at every step.
- There's not a good way to encode this information in the types you use. We'll work through an example of what we mean in "Encoding States and Behavior as Types" on page 393.

If someone calls your code and passes in values that don't make sense, it's best to return an error if you can so the user of the library can decide what they want to do in that case. However, in cases where continuing could be insecure or harmful, the best choice might be to call panic! and alert the person using your library to the bug in their code so they can fix it during development. Similarly, panic! is often appropriate if you're calling external code that is out of your control and it returns an invalid state that you have no way of fixing.

However, when failure is expected, it's more appropriate to return a Result than to make a panic! call. Examples include a parser being given malformed data or an HTTP request returning a status that indicates you have hit a rate limit. In these cases, returning a Result indicates that failure is an expected possibility that the calling code must decide how to handle.

When your code performs an operation that could put a user at risk if it's called using invalid values, your code should verify the values are valid first and panic if the values aren't valid. This is mostly for safety reasons: attempting to operate on invalid data can expose your code to vulnerabilities. This is the main reason the standard library will call panic! if you attempt an out-of-bounds memory access: trying to access memory that doesn't belong to the current data structure is a common security problem. Functions often have *contracts*: their behavior is only guaranteed if the inputs meet particular requirements. Panicking when the contract is violated makes sense because a contract violation always indicates a caller-side bug, and it's not a kind of error you want the calling code to have to explicitly handle. In fact, there's no reasonable way for calling code to recover; the calling *programmers* need to fix the code. Contracts for a function, especially when a violation will cause a panic, should be explained in the API documentation for the function.

However, having lots of error checks in all of your functions would be verbose and annoying. Fortunately, you can use Rust's type system (and thus the type checking done by the compiler) to do many of the checks for you. If your function has a particular type as a parameter, you can proceed with your code's logic knowing that the compiler has already ensured you have a valid value. For example, if you have a type rather than an Option, your program expects to have *something* rather than *nothing*. Your code then doesn't have to handle two cases for the Some and None variants: it will only have one case for definitely having a value. Code trying to pass nothing to your function won't even compile, so your function doesn't have to check for that case at runtime. Another example is using an unsigned integer type such as u32, which ensures the parameter is never negative.

Creating Custom Types for Validation

Let's take the idea of using Rust's type system to ensure we have a valid value one step further and look at creating a custom type for validation. Recall the guessing game in Chapter 2 in which our code asked the user to guess a number between 1 and 100. We never validated that the user's guess was between those numbers before checking it against our secret number; we only validated that the guess was positive. In this case, the consequences were not very dire: our output of "Too high" or "Too low" would still be correct. But it would be a useful enhancement to guide the user toward valid guesses and have different behavior when the user guesses a number that's out of range versus when the user types, for example, letters instead.

One way to do this would be to parse the guess as an i32 instead of only a u32 to allow potentially negative numbers, and then add a check for the number being in range, like so:

src/main.rs
```
loop {
    --snip--

    let guess: i32 = match guess.trim().parse() {
        Ok(num) => num,
        Err(_) => continue,
    };

    if guess < 1 || guess > 100 {
        println!("The secret number will be between 1 and 100.");
        continue;
    }

    match guess.cmp(&secret_number) {
        --snip--
}
```

The if expression checks whether our value is out of range, tells the user about the problem, and calls continue to start the next iteration of the loop and ask for another guess. After the if expression, we can proceed with the comparisons between guess and the secret number knowing that guess is between 1 and 100.

However, this is not an ideal solution: if it were absolutely critical that the program only operated on values between 1 and 100, and it had many functions with this requirement, having a check like this in every function would be tedious (and might impact performance).

Instead, we can make a new type and put the validations in a function to create an instance of the type rather than repeating the validations everywhere. That way, it's safe for functions to use the new type in their signatures and confidently use the values they receive. Listing 9-13 shows one way to define a Guess type that will only create an instance of Guess if the new function receives a value between 1 and 100.

src/lib.rs
```
❶ pub struct Guess {
    value: i32,
}

impl Guess {
  ❷ pub fn new(value: i32) -> Guess {
      ❸ if value < 1 || value > 100 {
          ❹ panic!(
```

```
                "Guess value must be between 1 and 100, got {}.",
                value
            );
        }

        ❺ Guess { value }
    }

    ❻ pub fn value(&self) -> i32 {
        self.value
    }
}
```

Listing 9-13: A Guess type that will only continue with values between 1 and 100

First we define a struct named Guess that has a field named value that holds an i32 ❶. This is where the number will be stored.

Then we implement an associated function named new on Guess that creates instances of Guess values ❷. The new function is defined to have one parameter named value of type i32 and to return a Guess. The code in the body of the new function tests value to make sure it's between 1 and 100 ❸. If value doesn't pass this test, we make a panic! call ❹, which will alert the programmer who is writing the calling code that they have a bug they need to fix, because creating a Guess with a value outside this range would violate the contract that Guess::new is relying on. The conditions in which Guess::new might panic should be discussed in its public-facing API documentation; we'll cover documentation conventions indicating the possibility of a panic! in the API documentation that you create in Chapter 14. If value does pass the test, we create a new Guess with its value field set to the value parameter and return the Guess ❺.

Next, we implement a method named value that borrows self, doesn't have any other parameters, and returns an i32 ❻. This kind of method is sometimes called a *getter* because its purpose is to get some data from its fields and return it. This public method is necessary because the value field of the Guess struct is private. It's important that the value field be private so code using the Guess struct is not allowed to set value directly: code outside the module *must* use the Guess::new function to create an instance of Guess, thereby ensuring there's no way for a Guess to have a value that hasn't been checked by the conditions in the Guess::new function.

A function that has a parameter or returns only numbers between 1 and 100 could then declare in its signature that it takes or returns a Guess rather than an i32 and wouldn't need to do any additional checks in its body.

Summary

Rust's error-handling features are designed to help you write more robust code. The panic! macro signals that your program is in a state it can't handle and lets you tell the process to stop instead of trying to proceed with invalid or incorrect values. The Result enum uses Rust's type system to indicate that operations might fail in a way that your code could recover from. You can use Result to tell code that calls your code that it needs to handle potential success or failure as well. Using panic! and Result in the appropriate situations will make your code more reliable in the face of inevitable problems.

Now that you've seen useful ways that the standard library uses generics with the Option and Result enums, we'll talk about how generics work and how you can use them in your code.

10

GENERIC TYPES, TRAITS, AND LIFETIMES

 Every programming language has tools for effectively handling the duplication of concepts. In Rust, one such tool is *generics*: abstract stand-ins for concrete types or other properties. We can express the behavior of generics or how they relate to other generics without knowing what will be in their place when compiling and running the code.

Functions can take parameters of some generic type, instead of a concrete type like i32 or String, in the same way they take parameters with unknown values to run the same code on multiple concrete values. In fact, we've already used generics in Chapter 6 with Option<T>, in Chapter 8 with Vec<T> and HashMap<K, V>, and in Chapter 9 with Result<T, E>. In this chapter, you'll explore how to define your own types, functions, and methods with generics!

First we'll review how to extract a function to reduce code duplication. We'll then use the same technique to make a generic function from two functions that differ only in the types of their parameters. We'll also explain how to use generic types in struct and enum definitions.

Then you'll learn how to use *traits* to define behavior in a generic way. You can combine traits with generic types to constrain a generic type to accept only those types that have a particular behavior, as opposed to just any type.

Finally, we'll discuss *lifetimes*: a variety of generics that give the compiler information about how references relate to each other. Lifetimes allow us to give the compiler enough information about borrowed values so that it can ensure references will be valid in more situations than it could without our help.

Removing Duplication by Extracting a Function

Generics allow us to replace specific types with a placeholder that represents multiple types to remove code duplication. Before diving into generics syntax, let's first look at how to remove duplication in a way that doesn't involve generic types by extracting a function that replaces specific values with a placeholder that represents multiple values. Then we'll apply the same technique to extract a generic function! By looking at how to recognize duplicated code you can extract into a function, you'll start to recognize duplicated code that can use generics.

We'll begin with the short program in Listing 10-1 that finds the largest number in a list.

src/main.rs
```
fn main() {
  ❶ let number_list = vec![34, 50, 25, 100, 65];

  ❷ let mut largest = &number_list[0];

  ❸ for number in &number_list {
      ❹ if number > largest {
          ❺ largest = number;
        }
    }

    println!("The largest number is {largest}");
}
```

Listing 10-1: Finding the largest number in a list of numbers

We store a list of integers in the variable number_list ❶ and place a reference to the first number in the list in a variable named largest ❷. We then iterate through all the numbers in the list ❸, and if the current number is greater than the number stored in largest ❹, we replace the reference in that variable ❺. However, if the current number is less than or equal to the largest number seen so far, the variable doesn't change, and the code moves on to the next number in the list. After considering all the numbers in the list, largest should refer to the largest number, which in this case is 100.

We've now been tasked with finding the largest number in two different lists of numbers. To do so, we can choose to duplicate the code in Listing 10-1 and use the same logic at two different places in the program, as shown in Listing 10-2.

src/main.rs
```
fn main() {
    let number_list = vec![34, 50, 25, 100, 65];

    let mut largest = &number_list[0];

    for number in &number_list {
        if number > largest {
            largest = number;
        }
    }

    println!("The largest number is {largest}");

    let number_list = vec![102, 34, 6000, 89, 54, 2, 43, 8];

    let mut largest = &number_list[0];

    for number in &number_list {
        if number > largest {
            largest = number;
        }
    }

    println!("The largest number is {largest}");
}
```

Listing 10-2: Code to find the largest number in two lists of numbers

Although this code works, duplicating code is tedious and error prone. We also have to remember to update the code in multiple places when we want to change it.

To eliminate this duplication, we'll create an abstraction by defining a function that operates on any list of integers passed in a parameter. This solution makes our code clearer and lets us express the concept of finding the largest number in a list abstractly.

In Listing 10-3, we extract the code that finds the largest number into a function named largest. Then we call the function to find the largest number in the two lists from Listing 10-2. We could also use the function on any other list of i32 values we might have in the future.

src/main.rs
```
fn largest(list: &[i32]) -> &i32 {
    let mut largest = &list[0];

    for item in list {
        if item > largest {
            largest = item;
        }
    }
}
```

```
        largest
}

fn main() {
    let number_list = vec![34, 50, 25, 100, 65];

    let result = largest(&number_list);
    println!("The largest number is {result}");

    let number_list = vec![102, 34, 6000, 89, 54, 2, 43, 8];

    let result = largest(&number_list);
    println!("The largest number is {result}");
}
```

Listing 10-3: Abstracted code to find the largest number in two lists

The largest function has a parameter called list, which represents any concrete slice of i32 values we might pass into the function. As a result, when we call the function, the code runs on the specific values that we pass in.

In summary, here are the steps we took to change the code from Listing 10-2 to Listing 10-3:

1. Identify duplicate code.
2. Extract the duplicate code into the body of the function, and specify the inputs and return values of that code in the function signature.
3. Update the two instances of duplicated code to call the function instead.

Next, we'll use these same steps with generics to reduce code duplication. In the same way that the function body can operate on an abstract list instead of specific values, generics allow code to operate on abstract types.

For example, say we had two functions: one that finds the largest item in a slice of i32 values and one that finds the largest item in a slice of char values. How would we eliminate that duplication? Let's find out!

Generic Data Types

We use generics to create definitions for items like function signatures or structs, which we can then use with many different concrete data types. Let's first look at how to define functions, structs, enums, and methods using generics. Then we'll discuss how generics affect code performance.

In Function Definitions

When defining a function that uses generics, we place the generics in the signature of the function where we would usually specify the data types of the parameters and return value. Doing so makes our code more flexible and provides more functionality to callers of our function while preventing code duplication.

Continuing with our largest function, Listing 10-4 shows two functions that both find the largest value in a slice. We'll then combine these into a single function that uses generics.

```rust
fn largest_i32(list: &[i32]) -> &i32 {
    let mut largest = &list[0];

    for item in list {
        if item > largest {
            largest = item;
        }
    }

    largest
}

fn largest_char(list: &[char]) -> &char {
    let mut largest = &list[0];

    for item in list {
        if item > largest {
            largest = item;
        }
    }

    largest
}

fn main() {
    let number_list = vec![34, 50, 25, 100, 65];

    let result = largest_i32(&number_list);
    println!("The largest number is {result}");

    let char_list = vec!['y', 'm', 'a', 'q'];

    let result = largest_char(&char_list);
    println!("The largest char is {result}");
}
```

Listing 10-4: Two functions that differ only in their names and in the types in their signatures

The largest_i32 function is the one we extracted in Listing 10-3 that finds the largest i32 in a slice. The largest_char function finds the largest char in a slice. The function bodies have the same code, so let's eliminate the duplication by introducing a generic type parameter in a single function.

To parameterize the types in a new single function, we need to name the type parameter, just as we do for the value parameters to a function. You can use any identifier as a type parameter name. But we'll use T because, by convention, type parameter names in Rust are short, often just one letter, and Rust's type-naming convention is UpperCamelCase. Short for *type*, T is the default choice of most Rust programmers.

When we use a parameter in the body of the function, we have to declare the parameter name in the signature so the compiler knows what that name means. Similarly, when we use a type parameter name in a function signature, we have to declare the type parameter name before we use it. To define the generic largest function, we place type name declarations inside angle brackets, <>, between the name of the function and the parameter list, like this:

```
fn largest<T>(list: &[T]) -> &T {
```

We read this definition as: the function largest is generic over some type T. This function has one parameter named list, which is a slice of values of type T. The largest function will return a reference to a value of the same type T.

Listing 10-5 shows the combined largest function definition using the generic data type in its signature. The listing also shows how we can call the function with either a slice of i32 values or char values. Note that this code won't compile yet, but we'll fix it later in this chapter.

src/main.rs
```
fn largest<T>(list: &[T]) -> &T {
    let mut largest = &list[0];

    for item in list {
        if item > largest {
            largest = item;
        }
    }

    largest
}

fn main() {
    let number_list = vec![34, 50, 25, 100, 65];

    let result = largest(&number_list);
    println!("The largest number is {result}");

    let char_list = vec!['y', 'm', 'a', 'q'];

    let result = largest(&char_list);
    println!("The largest char is {result}");
}
```

Listing 10-5: The largest function using generic type parameters; this doesn't compile yet

If we compile this code right now, we'll get this error:

```
error[E0369]: binary operation `>` cannot be applied to type `&T`
 --> src/main.rs:5:17
  |
5 |         if item > largest {
  |            ---- ^ ------- &T
  |            |
  |            &T
```

```
                      |
help: consider restricting type parameter `T`
                      |
1 |  fn largest<T: std::cmp::PartialOrd>(list: &[T]) -> &T {
                      |                  +++++++++++++++++++++++++
```

The help text mentions std::cmp::PartialOrd, which is a *trait*, and we're going to talk about traits in the next section. For now, know that this error states that the body of largest won't work for all possible types that T could be. Because we want to compare values of type T in the body, we can only use types whose values can be ordered. To enable comparisons, the standard library has the std::cmp::PartialOrd trait that you can implement on types (see Appendix C for more on this trait). By following the help text's suggestion, we restrict the types valid for T to only those that implement PartialOrd and this example will compile, because the standard library implements PartialOrd on both i32 and char.

In Struct Definitions

We can also define structs to use a generic type parameter in one or more fields using the <> syntax. Listing 10-6 defines a Point<T> struct to hold x and y coordinate values of any type.

src/main.rs ❶ struct Point<T> {
        ❷ x: T,
        ❸ y: T,
    }

    fn main() {
        let integer = Point { x: 5, y: 10 };
        let float = Point { x: 1.0, y: 4.0 };
    }

Listing 10-6: A Point<T> struct that holds x and y values of type T

The syntax for using generics in struct definitions is similar to that used in function definitions. First we declare the name of the type parameter inside angle brackets just after the name of the struct ❶. Then we use the generic type in the struct definition where we would otherwise specify concrete data types ❷❸.

Note that because we've used only one generic type to define Point<T>, this definition says that the Point<T> struct is generic over some type T, and the fields x and y are *both* that same type, whatever that type may be. If we create an instance of a Point<T> that has values of different types, as in Listing 10-7, our code won't compile.

src/main.rs   struct Point<T> {
        x: T,
        y: T,
    }

```
fn main() {
    let wont_work = Point { x: 5, y: 4.0 };
}
```

Listing 10-7: The fields x and y must be the same type because both have the same generic data type T.

In this example, when we assign the integer value 5 to x, we let the compiler know that the generic type T will be an integer for this instance of Point<T>. Then when we specify 4.0 for y, which we've defined to have the same type as x, we'll get a type mismatch error like this:

```
error[E0308]: mismatched types
 --> src/main.rs:7:38
  |
7 |     let wont_work = Point { x: 5, y: 4.0 };
  |                                      ^^^ expected integer, found floating-
point number
```

To define a Point struct where x and y are both generics but could have different types, we can use multiple generic type parameters. For example, in Listing 10-8, we change the definition of Point to be generic over types T and U where x is of type T and y is of type U.

src/main.rs
```
struct Point<T, U> {
    x: T,
    y: U,
}

fn main() {
    let both_integer = Point { x: 5, y: 10 };
    let both_float = Point { x: 1.0, y: 4.0 };
    let integer_and_float = Point { x: 5, y: 4.0 };
}
```

Listing 10-8: A Point<T, U> generic over two types so that x and y can be values of different types

Now all the instances of Point shown are allowed! You can use as many generic type parameters in a definition as you want, but using more than a few makes your code hard to read. If you're finding you need lots of generic types in your code, it could indicate that your code needs restructuring into smaller pieces.

In Enum Definitions

As we did with structs, we can define enums to hold generic data types in their variants. Let's take another look at the Option<T> enum that the standard library provides, which we used in Chapter 6:

```
enum Option<T> {
    Some(T),
    None,
}
```

This definition should now make more sense to you. As you can see, the Option<T> enum is generic over type T and has two variants: Some, which holds one value of type T, and a None variant that doesn't hold any value. By using the Option<T> enum, we can express the abstract concept of an optional value, and because Option<T> is generic, we can use this abstraction no matter what the type of the optional value is.

Enums can use multiple generic types as well. The definition of the Result enum that we used in Chapter 9 is one example:

```
enum Result<T, E> {
    Ok(T),
    Err(E),
}
```

The Result enum is generic over two types, T and E, and has two variants: Ok, which holds a value of type T, and Err, which holds a value of type E. This definition makes it convenient to use the Result enum anywhere we have an operation that might succeed (return a value of some type T) or fail (return an error of some type E). In fact, this is what we used to open a file in Listing 9-3, where T was filled in with the type std::fs::File when the file was opened successfully and E was filled in with the type std::io::Error when there were problems opening the file.

When you recognize situations in your code with multiple struct or enum definitions that differ only in the types of the values they hold, you can avoid duplication by using generic types instead.

In Method Definitions

We can implement methods on structs and enums (as we did in Chapter 5) and use generic types in their definitions too. Listing 10-9 shows the Point<T> struct we defined in Listing 10-6 with a method named x implemented on it.

src/main.rs
```
struct Point<T> {
    x: T,
    y: T,
}

impl<T> Point<T> {
    fn x(&self) -> &T {
        &self.x
    }
}

fn main() {
    let p = Point { x: 5, y: 10 };

    println!("p.x = {}", p.x());
}
```

Listing 10-9: Implementing a method named x on the Point<T> struct that will return a reference to the x field of type T

Here, we've defined a method named x on Point<T> that returns a reference to the data in the field x.

Note that we have to declare T just after impl so we can use T to specify that we're implementing methods on the type Point<T>. By declaring T as a generic type after impl, Rust can identify that the type in the angle brackets in Point is a generic type rather than a concrete type. We could have chosen a different name for this generic parameter than the generic parameter declared in the struct definition, but using the same name is conventional. Methods written within an impl that declares the generic type will be defined on any instance of the type, no matter what concrete type ends up substituting for the generic type.

We can also specify constraints on generic types when defining methods on the type. We could, for example, implement methods only on Point<f32> instances rather than on Point<T> instances with any generic type. In Listing 10-10 we use the concrete type f32, meaning we don't declare any types after impl.

src/main.rs
```
impl Point<f32> {
    fn distance_from_origin(&self) -> f32 {
        (self.x.powi(2) + self.y.powi(2)).sqrt()
    }
}
```

Listing 10-10: An `impl` block that only applies to a struct with a particular concrete type for the generic type parameter T

This code means the type Point<f32> will have a distance_from_origin method; other instances of Point<T> where T is not of type f32 will not have this method defined. The method measures how far our point is from the point at coordinates (0.0, 0.0) and uses mathematical operations that are available only for floating-point types.

Generic type parameters in a struct definition aren't always the same as those you use in that same struct's method signatures. Listing 10-11 uses the generic types X1 and Y1 for the Point struct and X2 Y2 for the mixup method signature to make the example clearer. The method creates a new Point instance with the x value from the self Point (of type X1) and the y value from the passed-in Point (of type Y2).

src/main.rs
```
struct Point<X1, Y1> {
    x: X1,
    y: Y1,
}

❶ impl<X1, Y1> Point<X1, Y1> {
    ❷ fn mixup<X2, Y2>(
        self,
        other: Point<X2, Y2>,
    ) -> Point<X1, Y2> {
        Point {
            x: self.x,
            y: other.y,
```

```
        }
      }
}

fn main() {
  ❸ let p1 = Point { x: 5, y: 10.4 };
  ❹ let p2 = Point { x: "Hello", y: 'c' };

  ❺ let p3 = p1.mixup(p2);

  ❻ println!("p3.x = {}, p3.y = {}", p3.x, p3.y);
}
```

Listing 10-11: A method that uses generic types different from its struct's definition

In main, we've defined a Point that has an i32 for x (with value 5) and
an f64 for y (with value 10.4 ❸). The p2 variable is a Point struct that has a
string slice for x (with value "Hello") and a char for y (with value c ❹). Calling
mixup on p1 with the argument p2 gives us p3 ❺, which will have an i32 for x
because x came from p1. The p3 variable will have a char for y because y came
from p2. The println! macro call ❻ will print p3.x = 5, p3.y = c.

The purpose of this example is to demonstrate a situation in which
some generic parameters are declared with impl and some are declared with
the method definition. Here, the generic parameters X1 and Y1 are declared
after impl ❶ because they go with the struct definition. The generic parameters X2 and Y2 are declared after fn mixup ❷ because they're only relevant
to the method.

Performance of Code Using Generics

You might be wondering whether there is a runtime cost when using
generic type parameters. The good news is that using generic types won't
make your program run any slower than it would with concrete types.

Rust accomplishes this by performing monomorphization of the code
using generics at compile time. *Monomorphization* is the process of turning
generic code into specific code by filling in the concrete types that are used
when compiled. In this process, the compiler does the opposite of the steps
we used to create the generic function in Listing 10-5: the compiler looks at
all the places where generic code is called and generates code for the concrete types the generic code is called with.

Let's look at how this works by using the standard library's generic
Option<T> enum:

```
let integer = Some(5);
let float = Some(5.0);
```

When Rust compiles this code, it performs monomorphization. During
that process, the compiler reads the values that have been used in Option<T>
instances and identifies two kinds of Option<T>: one is i32 and the other is f64.
As such, it expands the generic definition of Option<T> into two definitions

specialized to i32 and f64, thereby replacing the generic definition with the specific ones.

The monomorphized version of the code looks similar to the following (the compiler uses different names than what we're using here for illustration):

```rust
enum Option_i32 {
    Some(i32),
    None,
}

enum Option_f64 {
    Some(f64),
    None,
}

fn main() {
    let integer = Option_i32::Some(5);
    let float = Option_f64::Some(5.0);
}
```

src/main.rs

The generic Option<T> is replaced with the specific definitions created by the compiler. Because Rust compiles generic code into code that specifies the type in each instance, we pay no runtime cost for using generics. When the code runs, it performs just as it would if we had duplicated each definition by hand. The process of monomorphization makes Rust's generics extremely efficient at runtime.

Traits: Defining Shared Behavior

A *trait* defines the functionality a particular type has and can share with other types. We can use traits to define shared behavior in an abstract way. We can use *trait bounds* to specify that a generic type can be any type that has certain behavior.

NOTE   *Traits are similar to a feature often called* interfaces *in other languages, although with some differences.*

Defining a Trait

A type's behavior consists of the methods we can call on that type. Different types share the same behavior if we can call the same methods on all of those types. Trait definitions are a way to group method signatures together to define a set of behaviors necessary to accomplish some purpose.

For example, let's say we have multiple structs that hold various kinds and amounts of text: a NewsArticle struct that holds a news story filed in a particular location and a Tweet that can have, at most, 280 characters along with metadata that indicates whether it was a new tweet, a retweet, or a reply to another tweet.

We want to make a media aggregator library crate named `aggregator` that can display summaries of data that might be stored in a `NewsArticle` or `Tweet` instance. To do this, we need a summary from each type, and we'll request that summary by calling a `summarize` method on an instance. Listing 10-12 shows the definition of a public `Summary` trait that expresses this behavior.

```
pub trait Summary {
    fn summarize(&self) -> String;
}
```

Listing 10-12: A Summary trait that consists of the behavior provided by a summarize method

Here, we declare a trait using the `trait` keyword and then the trait's name, which is `Summary` in this case. We also declare the trait as `pub` so that crates depending on this crate can make use of this trait too, as we'll see in a few examples. Inside the curly brackets, we declare the method signatures that describe the behaviors of the types that implement this trait, which in this case is `fn summarize(&self) -> String`.

After the method signature, instead of providing an implementation within curly brackets, we use a semicolon. Each type implementing this trait must provide its own custom behavior for the body of the method. The compiler will enforce that any type that has the `Summary` trait will have the method `summarize` defined with this signature exactly.

A trait can have multiple methods in its body: the method signatures are listed one per line, and each line ends in a semicolon.

Implementing a Trait on a Type

Now that we've defined the desired signatures of the `Summary` trait's methods, we can implement it on the types in our media aggregator. Listing 10-13 shows an implementation of the `Summary` trait on the `NewsArticle` struct that uses the headline, the author, and the location to create the return value of `summarize`. For the `Tweet` struct, we define `summarize` as the username followed by the entire text of the tweet, assuming that the tweet content is already limited to 280 characters.

```
pub struct NewsArticle {
    pub headline: String,
    pub location: String,
    pub author: String,
    pub content: String,
}

impl Summary for NewsArticle {
    fn summarize(&self) -> String {
        format!(
            "{}, by {} ({})",
            self.headline,
            self.author,
            self.location
        )
```

```
        }
    }

pub struct Tweet {
    pub username: String,
    pub content: String,
    pub reply: bool,
    pub retweet: bool,
}

impl Summary for Tweet {
    fn summarize(&self) -> String {
        format!("{}: {}", self.username, self.content)
    }
}
```

Listing 10-13: Implementing the Summary trait on the NewsArticle and Tweet types

Implementing a trait on a type is similar to implementing regular methods. The difference is that after impl, we put the trait name we want to implement, then use the for keyword, and then specify the name of the type we want to implement the trait for. Within the impl block, we put the method signatures that the trait definition has defined. Instead of adding a semicolon after each signature, we use curly brackets and fill in the method body with the specific behavior that we want the methods of the trait to have for the particular type.

Now that the library has implemented the Summary trait on NewsArticle and Tweet, users of the crate can call the trait methods on instances of NewsArticle and Tweet in the same way we call regular methods. The only difference is that the user must bring the trait into scope as well as the types. Here's an example of how a binary crate could use our aggregator library crate:

```
use aggregator::{Summary, Tweet};

fn main() {
    let tweet = Tweet {
        username: String::from("horse_ebooks"),
        content: String::from(
            "of course, as you probably already know, people",
        ),
        reply: false,
        retweet: false,
    };

    println!("1 new tweet: {}", tweet.summarize());
}
```

This code prints 1 new tweet: horse_ebooks: of course, as you probably already know, people.

Other crates that depend on the aggregator crate can also bring the Summary trait into scope to implement Summary on their own types. One restriction to note is that we can implement a trait on a type only if either the trait or the type, or both, are local to our crate. For example, we can implement standard library traits like Display on a custom type like Tweet as part of our aggregator crate functionality because the type Tweet is local to our aggregator crate. We can also implement Summary on Vec<T> in our aggregator crate because the trait Summary is local to our aggregator crate.

But we can't implement external traits on external types. For example, we can't implement the Display trait on Vec<T> within our aggregator crate because Display and Vec<T> are both defined in the standard library and aren't local to our aggregator crate. This restriction is part of a property called *coherence*, and more specifically the *orphan rule*, so named because the parent type is not present. This rule ensures that other people's code can't break your code and vice versa. Without the rule, two crates could implement the same trait for the same type, and Rust wouldn't know which implementation to use.

Default Implementations

Sometimes it's useful to have default behavior for some or all of the methods in a trait instead of requiring implementations for all methods on every type. Then, as we implement the trait on a particular type, we can keep or override each method's default behavior.

In Listing 10-14, we specify a default string for the summarize method of the Summary trait instead of only defining the method signature, as we did in Listing 10-12.

src/lib.rs
```
pub trait Summary {
    fn summarize(&self) -> String {
        String::from("(Read more...)")
    }
}
```

Listing 10-14: Defining a Summary trait with a default implementation of the summarize method

To use a default implementation to summarize instances of NewsArticle, we specify an empty impl block with impl Summary for NewsArticle {}.

Even though we're no longer defining the summarize method on NewsArticle directly, we've provided a default implementation and specified that NewsArticle implements the Summary trait. As a result, we can still call the summarize method on an instance of NewsArticle, like this:

```
let article = NewsArticle {
    headline: String::from(
        "Penguins win the Stanley Cup Championship!"
    ),
    location: String::from("Pittsburgh, PA, USA"),
    author: String::from("Iceburgh"),
```

```
        content: String::from(
            "The Pittsburgh Penguins once again are the best \
            hockey team in the NHL.",
        ),
    };

    println!("New article available! {}", article.summarize());
```

This code prints New article available! (Read more...).

Creating a default implementation doesn't require us to change anything about the implementation of Summary on Tweet in Listing 10-13. The reason is that the syntax for overriding a default implementation is the same as the syntax for implementing a trait method that doesn't have a default implementation.

Default implementations can call other methods in the same trait, even if those other methods don't have a default implementation. In this way, a trait can provide a lot of useful functionality and only require implementors to specify a small part of it. For example, we could define the Summary trait to have a summarize_author method whose implementation is required, and then define a summarize method that has a default implementation that calls the summarize_author method:

```
pub trait Summary {
    fn summarize_author(&self) -> String;

    fn summarize(&self) -> String {
        format!(
            "(Read more from {}...)",
            self.summarize_author()
        )
    }
}
```

To use this version of Summary, we only need to define summarize_author when we implement the trait on a type:

```
impl Summary for Tweet {
    fn summarize_author(&self) -> String {
        format!("@{}", self.username)
    }
}
```

After we define summarize_author, we can call summarize on instances of the Tweet struct, and the default implementation of summarize will call the definition of summarize_author that we've provided. Because we've implemented summarize_author, the Summary trait has given us the behavior of the summarize method without requiring us to write any more code. Here's what that looks like:

```
let tweet = Tweet {
    username: String::from("horse_ebooks"),
    content: String::from(
```

```
        "of course, as you probably already know, people",
    ),
    reply: false,
    retweet: false,
};

println!("1 new tweet: {}", tweet.summarize());
```

This code prints 1 new tweet: (Read more from @horse_ebooks...).

Note that it isn't possible to call the default implementation from an overriding implementation of that same method.

Traits as Parameters

Now that you know how to define and implement traits, we can explore how to use traits to define functions that accept many different types. We'll use the Summary trait we implemented on the NewsArticle and Tweet types in Listing 10-13 to define a notify function that calls the summarize method on its item parameter, which is of some type that implements the Summary trait. To do this, we use the impl Trait syntax, like this:

```
pub fn notify(item: &impl Summary) {
    println!("Breaking news! {}", item.summarize());
}
```

Instead of a concrete type for the item parameter, we specify the impl keyword and the trait name. This parameter accepts any type that implements the specified trait. In the body of notify, we can call any methods on item that come from the Summary trait, such as summarize. We can call notify and pass in any instance of NewsArticle or Tweet. Code that calls the function with any other type, such as a String or an i32, won't compile because those types don't implement Summary.

Trait Bound Syntax

The impl Trait syntax works for straightforward cases but is actually syntax sugar for a longer form known as a *trait bound*; it looks like this:

```
pub fn notify<T: Summary>(item: &T) {
    println!("Breaking news! {}", item.summarize());
}
```

This longer form is equivalent to the example in the previous section but is more verbose. We place trait bounds with the declaration of the generic type parameter after a colon and inside angle brackets.

The impl Trait syntax is convenient and makes for more concise code in simple cases, while the fuller trait bound syntax can express more complexity in other cases. For example, we can have two parameters that implement Summary. Doing so with the impl Trait syntax looks like this:

```
pub fn notify(item1: &impl Summary, item2: &impl Summary) {
```

Using impl Trait is appropriate if we want this function to allow item1 and item2 to have different types (as long as both types implement Summary). If we want to force both parameters to have the same type, however, we must use a trait bound, like this:

```
pub fn notify<T: Summary>(item1: &T, item2: &T) {
```

The generic type T specified as the type of the item1 and item2 parameters constrains the function such that the concrete type of the value passed as an argument for item1 and item2 must be the same.

Specifying Multiple Trait Bounds with the + Syntax

We can also specify more than one trait bound. Say we wanted notify to use display formatting as well as summarize on item: we specify in the notify definition that item must implement both Display and Summary. We can do so using the + syntax:

```
pub fn notify(item: &(impl Summary + Display)) {
```

The + syntax is also valid with trait bounds on generic types:

```
pub fn notify<T: Summary + Display>(item: &T) {
```

With the two trait bounds specified, the body of notify can call summarize and use {} to format item.

Clearer Trait Bounds with where Clauses

Using too many trait bounds has its downsides. Each generic has its own trait bounds, so functions with multiple generic type parameters can contain lots of trait bound information between the function's name and its parameter list, making the function signature hard to read. For this reason, Rust has alternate syntax for specifying trait bounds inside a where clause after the function signature. So, instead of writing this:

```
fn some_function<T: Display + Clone, U: Clone + Debug>(t: &T, u: &U) -> i32 {
```

we can use a where clause, like this:

```
fn some_function<T, U>(t: &T, u: &U) -> i32
where
    T: Display + Clone,
    U: Clone + Debug,
{
```

This function's signature is less cluttered: the function name, parameter list, and return type are close together, similar to a function without lots of trait bounds.

Returning Types That Implement Traits

We can also use the impl Trait syntax in the return position to return a value of some type that implements a trait, as shown here:

```
fn returns_summarizable() -> impl Summary {
    Tweet {
        username: String::from("horse_ebooks"),
        content: String::from(
            "of course, as you probably already know, people",
        ),
        reply: false,
        retweet: false,
    }
}
```

By using impl Summary for the return type, we specify that the returns
_summarizable function returns some type that implements the Summary trait
without naming the concrete type. In this case, returns_summarizable returns
a Tweet, but the code calling this function doesn't need to know that.

The ability to specify a return type only by the trait it implements is
especially useful in the context of closures and iterators, which we cover
in Chapter 13. Closures and iterators create types that only the compiler
knows or types that are very long to specify. The impl Trait syntax lets you
concisely specify that a function returns some type that implements the
Iterator trait without needing to write out a very long type.

However, you can only use impl Trait if you're returning a single type.
For example, this code that returns either a NewsArticle or a Tweet with the
return type specified as impl Summary wouldn't work:

```
fn returns_summarizable(switch: bool) -> impl Summary {
    if switch {
        NewsArticle {
            headline: String::from(
                "Penguins win the Stanley Cup Championship!",
            ),
            location: String::from("Pittsburgh, PA, USA"),
            author: String::from("Iceburgh"),
            content: String::from(
                "The Pittsburgh Penguins once again are the best \
                 hockey team in the NHL.",
            ),
        }
    } else {
        Tweet {
            username: String::from("horse_ebooks"),
            content: String::from(
                "of course, as you probably already know, people",
            ),
            reply: false,
            retweet: false,
        }
    }
}
```

Returning either a NewsArticle or a Tweet isn't allowed due to restrictions around how the impl Trait syntax is implemented in the compiler. We'll cover how to write a function with this behavior in "Using Trait Objects That Allow for Values of Different Types" on page 379.

Using Trait Bounds to Conditionally Implement Methods

By using a trait bound with an impl block that uses generic type parameters, we can implement methods conditionally for types that implement the specified traits. For example, the type Pair<T> in Listing 10-15 always implements the new function to return a new instance of Pair<T> (recall from "Defining Methods" on page 97 that Self is a type alias for the type of the impl block, which in this case is Pair<T>). But in the next impl block, Pair<T> only implements the cmp_display method if its inner type T implements the PartialOrd trait that enables comparison *and* the Display trait that enables printing.

src/lib.rs
```
use std::fmt::Display;

struct Pair<T> {
    x: T,
    y: T,
}

impl<T> Pair<T> {
    fn new(x: T, y: T) -> Self {
        Self { x, y }
    }
}

impl<T: Display + PartialOrd> Pair<T> {
    fn cmp_display(&self) {
        if self.x >= self.y {
            println!("The largest member is x = {}", self.x);
        } else {
            println!("The largest member is y = {}", self.y);
        }
    }
}
```

Listing 10-15: Conditionally implementing methods on a generic type depending on trait bounds

We can also conditionally implement a trait for any type that implements another trait. Implementations of a trait on any type that satisfies the trait bounds are called *blanket implementations* and are used extensively in the Rust standard library. For example, the standard library implements the ToString trait on any type that implements the Display trait. The impl block in the standard library looks similar to this code:

```
impl<T: Display> ToString for T {
    --snip--
}
```

Because the standard library has this blanket implementation, we can call the to_string method defined by the ToString trait on any type that implements the Display trait. For example, we can turn integers into their corresponding String values like this because integers implement Display:

```
let s = 3.to_string();
```

Blanket implementations appear in the documentation for the trait in the "Implementors" section.

Traits and trait bounds let us write code that uses generic type parameters to reduce duplication but also specify to the compiler that we want the generic type to have particular behavior. The compiler can then use the trait bound information to check that all the concrete types used with our code provide the correct behavior. In dynamically typed languages, we would get an error at runtime if we called a method on a type which didn't define the method. But Rust moves these errors to compile time so we're forced to fix the problems before our code is even able to run. Additionally, we don't have to write code that checks for behavior at runtime because we've already checked at compile time. Doing so improves performance without having to give up the flexibility of generics.

Validating References with Lifetimes

Lifetimes are another kind of generic that we've already been using. Rather than ensuring that a type has the behavior we want, lifetimes ensure that references are valid as long as we need them to be.

One detail we didn't discuss in "References and Borrowing" on page 71 is that every reference in Rust has a *lifetime*, which is the scope for which that reference is valid. Most of the time, lifetimes are implicit and inferred, just like most of the time, types are inferred. We must annotate types only when multiple types are possible. In a similar way, we must annotate lifetimes when the lifetimes of references could be related in a few different ways. Rust requires us to annotate the relationships using generic lifetime parameters to ensure the actual references used at runtime will definitely be valid.

Annotating lifetimes is not even a concept most other programming languages have, so this is going to feel unfamiliar. Although we won't cover lifetimes in their entirety in this chapter, we'll discuss common ways you might encounter lifetime syntax so you can get comfortable with the concept.

Preventing Dangling References with Lifetimes

The main aim of lifetimes is to prevent *dangling references*, which cause a program to reference data other than the data it's intended to reference. Consider the program in Listing 10-16, which has an outer scope and an inner scope.

```
fn main() {
❶ let r;
```

```
    {
    ❷ let x = 5;
    ❸ r = &x;
❹ }

❺ println!("r: {r}");
}
```

Listing 10-16: An attempt to use a reference whose value has gone out of scope

NOTE *The examples in Listings 10-16, 10-17, and 10-23 declare variables without giving them an initial value, so the variable name exists in the outer scope. At first glance, this might appear to be in conflict with Rust's having no null values. However, if we try to use a variable before giving it a value, we'll get a compile-time error, which shows that Rust indeed does not allow null values.*

The outer scope declares a variable named r with no initial value ❶, and the inner scope declares a variable named x with the initial value of 5 ❷. Inside the inner scope, we attempt to set the value of r as a reference to x ❸. Then the inner scope ends ❹, and we attempt to print the value in r ❺. This code won't compile because the value that r is referring to has gone out of scope before we try to use it. Here is the error message:

```
error[E0597]: `x` does not live long enough
 --> src/main.rs:6:13
  |
6 |         r = &x;
  |             ^^ borrowed value does not live long enough
7 |     }
  |     - `x` dropped here while still borrowed
8 |
9 |     println!("r: {r}");
  |                   - borrow later used here
```

The error message says that the variable x "does not live long enough." The reason is that x will be out of scope when the inner scope ends on line 7. But r is still valid for the outer scope; because its scope is larger, we say that it "lives longer." If Rust allowed this code to work, r would be referencing memory that was deallocated when x went out of scope, and anything we tried to do with r wouldn't work correctly. So how does Rust determine that this code is invalid? It uses a borrow checker.

The Borrow Checker

The Rust compiler has a *borrow checker* that compares scopes to determine whether all borrows are valid. Listing 10-17 shows the same code as Listing 10-16 but with annotations showing the lifetimes of the variables.

```
fn main() {
    let r;                 // ---------+-- 'a
                           //          |
    {                      //          |
        let x = 5;         // -+-- 'b  |
        r = &x;            //  |       |
    }                      // -+       |
                           //          |
    println!("r: {r}");    //          |
}                          // ---------+
```

Listing 10-17: Annotations of the lifetimes of r and x, named 'a and 'b, respectively

Here, we've annotated the lifetime of r with 'a and the lifetime of x with 'b. As you can see, the inner 'b block is much smaller than the outer 'a lifetime block. At compile time, Rust compares the size of the two lifetimes and sees that r has a lifetime of 'a but that it refers to memory with a lifetime of 'b. The program is rejected because 'b is shorter than 'a: the subject of the reference doesn't live as long as the reference.

Listing 10-18 fixes the code so it doesn't have a dangling reference and it compiles without any errors.

```
fn main() {
    let x = 5;             // ----------+-- 'b
                           //           |
    let r = &x;            // --+-- 'a  |
                           //   |       |
    println!("r: {r}");    //   |       |
                           // --+       |
}                          // ----------+
```

Listing 10-18: A valid reference because the data has a longer lifetime than the reference

Here, x has the lifetime 'b, which in this case is larger than 'a. This means r can reference x because Rust knows that the reference in r will always be valid while x is valid.

Now that you know where the lifetimes of references are and how Rust analyzes lifetimes to ensure references will always be valid, let's explore generic lifetimes of parameters and return values in the context of functions.

Generic Lifetimes in Functions

We'll write a function that returns the longer of two string slices. This function will take two string slices and return a single string slice. After we've implemented the longest function, the code in Listing 10-19 should print The longest string is abcd.

src/main.rs
```
fn main() {
    let string1 = String::from("abcd");
    let string2 = "xyz";
```

```
    let result = longest(string1.as_str(), string2);
    println!("The longest string is {result}");
}
```

Listing 10-19: A main *function that calls the* longest *function to find the longer of two string slices*

Note that we want the function to take string slices, which are references, rather than strings, because we don't want the longest function to take ownership of its parameters. Refer to "String Slices as Parameters" on page 82 for more discussion about why the parameters we use in Listing 10-19 are the ones we want.

If we try to implement the longest function as shown in Listing 10-20, it won't compile.

src/main.rs
```
fn longest(x: &str, y: &str) -> &str {
    if x.len() > y.len() {
        x
    } else {
        y
    }
}
```

Listing 10-20: An implementation of the longest *function that returns the longer of two string slices but does not yet compile*

Instead, we get the following error that talks about lifetimes:

```
error[E0106]: missing lifetime specifier
 --> src/main.rs:9:33
  |
9 | fn longest(x: &str, y: &str) -> &str {
  |               ----     ----     ^ expected named lifetime parameter
  |
  = help: this function's return type contains a borrowed value,
but the signature does not say whether it is borrowed from `x` or `y`
help: consider introducing a named lifetime parameter
  |
9 | fn longest<'a>(x: &'a str, y: &'a str) -> &'a str {
  |           ++++     ++           ++          ++
```

The help text reveals that the return type needs a generic lifetime parameter on it because Rust can't tell whether the reference being returned refers to x or y. Actually, we don't know either, because the if block in the body of this function returns a reference to x and the else block returns a reference to y!

When we're defining this function, we don't know the concrete values that will be passed into this function, so we don't know whether the if case or the else case will execute. We also don't know the concrete lifetimes of the references that will be passed in, so we can't look at the scopes as we did in Listings 10-17 and 10-18 to determine whether the reference we return will always be valid. The borrow checker can't determine this either, because it doesn't know how the lifetimes of x and y relate to the lifetime of the return value. To fix this error, we'll add generic lifetime parameters that define the relationship between the references so the borrow checker can perform its analysis.

Lifetime Annotation Syntax

Lifetime annotations don't change how long any of the references live. Rather, they describe the relationships of the lifetimes of multiple references to each other without affecting the lifetimes. Just as functions can accept any type when the signature specifies a generic type parameter, functions can accept references with any lifetime by specifying a generic lifetime parameter.

Lifetime annotations have a slightly unusual syntax: the names of lifetime parameters must start with an apostrophe (') and are usually all lowercase and very short, like generic types. Most people use the name 'a for the first lifetime annotation. We place lifetime parameter annotations after the & of a reference, using a space to separate the annotation from the reference's type.

Here are some examples: a reference to an i32 without a lifetime parameter, a reference to an i32 that has a lifetime parameter named 'a, and a mutable reference to an i32 that also has the lifetime 'a.

```
&i32        // a reference
&'a i32     // a reference with an explicit lifetime
&'a mut i32 // a mutable reference with an explicit lifetime
```

One lifetime annotation by itself doesn't have much meaning because the annotations are meant to tell Rust how generic lifetime parameters of multiple references relate to each other. Let's examine how the lifetime annotations relate to each other in the context of the longest function.

Lifetime Annotations in Function Signatures

To use lifetime annotations in function signatures, we need to declare the generic *lifetime* parameters inside angle brackets between the function name and the parameter list, just as we did with generic *type* parameters.

We want the signature to express the following constraint: the returned reference will be valid as long as both the parameters are valid. This is the relationship between lifetimes of the parameters and the return value. We'll name the lifetime 'a and then add it to each reference, as shown in Listing 10-21.

src/main.rs
```
fn longest<'a>(x: &'a str, y: &'a str) -> &'a str {
    if x.len() > y.len() {
        x
    } else {
        y
    }
}
```

Listing 10-21: The longest function definition specifying that all the references in the signature must have the same lifetime 'a

This code should compile and produce the result we want when we use it with the main function in Listing 10-19.

The function signature now tells Rust that for some lifetime 'a, the function takes two parameters, both of which are string slices that live at least as long as lifetime 'a. The function signature also tells Rust that the string slice returned from the function will live at least as long as lifetime 'a. In practice, it means that the lifetime of the reference returned by the longest function is the same as the smaller of the lifetimes of the values referred to by the function arguments. These relationships are what we want Rust to use when analyzing this code.

Remember, when we specify the lifetime parameters in this function signature, we're not changing the lifetimes of any values passed in or returned. Rather, we're specifying that the borrow checker should reject any values that don't adhere to these constraints. Note that the longest function doesn't need to know exactly how long x and y will live, only that some scope can be substituted for 'a that will satisfy this signature.

When annotating lifetimes in functions, the annotations go in the function signature, not in the function body. The lifetime annotations become part of the contract of the function, much like the types in the signature. Having function signatures contain the lifetime contract means the analysis the Rust compiler does can be simpler. If there's a problem with the way a function is annotated or the way it is called, the compiler errors can point to the part of our code and the constraints more precisely. If, instead, the Rust compiler made more inferences about what we intended the relationships of the lifetimes to be, the compiler might only be able to point to a use of our code many steps away from the cause of the problem.

When we pass concrete references to longest, the concrete lifetime that is substituted for 'a is the part of the scope of x that overlaps with the scope of y. In other words, the generic lifetime 'a will get the concrete lifetime that is equal to the smaller of the lifetimes of x and y. Because we've annotated the returned reference with the same lifetime parameter 'a, the returned reference will also be valid for the length of the smaller of the lifetimes of x and y.

Let's look at how the lifetime annotations restrict the longest function by passing in references that have different concrete lifetimes. Listing 10-22 is a straightforward example.

src/main.rs

```
fn main() {
    let string1 = String::from("long string is long");

    {
        let string2 = String::from("xyz");
        let result = longest(string1.as_str(), string2.as_str());
        println!("The longest string is {result}");
    }
}
```

Listing 10-22: Using the longest *function with references to* String *values that have different concrete lifetimes*

In this example, string1 is valid until the end of the outer scope, string2 is valid until the end of the inner scope, and result references something that is valid until the end of the inner scope. Run this code and you'll see that the borrow checker approves; it will compile and print The longest string is long string is long.

Next, let's try an example that shows that the lifetime of the reference in result must be the smaller lifetime of the two arguments. We'll move the declaration of the result variable outside the inner scope but leave the assignment of the value to the result variable inside the scope with string2. Then we'll move the println! that uses result to outside the inner scope, after the inner scope has ended. The code in Listing 10-23 will not compile.

src/main.rs

```
fn main() {
    let string1 = String::from("long string is long");
    let result;
    {
        let string2 = String::from("xyz");
        result = longest(string1.as_str(), string2.as_str());
    }
    println!("The longest string is {result}");
}
```

Listing 10-23: Attempting to use result after string2 has gone out of scope

When we try to compile this code, we get this error:

```
error[E0597]: `string2` does not live long enough
  --> src/main.rs:6:44
   |
6  |         result = longest(string1.as_str(), string2.as_str());
   |                                             ^^^^^^^^^^^^^^^^^ borrowed value
does not live long enough
7  |     }
   |     - `string2` dropped here while still borrowed
8  |     println!("The longest string is {result}");
   |                                      ------ borrow later used here
```

The error shows that for result to be valid for the println! statement, string2 would need to be valid until the end of the outer scope. Rust knows this because we annotated the lifetimes of the function parameters and return values using the same lifetime parameter 'a.

As humans, we can look at this code and see that string1 is longer than string2, and therefore, result will contain a reference to string1. Because string1 has not gone out of scope yet, a reference to string1 will still be valid for the println! statement. However, the compiler can't see that the reference is valid in this case. We've told Rust that the lifetime of the reference returned by the longest function is the same as the smaller of the lifetimes of the references passed in. Therefore, the borrow checker disallows the code in Listing 10-23 as possibly having an invalid reference.

Try designing more experiments that vary the values and lifetimes of the references passed in to the longest function and how the returned reference is used. Make hypotheses about whether or not your experiments will pass the borrow checker before you compile; then check to see if you're right!

Thinking in Terms of Lifetimes

The way in which you need to specify lifetime parameters depends on what your function is doing. For example, if we changed the implementation of the longest function to always return the first parameter rather than the longest string slice, we wouldn't need to specify a lifetime on the y parameter. The following code will compile:

src/main.rs
```
fn longest<'a>(x: &'a str, y: &str) -> &'a str {
    x
}
```

We've specified a lifetime parameter 'a for the parameter x and the return type, but not for the parameter y, because the lifetime of y does not have any relationship with the lifetime of x or the return value.

When returning a reference from a function, the lifetime parameter for the return type needs to match the lifetime parameter for one of the parameters. If the reference returned does *not* refer to one of the parameters, it must refer to a value created within this function. However, this would be a dangling reference because the value will go out of scope at the end of the function. Consider this attempted implementation of the longest function that won't compile:

src/main.rs
```
fn longest<'a>(x: &str, y: &str) -> &'a str {
    let result = String::from("really long string");
    result.as_str()
}
```

Here, even though we've specified a lifetime parameter 'a for the return type, this implementation will fail to compile because the return value lifetime is not related to the lifetime of the parameters at all. Here is the error message we get:

```
error[E0515]: cannot return reference to local variable `result`
  --> src/main.rs:11:5
   |
11 |     result.as_str()
   |     ^^^^^^^^^^^^^^^ returns a reference to data owned by the
current function
```

The problem is that result goes out of scope and gets cleaned up at the end of the longest function. We're also trying to return a reference to result from the function. There is no way we can specify lifetime parameters that would change the dangling reference, and Rust won't let us create a dangling reference. In this case, the best fix would be to return an owned data type rather than a reference so the calling function is then responsible for cleaning up the value.

Ultimately, lifetime syntax is about connecting the lifetimes of various parameters and return values of functions. Once they're connected, Rust has enough information to allow memory-safe operations and disallow operations that would create dangling pointers or otherwise violate memory safety.

Lifetime Annotations in Struct Definitions

So far, the structs we've defined all hold owned types. We can define structs to hold references, but in that case we would need to add a lifetime annotation on every reference in the struct's definition. Listing 10-24 has a struct named ImportantExcerpt that holds a string slice.

src/main.rs ❶ struct ImportantExcerpt<'a> {
```
    ❷ part: &'a str,
    }

    fn main() {
      ❸ let novel = String::from(
            "Call me Ishmael. Some years ago..."
        );
      ❹ let first_sentence = novel
            .split('.')
            .next()
            .expect("Could not find a '.'");
      ❺ let i = ImportantExcerpt {
            part: first_sentence,
        };
    }
```

Listing 10-24: A struct that holds a reference, requiring a lifetime annotation

This struct has the single field part that holds a string slice, which is a reference ❷. As with generic data types, we declare the name of the generic lifetime parameter inside angle brackets after the name of the struct so we can use the lifetime parameter in the body of the struct definition ❶. This annotation means an instance of ImportantExcerpt can't outlive the reference it holds in its part field.

The main function here creates an instance of the ImportantExcerpt struct ❺ that holds a reference to the first sentence of the String ❹ owned by the variable novel ❸. The data in novel exists before the ImportantExcerpt instance is created. In addition, novel doesn't go out of scope until after the ImportantExcerpt goes out of scope, so the reference in the ImportantExcerpt instance is valid.

Lifetime Elision

You've learned that every reference has a lifetime and that you need to specify lifetime parameters for functions or structs that use references. However, we had a function in Listing 4-9, shown again in Listing 10-25, that compiled without lifetime annotations.

src/lib.rs fn first_word(s: &str) -> &str {
```
        let bytes = s.as_bytes();
```

```
    for (i, &item) in bytes.iter().enumerate() {
        if item == b' ' {
            return &s[0..i];
        }
    }

    &s[..]
}
```

Listing 10-25: A function we defined in Listing 4-9 that compiled without lifetime annotations, even though the parameter and return type are references

The reason this function compiles without lifetime annotations is historical: in early versions (pre-1.0) of Rust, this code wouldn't have compiled because every reference needed an explicit lifetime. At that time, the function signature would have been written like this:

```
fn first_word<'a>(s: &'a str) -> &'a str {
```

After writing a lot of Rust code, the Rust team found that Rust programmers were entering the same lifetime annotations over and over in particular situations. These situations were predictable and followed a few deterministic patterns. The developers programmed these patterns into the compiler's code so the borrow checker could infer the lifetimes in these situations and wouldn't need explicit annotations.

This piece of Rust history is relevant because it's possible that more deterministic patterns will emerge and be added to the compiler. In the future, even fewer lifetime annotations might be required.

The patterns programmed into Rust's analysis of references are called the *lifetime elision rules*. These aren't rules for programmers to follow; they're a set of particular cases that the compiler will consider, and if your code fits these cases, you don't need to write the lifetimes explicitly.

The elision rules don't provide full inference. If Rust deterministically applies the rules but there is still ambiguity as to what lifetimes the references have, the compiler won't guess what the lifetime of the remaining references should be. Instead of guessing, the compiler will give you an error that you can resolve by adding the lifetime annotations.

Lifetimes on function or method parameters are called *input lifetimes*, and lifetimes on return values are called *output lifetimes*.

The compiler uses three rules to figure out the lifetimes of the references when there aren't explicit annotations. The first rule applies to input lifetimes, and the second and third rules apply to output lifetimes. If the compiler gets to the end of the three rules and there are still references for which it can't figure out lifetimes, the compiler will stop with an error. These rules apply to fn definitions as well as impl blocks.

The first rule is that the compiler assigns a lifetime parameter to each parameter that's a reference. In other words, a function with one parameter gets one lifetime parameter: fn foo<'a>(x: &'a i32); a function with two parameters gets two separate lifetime parameters: fn foo<'a, 'b>(x: &'a i32, y: &'b i32); and so on.

The second rule is that, if there is exactly one input lifetime parameter, that lifetime is assigned to all output lifetime parameters: fn foo<'a>(x: &'a i32) -> &'a i32.

The third rule is that, if there are multiple input lifetime parameters, but one of them is &self or &mut self because this is a method, the lifetime of self is assigned to all output lifetime parameters. This third rule makes methods much nicer to read and write because fewer symbols are necessary.

Let's pretend we're the compiler. We'll apply these rules to figure out the lifetimes of the references in the signature of the first_word function in Listing 10-25. The signature starts without any lifetimes associated with the references:

```
fn first_word(s: &str) -> &str {
```

Then the compiler applies the first rule, which specifies that each parameter gets its own lifetime. We'll call it 'a as usual, so now the signature is this:

```
fn first_word<'a>(s: &'a str) -> &str {
```

The second rule applies because there is exactly one input lifetime. The second rule specifies that the lifetime of the one input parameter gets assigned to the output lifetime, so the signature is now this:

```
fn first_word<'a>(s: &'a str) -> &'a str {
```

Now all the references in this function signature have lifetimes, and the compiler can continue its analysis without needing the programmer to annotate the lifetimes in this function signature.

Let's look at another example, this time using the longest function that had no lifetime parameters when we started working with it in Listing 10-20:

```
fn longest(x: &str, y: &str) -> &str {
```

Let's apply the first rule: each parameter gets its own lifetime. This time we have two parameters instead of one, so we have two lifetimes:

```
fn longest<'a, 'b>(x: &'a str, y: &'b str) -> &str {
```

You can see that the second rule doesn't apply because there is more than one input lifetime. The third rule doesn't apply either, because longest is a function rather than a method, so none of the parameters are self. After working through all three rules, we still haven't figured out what the return type's lifetime is. This is why we got an error trying to compile the code in Listing 10-20: the compiler worked through the lifetime elision rules but still couldn't figure out all the lifetimes of the references in the signature.

Because the third rule really only applies in method signatures, we'll look at lifetimes in that context next to see why the third rule means we don't have to annotate lifetimes in method signatures very often.

Lifetime Annotations in Method Definitions

When we implement methods on a struct with lifetimes, we use the same syntax as that of generic type parameters, as shown in Listing 10-11. Where we declare and use the lifetime parameters depends on whether they're related to the struct fields or the method parameters and return values.

Lifetime names for struct fields always need to be declared after the impl keyword and then used after the struct's name because those lifetimes are part of the struct's type.

In method signatures inside the impl block, references might be tied to the lifetime of references in the struct's fields, or they might be independent. In addition, the lifetime elision rules often make it so that lifetime annotations aren't necessary in method signatures. Let's look at some examples using the struct named ImportantExcerpt that we defined in Listing 10-24.

First we'll use a method named level whose only parameter is a reference to self and whose return value is an i32, which is not a reference to anything:

```
impl<'a> ImportantExcerpt<'a> {
    fn level(&self) -> i32 {
        3
    }
}
```

The lifetime parameter declaration after impl and its use after the type name are required, but we're not required to annotate the lifetime of the reference to self because of the first elision rule.

Here is an example where the third lifetime elision rule applies:

```
impl<'a> ImportantExcerpt<'a> {
    fn announce_and_return_part(&self, announcement: &str) -> &str {
        println!("Attention please: {announcement}");
        self.part
    }
}
```

There are two input lifetimes, so Rust applies the first lifetime elision rule and gives both &self and announcement their own lifetimes. Then, because one of the parameters is &self, the return type gets the lifetime of &self, and all lifetimes have been accounted for.

The Static Lifetime

One special lifetime we need to discuss is 'static, which denotes that the affected reference *can* live for the entire duration of the program. All string literals have the 'static lifetime, which we can annotate as follows:

```
let s: &'static str = "I have a static lifetime.";
```

The text of this string is stored directly in the program's binary, which is always available. Therefore, the lifetime of all string literals is 'static.

You might see suggestions to use the 'static lifetime in error messages. But before specifying 'static as the lifetime for a reference, think about whether the reference you have actually lives the entire lifetime of your program or not, and whether you want it to. Most of the time, an error message suggesting the 'static lifetime results from attempting to create a dangling reference or a mismatch of the available lifetimes. In such cases, the solution is to fix those problems, not to specify the 'static lifetime.

Generic Type Parameters, Trait Bounds, and Lifetimes Together

Let's briefly look at the syntax of specifying generic type parameters, trait bounds, and lifetimes all in one function!

```
use std::fmt::Display;

fn longest_with_an_announcement<'a, T>(
    x: &'a str,
    y: &'a str,
    ann: T,
) -> &'a str
where
    T: Display,
{
    println!("Announcement! {ann}");
    if x.len() > y.len() {
        x
    } else {
        y
    }
}
```

This is the longest function from Listing 10-21 that returns the longer of two string slices. But now it has an extra parameter named ann of the generic type T, which can be filled in by any type that implements the Display trait as specified by the where clause. This extra parameter will be printed using {}, which is why the Display trait bound is necessary. Because lifetimes are a type of generic, the declarations of the lifetime parameter 'a and the generic type parameter T go in the same list inside the angle brackets after the function name.

Summary

We covered a lot in this chapter! Now that you know about generic type parameters, traits and trait bounds, and generic lifetime parameters, you're ready to write code without repetition that works in many different situations. Generic type parameters let you apply the code to different types. Traits and trait bounds ensure that even though the types are generic, they'll have the behavior the code needs. You learned how to use lifetime annotations to ensure that this flexible code won't have any dangling references. And all of this analysis happens at compile time, which doesn't affect runtime performance!

Believe it or not, there is much more to learn on the topics we discussed in this chapter: Chapter 17 discusses trait objects, which are another way to use traits. There are also more complex scenarios involving lifetime annotations that you will only need in very advanced scenarios; for those, you should read the Rust Reference at *https://doc.rust-lang.org/reference/trait -bounds.html*. But next, you'll learn how to write tests in Rust so you can make sure your code is working the way it should.

11

WRITING AUTOMATED TESTS

In his 1972 essay "The Humble Programmer," Edsger W. Dijkstra said that "program testing can be a very effective way to show the presence of bugs, but it is hopelessly inadequate for showing their absence." That doesn't mean we shouldn't try to test as much as we can!

Correctness in our programs is the extent to which our code does what we intend it to do. Rust is designed with a high degree of concern about the correctness of programs, but correctness is complex and not easy to prove. Rust's type system shoulders a huge part of this burden, but the type system cannot catch everything. As such, Rust includes support for writing automated software tests.

Say we write a function add_two that adds 2 to whatever number is passed to it. This function's signature accepts an integer as a parameter and returns an integer as a result. When we implement and compile that function, Rust does all the type checking and borrow checking that you've learned so far to ensure that, for instance, we aren't passing a String value or an invalid reference to this function. But Rust *can't* check that this function will do precisely what we intend, which is return the parameter plus 2 rather than, say, the parameter plus 10 or the parameter minus 50! That's where tests come in.

We can write tests that assert, for example, that when we pass 3 to the add_two function, the returned value is 5. We can run these tests whenever we make changes to our code to make sure any existing correct behavior has not changed.

Testing is a complex skill: although we can't cover in one chapter every detail about how to write good tests, in this chapter we will discuss the mechanics of Rust's testing facilities. We'll talk about the annotations and macros available to you when writing your tests, the default behavior and options provided for running your tests, and how to organize tests into unit tests and integration tests.

How to Write Tests

Tests are Rust functions that verify that the non-test code is functioning in the expected manner. The bodies of test functions typically perform these three actions:

- Set up any needed data or state.
- Run the code you want to test.
- Assert that the results are what you expect.

Let's look at the features Rust provides specifically for writing tests that take these actions, which include the test attribute, a few macros, and the should_panic attribute.

The Anatomy of a Test Function

At its simplest, a test in Rust is a function that's annotated with the test attribute. Attributes are metadata about pieces of Rust code; one example is the derive attribute we used with structs in Chapter 5. To change a function into a test function, add #[test] on the line before fn. When you run your tests with the cargo test command, Rust builds a test runner binary that runs the annotated functions and reports on whether each test function passes or fails.

Whenever we make a new library project with Cargo, a test module with a test function in it is automatically generated for us. This module gives you a template for writing your tests so you don't have to look up the exact structure and syntax every time you start a new project. You can add as many additional test functions and as many test modules as you want!

We'll explore some aspects of how tests work by experimenting with the template test before we actually test any code. Then we'll write some real-world tests that call some code that we've written and assert that its behavior is correct.

Let's create a new library project called adder that will add two numbers:

```
$ cargo new adder --lib
    Created library `adder` project
$ cd adder
```

The contents of the *src/lib.rs* file in your adder library should look like Listing 11-1.

```
#[cfg(test)]
mod tests {
  ❶ #[test]
    fn it_works() {
        let result = 2 + 2;
      ❷ assert_eq!(result, 4);
    }
}
```

Listing 11-1: The test module and function generated automatically by cargo new

For now, let's ignore the top two lines and focus on the function. Note the #[test] annotation ❶: this attribute indicates this is a test function, so the test runner knows to treat this function as a test. We might also have non-test functions in the tests module to help set up common scenarios or perform common operations, so we always need to indicate which functions are tests.

The example function body uses the assert_eq! macro ❷ to assert that result, which contains the result of adding 2 and 2, equals 4. This assertion serves as an example of the format for a typical test. Let's run it to see that this test passes.

The cargo test command runs all tests in our project, as shown in Listing 11-2.

```
$ cargo test
   Compiling adder v0.1.0 (file:///projects/adder)
    Finished test [unoptimized + debuginfo] target(s) in 0.57s
     Running unittests src/lib.rs (target/debug/deps/adder-
92948b65e88960b4)

❶ running 1 test
❷ test tests::it_works ... ok

❸ test result: ok. 1 passed; 0 failed; 0 ignored; 0 measured; 0
filtered out; finished in 0.00s

    ❹ Doc-tests adder

running 0 tests

test result: ok. 0 passed; 0 failed; 0 ignored; 0 measured; 0
filtered out; finished in 0.00s
```

Listing 11-2: The output from running the automatically generated test

Cargo compiled and ran the test. We see the line running 1 test ❶. The next line shows the name of the generated test function, called it_works, and that the result of running that test is ok ❷. The overall summary test result: ok. ❸ means that all the tests passed, and the portion that reads 1 passed; 0 failed totals the number of tests that passed or failed.

It's possible to mark a test as ignored so it doesn't run in a particular instance; we'll cover that in "Ignoring Some Tests Unless Specifically Requested" on page 235. Because we haven't done that here, the summary shows 0 ignored. We can also pass an argument to the cargo test command to run only tests whose name matches a string; this is called *filtering* and we'll cover it in "Running a Subset of Tests by Name" on page 233. Here we haven't filtered the tests being run, so the end of the summary shows 0 filtered out.

The 0 measured statistic is for benchmark tests that measure performance. Benchmark tests are, as of this writing, only available in nightly Rust. See the documentation about benchmark tests at *https://doc.rust-lang.org/unstable-book/ library-features/test.html* to learn more.

The next part of the test output starting at Doc-tests adder ❹ is for the results of any documentation tests. We don't have any documentation tests yet, but Rust can compile any code examples that appear in our API documentation. This feature helps keep your docs and your code in sync! We'll discuss how to write documentation tests in "Documentation Comments as Tests" on page 298. For now, we'll ignore the Doc-tests output.

Let's start to customize the test to our own needs. First, change the name of the it_works function to a different name, such as exploration, like so:

src/lib.rs
```
#[cfg(test)]
mod tests {
    #[test]
    fn exploration() {
        let result = 2 + 2;
        assert_eq!(result, 4);
    }
}
```

Then run cargo test again. The output now shows exploration instead of it_works:

```
running 1 test
test tests::exploration ... ok

test result: ok. 1 passed; 0 failed; 0 ignored; 0 measured; 0
filtered out; finished in 0.00s
```

Now we'll add another test, but this time we'll make a test that fails! Tests fail when something in the test function panics. Each test is run in a new thread, and when the main thread sees that a test thread has died, the test is marked as failed. In Chapter 9, we talked about how the simplest way to panic is to call the panic! macro. Enter the new test as a function named another, so your *src/lib.rs* file looks like Listing 11-3.

src/lib.rs
```
#[cfg(test)]
mod tests {
    #[test]
    fn exploration() {
        assert_eq!(2 + 2, 4);
    }
```

```
    #[test]
    fn another() {
        panic!("Make this test fail");
    }
}
```

Listing 11-3: Adding a second test that will fail because we call the panic! macro

Run the tests again using cargo test. The output should look like Listing 11-4, which shows that our exploration test passed and another failed.

```
running 2 tests
test tests::exploration ... ok
❶ test tests::another ... FAILED

❷ failures:

---- tests::another stdout ----
thread 'main' panicked at 'Make this test fail', src/lib.rs:10:9
note: run with `RUST_BACKTRACE=1` environment variable to display
a backtrace

❸ failures:
    tests::another

❹ test result: FAILED. 1 passed; 1 failed; 0 ignored; 0 measured; 0
filtered out; finished in 0.00s

error: test failed, to rerun pass '--lib'
```

Listing 11-4: Test results when one test passes and one test fails

Instead of ok, the line test tests::another shows FAILED ❶. Two new sections appear between the individual results and the summary: the first ❷ displays the detailed reason for each test failure. In this case, we get the details that another failed because it panicked at 'Make this test fail' on line 10 in the *src/lib.rs* file. The next section ❸ lists just the names of all the failing tests, which is useful when there are lots of tests and lots of detailed failing test output. We can use the name of a failing test to run just that test to more easily debug it; we'll talk more about ways to run tests in "Controlling How Tests Are Run" on page 230.

The summary line displays at the end ❹: overall, our test result is FAILED. We had one test pass and one test fail.

Now that you've seen what the test results look like in different scenarios, let's look at some macros other than panic! that are useful in tests.

Checking Results with the assert! Macro

The assert! macro, provided by the standard library, is useful when you want to ensure that some condition in a test evaluates to true. We give the assert! macro an argument that evaluates to a Boolean. If the value is true, nothing happens and the test passes. If the value is false, the assert! macro calls panic! to cause the test to fail. Using the assert! macro helps us check that our code is functioning in the way we intend.

In Listing 5-15, we used a Rectangle struct and a can_hold method, which are repeated here in Listing 11-5. Let's put this code in the *src/lib.rs* file, then write some tests for it using the assert! macro.

src/lib.rs
```
#[derive(Debug)]
struct Rectangle {
    width: u32,
    height: u32,
}

impl Rectangle {
    fn can_hold(&self, other: &Rectangle) -> bool {
        self.width > other.width && self.height > other.height
    }
}
```

Listing 11-5: Using the Rectangle struct and its can_hold method from Chapter 5

The can_hold method returns a Boolean, which means it's a perfect use case for the assert! macro. In Listing 11-6, we write a test that exercises the can_hold method by creating a Rectangle instance that has a width of 8 and a height of 7 and asserting that it can hold another Rectangle instance that has a width of 5 and a height of 1.

src/lib.rs
```
#[cfg(test)]
mod tests {
  ❶ use super::*;

    #[test]
  ❷ fn larger_can_hold_smaller() {
      ❸ let larger = Rectangle {
            width: 8,
            height: 7,
        };
        let smaller = Rectangle {
            width: 5,
            height: 1,
        };

      ❹ assert!(larger.can_hold(&smaller));
    }
}
```

Listing 11-6: A test for can_hold that checks whether a larger rectangle can indeed hold a smaller rectangle

Note that we've added a new line inside the tests module: use super::*; ❶. The tests module is a regular module that follows the usual visibility rules we covered in "Paths for Referring to an Item in the Module Tree" on page 125. Because the tests module is an inner module, we need to bring the code under test in the outer module into the scope of the inner module. We use a glob here, so anything we define in the outer module is available to this tests module.

We've named our test larger_can_hold_smaller ❷, and we've created the two Rectangle instances that we need ❸. Then we called the assert! macro and passed it the result of calling larger.can_hold(&smaller) ❹. This expression is supposed to return true, so our test should pass. Let's find out!

```
running 1 test
test tests::larger_can_hold_smaller ... ok

test result: ok. 1 passed; 0 failed; 0 ignored; 0 measured; 0
filtered out; finished in 0.00s
```

It does pass! Let's add another test, this time asserting that a smaller rectangle cannot hold a larger rectangle:

src/lib.rs
```
#[cfg(test)]
mod tests {
    use super::*;

    #[test]
    fn larger_can_hold_smaller() {
        --snip--
    }

    #[test]
    fn smaller_cannot_hold_larger() {
        let larger = Rectangle {
            width: 8,
            height: 7,
        };
        let smaller = Rectangle {
            width: 5,
            height: 1,
        };

        assert!(!smaller.can_hold(&larger));
    }
}
```

Because the correct result of the can_hold function in this case is false, we need to negate that result before we pass it to the assert! macro. As a result, our test will pass if can_hold returns false:

```
running 2 tests
test tests::larger_can_hold_smaller ... ok
test tests::smaller_cannot_hold_larger ... ok

test result: ok. 2 passed; 0 failed; 0 ignored; 0 measured; 0
filtered out; finished in 0.00s
```

Two tests that pass! Now let's see what happens to our test results when we introduce a bug in our code. We'll change the implementation of the can_hold method by replacing the greater-than sign with a less-than sign when it compares the widths:

```
--snip--

impl Rectangle {
    fn can_hold(&self, other: &Rectangle) -> bool {
        self.width < other.width && self.height > other.height
    }
}
```

Running the tests now produces the following:

```
running 2 tests
test tests::smaller_cannot_hold_larger ... ok
test tests::larger_can_hold_smaller ... FAILED

failures:

---- tests::larger_can_hold_smaller stdout ----
thread 'main' panicked at 'assertion failed:
larger.can_hold(&smaller)', src/lib.rs:28:9
note: run with `RUST_BACKTRACE=1` environment variable to display
a backtrace


failures:
    tests::larger_can_hold_smaller

test result: FAILED. 1 passed; 1 failed; 0 ignored; 0 measured; 0
filtered out; finished in 0.00s
```

Our tests caught the bug! Because larger.width is 8 and smaller.width is 5, the comparison of the widths in can_hold now returns false: 8 is not less than 5.

Testing Equality with the assert_eq! and assert_ne! Macros

A common way to verify functionality is to test for equality between the result of the code under test and the value you expect the code to return. You could do this by using the assert! macro and passing it an expression using the == operator. However, this is such a common test that the standard library provides a pair of macros—assert_eq! and assert_ne!—to perform this test more conveniently. These macros compare two arguments for equality or inequality, respectively. They'll also print the two values if the assertion fails, which makes it easier to see *why* the test failed; conversely, the assert! macro only indicates that it got a false value for the == expression, without printing the values that led to the false value.

In Listing 11-7, we write a function named add_two that adds 2 to its parameter, then we test this function using the assert_eq! macro.

```
src/lib.rs   pub fn add_two(a: i32) -> i32 {
                 a + 2
             }

             #[cfg(test)]
             mod tests {
                 use super::*;

                 #[test]
                 fn it_adds_two() {
                     assert_eq!(4, add_two(2));
                 }
             }
```

Listing 11-7: Testing the function add_two using the assert_eq! macro

Let's check that it passes!

```
running 1 test
test tests::it_adds_two ... ok

test result: ok. 1 passed; 0 failed; 0 ignored; 0 measured; 0
filtered out; finished in 0.00s
```

We pass 4 as the argument to assert_eq!, which is equal to the result of calling add_two(2). The line for this test is test tests::it_adds_two ... ok, and the ok text indicates that our test passed!

Let's introduce a bug into our code to see what assert_eq! looks like when it fails. Change the implementation of the add_two function to instead add 3:

```
pub fn add_two(a: i32) -> i32 {
    a + 3
}
```

Run the tests again:

```
running 1 test
test tests::it_adds_two ... FAILED

failures:

---- tests::it_adds_two stdout ----
❶ thread 'main' panicked at 'assertion failed: `(left == right)`
  ❷ left: `4`,
 ❸ right: `5`', src/lib.rs:11:9
 note: run with `RUST_BACKTRACE=1` environment variable to display
 a backtrace

failures:
    tests::it_adds_two

test result: FAILED. 0 passed; 1 failed; 0 ignored; 0 measured; 0
filtered out; finished in 0.00s
```

Our test caught the bug! The it_adds_two test failed, and the message tells us that the assertion that failed was assertion failed: `(left == right)` ❶ and what the left ❷ and right ❸ values are. This message helps us start debugging: the left argument was 4 but the right argument, where we had add_two(2), was 5. You can imagine that this would be especially helpful when we have a lot of tests going on.

Note that in some languages and test frameworks, the parameters to equality assertion functions are called expected and actual, and the order in which we specify the arguments matters. However, in Rust, they're called left and right, and the order in which we specify the value we expect and the value the code produces doesn't matter. We could write the assertion in this test as assert_eq!(add_two(2), 4), which would result in the same failure message that displays assertion failed: `(left == right)`.

The assert_ne! macro will pass if the two values we give it are not equal and fail if they're equal. This macro is most useful for cases when we're not sure what a value *will* be, but we know what the value definitely *shouldn't* be. For example, if we're testing a function that is guaranteed to change its input in some way, but the way in which the input is changed depends on the day of the week that we run our tests, the best thing to assert might be that the output of the function is not equal to the input.

Under the surface, the assert_eq! and assert_ne! macros use the operators == and !=, respectively. When the assertions fail, these macros print their arguments using debug formatting, which means the values being compared must implement the PartialEq and Debug traits. All primitive types and most of the standard library types implement these traits. For structs and enums that you define yourself, you'll need to implement PartialEq to assert equality of those types. You'll also need to implement Debug to print the values when the assertion fails. Because both traits are derivable traits, as mentioned in Listing 5-12, this is usually as straightforward as adding the #[derive(PartialEq, Debug)] annotation to your struct or enum definition. See Appendix C for more details about these and other derivable traits.

Adding Custom Failure Messages

You can also add a custom message to be printed with the failure message as optional arguments to the assert!, assert_eq!, and assert_ne! macros. Any arguments specified after the required arguments are passed along to the format! macro (discussed in "Concatenation with the + Operator or the format! Macro" on page 149), so you can pass a format string that contains {} placeholders and values to go in those placeholders. Custom messages are useful for documenting what an assertion means; when a test fails, you'll have a better idea of what the problem is with the code.

For example, let's say we have a function that greets people by name and we want to test that the name we pass into the function appears in the output:

src/lib.rs
```
pub fn greeting(name: &str) -> String {
    format!("Hello {name}!")
}
```

```
#[cfg(test)]
mod tests {
    use super::*;

    #[test]
    fn greeting_contains_name() {
        let result = greeting("Carol");
        assert!(result.contains("Carol"));
    }
}
```

The requirements for this program haven't been agreed upon yet, and we're pretty sure the Hello text at the beginning of the greeting will change. We decided we don't want to have to update the test when the requirements change, so instead of checking for exact equality to the value returned from the greeting function, we'll just assert that the output contains the text of the input parameter.

Now let's introduce a bug into this code by changing greeting to exclude name to see what the default test failure looks like:

```
pub fn greeting(name: &str) -> String {
    String::from("Hello!")
}
```

Running this test produces the following:

```
running 1 test
test tests::greeting_contains_name ... FAILED

failures:

---- tests::greeting_contains_name stdout ----
thread 'main' panicked at 'assertion failed:
result.contains(\"Carol\")', src/lib.rs:12:9
note: run with `RUST_BACKTRACE=1` environment variable to display
a backtrace


failures:
    tests::greeting_contains_name
```

This result just indicates that the assertion failed and which line the assertion is on. A more useful failure message would print the value from the greeting function. Let's add a custom failure message composed of a format string with a placeholder filled in with the actual value we got from the greeting function:

```
#[test]
fn greeting_contains_name() {
    let result = greeting("Carol");
    assert!(
```

```
            result.contains("Carol"),
            "Greeting did not contain name, value was `{result}`"
    );
}
```

Now when we run the test, we'll get a more informative error message:

```
---- tests::greeting_contains_name stdout ----
thread 'main' panicked at 'Greeting did not contain name, value
was `Hello!`', src/lib.rs:12:9
note: run with `RUST_BACKTRACE=1` environment variable to display
a backtrace
```

We can see the value we actually got in the test output, which would help us debug what happened instead of what we were expecting to happen.

Checking for Panics with should_panic

In addition to checking return values, it's important to check that our code handles error conditions as we expect. For example, consider the Guess type that we created in Listing 9-13. Other code that uses Guess depends on the guarantee that Guess instances will contain only values between 1 and 100. We can write a test that ensures that attempting to create a Guess instance with a value outside that range panics.

We do this by adding the attribute should_panic to our test function. The test passes if the code inside the function panics; the test fails if the code inside the function doesn't panic.

Listing 11-8 shows a test that checks that the error conditions of Guess::new happen when we expect them to.

```
src/lib.rs  pub struct Guess {
                value: i32,
            }

            impl Guess {
                pub fn new(value: i32) -> Guess {
                    if value < 1 || value > 100 {
                        panic!(
                            "Guess value must be between 1 and 100, got {}.",
                            value
                        );
                    }

                    Guess { value }
                }
            }

            #[cfg(test)]
            mod tests {
                use super::*;
```

```
#[test]
#[should_panic]
fn greater_than_100() {
    Guess::new(200);
}
}
```

Listing 11-8: Testing that a condition will cause a panic!

We place the #[should_panic] attribute after the #[test] attribute and before the test function it applies to. Let's look at the result when this test passes:

```
running 1 test
test tests::greater_than_100 - should panic ... ok

test result: ok. 1 passed; 0 failed; 0 ignored; 0 measured; 0
filtered out; finished in 0.00s
```

Looks good! Now let's introduce a bug in our code by removing the condition that the new function will panic if the value is greater than 100:

src/lib.rs

```
--snip--

impl Guess {
    pub fn new(value: i32) -> Guess {
        if value < 1 {
            panic!(
                "Guess value must be between 1 and 100, got {}.",
                value
            );
        }

        Guess { value }
    }
}
```

When we run the test in Listing 11-8, it will fail:

```
running 1 test
test tests::greater_than_100 - should panic ... FAILED

failures:

---- tests::greater_than_100 stdout ----
note: test did not panic as expected

failures:
    tests::greater_than_100

test result: FAILED. 0 passed; 1 failed; 0 ignored; 0 measured; 0
filtered out; finished in 0.00s
```

We don't get a very helpful message in this case, but when we look at the test function, we see that it's annotated with #[should_panic]. The failure we got means that the code in the test function did not cause a panic.

Tests that use should_panic can be imprecise. A should_panic test would pass even if the test panics for a different reason from the one we were expecting. To make should_panic tests more precise, we can add an optional expected parameter to the should_panic attribute. The test harness will make sure that the failure message contains the provided text. For example, consider the modified code for Guess in Listing 11-9 where the new function panics with different messages depending on whether the value is too small or too large.

src/lib.rs

```
--snip--

impl Guess {
    pub fn new(value: i32) -> Guess {
        if value < 1 {
            panic!(
                "Guess value must be greater than or equal to 1, got {}.",
                value
            );
        } else if value > 100 {
            panic!(
                "Guess value must be less than or equal to 100, got {}.",
                value
            );
        }

        Guess { value }
    }
}

#[cfg(test)]
mod tests {
    use super::*;

    #[test]
    #[should_panic(expected = "less than or equal to 100")]
    fn greater_than_100() {
        Guess::new(200);
    }
}
```

Listing 11-9: Testing for a panic! with a panic message containing a specified substring

This test will pass because the value we put in the should_panic attribute's expected parameter is a substring of the message that the Guess::new function panics with. We could have specified the entire panic message that we expect, which in this case would be Guess value must be less than or equal to 100, got 200. What you choose to specify depends on how much of the panic message is unique or dynamic and how precise you want your test to be. In this case, a substring of the panic message is enough to ensure that the code in the test function executes the else if value > 100 case.

To see what happens when a should_panic test with an expected message fails, let's again introduce a bug into our code by swapping the bodies of the if value < 1 and the else if value > 100 blocks:

src/lib.rs
```
--snip--
if value < 1 {
    panic!(
        "Guess value must be less than or equal to 100, got {}.",
        value
    );
} else if value > 100 {
    panic!(
        "Guess value must be greater than or equal to 1, got {}.",
        value
    );
}
--snip--
```

This time when we run the should_panic test, it will fail:

```
running 1 test
test tests::greater_than_100 - should panic ... FAILED

failures:

---- tests::greater_than_100 stdout ----
thread 'main' panicked at 'Guess value must be greater than or equal to 1, got
200.', src/lib.rs:13:13
note: run with `RUST_BACKTRACE=1` environment variable to display a backtrace
note: panic did not contain expected string
      panic message: `"Guess value must be greater than or equal to 1, got
200."`,
 expected substring: `"less than or equal to 100"`

failures:
    tests::greater_than_100

test result: FAILED. 0 passed; 1 failed; 0 ignored; 0 measured; 0 filtered out;
finished in 0.00s
```

The failure message indicates that this test did indeed panic as we expected, but the panic message did not include the expected string 'Guess value must be less than or equal to 100'. The panic message that we did get in this case was Guess value must be greater than or equal to 1, got 200. Now we can start figuring out where our bug is!

Using Result<T, E> in Tests

Our tests so far all panic when they fail. We can also write tests that use Result<T, E>! Here's the test from Listing 11-1, rewritten to use Result<T, E> and return an Err instead of panicking:

src/lib.rs

```
#[cfg(test)]
mod tests {
    #[test]
    fn it_works() -> Result<(), String> {
        if 2 + 2 == 4 {
            Ok(())
        } else {
            Err(String::from("two plus two does not equal four"))
        }
    }
}
```

The it_works function now has the Result<(), String> return type. In the body of the function, rather than calling the assert_eq! macro, we return Ok(()) when the test passes and an Err with a String inside when the test fails.

Writing tests so they return a Result<T, E> enables you to use the question mark operator in the body of tests, which can be a convenient way to write tests that should fail if any operation within them returns an Err variant.

You can't use the #[should_panic] annotation on tests that use Result<T, E>. To assert that an operation returns an Err variant, *don't* use the question mark operator on the Result<T, E> value. Instead, use assert!(value.is_err()).

Now that you know several ways to write tests, let's look at what is happening when we run our tests and explore the different options we can use with cargo test.

Controlling How Tests Are Run

Just as cargo run compiles your code and then runs the resultant binary, cargo test compiles your code in test mode and runs the resultant test binary. The default behavior of the binary produced by cargo test is to run all the tests in parallel and capture output generated during test runs, preventing the output from being displayed and making it easier to read the output related to the test results. You can, however, specify command line options to change this default behavior.

Some command line options go to cargo test, and some go to the resultant test binary. To separate these two types of arguments, you list the arguments that go to cargo test followed by the separator -- and then the ones that go to the test binary. Running cargo test --help displays the options you can use with cargo test, and running cargo test -- --help displays the options you can use after the separator.

Running Tests in Parallel or Consecutively

When you run multiple tests, by default they run in parallel using threads, meaning they finish running faster and you get feedback quicker. Because the tests are running at the same time, you must make sure your tests don't depend on each other or on any shared state, including a shared environment, such as the current working directory or environment variables.

For example, say each of your tests runs some code that creates a file on disk named *test-output.txt* and writes some data to that file. Then each test reads the data in that file and asserts that the file contains a particular value, which is different in each test. Because the tests run at the same time, one test might overwrite the file in the time between another test writing and reading the file. The second test will then fail, not because the code is incorrect but because the tests have interfered with each other while running in parallel. One solution is to make sure each test writes to a different file; another solution is to run the tests one at a time.

If you don't want to run the tests in parallel or if you want more fine-grained control over the number of threads used, you can send the --test -threads flag and the number of threads you want to use to the test binary. Take a look at the following example:

```
$ cargo test -- --test-threads=1
```

We set the number of test threads to 1, telling the program not to use any parallelism. Running the tests using one thread will take longer than running them in parallel, but the tests won't interfere with each other if they share state.

Showing Function Output

By default, if a test passes, Rust's test library captures anything printed to standard output. For example, if we call println! in a test and the test passes, we won't see the println! output in the terminal; we'll see only the line that indicates the test passed. If a test fails, we'll see whatever was printed to standard output with the rest of the failure message.

As an example, Listing 11-10 has a silly function that prints the value of its parameter and returns 10, as well as a test that passes and a test that fails.

src/lib.rs
```rust
fn prints_and_returns_10(a: i32) -> i32 {
    println!("I got the value {a}");
    10
}

#[cfg(test)]
mod tests {
    use super::*;

    #[test]
    fn this_test_will_pass() {
        let value = prints_and_returns_10(4);
        assert_eq!(10, value);
    }
```

```
        #[test]
        fn this_test_will_fail() {
            let value = prints_and_returns_10(8);
            assert_eq!(5, value);
        }
    }
```

Listing 11-10: Tests for a function that calls println!

When we run these tests with cargo test, we'll see the following output:

```
running 2 tests
test tests::this_test_will_pass ... ok
test tests::this_test_will_fail ... FAILED

failures:

---- tests::this_test_will_fail stdout ----
❶ I got the value 8
thread 'main' panicked at 'assertion failed: `(left == right)`
  left: `5`,
 right: `10`', src/lib.rs:19:9
note: run with `RUST_BACKTRACE=1` environment variable to display
a backtrace

failures:
    tests::this_test_will_fail

test result: FAILED. 1 passed; 1 failed; 0 ignored; 0 measured; 0
filtered out; finished in 0.00s
```

Note that nowhere in this output do we see I got the value 4, which is printed when the test that passes runs. That output has been captured. The output from the test that failed, I got the value 8 ❶, appears in the section of the test summary output, which also shows the cause of the test failure.

If we want to see printed values for passing tests as well, we can tell Rust to also show the output of successful tests with --show-output:

```
$ cargo test -- --show-output
```

When we run the tests in Listing 11-10 again with the --show-output flag, we see the following output:

```
running 2 tests
test tests::this_test_will_pass ... ok
test tests::this_test_will_fail ... FAILED

successes:

---- tests::this_test_will_pass stdout ----
I got the value 4
```

```
successes:
    tests::this_test_will_pass

failures:

---- tests::this_test_will_fail stdout ----
I got the value 8
thread 'main' panicked at 'assertion failed: `(left == right)`
  left: `5`,
 right: `10`', src/lib.rs:19:9
note: run with `RUST_BACKTRACE=1` environment variable to display
a backtrace

failures:
    tests::this_test_will_fail

test result: FAILED. 1 passed; 1 failed; 0 ignored; 0 measured; 0
filtered out; finished in 0.00s
```

Running a Subset of Tests by Name

Sometimes, running a full test suite can take a long time. If you're working on code in a particular area, you might want to run only the tests pertaining to that code. You can choose which tests to run by passing cargo test the name or names of the test(s) you want to run as an argument.

To demonstrate how to run a subset of tests, we'll first create three tests for our add_two function, as shown in Listing 11-11, and choose which ones to run.

src/lib.rs
```
pub fn add_two(a: i32) -> i32 {
    a + 2
}

#[cfg(test)]
mod tests {
    use super::*;

    #[test]
    fn add_two_and_two() {
        assert_eq!(4, add_two(2));
    }

    #[test]
    fn add_three_and_two() {
        assert_eq!(5, add_two(3));
    }

    #[test]
    fn one_hundred() {
        assert_eq!(102, add_two(100));
    }
}
```

Listing 11-11: Three tests with three different names

If we run the tests without passing any arguments, as we saw earlier, all the tests will run in parallel:

```
running 3 tests
test tests::add_three_and_two ... ok
test tests::add_two_and_two ... ok
test tests::one_hundred ... ok

test result: ok. 3 passed; 0 failed; 0 ignored; 0 measured; 0
filtered out; finished in 0.00s
```

Running Single Tests

We can pass the name of any test function to cargo test to run only that test:

```
$ cargo test one_hundred
   Compiling adder v0.1.0 (file:///projects/adder)
    Finished test [unoptimized + debuginfo] target(s) in 0.69s
     Running unittests src/lib.rs (target/debug/deps/adder-
92948b65e88960b4)

running 1 test
test tests::one_hundred ... ok

test result: ok. 1 passed; 0 failed; 0 ignored; 0 measured; 2
filtered out; finished in 0.00s
```

Only the test with the name one_hundred ran; the other two tests didn't match that name. The test output lets us know we had more tests that didn't run by displaying 2 filtered out at the end.

We can't specify the names of multiple tests in this way; only the first value given to cargo test will be used. But there is a way to run multiple tests.

Filtering to Run Multiple Tests

We can specify part of a test name, and any test whose name matches that value will be run. For example, because two of our tests' names contain add, we can run those two by running cargo test add:

```
$ cargo test add
   Compiling adder v0.1.0 (file:///projects/adder)
    Finished test [unoptimized + debuginfo] target(s) in 0.61s
     Running unittests src/lib.rs (target/debug/deps/adder-
92948b65e88960b4)

running 2 tests
test tests::add_three_and_two ... ok
test tests::add_two_and_two ... ok

test result: ok. 2 passed; 0 failed; 0 ignored; 0 measured; 1
filtered out; finished in 0.00s
```

This command ran all tests with add in the name and filtered out the test named one_hundred. Also note that the module in which a test appears becomes part of the test's name, so we can run all the tests in a module by filtering on the module's name.

Ignoring Some Tests Unless Specifically Requested

Sometimes a few specific tests can be very time-consuming to execute, so you might want to exclude them during most runs of cargo test. Rather than listing as arguments all tests you do want to run, you can instead annotate the time-consuming tests using the ignore attribute to exclude them, as shown here:

src/lib.rs
```
#[test]
fn it_works() {
    let result = 2 + 2;
    assert_eq!(result, 4);
}

#[test]
#[ignore]
fn expensive_test() {
    // code that takes an hour to run
}
```

After #[test], we add the #[ignore] line to the test we want to exclude. Now when we run our tests, it_works runs, but expensive_test doesn't:

```
$ cargo test
   Compiling adder v0.1.0 (file:///projects/adder)
    Finished test [unoptimized + debuginfo] target(s) in 0.60s
     Running unittests src/lib.rs (target/debug/deps/adder-92948b65e88960b4)

running 2 tests
test expensive_test ... ignored
test it_works ... ok

test result: ok. 1 passed; 0 failed; 1 ignored; 0 measured; 0
filtered out; finished in 0.00s
```

The expensive_test function is listed as ignored. If we want to run only the ignored tests, we can use cargo test -- --ignored:

```
$ cargo test -- --ignored
    Finished test [unoptimized + debuginfo] target(s) in 0.61s
     Running unittests src/lib.rs (target/debug/deps/adder-92948b65e88960b4)

running 1 test
test expensive_test ... ok

test result: ok. 1 passed; 0 failed; 0 ignored; 0 measured; 1
filtered out; finished in 0.00s
```

By controlling which tests run, you can make sure your cargo test results will be returned quickly. When you're at a point where it makes sense to check the results of the ignored tests and you have time to wait for the results, you can run cargo test -- --ignored instead. If you want to run all tests whether they're ignored or not, you can run cargo test -- --include-ignored.

Test Organization

As mentioned at the start of the chapter, testing is a complex discipline, and different people use different terminology and organization. The Rust community thinks about tests in terms of two main categories: unit tests and integration tests. *Unit tests* are small and more focused, testing one module in isolation at a time, and can test private interfaces. *Integration tests* are entirely external to your library and use your code in the same way any other external code would, using only the public interface and potentially exercising multiple modules per test.

Writing both kinds of tests is important to ensure that the pieces of your library are doing what you expect them to, separately and together.

Unit Tests

The purpose of unit tests is to test each unit of code in isolation from the rest of the code to quickly pinpoint where code is and isn't working as expected. You'll put unit tests in the *src* directory in each file with the code that they're testing. The convention is to create a module named tests in each file to contain the test functions and to annotate the module with cfg(test).

The Tests Module and #[cfg(test)]

The #[cfg(test)] annotation on the tests module tells Rust to compile and run the test code only when you run cargo test, not when you run cargo build. This saves compile time when you only want to build the library and saves space in the resultant compiled artifact because the tests are not included. You'll see that because integration tests go in a different directory, they don't need the #[cfg(test)] annotation. However, because unit tests go in the same files as the code, you'll use #[cfg(test)] to specify that they shouldn't be included in the compiled result.

Recall that when we generated the new adder project in the first section of this chapter, Cargo generated this code for us:

src/lib.rs
```
#[cfg(test)]
mod tests {
    #[test]
    fn it_works() {
        let result = 2 + 2;
        assert_eq!(result, 4);
    }
}
```

This code is the automatically generated tests module. The attribute cfg stands for *configuration* and tells Rust that the following item should only be included given a certain configuration option. In this case, the configuration option is test, which is provided by Rust for compiling and running tests. By using the cfg attribute, Cargo compiles our test code only if we actively run the tests with cargo test. This includes any helper functions that might be within this module, in addition to the functions annotated with #[test].

Testing Private Functions

There's debate within the testing community about whether or not private functions should be tested directly, and other languages make it difficult or impossible to test private functions. Regardless of which testing ideology you adhere to, Rust's privacy rules do allow you to test private functions. Consider the code in Listing 11-12 with the private function internal_adder.

src/lib.rs
```
pub fn add_two(a: i32) -> i32 {
    internal_adder(a, 2)
}

fn internal_adder(a: i32, b: i32) -> i32 {
    a + b
}

#[cfg(test)]
mod tests {
    use super::*;

    #[test]
    fn internal() {
        assert_eq!(4, internal_adder(2, 2));
    }
}
```

Listing 11-12: Testing a private function

Note that the internal_adder function is not marked as pub. Tests are just Rust code, and the tests module is just another module. As we discussed in "Paths for Referring to an Item in the Module Tree" on page 125, items in child modules can use the items in their ancestor modules. In this test, we bring all of the test module's parent's items into scope with use super::*, and then the test can call internal_adder. If you don't think private functions should be tested, there's nothing in Rust that will compel you to do so.

Integration Tests

In Rust, integration tests are entirely external to your library. They use your library in the same way any other code would, which means they can only call functions that are part of your library's public API. Their purpose is to test whether many parts of your library work together correctly. Units of code that work correctly on their own could have problems when integrated, so test coverage of the integrated code is important as well. To create integration tests, you first need a *tests* directory.

The tests Directory

We create a *tests* directory at the top level of our project directory, next to *src*. Cargo knows to look for integration test files in this directory. We can then make as many test files as we want, and Cargo will compile each of the files as an individual crate.

Let's create an integration test. With the code in Listing 11-12 still in the *src/lib.rs* file, make a *tests* directory, and create a new file named *tests/integration_test.rs*. Your directory structure should look like this:

```
adder
├── Cargo.lock
├── Cargo.toml
├── src
│   └── lib.rs
└── tests
    └── integration_test.rs
```

Enter the code in Listing 11-13 into the *tests/integration_test.rs* file.

tests/
integration
_test.rs

```
use adder;

#[test]
fn it_adds_two() {
    assert_eq!(4, adder::add_two(2));
}
```

Listing 11-13: An integration test of a function in the adder crate

Each file in the *tests* directory is a separate crate, so we need to bring our library into each test crate's scope. For that reason we add use adder; at the top of the code, which we didn't need in the unit tests.

We don't need to annotate any code in *tests/integration_test.rs* with #[cfg(test)]. Cargo treats the *tests* directory specially and compiles files in this directory only when we run cargo test. Run cargo test now:

```
$ cargo test
   Compiling adder v0.1.0 (file:///projects/adder)
    Finished test [unoptimized + debuginfo] target(s) in 1.31s
     Running unittests src/lib.rs (target/debug/deps/adder-
1082c4b063a8fbe6)

❶ running 1 test
test tests::internal ... ok

test result: ok. 1 passed; 0 failed; 0 ignored; 0 measured; 0
filtered out; finished in 0.00s

❷ Running tests/integration_test.rs
(target/debug/deps/integration_test-1082c4b063a8fbe6)

running 1 test
❸ test it_adds_two ... ok
```

❹ test result: ok. 1 passed; 0 failed; 0 ignored; 0 measured; 0
filtered out; finished in 0.00s

   Doc-tests adder

running 0 tests

test result: ok. 0 passed; 0 failed; 0 ignored; 0 measured; 0
filtered out; finished in 0.00s

The three sections of output include the unit tests, the integration test, and the doc tests. Note that if any test in a section fails, the following sections will not be run. For example, if a unit test fails, there won't be any output for integration and doc tests because those tests will only be run if all unit tests are passing.

The first section for the unit tests ❶ is the same as we've been seeing: one line for each unit test (one named `internal` that we added in Listing 11-12) and then a summary line for the unit tests.

The integration tests section starts with the line `Running tests/integration _test.rs` ❷. Next, there is a line for each test function in that integration test ❸ and a summary line for the results of the integration test ❹ just before the `Doc-tests adder` section starts.

Each integration test file has its own section, so if we add more files in the *tests* directory, there will be more integration test sections.

We can still run a particular integration test function by specifying the test function's name as an argument to cargo test. To run all the tests in a particular integration test file, use the --test argument of cargo test followed by the name of the file:

```
$ cargo test --test integration_test
    Finished test [unoptimized + debuginfo] target(s) in 0.64s
      Running tests/integration_test.rs
(target/debug/deps/integration_test-82e7799c1bc62298)

running 1 test
test it_adds_two ... ok

test result: ok. 1 passed; 0 failed; 0 ignored; 0 measured; 0
filtered out; finished in 0.00s
```

This command runs only the tests in the *tests/integration_test.rs* file.

Submodules in Integration Tests

As you add more integration tests, you might want to make more files in the *tests* directory to help organize them; for example, you can group the test functions by the functionality they're testing. As mentioned earlier, each file in the *tests* directory is compiled as its own separate crate, which is useful for creating separate scopes to more closely imitate the way end users will be using your crate. However, this means files in the *tests* directory don't share the same behavior as files in *src* do, as you learned in Chapter 7 regarding how to separate code into modules and files.

The different behavior of *tests* directory files is most noticeable when you have a set of helper functions to use in multiple integration test files and you try to follow the steps in "Separating Modules into Different Files" on page 138 to extract them into a common module. For example, if we create *tests/common.rs* and place a function named setup in it, we can add some code to setup that we want to call from multiple test functions in multiple test files:

tests/common.rs
```
pub fn setup() {
    // setup code specific to your library's tests would go here
}
```

When we run the tests again, we'll see a new section in the test output for the *common.rs* file, even though this file doesn't contain any test functions nor did we call the setup function from anywhere:

```
running 1 test
test tests::internal ... ok

test result: ok. 1 passed; 0 failed; 0 ignored; 0 measured; 0
filtered out; finished in 0.00s

    Running tests/common.rs (target/debug/deps/common-92948b65e88960b4)

running 0 tests

test result: ok. 0 passed; 0 failed; 0 ignored; 0 measured; 0
filtered out; finished in 0.00s

    Running tests/integration_test.rs
(target/debug/deps/integration_test-92948b65e88960b4)

running 1 test
test it_adds_two ... ok

test result: ok. 1 passed; 0 failed; 0 ignored; 0 measured; 0
filtered out; finished in 0.00s

   Doc-tests adder

running 0 tests

test result: ok. 0 passed; 0 failed; 0 ignored; 0 measured; 0
filtered out; finished in 0.00s
```

Having common appear in the test results with running 0 tests displayed for it is not what we wanted. We just wanted to share some code with the other integration test files. To avoid having common appear in the test output, instead of creating *tests/common.rs*, we'll create *tests/common/mod.rs*. The project directory now looks like this:

```
├── Cargo.lock
├── Cargo.toml
├── src
│   └── lib.rs
└── tests
    ├── common
    │   └── mod.rs
    └── integration_test.rs
```

This is the older naming convention that Rust also understands that we mentioned in "Alternate File Paths" on page 139. Naming the file this way tells Rust not to treat the common module as an integration test file. When we move the setup function code into *tests/common/mod.rs* and delete the *tests/common.rs* file, the section in the test output will no longer appear. Files in subdirectories of the *tests* directory don't get compiled as separate crates or have sections in the test output.

After we've created *tests/common/mod.rs*, we can use it from any of the integration test files as a module. Here's an example of calling the setup function from the it_adds_two test in *tests/integration_test.rs*:

tests/
integration
_test.rs

```
use adder;

mod common;

#[test]
fn it_adds_two() {
    common::setup();
    assert_eq!(4, adder::add_two(2));
}
```

Note that the mod common; declaration is the same as the module declaration we demonstrated in Listing 7-21. Then, in the test function, we can call the common::setup() function.

Integration Tests for Binary Crates

If our project is a binary crate that only contains a *src/main.rs* file and doesn't have a *src/lib.rs* file, we can't create integration tests in the *tests* directory and bring functions defined in the *src/main.rs* file into scope with a use statement. Only library crates expose functions that other crates can use; binary crates are meant to be run on their own.

This is one of the reasons Rust projects that provide a binary have a straightforward *src/main.rs* file that calls logic that lives in the *src/lib.rs* file. Using that structure, integration tests *can* test the library crate with use to make the important functionality available. If the important functionality works, the small amount of code in the *src/main.rs* file will work as well, and that small amount of code doesn't need to be tested.

Summary

Rust's testing features provide a way to specify how code should function to ensure it continues to work as you expect, even as you make changes. Unit tests exercise different parts of a library separately and can test private implementation details. Integration tests check that many parts of the library work together correctly, and they use the library's public API to test the code in the same way external code will use it. Even though Rust's type system and ownership rules help prevent some kinds of bugs, tests are still important to reduce logic bugs having to do with how your code is expected to behave.

Let's combine the knowledge you learned in this chapter and in previous chapters to work on a project!

12

AN I/O PROJECT: BUILDING A COMMAND LINE PROGRAM

This chapter is a recap of the many skills you've learned so far and an exploration of a few more standard library features. We'll build a command line tool that interacts with file and command line input/output to practice some of the Rust concepts you now have under your belt.

Rust's speed, safety, single binary output, and cross-platform support make it an ideal language for creating command line tools, so for our project, we'll make our own version of the classic command line search tool grep (*g*lobally search a *r*egular *e*xpression and *p*rint). In the simplest use case, grep searches a specified file for a specified string. To do so, grep takes as its arguments a file path and a string. Then it reads the file, finds lines in that file that contain the string argument, and prints those lines.

Along the way, we'll show how to make our command line tool use the terminal features that many other command line tools use. We'll read the value of an environment variable to allow the user to configure the behavior of our tool. We'll also print error messages to the standard error console stream (stderr) instead of standard output (stdout) so that, for example, the user can redirect successful output to a file while still seeing error messages onscreen.

One Rust community member, Andrew Gallant, has already created a fully featured, very fast version of grep, called ripgrep. By comparison, our version will be fairly simple, but this chapter will give you some of the background knowledge you need to understand a real-world project such as ripgrep.

Our grep project will combine a number of concepts you've learned so far:

- Organizing code (Chapter 7)
- Using vectors and strings (Chapter 8)
- Handling errors (Chapter 9)
- Using traits and lifetimes where appropriate (Chapter 10)
- Writing tests (Chapter 11)

We'll also briefly introduce closures, iterators, and trait objects, which Chapter 13 and Chapter 17 will cover in detail.

Accepting Command Line Arguments

Let's create a new project with, as always, cargo new. We'll call our project minigrep to distinguish it from the grep tool that you might already have on your system.

```
$ cargo new minigrep
    Created binary (application) `minigrep` project
$ cd minigrep
```

The first task is to make minigrep accept its two command line arguments: the file path and a string to search for. That is, we want to be able to run our program with cargo run, two hyphens to indicate the following arguments are for our program rather than for cargo, a string to search for, and a path to a file to search in, like so:

```
$ cargo run -- searchstring example-filename.txt
```

Right now, the program generated by cargo new cannot process arguments we give it. Some existing libraries on *https://crates.io* can help with writing a program that accepts command line arguments, but because you're just learning this concept, let's implement this capability ourselves.

Reading the Argument Values

To enable minigrep to read the values of command line arguments we pass to it, we'll need the std::env::args function provided in Rust's standard library. This function returns an iterator of the command line arguments passed to minigrep. We'll cover iterators fully in Chapter 13. For now, you only need to know two details about iterators: iterators produce a series of values, and we can call the collect method on an iterator to turn it into a collection, such as a vector, that contains all the elements the iterator produces.

The code in Listing 12-1 allows your minigrep program to read any command line arguments passed to it, and then collect the values into a vector.

src/main.rs
```rust
use std::env;

fn main() {
    let args: Vec<String> = env::args().collect();
    dbg!(args);
}
```

Listing 12-1: Collecting the command line arguments into a vector and printing them

First we bring the std::env module into scope with a use statement so we can use its args function. Notice that the std::env::args function is nested in two levels of modules. As we discussed in Chapter 7, in cases where the desired function is nested in more than one module, we've chosen to bring the parent module into scope rather than the function. By doing so, we can easily use other functions from std::env. It's also less ambiguous than adding use std::env::args and then calling the function with just args, because args might easily be mistaken for a function that's defined in the current module.

THE ARGS FUNCTION AND INVALID UNICODE

Note that std::env::args will panic if any argument contains invalid Unicode. If your program needs to accept arguments containing invalid Unicode, use std::env::args_os instead. That function returns an iterator that produces OsString values instead of String values. We've chosen to use std::env::args here for simplicity because OsString values differ per platform and are more complex to work with than String values.

On the first line of main, we call env::args, and we immediately use collect to turn the iterator into a vector containing all the values produced by the iterator. We can use the collect function to create many kinds of collections, so we explicitly annotate the type of args to specify that we want a vector of strings. Although you very rarely need to annotate types in Rust, collect is one function you do often need to annotate because Rust isn't able to infer the kind of collection you want.

Finally, we print the vector using the debug macro. Let's try running the code first with no arguments and then with two arguments:

```
$ cargo run
--snip--
[src/main.rs:5] args = [
    "target/debug/minigrep",
]
$ cargo run -- needle haystack
--snip--
```

```
[src/main.rs:5] args = [
    "target/debug/minigrep",
    "needle",
    "haystack",
]
```

Notice that the first value in the vector is "target/debug/minigrep", which is the name of our binary. This matches the behavior of the arguments list in C, letting programs use the name by which they were invoked in their execution. It's often convenient to have access to the program name in case you want to print it in messages or change the behavior of the program based on what command line alias was used to invoke the program. But for the purposes of this chapter, we'll ignore it and save only the two arguments we need.

Saving the Argument Values in Variables

The program is currently able to access the values specified as command line arguments. Now we need to save the values of the two arguments in variables so we can use the values throughout the rest of the program. We do that in Listing 12-2.

src/main.rs
```
use std::env;

fn main() {
    let args: Vec<String> = env::args().collect();

    let query = &args[1];
    let file_path = &args[2];

    println!("Searching for {}", query);
    println!("In file {}", file_path);
}
```

Listing 12-2: Creating variables to hold the query argument and file path argument

As we saw when we printed the vector, the program's name takes up the first value in the vector at args[0], so we're starting arguments at index 1. The first argument minigrep takes is the string we're searching for, so we put a reference to the first argument in the variable query. The second argument will be the file path, so we put a reference to the second argument in the variable file_path.

We temporarily print the values of these variables to prove that the code is working as we intend. Let's run this program again with the arguments test and sample.txt:

```
$ cargo run -- test sample.txt
   Compiling minigrep v0.1.0 (file:///projects/minigrep)
    Finished dev [unoptimized + debuginfo] target(s) in 0.0s
     Running `target/debug/minigrep test sample.txt`
Searching for test
In file sample.txt
```

Great, the program is working! The values of the arguments we need are being saved into the right variables. Later we'll add some error handling to deal with certain potential erroneous situations, such as when the user provides no arguments; for now, we'll ignore that situation and work on adding file-reading capabilities instead.

Reading a File

Now we'll add functionality to read the file specified in the file_path argument. First we need a sample file to test it with: we'll use a file with a small amount of text over multiple lines with some repeated words. Listing 12-3 has an Emily Dickinson poem that will work well! Create a file called *poem.txt* at the root level of your project, and enter the poem "I'm Nobody! Who are you?"

poem.txt
```
I'm nobody! Who are you?
Are you nobody, too?
Then there's a pair of us - don't tell!
They'd banish us, you know.

How dreary to be somebody!
How public, like a frog
To tell your name the livelong day
To an admiring bog!
```

Listing 12-3: A poem by Emily Dickinson makes a good test case.

With the text in place, edit *src/main.rs* and add code to read the file, as shown in Listing 12-4.

src/main.rs
```
use std::env;
❶ use std::fs;

fn main() {
    --snip--
    println!("In file {}", file_path);

❷  let contents = fs::read_to_string(file_path)
        .expect("Should have been able to read the file");

❸  println!("With text:\n{contents}");
}
```

Listing 12-4: Reading the contents of the file specified by the second argument

First we bring in a relevant part of the standard library with a use statement: we need std::fs to handle files ❶.

In main, the new statement fs::read_to_string takes the file_path, opens that file, and returns an std::io::Result<String> of the file's contents ❷.

After that, we again add a temporary println! statement that prints the value of contents after the file is read, so we can check that the program is working so far ❸.

Let's run this code with any string as the first command line argument (because we haven't implemented the searching part yet) and the *poem.txt* file as the second argument:

```
$ cargo run -- the poem.txt
   Compiling minigrep v0.1.0 (file:///projects/minigrep)
    Finished dev [unoptimized + debuginfo] target(s) in 0.0s
     Running `target/debug/minigrep the poem.txt`
Searching for the
In file poem.txt
With text:
I'm nobody! Who are you?
Are you nobody, too?
Then there's a pair of us - don't tell!
They'd banish us, you know.

How dreary to be somebody!
How public, like a frog
To tell your name the livelong day
To an admiring bog!
```

Great! The code read and then printed the contents of the file. But the code has a few flaws. At the moment, the main function has multiple responsibilities: generally, functions are clearer and easier to maintain if each function is responsible for only one idea. The other problem is that we're not handling errors as well as we could. The program is still small, so these flaws aren't a big problem, but as the program grows, it will be harder to fix them cleanly. It's a good practice to begin refactoring early on when developing a program because it's much easier to refactor smaller amounts of code. We'll do that next.

Refactoring to Improve Modularity and Error Handling

To improve our program, we'll fix four problems that have to do with the program's structure and how it's handling potential errors. First, our main function now performs two tasks: it parses arguments and reads files. As our program grows, the number of separate tasks the main function handles will increase. As a function gains responsibilities, it becomes more difficult to reason about, harder to test, and harder to change without breaking one of its parts. It's best to separate functionality so each function is responsible for one task.

This issue also ties into the second problem: although query and file _path are configuration variables to our program, variables like contents are used to perform the program's logic. The longer main becomes, the more variables we'll need to bring into scope; the more variables we have in scope, the harder it will be to keep track of the purpose of each. It's best to group the configuration variables into one structure to make their purpose clear.

The third problem is that we've used expect to print an error message when reading the file fails, but the error message just prints Should have been able to read the file. Reading a file can fail in a number of ways: for example, the file could be missing, or we might not have permission to open it. Right now, regardless of the situation, we'd print the same error message for everything, which wouldn't give the user any information!

Fourth, we use `expect` repeatedly to handle different errors, and if the user runs our program without specifying enough arguments, they'll get an `index out of bounds` error from Rust that doesn't clearly explain the problem. It would be best if all the error-handling code were in one place so future maintainers had only one place to consult the code if the error-handling logic needed to change. Having all the error-handling code in one place will also ensure that we're printing messages that will be meaningful to our end users.

Let's address these four problems by refactoring our project.

Separation of Concerns for Binary Projects

The organizational problem of allocating responsibility for multiple tasks to the `main` function is common to many binary projects. As a result, the Rust community has developed guidelines for splitting the separate concerns of a binary program when `main` starts getting large. This process has the following steps:

- Split your program into a *main.rs* file and a *lib.rs* file and move your program's logic to *lib.rs*.
- As long as your command line parsing logic is small, it can remain in *main.rs*.
- When the command line parsing logic starts getting complicated, extract it from *main.rs* and move it to *lib.rs*.

The responsibilities that remain in the `main` function after this process should be limited to the following:

- Calling the command line parsing logic with the argument values
- Setting up any other configuration
- Calling a `run` function in *lib.rs*
- Handling the error if `run` returns an error

This pattern is about separating concerns: *main.rs* handles running the program and *lib.rs* handles all the logic of the task at hand. Because you can't test the `main` function directly, this structure lets you test all of your program's logic by moving it into functions in *lib.rs*. The code that remains in *main.rs* will be small enough to verify its correctness by reading it. Let's rework our program by following this process.

Extracting the Argument Parser

We'll extract the functionality for parsing arguments into a function that `main` will call to prepare for moving the command line parsing logic to *src/lib.rs*. Listing 12-5 shows the new start of `main` that calls a new function `parse_config`, which we'll define in *src/main.rs* for the moment.

```
fn main() {
    let args: Vec<String> = env::args().collect();

    let (query, file_path) = parse_config(&args);

    --snip--
}

fn parse_config(args: &[String]) -> (&str, &str) {
    let query = &args[1];
    let file_path = &args[2];

    (query, file_path)
}
```

Listing 12-5: Extracting a parse_config function from main

We're still collecting the command line arguments into a vector, but instead of assigning the argument value at index 1 to the variable query and the argument value at index 2 to the variable file_path within the main function, we pass the whole vector to the parse_config function. The parse_config function then holds the logic that determines which argument goes in which variable and passes the values back to main. We still create the query and file_path variables in main, but main no longer has the responsibility of determining how the command line arguments and variables correspond.

This rework may seem like overkill for our small program, but we're refactoring in small, incremental steps. After making this change, run the program again to verify that the argument parsing still works. It's good to check your progress often, to help identify the cause of problems when they occur.

Grouping Configuration Values

We can take another small step to improve the parse_config function further. At the moment, we're returning a tuple, but then we immediately break that tuple into individual parts again. This is a sign that perhaps we don't have the right abstraction yet.

Another indicator that shows there's room for improvement is the config part of parse_config, which implies that the two values we return are related and are both part of one configuration value. We're not currently conveying this meaning in the structure of the data other than by grouping the two values into a tuple; we'll instead put the two values into one struct and give each of the struct fields a meaningful name. Doing so will make it easier for future maintainers of this code to understand how the different values relate to each other and what their purpose is.

Listing 12-6 shows the improvements to the parse_config function.

```
fn main() {
    let args: Vec<String> = env::args().collect();

  ❶ let config = parse_config(&args);
```

```
        println!("Searching for {}",❷ config.query);
        println!("In file {}",❸ config.file_path);

        let contents = fs::read_to_string(❹config.file_path)
            .expect("Should have been able to read the file");

        --snip--
    }

❺ struct Config {
        query: String,
        file_path: String,
    }

❻ fn parse_config(args: &[String]) -> Config {
    ❼ let query = args[1].clone();
    ❽ let file_path = args[2].clone();

        Config { query, file_path }
    }
```

Listing 12-6: Refactoring parse_config *to return an instance of a* Config *struct*

We've added a struct named Config defined to have fields named query and file_path ❺. The signature of parse_config now indicates that it returns a Config value ❻. In the body of parse_config, where we used to return string slices that reference String values in args, we now define Config to contain owned String values. The args variable in main is the owner of the argument values and is only letting the parse_config function borrow them, which means we'd violate Rust's borrowing rules if Config tried to take ownership of the values in args.

There are a number of ways we could manage the String data; the easiest, though somewhat inefficient, route is to call the clone method on the values ❼ ❽. This will make a full copy of the data for the Config instance to own, which takes more time and memory than storing a reference to the string data. However, cloning the data also makes our code very straightforward because we don't have to manage the lifetimes of the references; in this circumstance, giving up a little performance to gain simplicity is a worthwhile trade-off.

THE TRADE-OFFS OF USING CLONE

There's a tendency among many Rustaceans to avoid using clone to fix ownership problems because of its runtime cost. In Chapter 13, you'll learn how to use more efficient methods in this type of situation. But for now, it's okay to copy a few strings to continue making progress because you'll make these copies only once and your file path and query string are very small. It's better to have a working program that's a bit inefficient than to try to hyperoptimize code on your first pass. As you become more experienced with Rust, it'll be easier to start with the most efficient solution, but for now, it's perfectly acceptable to call clone.

We've updated main so it places the instance of Config returned by parse
_config into a variable named config ❶, and we updated the code that previ-
ously used the separate query and file_path variables so it now uses the fields
on the Config struct instead ❷ ❸ ❹.

Now our code more clearly conveys that query and file_path are related
and that their purpose is to configure how the program will work. Any code
that uses these values knows to find them in the config instance in the fields
named for their purpose.

Creating a Constructor for Config

So far, we've extracted the logic responsible for parsing the command line
arguments from main and placed it in the parse_config function. Doing
so helped us see that the query and file_path values were related, and that
relationship should be conveyed in our code. We then added a Config struct
to name the related purpose of query and file_path and to be able to return
the values' names as struct field names from the parse_config function.

So now that the purpose of the parse_config function is to create a
Config instance, we can change parse_config from a plain function to a function named new that is associated with the Config struct. Making this change
will make the code more idiomatic. We can create instances of types in the
standard library, such as String, by calling String::new. Similarly, by changing parse_config into a new function associated with Config, we'll be able
to create instances of Config by calling Config::new. Listing 12-7 shows the
changes we need to make.

src/main.rs
```
fn main() {
    let args: Vec<String> = env::args().collect();

❶   let config = Config::new(&args);

    --snip--
}

--snip--

❷ impl Config {
❸   fn new(args: &[String]) -> Config {
        let query = args[1].clone();
        let file_path = args[2].clone();

        Config { query, file_path }
    }
}
```

Listing 12-7: Changing parse_config *into* Config::new

We've updated main where we were calling parse_config to instead call
Config::new ❶. We've changed the name of parse_config to new ❸ and moved
it within an impl block ❷, which associates the new function with Config. Try
compiling this code again to make sure it works.

Fixing the Error Handling

Now we'll work on fixing our error handling. Recall that attempting to access the values in the args vector at index 1 or index 2 will cause the program to panic if the vector contains fewer than three items. Try running the program without any arguments; it will look like this:

```
$ cargo run
   Compiling minigrep v0.1.0 (file:///projects/minigrep)
    Finished dev [unoptimized + debuginfo] target(s) in 0.0s
     Running `target/debug/minigrep`
thread 'main' panicked at 'index out of bounds: the len is 1 but
the index is 1', src/main.rs:27:21
note: run with `RUST_BACKTRACE=1` environment variable to display
a backtrace
```

The line index out of bounds: the len is 1 but the index is 1 is an error message intended for programmers. It won't help our end users understand what they should do instead. Let's fix that now.

Improving the Error Message

In Listing 12-8, we add a check in the new function that will verify that the slice is long enough before accessing index 1 and index 2. If the slice isn't long enough, the program panics and displays a better error message.

src/main.rs
```
--snip--
fn new(args: &[String]) -> Config {
    if args.len() < 3 {
        panic!("not enough arguments");
    }
    --snip--
```

Listing 12-8: Adding a check for the number of arguments

This code is similar to the Guess::new function we wrote in Listing 9-13, where we called panic! when the value argument was out of the range of valid values. Instead of checking for a range of values here, we're checking that the length of args is at least 3 and the rest of the function can operate under the assumption that this condition has been met. If args has fewer than three items, this condition will be true, and we call the panic! macro to end the program immediately.

With these extra few lines of code in new, let's run the program without any arguments again to see what the error looks like now:

```
$ cargo run
   Compiling minigrep v0.1.0 (file:///projects/minigrep)
    Finished dev [unoptimized + debuginfo] target(s) in 0.0s
     Running `target/debug/minigrep`
thread 'main' panicked at 'not enough arguments',
src/main.rs:26:13
note: run with `RUST_BACKTRACE=1` environment variable to display
a backtrace
```

This output is better: we now have a reasonable error message. However, we also have extraneous information we don't want to give to our users. Perhaps the technique we used in Listing 9-13 isn't the best one to use here: a call to panic! is more appropriate for a programming problem than a usage problem, as discussed in Chapter 9. Instead, we'll use the other technique you learned about in Chapter 9—returning a Result that indicates either success or an error.

Returning a Result Instead of Calling panic!

We can instead return a Result value that will contain a Config instance in the successful case and will describe the problem in the error case. We're also going to change the function name from new to build because many programmers expect new functions to never fail. When Config::build is communicating to main, we can use the Result type to signal there was a problem. Then we can change main to convert an Err variant into a more practical error for our users without the surrounding text about thread 'main' and RUST_BACKTRACE that a call to panic! causes.

Listing 12-9 shows the changes we need to make to the return value of the function we're now calling Config::build and the body of the function needed to return a Result. Note that this won't compile until we update main as well, which we'll do in the next listing.

src/main.rs
```
impl Config {
    fn build(args: &[String]) -> Result<Config, &'static str> {
        if args.len() < 3 {
            return Err("not enough arguments");
        }

        let query = args[1].clone();
        let file_path = args[2].clone();

        Ok(Config { query, file_path })
    }
}
```

Listing 12-9: Returning a Result from Config::build

Our build function returns a Result with a Config instance in the success case and an &'static str in the error case. Our error values will always be string literals that have the 'static lifetime.

We've made two changes in the body of the function: instead of calling panic! when the user doesn't pass enough arguments, we now return an Err value, and we've wrapped the Config return value in an Ok. These changes make the function conform to its new type signature.

Returning an Err value from Config::build allows the main function to handle the Result value returned from the build function and exit the process more cleanly in the error case.

Calling Config::build and Handling Errors

To handle the error case and print a user-friendly message, we need to update main to handle the Result being returned by Config::build, as shown in Listing 12-10. We'll also take the responsibility of exiting the command line tool with a nonzero error code away from panic! and instead implement it by hand. A nonzero exit status is a convention to signal to the process that called our program that the program exited with an error state.

src/main.rs ❶ `use std::process;`

```
fn main() {
    let args: Vec<String> = env::args().collect();

❷  let config = Config::build(&args).❸unwrap_or_else(|❹err| {
❺      println!("Problem parsing arguments: {err}");
❻      process::exit(1);
    });

    --snip--
```

Listing 12-10: Exiting with an error code if building a Config fails

In this listing, we've used a method we haven't covered in detail yet: unwrap_or_else, which is defined on Result<T, E> by the standard library ❷. Using unwrap_or_else allows us to define some custom, non-panic! error handling. If the Result is an Ok value, this method's behavior is similar to unwrap: it returns the inner value that Ok is wrapping. However, if the value is an Err value, this method calls the code in the *closure*, which is an anonymous function we define and pass as an argument to unwrap_or_else ❸. We'll cover closures in more detail in Chapter 13. For now, you just need to know that unwrap_or_else will pass the inner value of the Err, which in this case is the static string "not enough arguments" that we added in Listing 12-9, to our closure in the argument err that appears between the vertical pipes ❹. The code in the closure can then use the err value when it runs.

We've added a new use line to bring process from the standard library into scope ❶. The code in the closure that will be run in the error case is only two lines: we print the err value ❺ and then call process::exit ❻. The process::exit function will stop the program immediately and return the number that was passed as the exit status code. This is similar to the panic!-based handling we used in Listing 12-8, but we no longer get all the extra output. Let's try it:

```
$ cargo run
   Compiling minigrep v0.1.0 (file:///projects/minigrep)
    Finished dev [unoptimized + debuginfo] target(s) in 0.48s
     Running `target/debug/minigrep`
Problem parsing arguments: not enough arguments
```

Great! This output is much friendlier for our users.

Extracting Logic from main

Now that we've finished refactoring the configuration parsing, let's turn to the program's logic. As we stated in "Separation of Concerns for Binary Projects" on page 249, we'll extract a function named run that will hold all the logic currently in the main function that isn't involved with setting up configuration or handling errors. When we're done, main will be concise and easy to verify by inspection, and we'll be able to write tests for all the other logic.

Listing 12-11 shows the extracted run function. For now, we're just making the small, incremental improvement of extracting the function. We're still defining the function in *src/main.rs*.

src/main.rs
```
fn main() {
    --snip--

    println!("Searching for {}", config.query);
    println!("In file {}", config.file_path);

    run(config);
}

fn run(config: Config) {
    let contents = fs::read_to_string(config.file_path)
        .expect("Should have been able to read the file");

    println!("With text:\n{contents}");
}

--snip--
```

Listing 12-11: Extracting a run function containing the rest of the program logic

The run function now contains all the remaining logic from main, starting from reading the file. The run function takes the Config instance as an argument.

Returning Errors from the run Function

With the remaining program logic separated into the run function, we can improve the error handling, as we did with Config::build in Listing 12-9. Instead of allowing the program to panic by calling expect, the run function will return a Result<T, E> when something goes wrong. This will let us further consolidate the logic around handling errors into main in a user-friendly way. Listing 12-12 shows the changes we need to make to the signature and body of run.

src/main.rs ❶ use std::error::Error;

```
    --snip--

❷ fn run(config: Config) -> Result<(), Box<dyn Error>> {
    let contents = fs::read_to_string(config.file_path)❸?;

    println!("With text:\n{contents}");
```

```
❹ Ok(())
}
```

Listing 12-12: Changing the run *function to return* Result

We've made three significant changes here. First, we changed the return type of the run function to Result<(), Box<dyn Error>> ❷. This function previously returned the unit type, (), and we keep that as the value returned in the Ok case.

For the error type, we used the *trait object* Box<dyn Error> (and we've brought std::error::Error into scope with a use statement at the top ❶). We'll cover trait objects in Chapter 17. For now, just know that Box<dyn Error> means the function will return a type that implements the Error trait, but we don't have to specify what particular type the return value will be. This gives us flexibility to return error values that may be of different types in different error cases. The dyn keyword is short for *dynamic*.

Second, we've removed the call to expect in favor of the ? operator ❸, as we talked about in Chapter 9. Rather than panic! on an error, ? will return the error value from the current function for the caller to handle.

Third, the run function now returns an Ok value in the success case ❹. We've declared the run function's success type as () in the signature, which means we need to wrap the unit type value in the Ok value. This Ok(()) syntax might look a bit strange at first, but using () like this is the idiomatic way to indicate that we're calling run for its side effects only; it doesn't return a value we need.

When you run this code, it will compile but will display a warning:

```
warning: unused `Result` that must be used
  --> src/main.rs:19:5
   |
19 |     run(config);
   |     ^^^^^^^^^^^
   |
   = note: `#[warn(unused_must_use)]` on by default
   = note: this `Result` may be an `Err` variant, which should be
handled
```

Rust tells us that our code ignored the Result value and the Result value might indicate that an error occurred. But we're not checking to see whether or not there was an error, and the compiler reminds us that we probably meant to have some error-handling code here! Let's rectify that problem now.

Handling Errors Returned from run in main

We'll check for errors and handle them using a technique similar to one we used with Config::build in Listing 12-10, but with a slight difference:

src/main.rs
```
fn main() {
    --snip--
```

```
    println!("Searching for {}", config.query);
    println!("In file {}", config.file_path);

    if let Err(e) = run(config) {
        println!("Application error: {e}");
        process::exit(1);
    }
}
```

We use if let rather than unwrap_or_else to check whether run returns an Err value and to call process::exit(1) if it does. The run function doesn't return a value that we want to unwrap in the same way that Config::build returns the Config instance. Because run returns () in the success case, we only care about detecting an error, so we don't need unwrap_or_else to return the unwrapped value, which would only be ().

The bodies of the if let and the unwrap_or_else functions are the same in both cases: we print the error and exit.

Splitting Code into a Library Crate

Our minigrep project is looking good so far! Now we'll split the *src/main.rs* file and put some code into the *src/lib.rs* file. That way, we can test the code and have a *src/main.rs* file with fewer responsibilities.

Let's move all the code that isn't in the main function from *src/main.rs* to *src/lib.rs*:

- The run function definition
- The relevant use statements
- The definition of Config
- The Config::build function definition

The contents of *src/lib.rs* should have the signatures shown in Listing 12-13 (we've omitted the bodies of the functions for brevity). Note that this won't compile until we modify *src/main.rs* in Listing 12-14.

src/lib.rs
```
use std::error::Error;
use std::fs;

pub struct Config {
    pub query: String,
    pub file_path: String,
}

impl Config {
    pub fn build(
        args: &[String],
    ) -> Result<Config, &'static str> {
        --snip--
    }
}
```

```
pub fn run(config: Config) -> Result<(), Box<dyn Error>> {
    --snip--
}
```

Listing 12-13: Moving `Config` *and* `run` *into* src/lib.rs

We've made liberal use of the `pub` keyword: on `Config`, on its fields and its build method, and on the run function. We now have a library crate that has a public API we can test!

Now we need to bring the code we moved to *src/lib.rs* into the scope of the binary crate in *src/main.rs*, as shown in Listing 12-14.

src/main.rs
```
use std::env;
use std::process;

use minigrep::Config;

fn main() {
    --snip--
    if let Err(e) = minigrep::run(config) {
        --snip--
    }
}
```

Listing 12-14: Using the `minigrep` *library crate in* src/main.rs

We add a use `minigrep::Config` line to bring the `Config` type from the library crate into the binary crate's scope, and we prefix the run function with our crate name. Now all the functionality should be connected and should work. Run the program with `cargo run` and make sure everything works correctly.

Whew! That was a lot of work, but we've set ourselves up for success in the future. Now it's much easier to handle errors, and we've made the code more modular. Almost all of our work will be done in *src/lib.rs* from here on out.

Let's take advantage of this newfound modularity by doing something that would have been difficult with the old code but is easy with the new code: we'll write some tests!

Developing the Library's Functionality with Test-Driven Development

Now that we've extracted the logic into *src/lib.rs* and left the argument collecting and error handling in *src/main.rs*, it's much easier to write tests for the core functionality of our code. We can call functions directly with various arguments and check return values without having to call our binary from the command line.

In this section, we'll add the searching logic to the `minigrep` program using the test-driven development (TDD) process with the following steps:

1. Write a test that fails and run it to make sure it fails for the reason you expect.

2. Write or modify just enough code to make the new test pass.

3. Refactor the code you just added or changed and make sure the tests continue to pass.

4. Repeat from step 1!

Though it's just one of many ways to write software, TDD can help drive code design. Writing the test before you write the code that makes the test pass helps to maintain high test coverage throughout the process.

We'll test-drive the implementation of the functionality that will actually do the searching for the query string in the file contents and produce a list of lines that match the query. We'll add this functionality in a function called search.

Writing a Failing Test

Because we don't need them anymore, let's remove the println! statements from *src/lib.rs* and *src/main.rs* that we used to check the program's behavior. Then, in *src/lib.rs*, we'll add a tests module with a test function, as we did in Chapter 11. The test function specifies the behavior we want the search function to have: it will take a query and the text to search, and it will return only the lines from the text that contain the query. Listing 12-15 shows this test, which won't compile yet.

src/lib.rs
```
#[cfg(test)]
mod tests {
    use super::*;

    #[test]
    fn one_result() {
        let query = "duct";
        let contents = "\
Rust:
safe, fast, productive.
Pick three.";

        assert_eq!(
            vec!["safe, fast, productive."],
            search(query, contents)
        );
    }
}
```

Listing 12-15: Creating a failing test for the search function we wish we had

This test searches for the string "duct". The text we're searching is three lines, only one of which contains "duct" (note that the backslash after the opening double quote tells Rust not to put a newline character at the beginning of the contents of this string literal). We assert that the value returned from the search function contains only the line we expect.

We aren't yet able to run this test and watch it fail because the test doesn't even compile: the search function doesn't exist yet! In accordance with TDD principles, we'll add just enough code to get the test to compile and run by adding a definition of the search function that always returns an empty vector, as shown in Listing 12-16. Then the test should compile and fail because an empty vector doesn't match a vector containing the line `"safe, fast, productive."`

src/lib.rs
```
pub fn search<'a>(
    query: &str,
    contents: &'a str,
) -> Vec<&'a str> {
    vec![]
}
```

Listing 12-16: Defining just enough of the search function so our test will compile

Notice that we need to define an explicit lifetime `'a` in the signature of search and use that lifetime with the `contents` argument and the return value. Recall in Chapter 10 that the lifetime parameters specify which argument lifetime is connected to the lifetime of the return value. In this case, we indicate that the returned vector should contain string slices that reference slices of the argument `contents` (rather than the argument `query`).

In other words, we tell Rust that the data returned by the search function will live as long as the data passed into the search function in the `contents` argument. This is important! The data referenced *by* a slice needs to be valid for the reference to be valid; if the compiler assumes we're making string slices of `query` rather than `contents`, it will do its safety checking incorrectly.

If we forget the lifetime annotations and try to compile this function, we'll get this error:

```
error[E0106]: missing lifetime specifier
  --> src/lib.rs:31:10
   |
29 |     query: &str,
   |            ----
30 |     contents: &str,
   |               ----
31 | ) -> Vec<&str> {
   |          ^ expected named lifetime parameter
   |
   = help: this function's return type contains a borrowed value, but the
signature does not say whether it is borrowed from `query` or `contents`
help: consider introducing a named lifetime parameter
   |
28 ~ pub fn search<'a>(
29 ~     query: &'a str,
30 ~     contents: &'a str,
31 ~ ) -> Vec<&'a str> {
   |
```

Rust can't possibly know which of the two arguments we need, so we need to tell it explicitly. Because `contents` is the argument that contains all of our text and we want to return the parts of that text that match, we know `contents` is the argument that should be connected to the return value using the lifetime syntax.

Other programming languages don't require you to connect arguments to return values in the signature, but this practice will get easier over time. You might want to compare this example with the examples in "Validating References with Lifetimes" on page 201.

Now let's run the test:

```
$ cargo test
   Compiling minigrep v0.1.0 (file:///projects/minigrep)
    Finished test [unoptimized + debuginfo] target(s) in 0.97s
     Running unittests src/lib.rs (target/debug/deps/minigrep-9cd200e5fac0fc94)

running 1 test
test tests::one_result ... FAILED

failures:

---- tests::one_result stdout ----
thread 'tests::one_result' panicked at 'assertion failed: `(left == right)`
  left: `["safe, fast, productive."]`,
 right: `[]`', src/lib.rs:47:9
note: run with `RUST_BACKTRACE=1` environment variable to display a backtrace


failures:
    tests::one_result

test result: FAILED. 0 passed; 1 failed; 0 ignored; 0 measured; 0 filtered out;
finished in 0.00s

error: test failed, to rerun pass '--lib'
```

Great, the test fails, exactly as we expected. Let's get the test to pass!

Writing Code to Pass the Test

Currently, our test is failing because we always return an empty vector. To fix that and implement search, our program needs to follow these steps:

1. Iterate through each line of the contents.
2. Check whether the line contains our query string.
3. If it does, add it to the list of values we're returning.
4. If it doesn't, do nothing.
5. Return the list of results that match.

Let's work through each step, starting with iterating through lines.

Iterating Through Lines with the lines Method

Rust has a helpful method to handle line-by-line iteration of strings, conveniently named lines, that works as shown in Listing 12-17. Note that this won't compile yet.

src/lib.rs

```
pub fn search<'a>(
    query: &str,
    contents: &'a str,
) -> Vec<&'a str> {
    for line in contents.lines() {
        // do something with line
    }
}
```

Listing 12-17: Iterating through each line in contents

The lines method returns an iterator. We'll talk about iterators in depth in Chapter 13, but recall that you saw this way of using an iterator in Listing 3-5, where we used a for loop with an iterator to run some code on each item in a collection.

Searching Each Line for the Query

Next, we'll check whether the current line contains our query string. Fortunately, strings have a helpful method named contains that does this for us! Add a call to the contains method in the search function, as shown in Listing 12-18. Note that this still won't compile yet.

src/lib.rs

```
pub fn search<'a>(
    query: &str,
    contents: &'a str,
) -> Vec<&'a str> {
    for line in contents.lines() {
        if line.contains(query) {
            // do something with line
        }
    }
}
```

Listing 12-18: Adding functionality to see whether the line contains the string in query

At the moment, we're building up functionality. To get the code to compile, we need to return a value from the body as we indicated we would in the function signature.

Storing Matching Lines

To finish this function, we need a way to store the matching lines that we want to return. For that, we can make a mutable vector before the for loop and call the push method to store a line in the vector. After the for loop, we return the vector, as shown in Listing 12-19.

src/lib.rs

```
pub fn search<'a>(
    query: &str,
    contents: &'a str,
) -> Vec<&'a str> {
    let mut results = Vec::new();
```

```
    for line in contents.lines() {
        if line.contains(query) {
            results.push(line);
        }
    }

    results
}
```

Listing 12-19: Storing the lines that match so we can return them

Now the search function should return only the lines that contain query, and our test should pass. Let's run the test:

```
$ cargo test
--snip--
running 1 test
test tests::one_result ... ok

test result: ok. 1 passed; 0 failed; 0 ignored; 0 measured; 0
filtered out; finished in 0.00s
```

Our test passed, so we know it works!

At this point, we could consider opportunities for refactoring the implementation of the search function while keeping the tests passing to maintain the same functionality. The code in the search function isn't too bad, but it doesn't take advantage of some useful features of iterators. We'll return to this example in Chapter 13, where we'll explore iterators in detail, and look at how to improve it.

Using the search Function in the run Function

Now that the search function is working and tested, we need to call search from our run function. We need to pass the config.query value and the contents that run reads from the file to the search function. Then run will print each line returned from search:

src/lib.rs
```
pub fn run(config: Config) -> Result<(), Box<dyn Error>> {
    let contents = fs::read_to_string(config.file_path)?;

    for line in search(&config.query, &contents) {
        println!("{line}");
    }

    Ok(())
}
```

We're still using a for loop to return each line from search and print it.

Now the entire program should work! Let's try it out, first with a word that should return exactly one line from the Emily Dickinson poem: *frog.*

```
$ cargo run -- frog poem.txt
   Compiling minigrep v0.1.0 (file:///projects/minigrep)
```

```
    Finished dev [unoptimized + debuginfo] target(s) in 0.38s
     Running `target/debug/minigrep frog poem.txt`
How public, like a frog
```

Cool! Now let's try a word that will match multiple lines, like *body*:

```
$ cargo run -- body poem.txt
    Finished dev [unoptimized + debuginfo] target(s) in 0.0s
     Running `target/debug/minigrep body poem.txt`
I'm nobody! Who are you?
Are you nobody, too?
How dreary to be somebody!
```

And finally, let's make sure that we don't get any lines when we search for a word that isn't anywhere in the poem, such as *monomorphization*:

```
$ cargo run -- monomorphization poem.txt
    Finished dev [unoptimized + debuginfo] target(s) in 0.0s
     Running `target/debug/minigrep monomorphization poem.txt`
```

Excellent! We've built our own mini version of a classic tool and learned a lot about how to structure applications. We've also learned a bit about file input and output, lifetimes, testing, and command line parsing.

To round out this project, we'll briefly demonstrate how to work with environment variables and how to print to standard error, both of which are useful when you're writing command line programs.

Working with Environment Variables

We'll improve minigrep by adding an extra feature: an option for case-insensitive searching that the user can turn on via an environment variable. We could make this feature a command line option and require that users enter it each time they want it to apply, but by instead making it an environment variable, we allow our users to set the environment variable once and have all their searches be case insensitive in that terminal session.

Writing a Failing Test for the Case-Insensitive Search Function

We first add a new search_case_insensitive function that will be called when the environment variable has a value. We'll continue to follow the TDD process, so the first step is again to write a failing test. We'll add a new test for the new search_case_insensitive function and rename our old test from one_result to case_sensitive to clarify the differences between the two tests, as shown in Listing 12-20.

src/lib.rs
```
#[cfg(test)]
mod tests {
    use super::*;

    #[test]
    fn case_sensitive() {
```

```
        let query = "duct";
        let contents = "\
Rust:
safe, fast, productive.
Pick three.
Duct tape.";

        assert_eq!(
            vec!["safe, fast, productive."],
            search(query, contents)
        );
    }

    #[test]
    fn case_insensitive() {
        let query = "rUsT";
        let contents = "\
Rust:
safe, fast, productive.
Pick three.
Trust me.";

        assert_eq!(
            vec!["Rust:", "Trust me."],
            search_case_insensitive(query, contents)
        );
    }
}
```

Listing 12-20: Adding a new failing test for the case-insensitive function we're about to add

Note that we've edited the old test's contents too. We've added a new line with the text "Duct tape." using a capital *D* that shouldn't match the query "duct" when we're searching in a case-sensitive manner. Changing the old test in this way helps ensure that we don't accidentally break the case-sensitive search functionality that we've already implemented. This test should pass now and should continue to pass as we work on the case-insensitive search.

The new test for the case-*insensitive* search uses "rUsT" as its query. In the search_case_insensitive function we're about to add, the query "rUsT" should match the line containing "Rust:" with a capital *R* and match the line "Trust me." even though both have different casing from the query. This is our failing test, and it will fail to compile because we haven't yet defined the search_case_insensitive function. Feel free to add a skeleton implementation that always returns an empty vector, similar to the way we did for the search function in Listing 12-16 to see the test compile and fail.

Implementing the search_case_insensitive Function

The search_case_insensitive function, shown in Listing 12-21, will be almost the same as the search function. The only difference is that we'll lowercase the query and each line so that whatever the case of the input arguments, they'll be the same case when we check whether the line contains the query.

src/lib.rs
```rust
pub fn search_case_insensitive<'a>(
    query: &str,
    contents: &'a str,
) -> Vec<&'a str> {
  ❶ let query = query.to_lowercase();
    let mut results = Vec::new();

    for line in contents.lines() {
        if ❷ line.to_lowercase().contains(❸&query) {
            results.push(line);
        }
    }

    results
}
```

Listing 12-21: Defining the search_case_insensitive function to lowercase the query and the line before comparing them

First we lowercase the query string and store it in a shadowed variable with the same name ❶. Calling to_lowercase on the query is necessary so that no matter whether the user's query is "rust", "RUST", "Rust", or "rUsT", we'll treat the query as if it were "rust" and be insensitive to the case. While to_lowercase will handle basic Unicode, it won't be 100 percent accurate. If we were writing a real application, we'd want to do a bit more work here, but this section is about environment variables, not Unicode, so we'll leave it at that here.

Note that query is now a String rather than a string slice because calling to_lowercase creates new data rather than referencing existing data. Say the query is "rUsT", as an example: that string slice doesn't contain a lowercase u or t for us to use, so we have to allocate a new String containing "rust". When we pass query as an argument to the contains method now, we need to add an ampersand ❸ because the signature of contains is defined to take a string slice.

Next, we add a call to to_lowercase on each line to lowercase all characters ❷. Now that we've converted line and query to lowercase, we'll find matches no matter what the case of the query is.

Let's see if this implementation passes the tests:

```
running 2 tests
test tests::case_insensitive ... ok
test tests::case_sensitive ... ok

test result: ok. 2 passed; 0 failed; 0 ignored; 0 measured; 0
filtered out; finished in 0.00s
```

Great! They passed. Now, let's call the new search_case_insensitive function from the run function. First we'll add a configuration option to the Config struct to switch between case-sensitive and case-insensitive search.

Adding this field will cause compiler errors because we aren't initializing this field anywhere yet:

src/lib.rs

```
pub struct Config {
    pub query: String,
    pub file_path: String,
    pub ignore_case: bool,
}
```

We added the ignore_case field that holds a Boolean. Next, we need the run function to check the ignore_case field's value and use that to decide whether to call the search function or the search_case_insensitive function, as shown in Listing 12-22. This still won't compile yet.

src/lib.rs

```
pub fn run(config: Config) -> Result<(), Box<dyn Error>> {
    let contents = fs::read_to_string(config.file_path)?;

    let results = if config.ignore_case {
        search_case_insensitive(&config.query, &contents)
    } else {
        search(&config.query, &contents)
    };

    for line in results {
        println!("{line}");
    }

    Ok(())
}
```

Listing 12-22: Calling either search or search_case_insensitive based on the value in config.ignore_case

Finally, we need to check for the environment variable. The functions for working with environment variables are in the env module in the standard library, so we bring that module into scope at the top of *src/lib.rs*. Then we'll use the var function from the env module to check to see if any value has been set for an environment variable named IGNORE_CASE, as shown in Listing 12-23.

src/lib.rs

```
use std::env;
--snip--

impl Config {
    pub fn build(
        args: &[String]
    ) -> Result<Config, &'static str> {
        if args.len() < 3 {
            return Err("not enough arguments");
        }
```

```
    let query = args[1].clone();
    let file_path = args[2].clone();

    let ignore_case = env::var("IGNORE_CASE").is_ok();

    Ok(Config {
        query,
        file_path,
        ignore_case,
    })
    }
}
```

Listing 12-23: Checking for any value in an environment variable named IGNORE_CASE

Here, we create a new variable, ignore_case. To set its value, we call the env::var function and pass it the name of the IGNORE_CASE environment variable. The env::var function returns a Result that will be the successful Ok variant that contains the value of the environment variable if the environment variable is set to any value. It will return the Err variant if the environment variable is not set.

We're using the is_ok method on the Result to check whether the environment variable is set, which means the program should do a case-insensitive search. If the IGNORE_CASE environment variable isn't set to anything, is_ok will return false and the program will perform a case-sensitive search. We don't care about the *value* of the environment variable, just whether it's set or unset, so we're checking is_ok rather than using unwrap, expect, or any of the other methods we've seen on Result.

We pass the value in the ignore_case variable to the Config instance so the run function can read that value and decide whether to call search_case _insensitive or search, as we implemented in Listing 12-22.

Let's give it a try! First we'll run our program without the environment variable set and with the query to, which should match any line that contains the word *to* in all lowercase:

```
$ cargo run -- to poem.txt
   Compiling minigrep v0.1.0 (file:///projects/minigrep)
    Finished dev [unoptimized + debuginfo] target(s) in 0.0s
     Running `target/debug/minigrep to poem.txt`
Are you nobody, too?
How dreary to be somebody!
```

Looks like that still works! Now let's run the program with IGNORE_CASE set to 1 but with the same query to:

```
$ IGNORE_CASE=1 cargo run -- to poem.txt
```

If you're using PowerShell, you will need to set the environment variable and run the program as separate commands:

```
PS> $Env:IGNORE_CASE=1; cargo run -- to poem.txt
```

This will make `IGNORE_CASE` persist for the remainder of your shell session. It can be unset with the `Remove-Item` cmdlet:

```
PS> Remove-Item Env:IGNORE_CASE
```

We should get lines that contain *to* that might have uppercase letters:

```
Are you nobody, too?
How dreary to be somebody!
To tell your name the livelong day
To an admiring bog!
```

Excellent, we also got lines containing *To*! Our `minigrep` program can now do case-insensitive searching controlled by an environment variable. Now you know how to manage options set using either command line arguments or environment variables.

Some programs allow arguments *and* environment variables for the same configuration. In those cases, the programs decide that one or the other takes precedence. For another exercise on your own, try controlling case sensitivity through either a command line argument or an environment variable. Decide whether the command line argument or the environment variable should take precedence if the program is run with one set to case sensitive and one set to ignore case.

The `std::env` module contains many more useful features for dealing with environment variables: check out its documentation to see what is available.

Writing Error Messages to Standard Error Instead of Standard Output

At the moment, we're writing all of our output to the terminal using the `println!` macro. In most terminals, there are two kinds of output: *standard output* (stdout) for general information and *standard error* (stderr) for error messages. This distinction enables users to choose to direct the successful output of a program to a file but still print error messages to the screen.

The `println!` macro is only capable of printing to standard output, so we have to use something else to print to standard error.

Checking Where Errors Are Written

First let's observe how the content printed by `minigrep` is currently being written to standard output, including any error messages we want to write to standard error instead. We'll do that by redirecting the standard output stream to a file while intentionally causing an error. We won't redirect the standard error stream, so any content sent to standard error will continue to display on the screen.

Command line programs are expected to send error messages to the standard error stream so we can still see error messages on the screen even if we redirect the standard output stream to a file. Our program is not currently well behaved: we're about to see that it saves the error message output to a file instead!

To demonstrate this behavior, we'll run the program with > and the file path, *output.txt*, that we want to redirect the standard output stream to. We won't pass any arguments, which should cause an error:

```
$ cargo run > output.txt
```

The > syntax tells the shell to write the contents of standard output to *output.txt* instead of the screen. We didn't see the error message we were expecting printed to the screen, so that means it must have ended up in the file. This is what *output.txt* contains:

```
Problem parsing arguments: not enough arguments
```

Yup, our error message is being printed to standard output. It's much more useful for error messages like this to be printed to standard error so only data from a successful run ends up in the file. We'll change that.

Printing Errors to Standard Error

We'll use the code in Listing 12-24 to change how error messages are printed. Because of the refactoring we did earlier in this chapter, all the code that prints error messages is in one function, main. The standard library provides the eprintln! macro that prints to the standard error stream, so let's change the two places we were calling println! to print errors to use eprintln! instead.

src/main.rs
```
fn main() {
    let args: Vec<String> = env::args().collect();

    let config = Config::build(&args).unwrap_or_else(|err| {
        eprintln!("Problem parsing arguments: {err}");
        process::exit(1);
    });

    if let Err(e) = minigrep::run(config) {
        eprintln!("Application error: {e}");
        process::exit(1);
    }
}
```

Listing 12-24: Writing error messages to standard error instead of standard output using eprintln!

Let's now run the program again in the same way, without any arguments and redirecting standard output with >:

```
$ cargo run > output.txt
Problem parsing arguments: not enough arguments
```

Now we see the error onscreen and *output.txt* contains nothing, which is the behavior we expect of command line programs.

Let's run the program again with arguments that don't cause an error but still redirect standard output to a file, like so:

```
$ cargo run -- to poem.txt > output.txt
```

We won't see any output to the terminal, and *output.txt* will contain our results:

output.txt
```
Are you nobody, too?
How dreary to be somebody!
```

This demonstrates that we're now using standard output for successful output and standard error for error output as appropriate.

Summary

This chapter recapped some of the major concepts you've learned so far and covered how to perform common I/O operations in Rust. By using command line arguments, files, environment variables, and the eprintln! macro for printing errors, you're now prepared to write command line applications. Combined with the concepts in previous chapters, your code will be well organized, store data effectively in the appropriate data structures, handle errors nicely, and be well tested.

Next, we'll explore some Rust features that were influenced by functional languages: closures and iterators.

13

FUNCTIONAL LANGUAGE FEATURES: ITERATORS AND CLOSURES

Rust's design has taken inspiration from many existing languages and techniques, and one significant influence is *functional programming*. Programming in a functional style often includes using functions as values by passing them in arguments, returning them from other functions, assigning them to variables for later execution, and so forth.

In this chapter, we won't debate the issue of what functional programming is or isn't but will instead discuss some features of Rust that are similar to features in many languages often referred to as functional.

More specifically, we'll cover:

- *Closures*, a function-like construct you can store in a variable
- *Iterators*, a way of processing a series of elements

- How to use closures and iterators to improve the I/O project in Chapter 12
- The performance of closures and iterators (spoiler alert: they're faster than you might think!)

We've already covered some other Rust features, such as pattern matching and enums, that are also influenced by the functional style. Because mastering closures and iterators is an important part of writing idiomatic, fast Rust code, we'll devote this entire chapter to them.

Closures: Anonymous Functions That Capture Their Environment

Rust's closures are anonymous functions you can save in a variable or pass as arguments to other functions. You can create the closure in one place and then call the closure elsewhere to evaluate it in a different context. Unlike functions, closures can capture values from the scope in which they're defined. We'll demonstrate how these closure features allow for code reuse and behavior customization.

Capturing the Environment with Closures

We'll first examine how we can use closures to capture values from the environment they're defined in for later use. Here's the scenario: every so often, our T-shirt company gives away an exclusive, limited-edition shirt to someone on our mailing list as a promotion. People on the mailing list can optionally add their favorite color to their profile. If the person chosen for a free shirt has their favorite color set, they get that color shirt. If the person hasn't specified a favorite color, they get whatever color the company currently has the most of.

There are many ways to implement this. For this example, we're going to use an enum called ShirtColor that has the variants Red and Blue (limiting the number of colors available for simplicity). We represent the company's inventory with an Inventory struct that has a field named shirts that contains a Vec<ShirtColor> representing the shirt colors currently in stock. The method giveaway defined on Inventory gets the optional shirt color preference of the free-shirt winner, and returns the shirt color the person will get. This setup is shown in Listing 13-1.

src/main.rs
```
#[derive(Debug, PartialEq, Copy, Clone)]
enum ShirtColor {
    Red,
    Blue,
}

struct Inventory {
    shirts: Vec<ShirtColor>,
}
```

```
impl Inventory {
    fn giveaway(
        &self,
        user_preference: Option<ShirtColor>,
    ) -> ShirtColor {
      ❶ user_preference.unwrap_or_else(|| self.most_stocked())
    }

    fn most_stocked(&self) -> ShirtColor {
        let mut num_red = 0;
        let mut num_blue = 0;

        for color in &self.shirts {
            match color {
                ShirtColor::Red => num_red += 1,
                ShirtColor::Blue => num_blue += 1,
            }
        }
        if num_red > num_blue {
            ShirtColor::Red
        } else {
            ShirtColor::Blue
        }
    }
}

fn main() {
    let store = Inventory {
      ❷ shirts: vec![
            ShirtColor::Blue,
            ShirtColor::Red,
            ShirtColor::Blue,
        ],
    };

    let user_pref1 = Some(ShirtColor::Red);
  ❸ let giveaway1 = store.giveaway(user_pref1);
    println!(
        "The user with preference {:?} gets {:?}",
        user_pref1, giveaway1
    );

    let user_pref2 = None;
  ❹ let giveaway2 = store.giveaway(user_pref2);
    println!(
        "The user with preference {:?} gets {:?}",
        user_pref2, giveaway2
    );
}
```

Listing 13-1: Shirt company giveaway situation

The store defined in main has two blue shirts and one red shirt remaining to distribute for this limited-edition promotion ❷. We call the giveaway method for a user with a preference for a red shirt ❸ and a user without any preference ❹.

Again, this code could be implemented in many ways, and here, to focus on closures, we've stuck to concepts you've already learned, except for the body of the giveaway method that uses a closure. In the giveaway method, we get the user preference as a parameter of type Option<ShirtColor> and call the unwrap_or_else method on user_preference ❶. The unwrap_or_else method on Option<T> is defined by the standard library. It takes one argument: a closure without any arguments that returns a value T (the same type stored in the Some variant of the Option<T>, in this case ShirtColor). If the Option<T> is the Some variant, unwrap_or_else returns the value from within the Some. If the Option<T> is the None variant, unwrap_or_else calls the closure and returns the value returned by the closure.

We specify the closure expression || self.most_stocked() as the argument to unwrap_or_else. This is a closure that takes no parameters itself (if the closure had parameters, they would appear between the two vertical pipes). The body of the closure calls self.most_stocked(). We're defining the closure here, and the implementation of unwrap_or_else will evaluate the closure later if the result is needed.

Running this code prints the following:

```
The user with preference Some(Red) gets Red
The user with preference None gets Blue
```

One interesting aspect here is that we've passed a closure that calls self.most_stocked() on the current Inventory instance. The standard library didn't need to know anything about the Inventory or ShirtColor types we defined, or the logic we want to use in this scenario. The closure captures an immutable reference to the self Inventory instance and passes it with the code we specify to the unwrap_or_else method. Functions, on the other hand, are not able to capture their environment in this way.

Closure Type Inference and Annotation

There are more differences between functions and closures. Closures don't usually require you to annotate the types of the parameters or the return value like fn functions do. Type annotations are required on functions because the types are part of an explicit interface exposed to your users. Defining this interface rigidly is important for ensuring that everyone agrees on what types of values a function uses and returns. Closures, on the other hand, aren't used in an exposed interface like this: they're stored in variables and used without naming them and exposing them to users of our library.

Closures are typically short and relevant only within a narrow context rather than in any arbitrary scenario. Within these limited contexts, the compiler can infer the types of the parameters and the return type, similar to how it's able to infer the types of most variables (there are rare cases where the compiler needs closure type annotations too).

As with variables, we can add type annotations if we want to increase explicitness and clarity at the cost of being more verbose than is strictly necessary. Annotating the types for a closure would look like the definition shown in Listing 13-2. In this example, we're defining a closure and storing it in a variable rather than defining the closure in the spot we pass it as an argument, as we did in Listing 13-1.

src/main.rs

```
let expensive_closure = |num: u32| -> u32 {
    println!("calculating slowly...");
    thread::sleep(Duration::from_secs(2));
    num
};
```

Listing 13-2: Adding optional type annotations of the parameter and return value types in the closure

With type annotations added, the syntax of closures looks more similar to the syntax of functions. Here, we define a function that adds 1 to its parameter and a closure that has the same behavior, for comparison. We've added some spaces to line up the relevant parts. This illustrates how closure syntax is similar to function syntax except for the use of pipes and the amount of syntax that is optional:

```
fn  add_one_v1   (x: u32) -> u32 { x + 1 }
let add_one_v2 = |x: u32| -> u32 { x + 1 };
let add_one_v3 = |x|             { x + 1 };
let add_one_v4 = |x|              x + 1  ;
```

The first line shows a function definition and the second line shows a fully annotated closure definition. In the third line, we remove the type annotations from the closure definition. In the fourth line, we remove the curly brackets, which are optional because the closure body has only one expression. These are all valid definitions that will produce the same behavior when they're called. The add_one_v3 and add_one_v4 lines require the closures to be evaluated to be able to compile because the types will be inferred from their usage. This is similar to let v = Vec::new(); needing either type annotations or values of some type to be inserted into the Vec for Rust to be able to infer the type.

For closure definitions, the compiler will infer one concrete type for each of their parameters and for their return value. For instance, Listing 13-3 shows the definition of a short closure that just returns the value it receives as a parameter. This closure isn't very useful except for the purposes of this example. Note that we haven't added any type annotations to the definition. Because there are no type annotations, we can call the closure with any type, which we've done here with String the first time. If we then try to call example _closure with an integer, we'll get an error.

src/main.rs

```
let example_closure = |x| x;

let s = example_closure(String::from("hello"));
let n = example_closure(5);
```

Listing 13-3: Attempting to call a closure whose types are inferred with two different types

The compiler gives us this error:

```
error[E0308]: mismatched types
 --> src/main.rs:5:29
  |
5 |     let n = example_closure(5);
  |                             ^- help: try using a conversion method:
`.to_string()`
  |                             |
  |                             expected struct `String`, found integer
```

The first time we call example_closure with the String value, the compiler infers the type of x and the return type of the closure to be String. Those types are then locked into the closure in example_closure, and we get a type error when we next try to use a different type with the same closure.

Capturing References or Moving Ownership

Closures can capture values from their environment in three ways, which directly map to the three ways a function can take a parameter: borrowing immutably, borrowing mutably, and taking ownership. The closure will decide which of these to use based on what the body of the function does with the captured values.

In Listing 13-4, we define a closure that captures an immutable reference to the vector named list because it only needs an immutable reference to print the value.

src/main.rs
```
fn main() {
    let list = vec![1, 2, 3];
    println!("Before defining closure: {:?}", list);

  ❶ let only_borrows = || println!("From closure: {:?}", list);

    println!("Before calling closure: {:?}", list);
  ❷ only_borrows();
    println!("After calling closure: {:?}", list);
}
```

Listing 13-4: Defining and calling a closure that captures an immutable reference

This example also illustrates that a variable can bind to a closure definition ❶, and we can later call the closure by using the variable name and parentheses as if the variable name were a function name ❷.

Because we can have multiple immutable references to list at the same time, list is still accessible from the code before the closure definition, after the closure definition but before the closure is called, and after the closure is called. This code compiles, runs, and prints:

```
Before defining closure: [1, 2, 3]
Before calling closure: [1, 2, 3]
From closure: [1, 2, 3]
After calling closure: [1, 2, 3]
```

Next, in Listing 13-5, we change the closure body so that it adds an element to the list vector. The closure now captures a mutable reference.

src/main.rs

```
fn main() {
    let mut list = vec![1, 2, 3];
    println!("Before defining closure: {:?}", list);

    let mut borrows_mutably = || list.push(7);

    borrows_mutably();
    println!("After calling closure: {:?}", list);
}
```

Listing 13-5: Defining and calling a closure that captures a mutable reference

This code compiles, runs, and prints:

```
Before defining closure: [1, 2, 3]
After calling closure: [1, 2, 3, 7]
```

Note that there's no longer a println! between the definition and the call of the borrows_mutably closure: when borrows_mutably is defined, it captures a mutable reference to list. We don't use the closure again after the closure is called, so the mutable borrow ends. Between the closure definition and the closure call, an immutable borrow to print isn't allowed because no other borrows are allowed when there's a mutable borrow. Try adding a println! there to see what error message you get!

If you want to force the closure to take ownership of the values it uses in the environment even though the body of the closure doesn't strictly need ownership, you can use the move keyword before the parameter list.

This technique is mostly useful when passing a closure to a new thread to move the data so that it's owned by the new thread. We'll discuss threads and why you would want to use them in detail in Chapter 16 when we talk about concurrency, but for now, let's briefly explore spawning a new thread using a closure that needs the move keyword. Listing 13-6 shows Listing 13-4 modified to print the vector in a new thread rather than in the main thread.

src/main.rs

```
use std::thread;

fn main() {
    let list = vec![1, 2, 3];
    println!("Before defining closure: {:?}", list);

❶  thread::spawn(move || {
      ❷  println!("From thread: {:?}", list)
    }).join().unwrap();
}
```

Listing 13-6: Using move to force the closure for the thread to take ownership of list

We spawn a new thread, giving the thread a closure to run as an argument. The closure body prints out the list. In Listing 13-4, the closure only captured `list` using an immutable reference because that's the least amount of access to `list` needed to print it. In this example, even though the closure body still only needs an immutable reference ❷, we need to specify that `list` should be moved into the closure by putting the `move` keyword ❶ at the beginning of the closure definition. The new thread might finish before the rest of the main thread finishes, or the main thread might finish first. If the main thread maintains ownership of `list` but ends before the new thread and drops `list`, the immutable reference in the thread would be invalid. Therefore, the compiler requires that `list` be moved into the closure given to the new thread so the reference will be valid. Try removing the `move` keyword or using `list` in the main thread after the closure is defined to see what compiler errors you get!

Moving Captured Values Out of Closures and the Fn Traits

Once a closure has captured a reference or captured ownership of a value from the environment where the closure is defined (thus affecting what, if anything, is moved *into* the closure), the code in the body of the closure defines what happens to the references or values when the closure is evaluated later (thus affecting what, if anything, is moved *out of* the closure).

A closure body can do any of the following: move a captured value out of the closure, mutate the captured value, neither move nor mutate the value, or capture nothing from the environment to begin with.

The way a closure captures and handles values from the environment affects which traits the closure implements, and traits are how functions and structs can specify what kinds of closures they can use. Closures will automatically implement one, two, or all three of these `Fn` traits, in an additive fashion, depending on how the closure's body handles the values:

- `FnOnce` applies to closures that can be called once. All closures implement at least this trait because all closures can be called. A closure that moves captured values out of its body will only implement `FnOnce` and none of the other `Fn` traits because it can only be called once.

- `FnMut` applies to closures that don't move captured values out of their body, but that might mutate the captured values. These closures can be called more than once.

- `Fn` applies to closures that don't move captured values out of their body and that don't mutate captured values, as well as closures that capture nothing from their environment. These closures can be called more than once without mutating their environment, which is important in cases such as calling a closure multiple times concurrently.

Let's look at the definition of the `unwrap_or_else` method on `Option<T>` that we used in Listing 13-1:

```
impl<T> Option<T> {
    pub fn unwrap_or_else<F>(self, f: F) -> T
    where
        F: FnOnce() -> T
    {
```

```
    match self {
        Some(x) => x,
        None => f(),
    }
}
}
```

Recall that T is the generic type representing the type of the value in the Some variant of an Option. That type T is also the return type of the unwrap_or_else function: code that calls unwrap_or_else on an Option<String>, for example, will get a String.

Next, notice that the unwrap_or_else function has the additional generic type parameter F. The F type is the type of the parameter named f, which is the closure we provide when calling unwrap_or_else.

The trait bound specified on the generic type F is FnOnce() -> T, which means F must be able to be called once, take no arguments, and return a T. Using FnOnce in the trait bound expresses the constraint that unwrap_or_else is only going to call f one time, at most. In the body of unwrap_or_else, we can see that if the Option is Some, f won't be called. If the Option is None, f will be called once. Because all closures implement FnOnce, unwrap_or_else accepts the largest variety of closures and is as flexible as it can be.

> **NOTE** *Functions can implement all three of the Fn traits too. If what we want to do doesn't require capturing a value from the environment, we can use the name of a function rather than a closure where we need something that implements one of the Fn traits. For example, on an Option<Vec<T>> value, we could call unwrap_or_else(Vec::new) to get a new, empty vector if the value is None.*

Now let's look at the standard library method sort_by_key, defined on slices, to see how that differs from unwrap_or_else and why sort_by_key uses FnMut instead of FnOnce for the trait bound. The closure gets one argument in the form of a reference to the current item in the slice being considered, and returns a value of type K that can be ordered. This function is useful when you want to sort a slice by a particular attribute of each item. In Listing 13-7, we have a list of Rectangle instances and we use sort_by_key to order them by their width attribute from low to high.

src/main.rs
```
#[derive(Debug)]
struct Rectangle {
    width: u32,
    height: u32,
}

fn main() {
    let mut list = [
        Rectangle { width: 10, height: 1 },
        Rectangle { width: 3, height: 5 },
        Rectangle { width: 7, height: 12 },
    ];
```

```
        list.sort_by_key(|r| r.width);
        println!("{:#?}", list);
}
```

Listing 13-7: Using sort_by_key to order rectangles by width

This code prints:

```
[
    Rectangle {
        width: 3,
        height: 5,
    },
    Rectangle {
        width: 7,
        height: 12,
    },
    Rectangle {
        width: 10,
        height: 1,
    },
]
```

The reason sort_by_key is defined to take an FnMut closure is that it calls the closure multiple times: once for each item in the slice. The closure |r| r.width doesn't capture, mutate, or move anything out from its environment, so it meets the trait bound requirements.

In contrast, Listing 13-8 shows an example of a closure that implements just the FnOnce trait, because it moves a value out of the environment. The compiler won't let us use this closure with sort_by_key.

src/main.rs
```
--snip--

fn main() {
    let mut list = [
        Rectangle { width: 10, height: 1 },
        Rectangle { width: 3, height: 5 },
        Rectangle { width: 7, height: 12 },
    ];

    let mut sort_operations = vec![];
    let value = String::from("by key called");

    list.sort_by_key(|r| {
        sort_operations.push(value);
        r.width
    });
    println!("{:#?}", list);
}
```

Listing 13-8: Attempting to use an FnOnce closure with sort_by_key

This is a contrived, convoluted way (that doesn't work) to try and count the number of times sort_by_key gets called when sorting list. This code attempts to do this counting by pushing value—a String from the closure's environment—into the sort_operations vector. The closure captures value and then moves value out of the closure by transferring ownership of value to the sort_operations vector. This closure can be called once; trying to call it a second time wouldn't work because value would no longer be in the environment to be pushed into sort_operations again! Therefore, this closure only implements FnOnce. When we try to compile this code, we get this error that value can't be moved out of the closure because the closure must implement FnMut:

```
error[E0507]: cannot move out of `value`, a captured variable in an `FnMut`
closure
  --> src/main.rs:18:30
   |
15 |         let value = String::from("by key called");
   |             ----- captured outer variable
16 |
17 |         list.sort_by_key(|r| {
   |  _____-
18 | |             sort_operations.push(value);
   | |                                  ^^^^^ move occurs because `value` has
type `String`, which does not implement the `Copy` trait
19 | |             r.width
20 | |         });
   | |_____- captured by this `FnMut` closure
```

The error points to the line in the closure body that moves value out of the environment. To fix this, we need to change the closure body so that it doesn't move values out of the environment. Keeping a counter in the environment and incrementing its value in the closure body is a more straightforward way to count the number of times sort_by_key is called. The closure in Listing 13-9 works with sort_by_key because it is only capturing a mutable reference to the num_sort_operations counter and can therefore be called more than once.

src/main.rs
```
--snip--

fn main() {
    --snip--

    let mut num_sort_operations = 0;
    list.sort_by_key(|r| {
        num_sort_operations += 1;
        r.width
    });
    println!(
        "{:#?}, sorted in {num_sort_operations} operations",
        list
    );
}
```

Listing 13-9: Using an FnMut closure with sort_by_key is allowed.

The Fn traits are important when defining or using functions or types that make use of closures. In the next section, we'll discuss iterators. Many iterator methods take closure arguments, so keep these closure details in mind as we continue!

Processing a Series of Items with Iterators

The iterator pattern allows you to perform some task on a sequence of items in turn. An iterator is responsible for the logic of iterating over each item and determining when the sequence has finished. When you use iterators, you don't have to reimplement that logic yourself.

In Rust, iterators are *lazy*, meaning they have no effect until you call methods that consume the iterator to use it up. For example, the code in Listing 13-10 creates an iterator over the items in the vector v1 by calling the iter method defined on Vec<T>. This code by itself doesn't do anything useful.

```
let v1 = vec![1, 2, 3];

let v1_iter = v1.iter();
```

Listing 13-10: Creating an iterator

The iterator is stored in the v1_iter variable. Once we've created an iterator, we can use it in a variety of ways. In Listing 3-5, we iterated over an array using a for loop to execute some code on each of its items. Under the hood, this implicitly created and then consumed an iterator, but we glossed over how exactly that works until now.

In the example in Listing 13-11, we separate the creation of the iterator from the use of the iterator in the for loop. When the for loop is called using the iterator in v1_iter, each element in the iterator is used in one iteration of the loop, which prints out each value.

```
let v1 = vec![1, 2, 3];

let v1_iter = v1.iter();

for val in v1_iter {
    println!("Got: {val}");
}
```

Listing 13-11: Using an iterator in a for loop

In languages that don't have iterators provided by their standard libraries, you would likely write this same functionality by starting a variable at index 0, using that variable to index into the vector to get a value, and incrementing the variable value in a loop until it reached the total number of items in the vector.

Iterators handle all of that logic for you, cutting down on repetitive code you could potentially mess up. Iterators give you more flexibility to use the same logic with many different kinds of sequences, not just data structures you can index into, like vectors. Let's examine how iterators do that.

The Iterator Trait and the next Method

All iterators implement a trait named Iterator that is defined in the standard library. The definition of the trait looks like this:

```
pub trait Iterator {
    type Item;

    fn next(&mut self) -> Option<Self::Item>;

    // methods with default implementations elided
}
```

Notice that this definition uses some new syntax: type Item and Self::Item, which are defining an *associated type* with this trait. We'll talk about associated types in depth in Chapter 19. For now, all you need to know is that this code says implementing the Iterator trait requires that you also define an Item type, and this Item type is used in the return type of the next method. In other words, the Item type will be the type returned from the iterator.

The Iterator trait only requires implementors to define one method: the next method, which returns one item of the iterator at a time, wrapped in Some, and, when iteration is over, returns None.

We can call the next method on iterators directly; Listing 13-12 demonstrates what values are returned from repeated calls to next on the iterator created from the vector.

src/lib.rs
```
#[test]
fn iterator_demonstration() {
    let v1 = vec![1, 2, 3];

    let mut v1_iter = v1.iter();

    assert_eq!(v1_iter.next(), Some(&1));
    assert_eq!(v1_iter.next(), Some(&2));
    assert_eq!(v1_iter.next(), Some(&3));
    assert_eq!(v1_iter.next(), None);
}
```

Listing 13-12: Calling the next method on an iterator

Note that we needed to make v1_iter mutable: calling the next method on an iterator changes internal state that the iterator uses to keep track of where it is in the sequence. In other words, this code *consumes*, or uses up, the iterator. Each call to next eats up an item from the iterator. We didn't need to make v1_iter mutable when we used a for loop because the loop took ownership of v1_iter and made it mutable behind the scenes.

Also note that the values we get from the calls to next are immutable references to the values in the vector. The iter method produces an iterator over immutable references. If we want to create an iterator that takes ownership of v1 and returns owned values, we can call into_iter instead of iter. Similarly, if we want to iterate over mutable references, we can call iter_mut instead of iter.

Methods That Consume the Iterator

The Iterator trait has a number of different methods with default implementations provided by the standard library; you can find out about these methods by looking in the standard library API documentation for the Iterator trait. Some of these methods call the next method in their definition, which is why you're required to implement the next method when implementing the Iterator trait.

Methods that call next are called *consuming adapters* because calling them uses up the iterator. One example is the sum method, which takes ownership of the iterator and iterates through the items by repeatedly calling next, thus consuming the iterator. As it iterates through, it adds each item to a running total and returns the total when iteration is complete. Listing 13-13 has a test illustrating a use of the sum method.

src/lib.rs
```
#[test]
fn iterator_sum() {
    let v1 = vec![1, 2, 3];

    let v1_iter = v1.iter();

    let total: i32 = v1_iter.sum();

    assert_eq!(total, 6);
}
```

Listing 13-13: Calling the sum method to get the total of all items in the iterator

We aren't allowed to use v1_iter after the call to sum because sum takes ownership of the iterator we call it on.

Methods That Produce Other Iterators

Iterator adapters are methods defined on the Iterator trait that don't consume the iterator. Instead, they produce different iterators by changing some aspect of the original iterator.

Listing 13-14 shows an example of calling the iterator adapter method map, which takes a closure to call on each item as the items are iterated through. The map method returns a new iterator that produces the modified items. The closure here creates a new iterator in which each item from the vector will be incremented by 1.

src/main.rs
```
let v1: Vec<i32> = vec![1, 2, 3];

v1.iter().map(|x| x + 1);
```

Listing 13-14: Calling the iterator adapter map to create a new iterator

However, this code produces a warning:

```
warning: unused `Map` that must be used
 --> src/main.rs:4:5
  |
```

```
4 |        v1.iter().map(|x| x + 1);
  |        ^^^^^^^^^^^^^^^^^^^^^^^^^
  |
  = note: `#[warn(unused_must_use)]` on by default
  = note: iterators are lazy and do nothing unless consumed
```

The code in Listing 13-14 doesn't do anything; the closure we've specified never gets called. The warning reminds us why: iterator adapters are lazy, and we need to consume the iterator here.

To fix this warning and consume the iterator, we'll use the collect method, which we used with env::args in Listing 12-1. This method consumes the iterator and collects the resultant values into a collection data type.

In Listing 13-15, we collect into a vector the results of iterating over the iterator that's returned from the call to map. This vector will end up containing each item from the original vector, incremented by 1.

src/main.rs
```
let v1: Vec<i32> = vec![1, 2, 3];

let v2: Vec<_> = v1.iter().map(|x| x + 1).collect();

assert_eq!(v2, vec![2, 3, 4]);
```

Listing 13-15: Calling the map *method to create a new iterator, and then calling the* collect *method to consume the new iterator and create a vector*

Because map takes a closure, we can specify any operation we want to perform on each item. This is a great example of how closures let you customize some behavior while reusing the iteration behavior that the Iterator trait provides.

You can chain multiple calls to iterator adapters to perform complex actions in a readable way. But because all iterators are lazy, you have to call one of the consuming adapter methods to get results from calls to iterator adapters.

Using Closures That Capture Their Environment

Many iterator adapters take closures as arguments, and commonly the closures we'll specify as arguments to iterator adapters will be closures that capture their environment.

For this example, we'll use the filter method that takes a closure. The closure gets an item from the iterator and returns a bool. If the closure returns true, the value will be included in the iteration produced by filter. If the closure returns false, the value won't be included.

In Listing 13-16, we use filter with a closure that captures the shoe_size variable from its environment to iterate over a collection of Shoe struct instances. It will return only shoes that are the specified size.

src/lib.rs
```
#[derive(PartialEq, Debug)]
struct Shoe {
    size: u32,
    style: String,
}
```

```
fn shoes_in_size(shoes: Vec<Shoe>, shoe_size: u32) -> Vec<Shoe> {
    shoes.into_iter().filter(|s| s.size == shoe_size).collect()
}

#[cfg(test)]
mod tests {
    use super::*;

    #[test]
    fn filters_by_size() {
        let shoes = vec![
            Shoe {
                size: 10,
                style: String::from("sneaker"),
            },
            Shoe {
                size: 13,
                style: String::from("sandal"),
            },
            Shoe {
                size: 10,
                style: String::from("boot"),
            },
        ];

        let in_my_size = shoes_in_size(shoes, 10);

        assert_eq!(
            in_my_size,
            vec![
                Shoe {
                    size: 10,
                    style: String::from("sneaker")
                },
                Shoe {
                    size: 10,
                    style: String::from("boot")
                },
            ]
        );
    }
}
```

Listing 13-16: Using the `filter` method with a closure that captures `shoe_size`

The shoes_in_size function takes ownership of a vector of shoes and
a shoe size as parameters. It returns a vector containing only shoes of the
specified size.

In the body of shoes_in_size, we call into_iter to create an iterator that
takes ownership of the vector. Then we call filter to adapt that iterator into
a new iterator that only contains elements for which the closure returns true.

The closure captures the shoe_size parameter from the environment
and compares the value with each shoe's size, keeping only shoes of the size

specified. Finally, calling collect gathers the values returned by the adapted iterator into a vector that's returned by the function.

The test shows that when we call shoes_in_size, we get back only shoes that have the same size as the value we specified.

Improving Our I/O Project

With this new knowledge about iterators, we can improve the I/O project in Chapter 12 by using iterators to make places in the code clearer and more concise. Let's look at how iterators can improve our implementation of the Config::build function and the search function.

Removing a clone Using an Iterator

In Listing 12-6, we added code that took a slice of String values and created an instance of the Config struct by indexing into the slice and cloning the values, allowing the Config struct to own those values. In Listing 13-17, we've reproduced the implementation of the Config::build function as it was in Listing 12-23.

```
impl Config {
    pub fn build(
        args: &[String]
    ) -> Result<Config, &'static str> {
        if args.len() < 3 {
            return Err("not enough arguments");
        }

        let query = args[1].clone();
        let file_path = args[2].clone();

        let ignore_case = env::var("IGNORE_CASE").is_ok();

        Ok(Config {
            query,
            file_path,
            ignore_case,
        })
    }
}
```

src/lib.rs

Listing 13-17: Reproduction of the Config::build function from Listing 12-23

At the time, we said not to worry about the inefficient clone calls because we would remove them in the future. Well, that time is now!

We needed clone here because we have a slice with String elements in the parameter args, but the build function doesn't own args. To return ownership of a Config instance, we had to clone the values from the query and filename fields of Config so the Config instance can own its values.

With our new knowledge about iterators, we can change the build function to take ownership of an iterator as its argument instead of borrowing a slice. We'll use the iterator functionality instead of the code that checks the length of the slice and indexes into specific locations. This will clarify what the `Config::build` function is doing because the iterator will access the values.

Once `Config::build` takes ownership of the iterator and stops using indexing operations that borrow, we can move the `String` values from the iterator into `Config` rather than calling `clone` and making a new allocation.

Using the Returned Iterator Directly

Open your I/O project's *src/main.rs* file, which should look like this:

src/main.rs
```
fn main() {
    let args: Vec<String> = env::args().collect();

    let config = Config::build(&args).unwrap_or_else(|err| {
        eprintln!("Problem parsing arguments: {err}");
        process::exit(1);
    });

    --snip--
}
```

We'll first change the start of the `main` function that we had in Listing 12-24 to the code in Listing 13-18, which this time uses an iterator. This won't compile until we update `Config::build` as well.

src/main.rs
```
fn main() {
    let config =
        Config::build(env::args()).unwrap_or_else(|err| {
            eprintln!("Problem parsing arguments: {err}");
            process::exit(1);
        });

    --snip--
}
```

Listing 13-18: Passing the return value of `env::args` to `Config::build`

The `env::args` function returns an iterator! Rather than collecting the iterator values into a vector and then passing a slice to `Config::build`, now we're passing ownership of the iterator returned from `env::args` to `Config::build` directly.

Next, we need to update the definition of `Config::build`. In your I/O project's *src/lib.rs* file, let's change the signature of `Config::build` to look like Listing 13-19. This still won't compile, because we need to update the function body.

src/lib.rs
```
impl Config {
    pub fn build(
        mut args: impl Iterator<Item = String>,
    ) -> Result<Config, &'static str> {
        --snip--
```

Listing 13-19: Updating the signature of `Config::build` to expect an iterator

The standard library documentation for the env::args function shows that the type of the iterator it returns is std::env::Args, and that type implements the Iterator trait and returns String values.

We've updated the signature of the Config::build function so the parameter args has a generic type with the trait bounds impl Iterator<Item = String> instead of &[String]. This usage of the impl Trait syntax we discussed in "Traits as Parameters" on page 197 means that args can be any type that implements the Iterator type and returns String items.

Because we're taking ownership of args and we'll be mutating args by iterating over it, we can add the mut keyword into the specification of the args parameter to make it mutable.

Using Iterator Trait Methods Instead of Indexing

Next, we'll fix the body of Config::build. Because args implements the Iterator trait, we know we can call the next method on it! Listing 13-20 updates the code from Listing 12-23 to use the next method.

src/lib.rs
```
impl Config {
    pub fn build(
        mut args: impl Iterator<Item = String>,
    ) -> Result<Config, &'static str> {
        args.next();

        let query = match args.next() {
            Some(arg) => arg,
            None => return Err("Didn't get a query string"),
        };

        let file_path = match args.next() {
            Some(arg) => arg,
            None => return Err("Didn't get a file path"),
        };

        let ignore_case = env::var("IGNORE_CASE").is_ok();

        Ok(Config {
            query,
            file_path,
            ignore_case,
        })
    }
}
```

Listing 13-20: Changing the body of Config::build to use iterator methods

Remember that the first value in the return value of env::args is the name of the program. We want to ignore that and get to the next value, so first we call next and do nothing with the return value. Then we call next to get the value we want to put in the query field of Config. If next returns Some, we use a match to extract the value. If it returns None, it means not enough arguments were given and we return early with an Err value. We do the same thing for the filename value.

Making Code Clearer with Iterator Adapters

We can also take advantage of iterators in the search function in our I/O project, which is reproduced here in Listing 13-21 as it was in Listing 12-19.

src/lib.rs
```
pub fn search<'a>(
    query: &str,
    contents: &'a str,
) -> Vec<&'a str> {
    let mut results = Vec::new();

    for line in contents.lines() {
        if line.contains(query) {
            results.push(line);
        }
    }

    results
}
```

Listing 13-21: The implementation of the search function from Listing 12-19

We can write this code in a more concise way using iterator adapter methods. Doing so also lets us avoid having a mutable intermediate results vector. The functional programming style prefers to minimize the amount of mutable state to make code clearer. Removing the mutable state might enable a future enhancement to make searching happen in parallel because we wouldn't have to manage concurrent access to the results vector. Listing 13-22 shows this change.

src/lib.rs
```
pub fn search<'a>(
    query: &str,
    contents: &'a str,
) -> Vec<&'a str> {
    contents
        .lines()
        .filter(|line| line.contains(query))
        .collect()
}
```

Listing 13-22: Using iterator adapter methods in the implementation of the search function

Recall that the purpose of the search function is to return all lines in contents that contain the query. Similar to the filter example in Listing 13-16, this code uses the filter adapter to keep only the lines for which line.contains (query) returns true. We then collect the matching lines into another vector with collect. Much simpler! Feel free to make the same change to use iterator methods in the search_case_insensitive function as well.

Choosing Between Loops and Iterators

The next logical question is which style you should choose in your own code and why: the original implementation in Listing 13-21 or the version using iterators in Listing 13-22. Most Rust programmers prefer to use the iterator style. It's a bit tougher to get the hang of at first, but once you get a feel for the various iterator adapters and what they do, iterators can be easier to understand. Instead of fiddling with the various bits of looping and building new vectors, the code focuses on the high-level objective of the loop. This abstracts away some of the commonplace code so it's easier to see the concepts that are unique to this code, such as the filtering condition each element in the iterator must pass.

But are the two implementations truly equivalent? The intuitive assumption might be that the lower-level loop will be faster. Let's talk about performance.

Comparing Performance: Loops vs. Iterators

To determine whether to use loops or iterators, you need to know which implementation is faster: the version of the search function with an explicit for loop or the version with iterators.

We ran a benchmark by loading the entire contents of *The Adventures of Sherlock Holmes* by Sir Arthur Conan Doyle into a String and looking for the word *the* in the contents. Here are the results of the benchmark on the version of search using the for loop and the version using iterators:

```
test bench_search_for  ... bench:  19,620,300 ns/iter (+/- 915,700)
test bench_search_iter ... bench:  19,234,900 ns/iter (+/- 657,200)
```

The iterator version was slightly faster! We won't explain the benchmark code here because the point is not to prove that the two versions are equivalent but to get a general sense of how these two implementations compare performance-wise.

For a more comprehensive benchmark, you should check using various texts of various sizes as the contents, different words and words of different lengths as the query, and all kinds of other variations. The point is this: iterators, although a high-level abstraction, get compiled down to roughly the same code as if you'd written the lower-level code yourself. Iterators are one of Rust's *zero-cost abstractions*, by which we mean that using the abstraction imposes no additional runtime overhead. This is analogous to how Bjarne Stroustrup, the original designer and implementor of C++, defines *zero-overhead* in "Foundations of C++" (2012):

> In general, C++ implementations obey the zero-overhead principle: What you don't use, you don't pay for. And further: What you do use, you couldn't hand code any better.

As another example, the following code is taken from an audio decoder. The decoding algorithm uses the linear prediction mathematical operation to estimate future values based on a linear function of the previous samples. This code uses an iterator chain to do some math on three variables in scope: a buffer slice of data, an array of 12 coefficients, and an amount by which to shift data in qlp_shift. We've declared the variables within this example but not given them any values; although this code doesn't have much meaning outside of its context, it's still a concise, real-world example of how Rust translates high-level ideas to low-level code.

```
let buffer: &mut [i32];
let coefficients: [i64; 12];
let qlp_shift: i16;

for i in 12..buffer.len() {
    let prediction = coefficients.iter()
                                 .zip(&buffer[i - 12..i])
                                 .map(|(&c, &s)| c * s as i64)
                                 .sum::<i64>() >> qlp_shift;
    let delta = buffer[i];
    buffer[i] = prediction as i32 + delta;
}
```

To calculate the value of prediction, this code iterates through each of the 12 values in coefficients and uses the zip method to pair the coefficient values with the previous 12 values in buffer. Then, for each pair, it multiplies the values together, sums all the results, and shifts the bits in the sum qlp_shift bits to the right.

Calculations in applications like audio decoders often prioritize performance most highly. Here, we're creating an iterator, using two adapters, and then consuming the value. What assembly code would this Rust code compile to? Well, as of this writing, it compiles down to the same assembly you'd write by hand. There's no loop at all corresponding to the iteration over the values in coefficients: Rust knows that there are 12 iterations, so it "unrolls" the loop. *Unrolling* is an optimization that removes the overhead of the loop controlling code and instead generates repetitive code for each iteration of the loop.

All of the coefficients get stored in registers, which means accessing the values is very fast. There are no bounds checks on the array access at runtime. All of these optimizations that Rust is able to apply make the resultant code extremely efficient. Now that you know this, you can use iterators and closures without fear! They make code seem like it's higher level but don't impose a runtime performance penalty for doing so.

Summary

Closures and iterators are Rust features inspired by functional programming language ideas. They contribute to Rust's capability to clearly express high-level ideas at low-level performance. The implementations of closures and iterators are such that runtime performance is not affected. This is part of Rust's goal to strive to provide zero-cost abstractions.

Now that we've improved the expressiveness of our I/O project, let's look at some more features of cargo that will help us share the project with the world.

14

MORE ABOUT CARGO AND CRATES.IO

So far, we've used only the most basic features of Cargo to build, run, and test our code, but it can do a lot more. In this chapter, we'll discuss some of its other, more advanced features to show you how to do the following:

- Customize your build through release profiles.
- Publish libraries on *https://crates.io*.
- Organize large projects with workspaces.
- Install binaries from *https://crates.io*.
- Extend Cargo using custom commands.

Cargo can do even more than the functionality we cover in this chapter, so for a full explanation of all its features, see its documentation at *https://doc.rust-lang.org/cargo*.

Customizing Builds with Release Profiles

In Rust, *release profiles* are predefined and customizable profiles with different configurations that allow a programmer to have more control over various options for compiling code. Each profile is configured independently of the others.

Cargo has two main profiles: the dev profile Cargo uses when you run cargo build, and the release profile Cargo uses when you run cargo build --release. The dev profile is defined with good defaults for development, and the release profile has good defaults for release builds.

These profile names might be familiar from the output of your builds:

```
$ cargo build
    Finished dev [unoptimized + debuginfo] target(s) in 0.0s
$ cargo build --release
    Finished release [optimized] target(s) in 0.0s
```

The dev and release are these different profiles used by the compiler.

Cargo has default settings for each of the profiles that apply when you haven't explicitly added any [profile.*] sections in the project's *Cargo.toml* file. By adding [profile.*] sections for any profile you want to customize, you override any subset of the default settings. For example, here are the default values for the opt-level setting for the dev and release profiles:

Cargo.toml
```
[profile.dev]
opt-level = 0

[profile.release]
opt-level = 3
```

The opt-level setting controls the number of optimizations Rust will apply to your code, with a range of 0 to 3. Applying more optimizations extends compiling time, so if you're in development and compiling your code often, you'll want fewer optimizations to compile faster even if the resultant code runs slower. The default opt-level for dev is therefore 0. When you're ready to release your code, it's best to spend more time compiling. You'll only compile in release mode once, but you'll run the compiled program many times, so release mode trades longer compile time for code that runs faster. That is why the default opt-level for the release profile is 3.

You can override a default setting by adding a different value for it in *Cargo.toml*. For example, if we want to use optimization level 1 in the development profile, we can add these two lines to our project's *Cargo.toml* file:

Cargo.toml
```
[profile.dev]
opt-level = 1
```

This code overrides the default setting of 0. Now when we run cargo build, Cargo will use the defaults for the dev profile plus our customization to opt-level. Because we set opt-level to 1, Cargo will apply more optimizations than the default, but not as many as in a release build.

For the full list of configuration options and defaults for each profile, see Cargo's documentation at *https://doc.rust-lang.org/cargo/reference/profiles.html*.

Publishing a Crate to Crates.io

We've used packages from *https://crates.io* as dependencies of our project, but you can also share your code with other people by publishing your own packages. The crate registry at *https://crates.io* distributes the source code of your packages, so it primarily hosts code that is open source.

Rust and Cargo have features that make your published package easier for people to find and use. We'll talk about some of these features next and then explain how to publish a package.

Making Useful Documentation Comments

Accurately documenting your packages will help other users know how and when to use them, so it's worth investing the time to write documentation. In Chapter 3, we discussed how to comment Rust code using two slashes, //. Rust also has a particular kind of comment for documentation, known conveniently as a *documentation comment*, that will generate HTML documentation. The HTML displays the contents of documentation comments for public API items intended for programmers interested in knowing how to *use* your crate as opposed to how your crate is *implemented*.

Documentation comments use three slashes, ///, instead of two and support Markdown notation for formatting the text. Place documentation comments just before the item they're documenting. Listing 14-1 shows documentation comments for an add_one function in a crate named my_crate.

```
src/lib.rs   /// Adds one to the number given.
             ///
             /// # Examples
             ///
             /// ```
             /// let arg = 5;
             /// let answer = my_crate::add_one(arg);
             ///
             /// assert_eq!(6, answer);
             /// ```
             pub fn add_one(x: i32) -> i32 {
                 x + 1
             }
```

Listing 14-1: A documentation comment for a function

Here, we give a description of what the add_one function does, start a section with the heading Examples, and then provide code that demonstrates how to use the add_one function. We can generate the HTML documentation from this documentation comment by running cargo doc. This command runs the rustdoc tool distributed with Rust and puts the generated HTML documentation in the *target/doc* directory.

For convenience, running cargo doc --open will build the HTML for your current crate's documentation (as well as the documentation for all of your crate's dependencies) and open the result in a web browser. Navigate to the add_one function and you'll see how the text in the documentation comments is rendered, as shown in Figure 14-1.

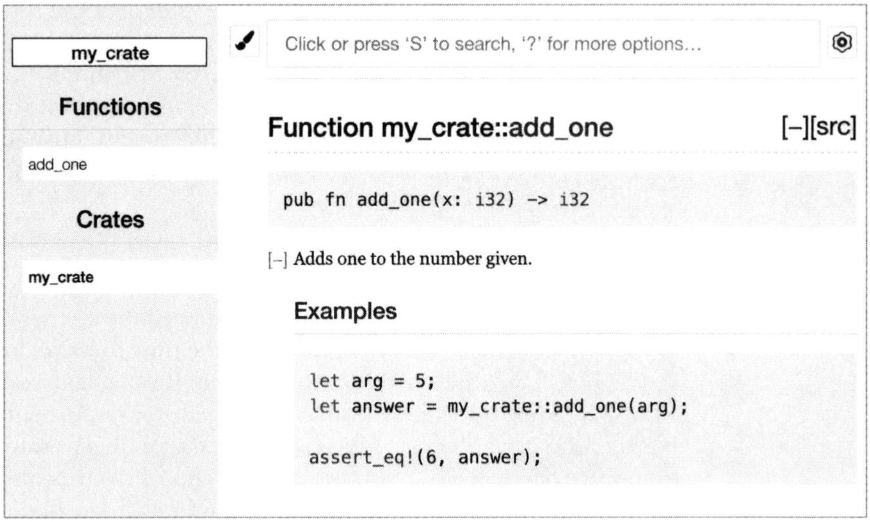

Figure 14-1: HTML documentation for the add_one function

Commonly Used Sections

We used the # Examples Markdown heading in Listing 14-1 to create a section in the HTML with the title "Examples." Here are some other sections that crate authors commonly use in their documentation:

Panics   The scenarios in which the function being documented could panic. Callers of the function who don't want their programs to panic should make sure they don't call the function in these situations.

Errors   If the function returns a Result, describing the kinds of errors that might occur and what conditions might cause those errors to be returned can be helpful to callers so they can write code to handle the different kinds of errors in different ways.

Safety   If the function is unsafe to call (we discuss unsafety in Chapter 19), there should be a section explaining why the function is unsafe and covering the invariants that the function expects callers to uphold.

Most documentation comments don't need all of these sections, but this is a good checklist to remind you of the aspects of your code users will be interested in knowing about.

Documentation Comments as Tests

Adding example code blocks in your documentation comments can help demonstrate how to use your library, and doing so has an additional bonus:

running cargo test will run the code examples in your documentation as tests! Nothing is better than documentation with examples. But nothing is worse than examples that don't work because the code has changed since the documentation was written. If we run cargo test with the documentation for the add_one function from Listing 14-1, we will see a section in the test results that looks like this:

```
Doc-tests my_crate

running 1 test
test src/lib.rs - add_one (line 5) ... ok

test result: ok. 1 passed; 0 failed; 0 ignored; 0 measured; 0
filtered out; finished in 0.27s
```

Now, if we change either the function or the example so the assert_eq! in the example panics, and run cargo test again, we'll see that the doc tests catch that the example and the code are out of sync with each other!

Commenting Contained Items

The doc comment //! adds documentation to the item that *contains* the comments rather than to the items *following* the comments. We typically use these doc comments inside the crate root file (*src/lib.rs* by convention) or inside a module to document the crate or the module as a whole.

For example, to add documentation that describes the purpose of the my_crate crate that contains the add_one function, we add documentation comments that start with //! to the beginning of the *src/lib.rs* file, as shown in Listing 14-2.

src/lib.rs
```
//! # My Crate
//!
//! `my_crate` is a collection of utilities to make performing
//! certain calculations more convenient.

/// Adds one to the number given.
--snip--
```

Listing 14-2: Documentation for the my_crate crate as a whole

Notice there isn't any code after the last line that begins with //!. Because we started the comments with //! instead of ///, we're documenting the item that contains this comment rather than an item that follows this comment. In this case, that item is the *src/lib.rs* file, which is the crate root. These comments describe the entire crate.

When we run cargo doc --open, these comments will display on the front page of the documentation for my_crate above the list of public items in the crate, as shown in Figure 14-2.

Documentation comments within items are useful for describing crates and modules especially. Use them to explain the overall purpose of the container to help your users understand the crate's organization.

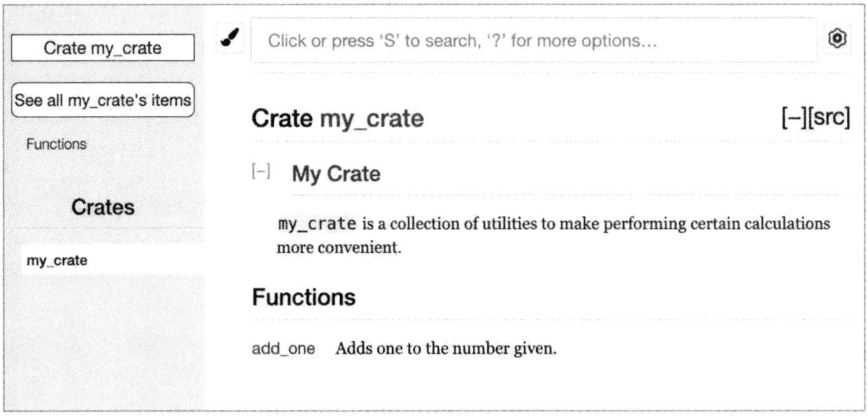

Figure 14-2: Rendered documentation for my_crate, including the comment describing the crate as a whole

Exporting a Convenient Public API with pub use

The structure of your public API is a major consideration when publishing a crate. People who use your crate are less familiar with the structure than you are and might have difficulty finding the pieces they want to use if your crate has a large module hierarchy.

In Chapter 7, we covered how to make items public using the pub keyword, and how to bring items into a scope with the use keyword. However, the structure that makes sense to you while you're developing a crate might not be very convenient for your users. You might want to organize your structs in a hierarchy containing multiple levels, but then people who want to use a type you've defined deep in the hierarchy might have trouble finding out that type exists. They might also be annoyed at having to enter use my_crate::*some_module*::*another_module*::*UsefulType*; rather than use my_crate::*UsefulType*;.

The good news is that if the structure *isn't* convenient for others to use from another library, you don't have to rearrange your internal organization: instead, you can re-export items to make a public structure that's different from your private structure by using pub use. *Re-exporting* takes a public item in one location and makes it public in another location, as if it were defined in the other location instead.

For example, say we made a library named art for modeling artistic concepts. Within this library are two modules: a kinds module containing two enums named PrimaryColor and SecondaryColor and a utils module containing a function named mix, as shown in Listing 14-3.

```
src/lib.rs    //! # Art
              //!
              //! A library for modeling artistic concepts.

              pub mod kinds {
                  /// The primary colors according to the RYB color model.
                  pub enum PrimaryColor {
```

```
        Red,
        Yellow,
        Blue,
    }

    /// The secondary colors according to the RYB color model.
    pub enum SecondaryColor {
        Orange,
        Green,
        Purple,
    }
}

pub mod utils {
    use crate::kinds::*;

    /// Combines two primary colors in equal amounts to create
    /// a secondary color.
    pub fn mix(
        c1: PrimaryColor,
        c2: PrimaryColor,
    ) -> SecondaryColor {
        --snip--
    }
}
```

Listing 14-3: An art library with items organized into kinds and utils modules

Figure 14-3 shows what the front page of the documentation for this crate generated by cargo doc would look like.

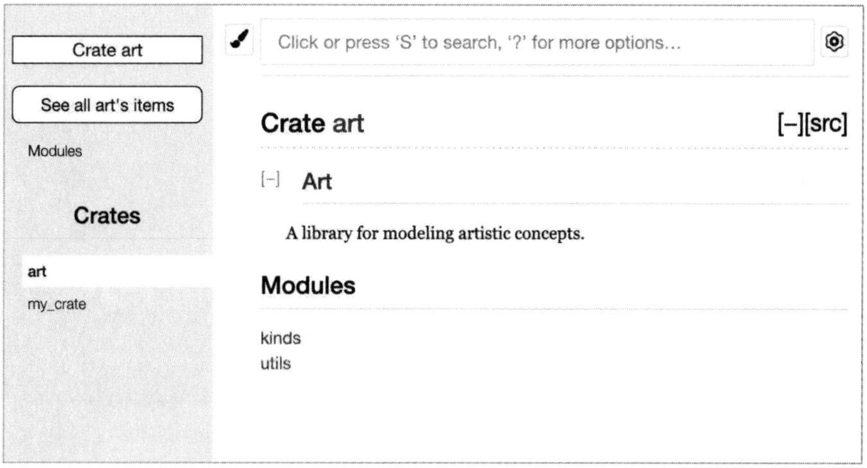

Figure 14-3: Front page of the documentation for art that lists the kinds and utils modules

Note that the PrimaryColor and SecondaryColor types aren't listed on the front page, nor is the mix function. We have to click kinds and utils to see them.

Another crate that depends on this library would need use statements that bring the items from art into scope, specifying the module structure that's currently defined. Listing 14-4 shows an example of a crate that uses the PrimaryColor and mix items from the art crate.

src/main.rs
```
use art::kinds::PrimaryColor;
use art::utils::mix;

fn main() {
    let red = PrimaryColor::Red;
    let yellow = PrimaryColor::Yellow;
    mix(red, yellow);
}
```

Listing 14-4: A crate using the art crate's items with its internal structure exported

The author of the code in Listing 14-4, which uses the art crate, had to figure out that PrimaryColor is in the kinds module and mix is in the utils module. The module structure of the art crate is more relevant to developers working on the art crate than to those using it. The internal structure doesn't contain any useful information for someone trying to understand how to use the art crate, but rather causes confusion because developers who use it have to figure out where to look, and must specify the module names in the use statements.

To remove the internal organization from the public API, we can modify the art crate code in Listing 14-3 to add pub use statements to re-export the items at the top level, as shown in Listing 14-5.

src/lib.rs
```
//! # Art
//!
//! A library for modeling artistic concepts.

pub use self::kinds::PrimaryColor;
pub use self::kinds::SecondaryColor;
pub use self::utils::mix;

pub mod kinds {
    --snip--
}

pub mod utils {
    --snip--
}
```

Listing 14-5: Adding pub use statements to re-export items

The API documentation that cargo doc generates for this crate will now list and link re-exports on the front page, as shown in Figure 14-4, making the PrimaryColor and SecondaryColor types and the mix function easier to find.

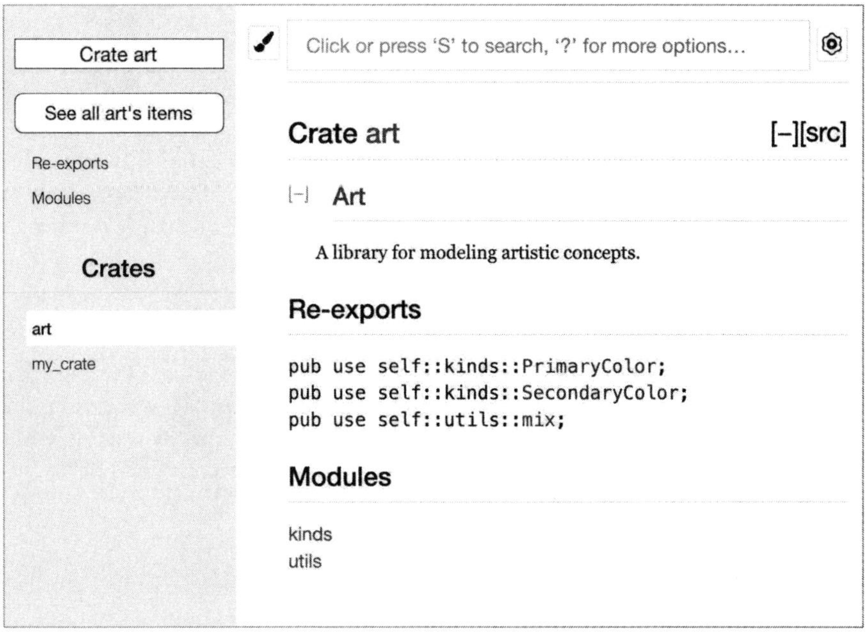

Figure 14-4: The front page of the documentation for art that lists the re-exports

The art crate users can still see and use the internal structure from Listing 14-3 as demonstrated in Listing 14-4, or they can use the more convenient structure in Listing 14-5, as shown in Listing 14-6.

src/main.rs
```
use art::mix;
use art::PrimaryColor;

fn main() {
    --snip--
}
```

Listing 14-6: A program using the re-exported items from the art crate

In cases where there are many nested modules, re-exporting the types at the top level with pub use can make a significant difference in the experience of people who use the crate. Another common use of pub use is to re-export definitions of a dependency in the current crate to make that crate's definitions part of your crate's public API.

Creating a useful public API structure is more of an art than a science, and you can iterate to find the API that works best for your users. Choosing pub use gives you flexibility in how you structure your crate internally and decouples that internal structure from what you present to your users. Look at some of the code of crates you've installed to see if their internal structure differs from their public API.

Setting Up a Crates.io Account

Before you can publish any crates, you need to create an account on *https://crates.io* and get an API token. To do so, visit the home page at *https://crates.io* and log in via a GitHub account. (The GitHub account is currently a requirement, but the site might support other ways of creating an account in the future.) Once you're logged in, visit your account settings at *https://crates.io/me* and retrieve your API key. Then run the cargo login command with your API key, like this:

```
$ cargo login abcdefghijklmnopqrstuvwxyz012345
```

This command will inform Cargo of your API token and store it locally in *~/.cargo/credentials*. Note that this token is a *secret*: do not share it with anyone else. If you do share it with anyone for any reason, you should revoke it and generate a new token on *https://crates.io*.

Adding Metadata to a New Crate

Let's say you have a crate you want to publish. Before publishing, you'll need to add some metadata in the [package] section of the crate's *Cargo.toml* file.

Your crate will need a unique name. While you're working on a crate locally, you can name a crate whatever you'd like. However, crate names on *https://crates.io* are allocated on a first-come, first-served basis. Once a crate name is taken, no one else can publish a crate with that name. Before attempting to publish a crate, search for the name you want to use. If the name has been used, you will need to find another name and edit the name field in the *Cargo.toml* file under the [package] section to use the new name for publishing, like so:

Cargo.toml
```
[package]
name = "guessing_game"
```

Even if you've chosen a unique name, when you run cargo publish to publish the crate at this point, you'll get a warning and then an error:

```
$ cargo publish
    Updating crates.io index
warning: manifest has no description, license, license-file, documentation,
homepage or repository.
See https://doc.rust-lang.org/cargo/reference/manifest.html#package-metadata
for more info.
--snip--
error: failed to publish to registry at https://crates.io

Caused by:
  the remote server responded with an error: missing or empty metadata fields:
description, license. Please see https://doc.rust-lang.org/cargo/reference
/manifest.html for how to upload metadata
```

This results in an error because you're missing some crucial information: a description and license are required so people will know what your crate does and under what terms they can use it. In *Cargo.toml*, add a description that's just a sentence or two, because it will appear with your crate in search results. For the `license` field, you need to give a *license identifier value*. The Linux Foundation's Software Package Data Exchange (SPDX) at *https://spdx.org/licenses* lists the identifiers you can use for this value. For example, to specify that you've licensed your crate using the MIT License, add the `MIT` identifier:

Cargo.toml
```
[package]
name = "guessing_game"
license = "MIT"
```

If you want to use a license that doesn't appear in the SPDX, you need to place the text of that license in a file, include the file in your project, and then use `license-file` to specify the name of that file instead of using the `license` key.

Guidance on which license is appropriate for your project is beyond the scope of this book. Many people in the Rust community license their projects in the same way as Rust by using a dual license of `MIT OR Apache-2.0`. This practice demonstrates that you can also specify multiple license identifiers separated by `OR` to have multiple licenses for your project.

With a unique name, the version, your description, and a license added, the *Cargo.toml* file for a project that is ready to publish might look like this:

Cargo.toml
```
[package]
name = "guessing_game"
version = "0.1.0"
edition = "2021"
description = "A fun game where you guess what number the
computer has chosen."
license = "MIT OR Apache-2.0"

[dependencies]
```

Cargo's documentation at *https://doc.rust-lang.org/cargo* describes other metadata you can specify to ensure that others can discover and use your crate more easily.

Publishing to Crates.io

Now that you've created an account, saved your API token, chosen a name for your crate, and specified the required metadata, you're ready to publish! Publishing a crate uploads a specific version to *https://crates.io* for others to use.

Be careful, because a publish is *permanent*. The version can never be overwritten, and the code cannot be deleted. One major goal of Crates.io is to act as a permanent archive of code so that builds of all projects that depend on crates from *https://crates.io* will continue to work. Allowing version deletions would make fulfilling that goal impossible. However, there is no limit to the number of crate versions you can publish.

Run the `cargo publish` command again. It should succeed now:

```
$ cargo publish
    Updating crates.io index
   Packaging guessing_game v0.1.0 (file:///projects/guessing_game)
   Verifying guessing_game v0.1.0 (file:///projects/guessing_game)
   Compiling guessing_game v0.1.0
(file:///projects/guessing_game/target/package/guessing_game-0.1.0)
    Finished dev [unoptimized + debuginfo] target(s) in 0.19s
   Uploading guessing_game v0.1.0 (file:///projects/guessing_game)
```

Congratulations! You've now shared your code with the Rust community, and anyone can easily add your crate as a dependency of their project.

Publishing a New Version of an Existing Crate

When you've made changes to your crate and are ready to release a new version, you change the `version` value specified in your *Cargo.toml* file and republish. Use the Semantic Versioning rules at *https://semver.org* to decide what an appropriate next version number is, based on the kinds of changes you've made. Then run `cargo publish` to upload the new version.

Deprecating Versions from Crates.io with cargo yank

Although you can't remove previous versions of a crate, you can prevent any future projects from adding them as a new dependency. This is useful when a crate version is broken for one reason or another. In such situations, Cargo supports yanking a crate version.

Yanking a version prevents new projects from depending on that version while allowing all existing projects that depend on it to continue. Essentially, a yank means that all projects with a *Cargo.lock* will not break, and any future *Cargo.lock* files generated will not use the yanked version.

To yank a version of a crate, in the directory of the crate that you've previously published, run `cargo yank` and specify which version you want to yank. For example, if we've published a crate named guessing_game version 1.0.1 and we want to yank it, in the project directory for guessing_game we'd run:

```
$ cargo yank --vers 1.0.1
    Updating crates.io index
        Yank guessing_game@1.0.1
```

By adding `--undo` to the command, you can also undo a yank and allow projects to start depending on a version again:

```
$ cargo yank --vers 1.0.1 --undo
    Updating crates.io index
      Unyank guessing_game@1.0.1
```

A yank *does not* delete any code. It cannot, for example, delete accidentally uploaded secrets. If that happens, you must reset those secrets immediately.

Cargo Workspaces

In Chapter 12, we built a package that included a binary crate and a library crate. As your project develops, you might find that the library crate continues to get bigger and you want to split your package further into multiple library crates. Cargo offers a feature called *workspaces* that can help manage multiple related packages that are developed in tandem.

Creating a Workspace

A *workspace* is a set of packages that share the same *Cargo.lock* and output directory. Let's make a project using a workspace—we'll use trivial code so we can concentrate on the structure of the workspace. There are multiple ways to structure a workspace, so we'll just show one common way. We'll have a workspace containing a binary and two libraries. The binary, which will provide the main functionality, will depend on the two libraries. One library will provide an add_one function and the other library an add_two function. These three crates will be part of the same workspace. We'll start by creating a new directory for the workspace:

```
$ mkdir add
$ cd add
```

Next, in the *add* directory, we create the *Cargo.toml* file that will configure the entire workspace. This file won't have a [package] section. Instead, it will start with a [workspace] section that will allow us to add members to the workspace by specifying the path to the package with our binary crate; in this case, that path is *adder*:

Cargo.toml
```
[workspace]

members = [
    "adder",
]
```

Next, we'll create the adder binary crate by running cargo new within the *add* directory:

```
$ cargo new adder
    Created binary (application) `adder` package
```

At this point, we can build the workspace by running cargo build. The files in your *add* directory should look like this:

```
├── Cargo.lock
├── Cargo.toml
├── adder
│   ├── Cargo.toml
│   └── src
│       └── main.rs
└── target
```

The workspace has one *target* directory at the top level that the compiled artifacts will be placed into; the adder package doesn't have its own *target* directory. Even if we were to run cargo build from inside the *adder* directory, the compiled artifacts would still end up in *add/target* rather than *add/adder/target*. Cargo structures the *target* directory in a workspace like this because the crates in a workspace are meant to depend on each other. If each crate had its own *target* directory, each crate would have to recompile each of the other crates in the workspace to place the artifacts in its own *target* directory. By sharing one *target* directory, the crates can avoid unnecessary rebuilding.

Creating the Second Package in the Workspace

Next, let's create another member package in the workspace and call it add_one. Change the top-level *Cargo.toml* to specify the *add_one* path in the members list:

Cargo.toml
```
[workspace]

members = [
    "adder",
    "add_one",
]
```

Then generate a new library crate named add_one:

```
$ cargo new add_one --lib
    Created library `add_one` package
```

Your *add* directory should now have these directories and files:

```
├── Cargo.lock
├── Cargo.toml
├── add_one
│   ├── Cargo.toml
│   └── src
│       └── lib.rs
├── adder
│   ├── Cargo.toml
│   └── src
│       └── main.rs
└── target
```

In the *add_one/src/lib.rs* file, let's add an add_one function:

add_one/
src/lib.rs
```
pub fn add_one(x: i32) -> i32 {
    x + 1
}
```

Now we can have the adder package with our binary depend on the add_one package that has our library. First we'll need to add a path dependency on add_one to *adder/Cargo.toml*:

adder/
Cargo.toml

```
[dependencies]
add_one = { path = "../add_one" }
```

Cargo doesn't assume that crates in a workspace will depend on each other, so we need to be explicit about the dependency relationships.

Next, let's use the add_one function (from the add_one crate) in the adder crate. Open the *adder/src/main.rs* file and add a use line at the top to bring the new add_one library crate into scope. Then change the main function to call the add_one function, as in Listing 14-7.

adder/src/
main.rs

```
use add_one;

fn main() {
    let num = 10;
    println!(
        "Hello, world! {num} plus one is {}!",
        add_one::add_one(num)
    );
}
```

Listing 14-7: Using the add_one library crate from the adder crate

Let's build the workspace by running cargo build in the top-level *add* directory!

```
$ cargo build
   Compiling add_one v0.1.0 (file:///projects/add/add_one)
   Compiling adder v0.1.0 (file:///projects/add/adder)
    Finished dev [unoptimized + debuginfo] target(s) in 0.68s
```

To run the binary crate from the *add* directory, we can specify which package in the workspace we want to run by using the -p argument and the package name with cargo run:

```
$ cargo run -p adder
    Finished dev [unoptimized + debuginfo] target(s) in 0.0s
     Running `target/debug/adder`
Hello, world! 10 plus one is 11!
```

This runs the code in *adder/src/main.rs*, which depends on the add_one crate.

Depending on an External Package in a Workspace

Notice that the workspace has only one *Cargo.lock* file at the top level, rather than having a *Cargo.lock* in each crate's directory. This ensures that all crates are using the same version of all dependencies. If we add the rand package to the *adder/Cargo.toml* and *add_one/Cargo.toml* files, Cargo will resolve both of those to one version of rand and record that in the one *Cargo.lock*. Making all crates in the workspace use the same dependencies means the crates will always be compatible with each other. Let's add the rand crate to the [dependencies] section in the *add_one/Cargo.toml* file so we can use the rand crate in the add_one crate:

add_one/
Cargo.toml

```
[dependencies]
rand = "0.8.5"
```

We can now add use rand; to the *add_one/src/lib.rs* file, and building the whole workspace by running cargo build in the *add* directory will bring in and compile the rand crate. We will get one warning because we aren't referring to the rand we brought into scope:

```
$ cargo build
    Updating crates.io index
  Downloaded rand v0.8.5
    --snip--
  Compiling rand v0.8.5
  Compiling add_one v0.1.0 (file:///projects/add/add_one)
  Compiling adder v0.1.0 (file:///projects/add/adder)
    Finished dev [unoptimized + debuginfo] target(s) in 10.18s
```

The top-level *Cargo.lock* now contains information about the dependency of add_one on rand. However, even though rand is used somewhere in the workspace, we can't use it in other crates in the workspace unless we add rand to their *Cargo.toml* files as well. For example, if we add use rand; to the *adder/src/main.rs* file for the adder package, we'll get an error:

```
$ cargo build
    --snip--
  Compiling adder v0.1.0 (file:///projects/add/adder)
error[E0432]: unresolved import `rand`
 --> adder/src/main.rs:2:5
  |
2 | use rand;
  |     ^^^^ no external crate `rand`
```

To fix this, edit the *Cargo.toml* file for the adder package and indicate that rand is a dependency for it as well. Building the adder package will add rand to the list of dependencies for adder in *Cargo.lock*, but no additional copies of rand will be downloaded. Cargo has ensured that every crate in every package in the workspace using the rand package will be using the same version, saving us space and ensuring that the crates in the workspace will be compatible with each other.

Adding a Test to a Workspace

For another enhancement, let's add a test of the add_one::add_one function within the add_one crate:

add_one/
src/lib.rs

```rust
pub fn add_one(x: i32) -> i32 {
    x + 1
}
```

```
#[cfg(test)]
mod tests {
    use super::*;

    #[test]
    fn it_works() {
        assert_eq!(3, add_one(2));
    }
}
```

Now run cargo test in the top-level *add* directory. Running cargo test in a workspace structured like this one will run the tests for all the crates in the workspace:

```
$ cargo test
   Compiling add_one v0.1.0 (file:///projects/add/add_one)
   Compiling adder v0.1.0 (file:///projects/add/adder)
    Finished test [unoptimized + debuginfo] target(s) in 0.27s
     Running unittests src/lib.rs (target/debug/deps/add_one-f0253159197f7841)

running 1 test
test tests::it_works ... ok

test result: ok. 1 passed; 0 failed; 0 ignored; 0 measured; 0 filtered out;
finished in 0.00s

     Running unittests src/main.rs (target/debug/deps/adder-49979ff40686fa8e)

running 0 tests

test result: ok. 0 passed; 0 failed; 0 ignored; 0 measured; 0 filtered out;
finished in 0.00s

   Doc-tests add_one

running 0 tests

test result: ok. 0 passed; 0 failed; 0 ignored; 0 measured; 0 filtered out;
finished in 0.00s
```

The first section of the output shows that the it_works test in the add _one crate passed. The next section shows that zero tests were found in the adder crate, and then the last section shows zero documentation tests were found in the add_one crate.

We can also run tests for one particular crate in a workspace from the top-level directory by using the -p flag and specifying the name of the crate we want to test:

```
$ cargo test -p add_one
    Finished test [unoptimized + debuginfo] target(s) in 0.00s
     Running unittests src/lib.rs (target/debug/deps/add_one-b3235fea9a156f74)
```

```
running 1 test
test tests::it_works ... ok

test result: ok. 1 passed; 0 failed; 0 ignored; 0 measured; 0 filtered out;
finished in 0.00s

   Doc-tests add_one

running 0 tests

test result: ok. 0 passed; 0 failed; 0 ignored; 0 measured; 0 filtered out;
finished in 0.00s
```

This output shows cargo test only ran the tests for the add_one crate and didn't run the adder crate tests.

If you publish the crates in the workspace to *https://crates.io*, each crate in the workspace will need to be published separately. Like cargo test, we can publish a particular crate in our workspace by using the -p flag and specifying the name of the crate we want to publish.

For additional practice, add an add_two crate to this workspace in a similar way as the add_one crate!

As your project grows, consider using a workspace: it provides easier-to-understand, smaller, individual components than one big blob of code. Furthermore, keeping the crates in a workspace can make coordination between crates easier if they are often changed at the same time.

Installing Binaries with cargo install

The cargo install command allows you to install and use binary crates locally. This isn't intended to replace system packages; it's meant to be a convenient way for Rust developers to install tools that others have shared on *https://crates.io*. Note that you can only install packages that have binary targets. A *binary target* is the runnable program that is created if the crate has a *src/main.rs* file or another file specified as a binary, as opposed to a library target that isn't runnable on its own but is suitable for including within other programs. Usually, crates have information in the README file about whether a crate is a library, has a binary target, or both.

All binaries installed with cargo install are stored in the installation root's *bin* folder. If you installed Rust using *rustup.rs* and don't have any custom configurations, this directory will be *$HOME/.cargo/bin*. Ensure that directory is in your $PATH to be able to run programs you've installed with cargo install.

For example, in Chapter 12 we mentioned that there's a Rust implementation of the grep tool called ripgrep for searching files. To install ripgrep, we can run the following:

```
$ cargo install ripgrep
    Updating crates.io index
  Downloaded ripgrep v13.0.0
  Downloaded 1 crate (243.3 KB) in 0.88s
```

```
Installing ripgrep v13.0.0
 --snip--
 Compiling ripgrep v13.0.0
  Finished release [optimized + debuginfo] target(s) in 3m 10s
Installing ~/.cargo/bin/rg
  Installed package `ripgrep v13.0.0` (executable `rg`)
```

The second-to-last line of the output shows the location and the name of the installed binary, which in the case of ripgrep is rg. As long as the installation directory is in your $PATH, as mentioned previously, you can then run rg --help and start using a faster, Rustier tool for searching files!

Extending Cargo with Custom Commands

Cargo is designed so you can extend it with new subcommands without having to modify it. If a binary in your $PATH is named cargo-something, you can run it as if it were a Cargo subcommand by running cargo something. Custom commands like this are also listed when you run cargo --list. Being able to use cargo install to install extensions and then run them just like the built-in Cargo tools is a super-convenient benefit of Cargo's design!

Summary

Sharing code with Cargo and *https://crates.io* is part of what makes the Rust ecosystem useful for many different tasks. Rust's standard library is small and stable, but crates are easy to share, use, and improve on a timeline different from that of the language. Don't be shy about sharing code that's useful to you on *https://crates.io*; it's likely that it will be useful to someone else as well!

15

SMART POINTERS

A *pointer* is a general concept for a variable that contains an address in memory. This address refers to, or "points at," some other data. The most common kind of pointer in Rust is a reference, which you learned about in Chapter 4. References are indicated by the & symbol and borrow the value they point to. They don't have any special capabilities other than referring to data, and they have no overhead.

Smart pointers, on the other hand, are data structures that act like a pointer but also have additional metadata and capabilities. The concept of smart pointers isn't unique to Rust: smart pointers originated in C++ and exist in other languages as well. Rust has a variety of smart pointers defined in the standard library that provide functionality beyond that provided by references. To explore the general concept, we'll look at a couple of different examples of smart pointers, including a *reference counting* smart pointer type. This pointer enables you to allow data to have multiple owners by keeping track of the number of owners and, when no owners remain, cleaning up the data.

Rust, with its concept of ownership and borrowing, has an additional difference between references and smart pointers: while references only borrow data, in many cases smart pointers *own* the data they point to.

Though we didn't call them as such at the time, we've already encountered a few smart pointers in this book, including String and Vec<T> in Chapter 8. Both of these types count as smart pointers because they own some memory and allow you to manipulate it. They also have metadata and extra capabilities or guarantees. String, for example, stores its capacity as metadata and has the extra ability to ensure its data will always be valid UTF-8.

Smart pointers are usually implemented using structs. Unlike an ordinary struct, smart pointers implement the Deref and Drop traits. The Deref trait allows an instance of the smart pointer struct to behave like a reference so you can write your code to work with either references or smart pointers. The Drop trait allows you to customize the code that's run when an instance of the smart pointer goes out of scope. In this chapter, we'll discuss both of these traits and demonstrate why they're important to smart pointers.

Given that the smart pointer pattern is a general design pattern used frequently in Rust, this chapter won't cover every existing smart pointer. Many libraries have their own smart pointers, and you can even write your own. We'll cover the most common smart pointers in the standard library:

- Box<T>, for allocating values on the heap
- Rc<T>, a reference counting type that enables multiple ownership
- Ref<T> and RefMut<T>, accessed through RefCell<T>, a type that enforces the borrowing rules at runtime instead of compile time

In addition, we'll cover the *interior mutability* pattern where an immutable type exposes an API for mutating an interior value. We'll also discuss reference cycles: how they can leak memory and how to prevent them.

Let's dive in!

Using Box<T> to Point to Data on the Heap

The most straightforward smart pointer is a box, whose type is written Box<T>. *Boxes* allow you to store data on the heap rather than the stack. What remains on the stack is the pointer to the heap data. Refer to Chapter 4 to review the difference between the stack and the heap.

Boxes don't have performance overhead, other than storing their data on the heap instead of on the stack. But they don't have many extra capabilities either. You'll use them most often in these situations:

- When you have a type whose size can't be known at compile time and you want to use a value of that type in a context that requires an exact size
- When you have a large amount of data and you want to transfer ownership but ensure the data won't be copied when you do so
- When you want to own a value and you care only that it's a type that implements a particular trait rather than being of a specific type

We'll demonstrate the first situation in "Enabling Recursive Types with Boxes" later in this chapter. In the second case, transferring ownership of a large amount of data can take a long time because the data is copied around on the stack. To improve performance in this situation, we can store the large amount of data on the heap in a box. Then, only the small amount of pointer data is copied around on the stack, while the data it references stays in one place on the heap. The third case is known as a *trait object*, and "Using Trait Objects That Allow for Values of Different Types" on page 379 is devoted to that topic. So what you learn here you'll apply again in that section!

Using Box<T> to Store Data on the Heap

Before we discuss the heap storage use case for Box<T>, we'll cover the syntax and how to interact with values stored within a Box<T>.

Listing 15-1 shows how to use a box to store an i32 value on the heap.

src/main.rs
```
fn main() {
    let b = Box::new(5);
    println!("b = {b}");
}
```

Listing 15-1: Storing an i32 value on the heap using a box

We define the variable b to have the value of a Box that points to the value 5, which is allocated on the heap. This program will print b = 5; in this case, we can access the data in the box similarly to how we would if this data were on the stack. Just like any owned value, when a box goes out of scope, as b does at the end of main, it will be deallocated. The deallocation happens both for the box (stored on the stack) and the data it points to (stored on the heap).

Putting a single value on the heap isn't very useful, so you won't use boxes by themselves in this way very often. Having values like a single i32 on the stack, where they're stored by default, is more appropriate in the majority of situations. Let's look at a case where boxes allow us to define types that we wouldn't be allowed to define if we didn't have boxes.

Enabling Recursive Types with Boxes

A value of a *recursive type* can have another value of the same type as part of itself. Recursive types pose an issue because, at compile time, Rust needs to know how much space a type takes up. However, the nesting of values of recursive types could theoretically continue infinitely, so Rust can't know how much space the value needs. Because boxes have a known size, we can enable recursive types by inserting a box in the recursive type definition.

As an example of a recursive type, let's explore the *cons list*. This is a data type commonly found in functional programming languages. The cons list type we'll define is straightforward except for the recursion; therefore, the concepts in the example we'll work with will be useful any time you get into more complex situations involving recursive types.

More Information About the Cons List

A *cons list* is a data structure that comes from the Lisp programming language and its dialects, is made up of nested pairs, and is the Lisp version of a linked list. Its name comes from the cons function (short for *construct function*) in Lisp that constructs a new pair from its two arguments. By calling cons on a pair consisting of a value and another pair, we can construct cons lists made up of recursive pairs.

For example, here's a pseudocode representation of a cons list containing the list 1, 2, 3 with each pair in parentheses:

```
(1, (2, (3, Nil)))
```

Each item in a cons list contains two elements: the value of the current item and the next item. The last item in the list contains only a value called Nil without a next item. A cons list is produced by recursively calling the cons function. The canonical name to denote the base case of the recursion is Nil. Note that this is not the same as the "null" or "nil" concept discussed in Chapter 6, which is an invalid or absent value.

The cons list isn't a commonly used data structure in Rust. Most of the time when you have a list of items in Rust, Vec<T> is a better choice to use. Other, more complex recursive data types *are* useful in various situations, but by starting with the cons list in this chapter, we can explore how boxes let us define a recursive data type without much distraction.

Listing 15-2 contains an enum definition for a cons list. Note that this code won't compile yet because the List type doesn't have a known size, which we'll demonstrate.

src/main.rs
```
enum List {
    Cons(i32, List),
    Nil,
}
```

Listing 15-2: The first attempt at defining an enum to represent a cons list data structure of i32 values

NOTE   *We're implementing a cons list that holds only i32 values for the purposes of this example. We could have implemented it using generics, as we discussed in Chapter 10, to define a cons list type that could store values of any type.*

Using the List type to store the list 1, 2, 3 would look like the code in Listing 15-3.

src/main.rs
```
--snip--

use crate::List::{Cons, Nil};

fn main() {
    let list = Cons(1, Cons(2, Cons(3, Nil)));
}
```

Listing 15-3: Using the List enum to store the list 1, 2, 3

The first Cons value holds 1 and another List value. This List value is another Cons value that holds 2 and another List value. This List value is one more Cons value that holds 3 and a List value, which is finally Nil, the non-recursive variant that signals the end of the list.

If we try to compile the code in Listing 15-3, we get the error shown in Listing 15-4.

```
error[E0072]: recursive type `List` has infinite size
 --> src/main.rs:1:1
  |
1 | enum List {
  | ^^^^^^^^^ recursive type has infinite size
2 |     Cons(i32, List),
  |               ---- recursive without indirection
  |
help: insert some indirection (e.g., a `Box`, `Rc`, or `&`) to make `List`
representable
  |
2 |     Cons(i32, Box<List>),
  |               ++++    +
```

Listing 15-4: The error we get when attempting to define a recursive enum

The error shows this type "has infinite size." The reason is that we've defined List with a variant that is recursive: it holds another value of itself directly. As a result, Rust can't figure out how much space it needs to store a List value. Let's break down why we get this error. First we'll look at how Rust decides how much space it needs to store a value of a non-recursive type.

Computing the Size of a Non-Recursive Type

Recall the Message enum we defined in Listing 6-2 when we discussed enum definitions in Chapter 6:

```
enum Message {
    Quit,
    Move { x: i32, y: i32 },
    Write(String),
    ChangeColor(i32, i32, i32),
}
```

To determine how much space to allocate for a Message value, Rust goes through each of the variants to see which variant needs the most space. Rust sees that Message::Quit doesn't need any space, Message::Move needs enough space to store two i32 values, and so forth. Because only one variant will be used, the most space a Message value will need is the space it would take to store the largest of its variants.

Contrast this with what happens when Rust tries to determine how much space a recursive type like the List enum in Listing 15-2 needs. The compiler starts by looking at the Cons variant, which holds a value of type i32 and a value of type List. Therefore, Cons needs an amount of space equal to the size of an i32 plus the size of a List. To figure out how much memory the List type needs, the compiler looks at the variants, starting with the Cons variant. The Cons variant holds a value of type i32 and a value of type List, and this process continues infinitely, as shown in Figure 15-1.

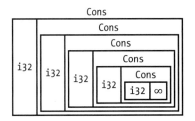

Figure 15-1: An infinite List consisting of infinite Cons variants

Using Box<T> to Get a Recursive Type with a Known Size

Because Rust can't figure out how much space to allocate for recursively defined types, the compiler gives an error with this helpful suggestion:

```
help: insert some indirection (e.g., a `Box`, `Rc`, or `&`) to make `List`
representable
  |
2 |     Cons(i32, Box<List>),
  |              ++++    +
```

In this suggestion, *indirection* means that instead of storing a value directly, we should change the data structure to store the value indirectly by storing a pointer to the value instead.

Because a Box<T> is a pointer, Rust always knows how much space a Box<T> needs: a pointer's size doesn't change based on the amount of data it's pointing to. This means we can put a Box<T> inside the Cons variant instead of another List value directly. The Box<T> will point to the next List value that will be on the heap rather than inside the Cons variant. Conceptually, we still have a list, created with lists holding other lists, but this implementation is now more like placing the items next to one another rather than inside one another.

We can change the definition of the List enum in Listing 15-2 and the usage of the List in Listing 15-3 to the code in Listing 15-5, which will compile.

src/main.rs
```
enum List {
    Cons(i32, Box<List>),
    Nil,
}

use crate::List::{Cons, Nil};

fn main() {
    let list = Cons(
        1,
```

```
        Box::new(Cons(
            2,
            Box::new(Cons(
                3,
                Box::new(Nil)
            ))
        ))
    );
}
```

Listing 15-5: Definition of List that uses Box<T> in order to have a known size

The Cons variant needs the size of an i32 plus the space to store the box's pointer data. The Nil variant stores no values, so it needs less space than the Cons variant. We now know that any List value will take up the size of an i32 plus the size of a box's pointer data. By using a box, we've broken the infinite, recursive chain, so the compiler can figure out the size it needs to store a List value. Figure 15-2 shows what the Cons variant looks like now.

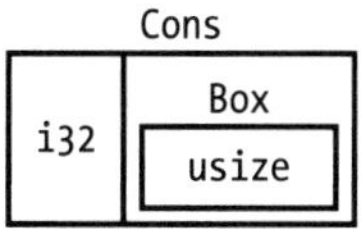

Figure 15-2: A List that is not infinitely sized, because Cons holds a Box

Boxes provide only the indirection and heap allocation; they don't have any other special capabilities, like those we'll see with the other smart pointer types. They also don't have the performance overhead that these special capabilities incur, so they can be useful in cases like the cons list where the indirection is the only feature we need. We'll look at more use cases for boxes in Chapter 17.

The Box<T> type is a smart pointer because it implements the Deref trait, which allows Box<T> values to be treated like references. When a Box<T> value goes out of scope, the heap data that the box is pointing to is cleaned up as well because of the Drop trait implementation. These two traits will be even more important to the functionality provided by the other smart pointer types we'll discuss in the rest of this chapter. Let's explore these two traits in more detail.

Treating Smart Pointers Like Regular References with Deref

Implementing the Deref trait allows you to customize the behavior of the *dereference operator* * (not to be confused with the multiplication or glob operator). By implementing Deref in such a way that a smart pointer can be treated like a regular reference, you can write code that operates on references and use that code with smart pointers too.

Let's first look at how the dereference operator works with regular references. Then we'll try to define a custom type that behaves like Box<T>, and see why the dereference operator doesn't work like a reference on our newly defined type. We'll explore how implementing the Deref trait makes it possible for smart pointers to work in ways similar to references. Then we'll look at Rust's *deref coercion* feature and how it lets us work with either references or smart pointers.

NOTE *There's one big difference between the MyBox<T> type we're about to build and the real Box<T>: our version will not store its data on the heap. We are focusing this example on Deref, so where the data is actually stored is less important than the pointer-like behavior.*

Following the Pointer to the Value

A regular reference is a type of pointer, and one way to think of a pointer is as an arrow to a value stored somewhere else. In Listing 15-6, we create a reference to an i32 value and then use the dereference operator to follow the reference to the value.

src/main.rs
```
fn main() {
  ❶ let x = 5;
  ❷ let y = &x;

  ❸ assert_eq!(5, x);
  ❹ assert_eq!(5, *y);
}
```

Listing 15-6: Using the dereference operator to follow a reference to an i32 value

The variable x holds an i32 value 5 ❶. We set y equal to a reference to x ❷. We can assert that x is equal to 5 ❸. However, if we want to make an assertion about the value in y, we have to use *y to follow the reference to the value it's pointing to (hence *dereference*) so the compiler can compare the actual value ❹. Once we dereference y, we have access to the integer value y is pointing to that we can compare with 5.

If we tried to write assert_eq!(5, y); instead, we would get this compilation error:

```
error[E0277]: can't compare `{integer}` with `&{integer}`
  --> src/main.rs:6:5
   |
6  |     assert_eq!(5, y);
   |     ^^^^^^^^^^^^^^^^^ no implementation for `{integer} ==
&{integer}`
   |
   = help: the trait `PartialEq<&{integer}>` is not implemented
for `{integer}`
```

Comparing a number and a reference to a number isn't allowed because they're different types. We must use the dereference operator to follow the reference to the value it's pointing to.

Using Box<T> Like a Reference

We can rewrite the code in Listing 15-6 to use a Box<T> instead of a reference; the dereference operator used on the Box<T> in Listing 15-7 functions in the same way as the dereference operator used on the reference in Listing 15-6.

src/main.rs
```
fn main() {
    let x = 5;
 ❶ let y = Box::new(x);

    assert_eq!(5, x);
 ❷ assert_eq!(5, *y);
}
```

Listing 15-7: Using the dereference operator on a Box<i32>

The main difference between Listing 15-7 and Listing 15-6 is that here we set y to be an instance of a box pointing to a copied value of x rather than a reference pointing to the value of x ❶. In the last assertion ❷, we can use the dereference operator to follow the box's pointer in the same way that we did when y was a reference. Next, we'll explore what is special about Box<T> that enables us to use the dereference operator by defining our own box type.

Defining Our Own Smart Pointer

Let's build a smart pointer similar to the Box<T> type provided by the standard library to experience how smart pointers behave differently from references by default. Then we'll look at how to add the ability to use the dereference operator.

The Box<T> type is ultimately defined as a tuple struct with one element, so Listing 15-8 defines a MyBox<T> type in the same way. We'll also define a new function to match the new function defined on Box<T>.

src/main.rs
```
❶ struct MyBox<T>(T);

impl<T> MyBox<T> {
 ❷ fn new(x: T) -> MyBox<T> {
     ❸ MyBox(x)
    }
}
```

Listing 15-8: Defining a MyBox<T> type

We define a struct named MyBox and declare a generic parameter T ❶ because we want our type to hold values of any type. The MyBox type is a tuple struct with one element of type T. The MyBox::new function takes one parameter of type T ❷ and returns a MyBox instance that holds the value passed in ❸.

Let's try adding the main function in Listing 15-7 to Listing 15-8 and changing it to use the MyBox<T> type we've defined instead of Box<T>. The code in Listing 15-9 won't compile because Rust doesn't know how to deref-erence MyBox.

src/main.rs

```
fn main() {
    let x = 5;
    let y = MyBox::new(x);

    assert_eq!(5, x);
    assert_eq!(5, *y);
}
```

Listing 15-9: Attempting to use MyBox<T> in the same way we used references and Box<T>

Here's the resultant compilation error:

```
error[E0614]: type `MyBox<{integer}>` cannot be dereferenced
  --> src/main.rs:14:19
   |
14 |     assert_eq!(5, *y);
   |                   ^^
```

Our MyBox<T> type can't be dereferenced because we haven't implemented that ability on our type. To enable dereferencing with the * operator, we implement the Deref trait.

Implementing the Deref Trait

As discussed in "Implementing a Trait on a Type" on page 193, to imple-ment a trait we need to provide implementations for the trait's required methods. The Deref trait, provided by the standard library, requires us to implement one method named deref that borrows self and returns a refer-ence to the inner data. Listing 15-10 contains an implementation of Deref to add to the definition of MyBox<T>.

src/main.rs

```
use std::ops::Deref;

impl<T> Deref for MyBox<T> {
  ❶ type Target = T;

    fn deref(&self) -> &Self::Target {
      ❷ &self.0
    }
}
```

Listing 15-10: Implementing Deref on MyBox<T>

The type Target = T; syntax ❶ defines an associated type for the Deref trait to use. Associated types are a slightly different way of declaring a generic parameter, but you don't need to worry about them for now; we'll cover them in more detail in Chapter 19.

We fill in the body of the deref method with &self.0 so deref returns a reference to the value we want to access with the * operator ❷; recall from "Using Tuple Structs Without Named Fields to Create Different Types" on page 89 that .0 accesses the first value in a tuple struct. The main function in Listing 15-9 that calls * on the MyBox<T> value now compiles, and the assertions pass!

Without the Deref trait, the compiler can only dereference & references. The deref method gives the compiler the ability to take a value of any type that implements Deref and call the deref method to get an & reference that it knows how to dereference.

When we entered *y in Listing 15-9, behind the scenes Rust actually ran this code:

```
*(y.deref())
```

Rust substitutes the * operator with a call to the deref method and then a plain dereference so we don't have to think about whether or not we need to call the deref method. This Rust feature lets us write code that functions identically whether we have a regular reference or a type that implements Deref.

The reason the deref method returns a reference to a value, and that the plain dereference outside the parentheses in *(y.deref()) is still necessary, has to do with the ownership system. If the deref method returned the value directly instead of a reference to the value, the value would be moved out of self. We don't want to take ownership of the inner value inside MyBox<T> in this case or in most cases where we use the dereference operator.

Note that the * operator is replaced with a call to the deref method and then a call to the * operator just once, each time we use a * in our code. Because the substitution of the * operator does not recurse infinitely, we end up with data of type i32, which matches the 5 in assert_eq! in Listing 15-9.

Implicit Deref Coercions with Functions and Methods

Deref coercion converts a reference to a type that implements the Deref trait into a reference to another type. For example, deref coercion can convert &String to &str because String implements the Deref trait such that it returns &str. Deref coercion is a convenience Rust performs on arguments to functions and methods, and works only on types that implement the Deref trait. It happens automatically when we pass a reference to a particular type's value as an argument to a function or method that doesn't match the parameter type in the function or method definition. A sequence of calls to the deref method converts the type we provided into the type the parameter needs.

Deref coercion was added to Rust so that programmers writing function and method calls don't need to add as many explicit references and dereferences with & and *. The deref coercion feature also lets us write more code that can work for either references or smart pointers.

To see deref coercion in action, let's use the MyBox<T> type we defined in Listing 15-8 as well as the implementation of Deref that we added in Listing 15-10. Listing 15-11 shows the definition of a function that has a string slice parameter.

```
fn hello(name: &str) {
    println!("Hello, {name}!");
}
```

Listing 15-11: A hello function that has the parameter name of type &str

We can call the hello function with a string slice as an argument, such as hello("Rust");, for example. Deref coercion makes it possible to call hello with a reference to a value of type MyBox<String>, as shown in Listing 15-12.

```
fn main() {
    let m = MyBox::new(String::from("Rust"));
    hello(&m);
}
```

Listing 15-12: Calling hello with a reference to a MyBox<String> value, which works because of deref coercion

Here we're calling the hello function with the argument &m, which is a reference to a MyBox<String> value. Because we implemented the Deref trait on MyBox<T> in Listing 15-10, Rust can turn &MyBox<String> into &String by calling deref. The standard library provides an implementation of Deref on String that returns a string slice, and this is in the API documentation for Deref. Rust calls deref again to turn the &String into &str, which matches the hello function's definition.

If Rust didn't implement deref coercion, we would have to write the code in Listing 15-13 instead of the code in Listing 15-12 to call hello with a value of type &MyBox<String>.

```
fn main() {
    let m = MyBox::new(String::from("Rust"));
    hello(&(*m)[..]);
}
```

Listing 15-13: The code we would have to write if Rust didn't have deref coercion

The (*m) dereferences the MyBox<String> into a String. Then the & and [..] take a string slice of the String that is equal to the whole string to match the signature of hello. This code without deref coercions is harder to read, write, and understand with all of these symbols involved. Deref coercion allows Rust to handle these conversions for us automatically.

When the Deref trait is defined for the types involved, Rust will analyze the types and use Deref::deref as many times as necessary to get a reference to match the parameter's type. The number of times that Deref::deref needs to be inserted is resolved at compile time, so there is no runtime penalty for taking advantage of deref coercion!

How Deref Coercion Interacts with Mutability

Similar to how you use the Deref trait to override the * operator on immutable references, you can use the DerefMut trait to override the * operator on mutable references.

Rust does deref coercion when it finds types and trait implementations in three cases:

1. From &T to &U when T: Deref<Target=U>
2. From &mut T to &mut U when T: DerefMut<Target=U>
3. From &mut T to &U when T: Deref<Target=U>

The first two cases are the same except that the second implements mutability. The first case states that if you have a &T, and T implements Deref to some type U, you can get a &U transparently. The second case states that the same deref coercion happens for mutable references.

The third case is trickier: Rust will also coerce a mutable reference to an immutable one. But the reverse is *not* possible: immutable references will never coerce to mutable references. Because of the borrowing rules, if you have a mutable reference, that mutable reference must be the only reference to that data (otherwise, the program wouldn't compile). Converting one mutable reference to one immutable reference will never break the borrowing rules. Converting an immutable reference to a mutable reference would require that the initial immutable reference is the only immutable reference to that data, but the borrowing rules don't guarantee that. Therefore, Rust can't make the assumption that converting an immutable reference to a mutable reference is possible.

Running Code on Cleanup with the Drop Trait

The second trait important to the smart pointer pattern is Drop, which lets you customize what happens when a value is about to go out of scope. You can provide an implementation for the Drop trait on any type, and that code can be used to release resources like files or network connections.

We're introducing Drop in the context of smart pointers because the functionality of the Drop trait is almost always used when implementing a smart pointer. For example, when a Box<T> is dropped, it will deallocate the space on the heap that the box points to.

In some languages, for some types, the programmer must call code to free memory or resources every time they finish using an instance of those types. Examples include file handles, sockets, and locks. If they forget, the system might become overloaded and crash. In Rust, you can specify that a particular bit of code be run whenever a value goes out of scope, and the compiler will insert this code automatically. As a result, you don't need to be careful about placing cleanup code everywhere in a program that an instance of a particular type is finished with—you still won't leak resources!

You specify the code to run when a value goes out of scope by implementing the Drop trait. The Drop trait requires you to implement one method named drop that takes a mutable reference to self. To see when Rust calls drop, let's implement drop with println! statements for now.

Listing 15-14 shows a `CustomSmartPointer` struct whose only custom functionality is that it will print `Dropping CustomSmartPointer!` when the instance goes out of scope, to show when Rust runs the drop method.

src/main.rs

```
struct CustomSmartPointer {
    data: String,
}

❶ impl Drop for CustomSmartPointer {
    fn drop(&mut self) {
      ❷ println!(
            "Dropping CustomSmartPointer with data `{}`!",
            self.data
        );
    }
}

fn main() {
  ❸ let c = CustomSmartPointer {
        data: String::from("my stuff"),
    };
  ❹ let d = CustomSmartPointer {
        data: String::from("other stuff"),
    };
  ❺ println!("CustomSmartPointers created.");
❻ }
```

Listing 15-14: A *CustomSmartPointer* struct that implements the *Drop* trait where we would put our cleanup code

The `Drop` trait is included in the prelude, so we don't need to bring it into scope. We implement the `Drop` trait on `CustomSmartPointer` ❶ and provide an implementation for the drop method that calls `println!` ❷. The body of the drop method is where you would place any logic that you wanted to run when an instance of your type goes out of scope. We're printing some text here to demonstrate visually when Rust will call drop.

In main, we create two instances of `CustomSmartPointer` at ❸ and ❹ and then print `CustomSmartPointers created` ❺. At the end of main ❻, our instances of `CustomSmartPointer` will go out of scope, and Rust will call the code we put in the drop method ❷, printing our final message. Note that we didn't need to call the drop method explicitly.

When we run this program, we'll see the following output:

```
CustomSmartPointers created.
Dropping CustomSmartPointer with data `other stuff`!
Dropping CustomSmartPointer with data `my stuff`!
```

Rust automatically called drop for us when our instances went out of scope, calling the code we specified. Variables are dropped in the reverse order of their creation, so d was dropped before c. This example's purpose is to give you a visual guide to how the drop method works; usually you would specify the cleanup code that your type needs to run rather than a print message.

Unfortunately, it's not straightforward to disable the automatic drop functionality. Disabling drop isn't usually necessary; the whole point of the Drop trait is that it's taken care of automatically. Occasionally, however, you might want to clean up a value early. One example is when using smart pointers that manage locks: you might want to force the drop method that releases the lock so that other code in the same scope can acquire the lock. Rust doesn't let you call the Drop trait's drop method manually; instead, you have to call the std::mem::drop function provided by the standard library if you want to force a value to be dropped before the end of its scope.

If we try to call the Drop trait's drop method manually by modifying the main function from Listing 15-14, as shown in Listing 15-15, we'll get a compiler error.

src/main.rs
```
fn main() {
    let c = CustomSmartPointer {
        data: String::from("some data"),
    };
    println!("CustomSmartPointer created.");
    c.drop();
    println!(
        "CustomSmartPointer dropped before the end of main."
    );
}
```

Listing 15-15: Attempting to call the drop method from the Drop trait manually to clean up early

When we try to compile this code, we'll get this error:

```
error[E0040]: explicit use of destructor method
  --> src/main.rs:16:7
   |
16 |     c.drop();
   |     --^^^^--
   |     | |
   |     | explicit destructor calls not allowed
   |     help: consider using `drop` function: `drop(c)`
```

This error message states that we're not allowed to explicitly call drop. The error message uses the term *destructor*, which is the general programming term for a function that cleans up an instance. A destructor is analogous to a *constructor*, which creates an instance. The drop function in Rust is one particular destructor.

Rust doesn't let us call drop explicitly because Rust would still automatically call drop on the value at the end of main. This would cause a *double free* error because Rust would be trying to clean up the same value twice.

We can't disable the automatic insertion of drop when a value goes out of scope, and we can't call the drop method explicitly. So, if we need to force a value to be cleaned up early, we use the std::mem::drop function.

The std::mem::drop function is different from the drop method in the Drop trait. We call it by passing as an argument the value we want to force-drop.

The function is in the prelude, so we can modify `main` in Listing 15-15 to call the `drop` function, as shown in Listing 15-16.

src/main.rs
```
fn main() {
    let c = CustomSmartPointer {
        data: String::from("some data"),
    };
    println!("CustomSmartPointer created.");
    drop(c);
    println!(
        "CustomSmartPointer dropped before the end of main."
    );
}
```

Listing 15-16: Calling `std::mem::drop` to explicitly drop a value before it goes out of scope

Running this code will print the following:

```
CustomSmartPointer created.
Dropping CustomSmartPointer with data `some data`!
CustomSmartPointer dropped before the end of main.
```

The text `Dropping CustomSmartPointer with data `some data`!` is printed between the `CustomSmartPointer created.` and `CustomSmartPointer dropped before the end of main.` text, showing that the drop method code is called to drop `c` at that point.

You can use code specified in a `Drop` trait implementation in many ways to make cleanup convenient and safe: for instance, you could use it to create your own memory allocator! With the `Drop` trait and Rust's ownership system, you don't have to remember to clean up because Rust does it automatically.

You also don't have to worry about problems resulting from accidentally cleaning up values still in use: the ownership system that makes sure references are always valid also ensures that `drop` gets called only once when the value is no longer being used.

Now that we've examined `Box<T>` and some of the characteristics of smart pointers, let's look at a few other smart pointers defined in the standard library.

Rc<T>, the Reference Counted Smart Pointer

In the majority of cases, ownership is clear: you know exactly which variable owns a given value. However, there are cases when a single value might have multiple owners. For example, in graph data structures, multiple edges might point to the same node, and that node is conceptually owned by all of the edges that point to it. A node shouldn't be cleaned up unless it doesn't have any edges pointing to it and so has no owners.

You have to enable multiple ownership explicitly by using the Rust type `Rc<T>`, which is an abbreviation for *reference counting*. The `Rc<T>` type keeps track of the number of references to a value to determine whether or not the value is still in use. If there are zero references to a value, the value can be cleaned up without any references becoming invalid.

Imagine Rc<T> as a TV in a family room. When one person enters to watch TV, they turn it on. Others can come into the room and watch the TV. When the last person leaves the room, they turn off the TV because it's no longer being used. If someone turns off the TV while others are still watching it, there would be an uproar from the remaining TV watchers!

We use the Rc<T> type when we want to allocate some data on the heap for multiple parts of our program to read and we can't determine at compile time which part will finish using the data last. If we knew which part would finish last, we could just make that part the data's owner, and the normal ownership rules enforced at compile time would take effect.

Note that Rc<T> is only for use in single-threaded scenarios. When we discuss concurrency in Chapter 16, we'll cover how to do reference counting in multithreaded programs.

Using Rc<T> to Share Data

Let's return to our cons list example in Listing 15-5. Recall that we defined it using Box<T>. This time, we'll create two lists that both share ownership of a third list. Conceptually, this looks similar to Figure 15-3.

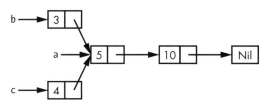

Figure 15-3: Two lists, b and c, sharing ownership of a third list, a

We'll create list a that contains 5 and then 10. Then we'll make two more lists: b that starts with 3 and c that starts with 4. Both b and c lists will then continue on to the first a list containing 5 and 10. In other words, both lists will share the first list containing 5 and 10.

Trying to implement this scenario using our definition of List with Box<T> won't work, as shown in Listing 15-17.

src/main.rs
```
enum List {
    Cons(i32, Box<List>),
    Nil,
}

use crate::List::{Cons, Nil};

fn main() {
    let a = Cons(5, Box::new(Cons(10, Box::new(Nil))));
  ❶ let b = Cons(3, Box::new(a));
  ❷ let c = Cons(4, Box::new(a));
}
```

Listing 15-17: Demonstrating that we're not allowed to have two lists using Box<T> that try to share ownership of a third list

When we compile this code, we get this error:

```
error[E0382]: use of moved value: `a`
  --> src/main.rs:11:30
   |
9  |     let a = Cons(5, Box::new(Cons(10, Box::new(Nil))));
   |         - move occurs because `a` has type `List`, which
does not implement the `Copy` trait
10 |     let b = Cons(3, Box::new(a));
   |                              - value moved here
11 |     let c = Cons(4, Box::new(a));
   |                              ^ value used here after move
```

The Cons variants own the data they hold, so when we create the b list ❶, a is moved into b and b owns a. Then, when we try to use a again when creating c ❷, we're not allowed to because a has been moved.

We could change the definition of Cons to hold references instead, but then we would have to specify lifetime parameters. By specifying lifetime parameters, we would be specifying that every element in the list will live at least as long as the entire list. This is the case for the elements and lists in Listing 15-17, but not in every scenario.

Instead, we'll change our definition of List to use Rc<T> in place of Box<T>, as shown in Listing 15-18. Each Cons variant will now hold a value and an Rc<T> pointing to a List. When we create b, instead of taking ownership of a, we'll clone the Rc<List> that a is holding, thereby increasing the number of references from one to two and letting a and b share ownership of the data in that Rc<List>. We'll also clone a when creating c, increasing the number of references from two to three. Every time we call Rc::clone, the reference count to the data within the Rc<List> will increase, and the data won't be cleaned up unless there are zero references to it.

src/main.rs

```
enum List {
    Cons(i32, Rc<List>),
    Nil,
}

use crate::List::{Cons, Nil};
❶ use std::rc::Rc;

fn main() {
❷   let a = Rc::new(Cons(5, Rc::new(Cons(10, Rc::new(Nil)))));
❸   let b = Cons(3, Rc::clone(&a));
❹   let c = Cons(4, Rc::clone(&a));
}
```

Listing 15-18: A definition of List that uses Rc<T>

We need to add a use statement to bring Rc<T> into scope ❶ because it's not in the prelude. In main, we create the list holding 5 and 10 and store it in a new Rc<List> in a ❷. Then, when we create b ❸ and c ❹, we call the Rc::clone function and pass a reference to the Rc<List> in a as an argument.

We could have called a.clone() rather than Rc::clone(&a), but Rust's convention is to use Rc::clone in this case. The implementation of Rc::clone doesn't make a deep copy of all the data like most types' implementations of clone do. The call to Rc::clone only increments the reference count, which doesn't take much time. Deep copies of data can take a lot of time. By using Rc::clone for reference counting, we can visually distinguish between the deep-copy kinds of clones and the kinds of clones that increase the reference count. When looking for performance problems in the code, we only need to consider the deep-copy clones and can disregard calls to Rc::clone.

Cloning an Rc<T> Increases the Reference Count

Let's change our working example in Listing 15-18 so we can see the reference counts changing as we create and drop references to the Rc<List> in a.

In Listing 15-19, we'll change main so it has an inner scope around list c; then we can see how the reference count changes when c goes out of scope.

src/main.rs

```
--snip--

fn main() {
    let a = Rc::new(Cons(5, Rc::new(Cons(10, Rc::new(Nil)))));
    println!(
        "count after creating a = {}",
        Rc::strong_count(&a)
    );
    let b = Cons(3, Rc::clone(&a));
    println!(
        "count after creating b = {}",
        Rc::strong_count(&a)
    );
    {
        let c = Cons(4, Rc::clone(&a));
        println!(
            "count after creating c = {}",
            Rc::strong_count(&a)
        );
    }
    println!(
        "count after c goes out of scope = {}",
        Rc::strong_count(&a)
    );
}
```

Listing 15-19: Printing the reference count

At each point in the program where the reference count changes, we print the reference count, which we get by calling the Rc::strong_count function. This function is named strong_count rather than count because the Rc<T> type also has a weak_count; we'll see what weak_count is used for in "Preventing Reference Cycles Using Weak<T>" on page 346.

This code prints the following:

```
count after creating a = 1
count after creating b = 2
count after creating c = 3
count after c goes out of scope = 2
```

We can see that the Rc<List> in a has an initial reference count of 1; then each time we call clone, the count goes up by 1. When c goes out of scope, the count goes down by 1. We don't have to call a function to decrease the reference count like we have to call Rc::clone to increase the reference count: the implementation of the Drop trait decreases the reference count automatically when an Rc<T> value goes out of scope.

What we can't see in this example is that when b and then a go out of scope at the end of main, the count is then 0, and the Rc<List> is cleaned up completely. Using Rc<T> allows a single value to have multiple owners, and the count ensures that the value remains valid as long as any of the owners still exist.

Via immutable references, Rc<T> allows you to share data between multiple parts of your program for reading only. If Rc<T> allowed you to have multiple mutable references too, you might violate one of the borrowing rules discussed in Chapter 4: multiple mutable borrows to the same place can cause data races and inconsistencies. But being able to mutate data is very useful! In the next section, we'll discuss the interior mutability pattern and the RefCell<T> type that you can use in conjunction with an Rc<T> to work with this immutability restriction.

RefCell<T> and the Interior Mutability Pattern

Interior mutability is a design pattern in Rust that allows you to mutate data even when there are immutable references to that data; normally, this action is disallowed by the borrowing rules. To mutate data, the pattern uses unsafe code inside a data structure to bend Rust's usual rules that govern mutation and borrowing. Unsafe code indicates to the compiler that we're checking the rules manually instead of relying on the compiler to check them for us; we will discuss unsafe code more in Chapter 19.

We can use types that use the interior mutability pattern only when we can ensure that the borrowing rules will be followed at runtime, even though the compiler can't guarantee that. The unsafe code involved is then wrapped in a safe API, and the outer type is still immutable.

Let's explore this concept by looking at the RefCell<T> type that follows the interior mutability pattern.

Enforcing Borrowing Rules at Runtime with RefCell<T>

Unlike Rc<T>, the RefCell<T> type represents single ownership over the data it holds. So what makes RefCell<T> different from a type like Box<T>? Recall the borrowing rules you learned in Chapter 4:

- At any given time, you can have *either* one mutable reference or any number of immutable references (but not both).
- References must always be valid.

With references and Box<T>, the borrowing rules' invariants are enforced at compile time. With RefCell<T>, these invariants are enforced *at runtime*. With references, if you break these rules, you'll get a compiler error. With RefCell<T>, if you break these rules, your program will panic and exit.

The advantages of checking the borrowing rules at compile time are that errors will be caught sooner in the development process, and there is no impact on runtime performance because all the analysis is completed beforehand. For those reasons, checking the borrowing rules at compile time is the best choice in the majority of cases, which is why this is Rust's default.

The advantage of checking the borrowing rules at runtime instead is that certain memory-safe scenarios are then allowed, where they would've been disallowed by the compile-time checks. Static analysis, like the Rust compiler, is inherently conservative. Some properties of code are impossible to detect by analyzing the code: the most famous example is the Halting Problem, which is beyond the scope of this book but is an interesting topic to research.

Because some analysis is impossible, if the Rust compiler can't be sure the code complies with the ownership rules, it might reject a correct program; in this way, it's conservative. If Rust accepted an incorrect program, users wouldn't be able to trust the guarantees Rust makes. However, if Rust rejects a correct program, the programmer will be inconvenienced, but nothing catastrophic can occur. The RefCell<T> type is useful when you're sure your code follows the borrowing rules but the compiler is unable to understand and guarantee that.

Similar to Rc<T>, RefCell<T> is only for use in single-threaded scenarios and will give you a compile-time error if you try using it in a multithreaded context. We'll talk about how to get the functionality of RefCell<T> in a multithreaded program in Chapter 16.

Here is a recap of the reasons to choose Box<T>, Rc<T>, or RefCell<T>:

- Rc<T> enables multiple owners of the same data; Box<T> and RefCell<T> have single owners.
- Box<T> allows immutable or mutable borrows checked at compile time; Rc<T> allows only immutable borrows checked at compile time; RefCell<T> allows immutable or mutable borrows checked at runtime.
- Because RefCell<T> allows mutable borrows checked at runtime, you can mutate the value inside the RefCell<T> even when the RefCell<T> is immutable.

Mutating the value inside an immutable value is the *interior mutability* pattern. Let's look at a situation in which interior mutability is useful and examine how it's possible.

Interior Mutability: A Mutable Borrow to an Immutable Value

A consequence of the borrowing rules is that when you have an immutable value, you can't borrow it mutably. For example, this code won't compile:

src/main.rs
```
fn main() {
    let x = 5;
    let y = &mut x;
}
```

If you tried to compile this code, you'd get the following error:

```
error[E0596]: cannot borrow `x` as mutable, as it is not declared
as mutable
 --> src/main.rs:3:13
  |
2 |     let x = 5;
  |         - help: consider changing this to be mutable: `mut x`
3 |     let y = &mut x;
  |             ^^^^^^ cannot borrow as mutable
```

However, there are situations in which it would be useful for a value to mutate itself in its methods but appear immutable to other code. Code outside the value's methods would not be able to mutate the value. Using RefCell<T> is one way to get the ability to have interior mutability, but RefCell<T> doesn't get around the borrowing rules completely: the borrow checker in the compiler allows this interior mutability, and the borrowing rules are checked at runtime instead. If you violate the rules, you'll get a panic! instead of a compiler error.

Let's work through a practical example where we can use RefCell<T> to mutate an immutable value and see why that is useful.

A Use Case for Interior Mutability: Mock Objects

Sometimes during testing a programmer will use a type in place of another type, in order to observe particular behavior and assert that it's implemented correctly. This placeholder type is called a *test double*. Think of it in the sense of a stunt double in filmmaking, where a person steps in and substitutes for an actor to do a particularly tricky scene. Test doubles stand in for other types when we're running tests. *Mock objects* are specific types of test doubles that record what happens during a test so you can assert that the correct actions took place.

Rust doesn't have objects in the same sense as other languages have objects, and Rust doesn't have mock object functionality built into the standard library as some other languages do. However, you can definitely create a struct that will serve the same purposes as a mock object.

Here's the scenario we'll test: we'll create a library that tracks a value against a maximum value and sends messages based on how close to the maximum value the current value is. This library could be used to keep track of a user's quota for the number of API calls they're allowed to make, for example.

Our library will only provide the functionality of tracking how close to the maximum a value is and what the messages should be at what times. Applications that use our library will be expected to provide the mechanism for sending the messages: the application could put a message in the application, send an email, send a text message, or do something else. The library doesn't need to know that detail. All it needs is something that implements a trait we'll provide called Messenger. Listing 15-20 shows the library code.

```
src/lib.rs   pub trait Messenger {
        ❶ fn send(&self, msg: &str);
        }

        pub struct LimitTracker<'a, T: Messenger> {
            messenger: &'a T,
            value: usize,
            max: usize,
        }

        impl<'a, T> LimitTracker<'a, T>
        where
            T: Messenger,
        {
            pub fn new(
                messenger: &'a T,
                max: usize
            ) -> LimitTracker<'a, T> {
                LimitTracker {
                    messenger,
                    value: 0,
                    max,
                }
            }

        ❷ pub fn set_value(&mut self, value: usize) {
                self.value = value;

                let percentage_of_max =
                    self.value as f64 / self.max as f64;

                if percentage_of_max >= 1.0 {
                    self.messenger
                        .send("Error: You are over your quota!");
                } else if percentage_of_max >= 0.9 {
                    self.messenger
                        .send("Urgent: You're at 90% of your quota!");
                } else if percentage_of_max >= 0.75 {
                    self.messenger
                        .send("Warning: You're at 75% of your quota!");
                }
            }
        }
```

Listing 15-20: A library to keep track of how close a value is to a maximum value and warn when the value is at certain levels

One important part of this code is that the Messenger trait has one method called send that takes an immutable reference to self and the text of the message ❶. This trait is the interface our mock object needs to implement so that the mock can be used in the same way a real object is. The other important part is that we want to test the behavior of the set_value method on the LimitTracker ❷. We can change what we pass in for the value parameter, but set_value doesn't return anything for us to make assertions on. We want to be able to say that if we create a LimitTracker with something that implements the Messenger trait and a particular value for max, when we pass different numbers for value the messenger is told to send the appropriate messages.

We need a mock object that, instead of sending an email or text message when we call send, will only keep track of the messages it's told to send. We can create a new instance of the mock object, create a LimitTracker that uses the mock object, call the set_value method on LimitTracker, and then check that the mock object has the messages we expect. Listing 15-21 shows an attempt to implement a mock object to do just that, but the borrow checker won't allow it.

src/lib.rs

```
#[cfg(test)]
mod tests {
    use super::*;

❶ struct MockMessenger {
    ❷ sent_messages: Vec<String>,
    }

    impl MockMessenger {
    ❸ fn new() -> MockMessenger {
            MockMessenger {
                sent_messages: vec![],
            }
        }
    }

❹ impl Messenger for MockMessenger {
        fn send(&self, message: &str) {
        ❺ self.sent_messages.push(String::from(message));
        }
    }

    #[test]
❻ fn it_sends_an_over_75_percent_warning_message() {
        let mock_messenger = MockMessenger::new();
        let mut limit_tracker = LimitTracker::new(
            &mock_messenger,
            100
        );

        limit_tracker.set_value(80);

        assert_eq!(mock_messenger.sent_messages.len(), 1);
    }
}
```

Listing 15-21: An attempt to implement a MockMessenger that isn't allowed by the borrow checker

This test code defines a MockMessenger struct ❶ that has a sent_messages field with a Vec of String values ❷ to keep track of the messages it's told to send. We also define an associated function new ❸ to make it convenient to create new MockMessenger values that start with an empty list of messages. We then implement the Messenger trait for MockMessenger ❹ so we can give a MockMessenger to a LimitTracker. In the definition of the send method ❺, we take the message passed in as a parameter and store it in the MockMessenger list of sent_messages.

In the test, we're testing what happens when the LimitTracker is told to set value to something that is more than 75 percent of the max value ❻. First we create a new MockMessenger, which will start with an empty list of messages. Then we create a new LimitTracker and give it a reference to the new MockMessenger and a max value of 100. We call the set_value method on the LimitTracker with a value of 80, which is more than 75 percent of 100. Then we assert that the list of messages that the MockMessenger is keeping track of should now have one message in it.

However, there's one problem with this test, as shown here:

```
error[E0596]: cannot borrow `self.sent_messages` as mutable, as it is behind a
`&` reference
  --> src/lib.rs:58:13
   |
2  |         fn send(&self, msg: &str);
   |                 ----- help: consider changing that to be a mutable reference:
`&mut self`
...
58 |             self.sent_messages.push(String::from(message));
   |             ^^^^^^^^^^^^^^^^^^^^^^^^^^^^^^^^^^^^^^^^^^^^^^^^ `self` is a
`&` reference, so the data it refers to cannot be borrowed as mutable
```

We can't modify the MockMessenger to keep track of the messages because the send method takes an immutable reference to self. We also can't take the suggestion from the error text to use &mut self instead because then the signature of send wouldn't match the signature in the Messenger trait definition (feel free to try it and see what error message you get).

This is a situation in which interior mutability can help! We'll store the sent_messages within a RefCell<T>, and then the send method will be able to modify sent_messages to store the messages we've seen. Listing 15-22 shows what that looks like.

src/lib.rs
```
#[cfg(test)]
mod tests {
    use super::*;
    use std::cell::RefCell;

    struct MockMessenger {
      ❶ sent_messages: RefCell<Vec<String>>,
    }
```

```
impl MockMessenger {
    fn new() -> MockMessenger {
        MockMessenger {
          ❷ sent_messages: RefCell::new(vec![]),
        }
    }
}

impl Messenger for MockMessenger {
    fn send(&self, message: &str) {
        self.sent_messages
          ❸ .borrow_mut()
            .push(String::from(message));
    }
}

#[test]
fn it_sends_an_over_75_percent_warning_message() {
    --snip--

    assert_eq!(
      ❹ mock_messenger.sent_messages.borrow().len(),
        1
    );
}
}
```

Listing 15-22: Using RefCell<T> to mutate an inner value while the outer value is considered immutable

The sent_messages field is now of type RefCell<Vec<String>> ❶ instead of Vec<String>. In the new function, we create a new RefCell<Vec<String>> instance around the empty vector ❷.

For the implementation of the send method, the first parameter is still an immutable borrow of self, which matches the trait definition. We call borrow_mut on the RefCell<Vec<String>> in self.sent_messages ❸ to get a mutable reference to the value inside the RefCell<Vec<String>>, which is the vector. Then we can call push on the mutable reference to the vector to keep track of the messages sent during the test.

The last change we have to make is in the assertion: to see how many items are in the inner vector, we call borrow on the RefCell<Vec<String>> to get an immutable reference to the vector ❹.

Now that you've seen how to use RefCell<T>, let's dig into how it works!

Keeping Track of Borrows at Runtime with RefCell<T>

When creating immutable and mutable references, we use the & and &mut syntax, respectively. With RefCell<T>, we use the borrow and borrow_mut methods, which are part of the safe API that belongs to RefCell<T>. The borrow method returns the smart pointer type Ref<T>, and borrow_mut returns the smart pointer type RefMut<T>. Both types implement Deref, so we can treat them like regular references.

The RefCell<T> keeps track of how many Ref<T> and RefMut<T> smart pointers are currently active. Every time we call borrow, the RefCell<T> increases its count of how many immutable borrows are active. When a Ref<T> value goes out of scope, the count of immutable borrows goes down by 1. Just like the compile-time borrowing rules, RefCell<T> lets us have many immutable borrows or one mutable borrow at any point in time.

If we try to violate these rules, rather than getting a compiler error as we would with references, the implementation of RefCell<T> will panic at runtime. Listing 15-23 shows a modification of the implementation of send in Listing 15-22. We're deliberately trying to create two mutable borrows active for the same scope to illustrate that RefCell<T> prevents us from doing this at runtime.

src/lib.rs
```
impl Messenger for MockMessenger {
    fn send(&self, message: &str) {
        let mut one_borrow = self.sent_messages.borrow_mut();
        let mut two_borrow = self.sent_messages.borrow_mut();

        one_borrow.push(String::from(message));
        two_borrow.push(String::from(message));
    }
}
```

Listing 15-23: Creating two mutable references in the same scope to see that RefCell<T> will panic

We create a variable one_borrow for the RefMut<T> smart pointer returned from borrow_mut. Then we create another mutable borrow in the same way in the variable two_borrow. This makes two mutable references in the same scope, which isn't allowed. When we run the tests for our library, the code in Listing 15-23 will compile without any errors, but the test will fail:

```
---- tests::it_sends_an_over_75_percent_warning_message stdout ----
thread 'main' panicked at 'already borrowed: BorrowMutError', src/lib.rs:60:53
note: run with `RUST_BACKTRACE=1` environment variable to display a backtrace
```

Notice that the code panicked with the message already borrowed: BorrowMutError. This is how RefCell<T> handles violations of the borrowing rules at runtime.

Choosing to catch borrowing errors at runtime rather than compile time, as we've done here, means you'd potentially be finding mistakes in your code later in the development process: possibly not until your code was deployed to production. Also, your code would incur a small runtime performance penalty as a result of keeping track of the borrows at runtime rather than compile time. However, using RefCell<T> makes it possible to write a mock object that can modify itself to keep track of the messages it has seen while you're using it in a context where only immutable values are allowed. You can use RefCell<T> despite its trade-offs to get more functionality than regular references provide.

Allowing Multiple Owners of Mutable Data with Rc<T> and RefCell<T>

A common way to use RefCell<T> is in combination with Rc<T>. Recall that Rc<T> lets you have multiple owners of some data, but it only gives immutable access to that data. If you have an Rc<T> that holds a RefCell<T>, you can get a value that can have multiple owners *and* that you can mutate!

For example, recall the cons list example in Listing 15-18 where we used Rc<T> to allow multiple lists to share ownership of another list. Because Rc<T> holds only immutable values, we can't change any of the values in the list once we've created them. Let's add in RefCell<T> for its ability to change the values in the lists. Listing 15-24 shows that by using a RefCell<T> in the Cons definition, we can modify the value stored in all the lists.

src/main.rs
```
#[derive(Debug)]
enum List {
    Cons(Rc<RefCell<i32>>, Rc<List>),
    Nil,
}

use crate::List::{Cons, Nil};
use std::cell::RefCell;
use std::rc::Rc;

fn main() {
  ❶ let value = Rc::new(RefCell::new(5));

  ❷ let a = Rc::new(Cons(Rc::clone(&value), Rc::new(Nil)));

    let b = Cons(Rc::new(RefCell::new(3)), Rc::clone(&a));
    let c = Cons(Rc::new(RefCell::new(4)), Rc::clone(&a));

  ❸ *value.borrow_mut() += 10;

    println!("a after = {:?}", a);
    println!("b after = {:?}", b);
    println!("c after = {:?}", c);
}
```

Listing 15-24: Using Rc<RefCell<i32>> to create a List that we can mutate

We create a value that is an instance of Rc<RefCell<i32>> and store it in a variable named value ❶ so we can access it directly later. Then we create a List in a with a Cons variant that holds value ❷. We need to clone value so both a and value have ownership of the inner 5 value rather than transferring ownership from value to a or having a borrow from value.

We wrap the list a in an Rc<T> so that when we create lists b and c, they can both refer to a, which is what we did in Listing 15-18.

After we've created the lists in a, b, and c, we want to add 10 to the value in value ❸. We do this by calling borrow_mut on value, which uses the automatic dereferencing feature we discussed in "Where's the -> Operator?" on page 99 to dereference the Rc<T> to the inner RefCell<T> value. The borrow_mut method returns a RefMut<T> smart pointer, and we use the dereference operator on it and change the inner value.

When we print a, b, and c, we can see that they all have the modified value of 15 rather than 5:

```
a after = Cons(RefCell { value: 15 }, Nil)
b after = Cons(RefCell { value: 3 }, Cons(RefCell { value: 15 }, Nil))
c after = Cons(RefCell { value: 4 }, Cons(RefCell { value: 15 }, Nil))
```

This technique is pretty neat! By using RefCell<T>, we have an outwardly immutable List value. But we can use the methods on RefCell<T> that provide access to its interior mutability so we can modify our data when we need to. The runtime checks of the borrowing rules protect us from data races, and it's sometimes worth trading a bit of speed for this flexibility in our data structures. Note that RefCell<T> does not work for multithreaded code! Mutex<T> is the thread-safe version of RefCell<T>, and we'll discuss Mutex<T> in Chapter 16.

Reference Cycles Can Leak Memory

Rust's memory safety guarantees make it difficult, but not impossible, to accidentally create memory that is never cleaned up (known as a *memory leak*). Preventing memory leaks entirely is not one of Rust's guarantees, meaning memory leaks are memory safe in Rust. We can see that Rust allows memory leaks by using Rc<T> and RefCell<T>: it's possible to create references where items refer to each other in a cycle. This creates memory leaks because the reference count of each item in the cycle will never reach 0, and the values will never be dropped.

Creating a Reference Cycle

Let's look at how a reference cycle might happen and how to prevent it, starting with the definition of the List enum and a tail method in Listing 15-25.

src/main.rs
```
use crate::List::{Cons, Nil};
use std::cell::RefCell;
use std::rc::Rc;

#[derive(Debug)]
enum List {
❶ Cons(i32, RefCell<Rc<List>>),
    Nil,
}
```

```
impl List {
  ❷ fn tail(&self) -> Option<&RefCell<Rc<List>>> {
        match self {
            Cons(_, item) => Some(item),
            Nil => None,
        }
    }
}
```

Listing 15-25: A cons list definition that holds a `RefCell<T>` so we can modify what a Cons variant is referring to

We're using another variation of the List definition from Listing 15-5. The second element in the Cons variant is now RefCell<Rc<List>> ❶, meaning that instead of having the ability to modify the i32 value as we did in Listing 15-24, we want to modify the List value a Cons variant is pointing to. We're also adding a tail method ❷ to make it convenient for us to access the second item if we have a Cons variant.

In Listing 15-26, we're adding a main function that uses the definitions in Listing 15-25. This code creates a list in a and a list in b that points to the list in a. Then it modifies the list in a to point to b, creating a reference cycle. There are println! statements along the way to show what the reference counts are at various points in this process.

src/main.rs

```
fn main() {
  ❶ let a = Rc::new(Cons(5, RefCell::new(Rc::new(Nil))));

    println!("a initial rc count = {}", Rc::strong_count(&a));
    println!("a next item = {:?}", a.tail());

  ❷ let b = Rc::new(Cons(10, RefCell::new(Rc::clone(&a))));

    println!(
        "a rc count after b creation = {}",
        Rc::strong_count(&a)
    );
    println!("b initial rc count = {}", Rc::strong_count(&b));
    println!("b next item = {:?}", b.tail());

  ❸ if let Some(link) = a.tail() {
      ❹ *link.borrow_mut() = Rc::clone(&b);
    }

    println!(
        "b rc count after changing a = {}",
        Rc::strong_count(&b)
    );
    println!(
        "a rc count after changing a = {}",
        Rc::strong_count(&a)
    );
```

```
// Uncomment the next line to see that we have a cycle;
// it will overflow the stack.
// println!("a next item = {:?}", a.tail());
}
```

Listing 15-26: Creating a reference cycle of two List values pointing to each other

We create an Rc<List> instance holding a List value in the variable a with an initial list of 5, Nil ❶. We then create an Rc<List> instance holding another List value in the variable b that contains the value 10 and points to the list in a ❷.

We modify a so it points to b instead of Nil, creating a cycle. We do that by using the tail method to get a reference to the RefCell<Rc<List>> in a, which we put in the variable link ❸. Then we use the borrow_mut method on the RefCell<Rc<List>> to change the value inside from an Rc<List> that holds a Nil value to the Rc<List> in b ❹.

When we run this code, keeping the last println! commented out for the moment, we'll get this output:

```
a initial rc count = 1
a next item = Some(RefCell { value: Nil })
a rc count after b creation = 2
b initial rc count = 1
b next item = Some(RefCell { value: Cons(5, RefCell { value: Nil }) })
b rc count after changing a = 2
a rc count after changing a = 2
```

The reference count of the Rc<List> instances in both a and b is 2 after we change the list in a to point to b. At the end of main, Rust drops the variable b, which decreases the reference count of the b Rc<List> instance from 2 to 1. The memory that Rc<List> has on the heap won't be dropped at this point because its reference count is 1, not 0. Then Rust drops a, which decreases the reference count of the a Rc<List> instance from 2 to 1 as well. This instance's memory can't be dropped either, because the other Rc<List> instance still refers to it. The memory allocated to the list will remain uncollected forever. To visualize this reference cycle, we've created the diagram in Figure 15-4.

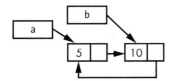

Figure 15-4: A reference cycle of lists a and b pointing to each other

If you uncomment the last println! and run the program, Rust will try to print this cycle with a pointing to b pointing to a, and so forth, until it overflows the stack.

Compared to a real-world program, the consequences of creating a reference cycle in this example aren't very dire: right after we create the reference cycle, the program ends. However, if a more complex program allocated lots of memory in a cycle and held onto it for a long time, the program would use more memory than it needed and might overwhelm the system, causing it to run out of available memory.

Creating reference cycles is not easily done, but it's not impossible either. If you have RefCell<T> values that contain Rc<T> values or similar nested combinations of types with interior mutability and reference counting, you must ensure that you don't create cycles; you can't rely on Rust to catch them. Creating a reference cycle would be a logic bug in your program that you should use automated tests, code reviews, and other software development practices to minimize.

Another solution for avoiding reference cycles is reorganizing your data structures so that some references express ownership and some references don't. As a result, you can have cycles made up of some ownership relationships and some non-ownership relationships, and only the ownership relationships affect whether or not a value can be dropped. In Listing 15-25, we always want Cons variants to own their list, so reorganizing the data structure isn't possible. Let's look at an example using graphs made up of parent nodes and child nodes to see when non-ownership relationships are an appropriate way to prevent reference cycles.

Preventing Reference Cycles Using Weak<T>

So far, we've demonstrated that calling Rc::clone increases the strong_count of an Rc<T> instance, and an Rc<T> instance is only cleaned up if its strong _count is 0. You can also create a weak reference to the value within an Rc<T> instance by calling Rc::downgrade and passing a reference to the Rc<T>. *Strong references* are how you can share ownership of an Rc<T> instance. *Weak references* don't express an ownership relationship, and their count doesn't affect when an Rc<T> instance is cleaned up. They won't cause a reference cycle because any cycle involving some weak references will be broken once the strong reference count of values involved is 0.

When you call Rc::downgrade, you get a smart pointer of type Weak<T>. Instead of increasing the strong_count in the Rc<T> instance by 1, calling Rc::downgrade increases the weak_count by 1. The Rc<T> type uses weak_count to keep track of how many Weak<T> references exist, similar to strong_count. The difference is the weak_count doesn't need to be 0 for the Rc<T> instance to be cleaned up.

Because the value that Weak<T> references might have been dropped, to do anything with the value that a Weak<T> is pointing to you must make sure the value still exists. Do this by calling the upgrade method on a Weak<T> instance, which will return an Option<Rc<T>>. You'll get a result of Some if the Rc<T> value has not been dropped yet and a result of None if the Rc<T> value has been dropped. Because upgrade returns an Option<Rc<T>>, Rust will ensure that the Some case and the None case are handled, and there won't be an invalid pointer.

As an example, rather than using a list whose items know only about the next item, we'll create a tree whose items know about their children items *and* their parent items.

Creating a Tree Data Structure: A Node with Child Nodes

To start, we'll build a tree with nodes that know about their child nodes. We'll create a struct named Node that holds its own i32 value as well as references to its children Node values:

src/main.rs
```
use std::cell::RefCell;
use std::rc::Rc;

#[derive(Debug)]
struct Node {
    value: i32,
    children: RefCell<Vec<Rc<Node>>>,
}
```

We want a Node to own its children, and we want to share that ownership with variables so we can access each Node in the tree directly. To do this, we define the Vec<T> items to be values of type Rc<Node>. We also want to modify which nodes are children of another node, so we have a RefCell<T> in children around the Vec<Rc<Node>>.

Next, we'll use our struct definition and create one Node instance named leaf with the value 3 and no children, and another instance named branch with the value 5 and leaf as one of its children, as shown in Listing 15-27.

src/main.rs
```
fn main() {
    let leaf = Rc::new(Node {
        value: 3,
        children: RefCell::new(vec![]),
    });

    let branch = Rc::new(Node {
        value: 5,
        children: RefCell::new(vec![Rc::clone(&leaf)]),
    });
}
```

Listing 15-27: Creating a leaf node with no children and a branch node with leaf as one of its children

We clone the Rc<Node> in leaf and store that in branch, meaning the Node in leaf now has two owners: leaf and branch. We can get from branch to leaf through branch.children, but there's no way to get from leaf to branch. The reason is that leaf has no reference to branch and doesn't know they're related. We want leaf to know that branch is its parent. We'll do that next.

Adding a Reference from a Child to Its Parent

To make the child node aware of its parent, we need to add a parent field to our Node struct definition. The trouble is in deciding what the type of parent should be. We know it can't contain an Rc<T> because that would create a reference cycle with leaf.parent pointing to branch and branch.children pointing to leaf, which would cause their strong_count values to never be 0.

Thinking about the relationships another way, a parent node should own its children: if a parent node is dropped, its child nodes should be dropped as well. However, a child should not own its parent: if we drop a child node, the parent should still exist. This is a case for weak references!

So, instead of Rc<T>, we'll make the type of parent use Weak<T>, specifically a RefCell<Weak<Node>>. Now our Node struct definition looks like this:

src/main.rs
```
use std::cell::RefCell;
use std::rc::{Rc, Weak};

#[derive(Debug)]
struct Node {
    value: i32,
    parent: RefCell<Weak<Node>>,
    children: RefCell<Vec<Rc<Node>>>,
}
```

A node will be able to refer to its parent node but doesn't own its parent. In Listing 15-28, we update main to use this new definition so the leaf node will have a way to refer to its parent, branch.

src/main.rs
```
fn main() {
    let leaf = Rc::new(Node {
        value: 3,
      ❶ parent: RefCell::new(Weak::new()),
        children: RefCell::new(vec![]),
    });

  ❷ println!(
        "leaf parent = {:?}",
        leaf.parent.borrow().upgrade()
    );

    let branch = Rc::new(Node {
        value: 5,
      ❸ parent: RefCell::new(Weak::new()),
        children: RefCell::new(vec![Rc::clone(&leaf)]),
    });

  ❹ *leaf.parent.borrow_mut() = Rc::downgrade(&branch);

  ❺ println!(
        "leaf parent = {:?}",
        leaf.parent.borrow().upgrade()
    );
}
```

Listing 15-28: A leaf node with a weak reference to its parent node, branch

Creating the `leaf` node looks similar to Listing 15-27 with the exception of the parent field: leaf starts out without a parent, so we create a new, empty `Weak<Node>` reference instance ❶.

At this point, when we try to get a reference to the parent of leaf by using the `upgrade` method, we get a `None` value. We see this in the output from the first `println!` statement ❷:

```
leaf parent = None
```

When we create the `branch` node, it will also have a new `Weak<Node>` reference in the parent field ❸ because branch doesn't have a parent node. We still have `leaf` as one of the children of branch. Once we have the `Node` instance in branch, we can modify leaf to give it a `Weak<Node>` reference to its parent ❹. We use the `borrow_mut` method on the `RefCell<Weak<Node>>` in the parent field of leaf, and then we use the `Rc::downgrade` function to create a `Weak<Node>` reference to branch from the `Rc<Node>` in branch.

When we print the parent of leaf again ❺, this time we'll get a `Some` variant holding branch: now leaf can access its parent! When we print leaf, we also avoid the cycle that eventually ended in a stack overflow like we had in Listing 15-26; the `Weak<Node>` references are printed as `(Weak)`:

```
leaf parent = Some(Node { value: 5, parent: RefCell { value: (Weak) },
children: RefCell { value: [Node { value: 3, parent: RefCell { value: (Weak) },
children: RefCell { value: [] } }] } })
```

The lack of infinite output indicates that this code didn't create a reference cycle. We can also tell this by looking at the values we get from calling `Rc::strong_count` and `Rc::weak_count`.

Visualizing Changes to strong_count and weak_count

Let's look at how the `strong_count` and `weak_count` values of the `Rc<Node>` instances change by creating a new inner scope and moving the creation of branch into that scope. By doing so, we can see what happens when branch is created and then dropped when it goes out of scope. The modifications are shown in Listing 15-29.

src/main.rs
```
fn main() {
    let leaf = Rc::new(Node {
        value: 3,
        parent: RefCell::new(Weak::new()),
        children: RefCell::new(vec![]),
    });

  ❶ println!(
        "leaf strong = {}, weak = {}",
        Rc::strong_count(&leaf),
        Rc::weak_count(&leaf),
    );
```

```
❷ {
        let branch = Rc::new(Node {
            value: 5,
            parent: RefCell::new(Weak::new()),
            children: RefCell::new(vec![Rc::clone(&leaf)]),
        });

        *leaf.parent.borrow_mut() = Rc::downgrade(&branch);

    ❸ println!(
            "branch strong = {}, weak = {}",
            Rc::strong_count(&branch),
            Rc::weak_count(&branch),
        );

    ❹ println!(
            "leaf strong = {}, weak = {}",
            Rc::strong_count(&leaf),
            Rc::weak_count(&leaf),
        );
❺ }

❻ println!(
        "leaf parent = {:?}",
        leaf.parent.borrow().upgrade()
    );
❼ println!(
        "leaf strong = {}, weak = {}",
        Rc::strong_count(&leaf),
        Rc::weak_count(&leaf),
    );
}
```

Listing 15-29: Creating branch in an inner scope and examining strong and weak reference counts

After leaf is created, its Rc<Node> has a strong count of 1 and a weak count of 0 ❶. In the inner scope ❷, we create branch and associate it with leaf, at which point, when we print the counts ❸, the Rc<Node> in branch will have a strong count of 1 and a weak count of 1 (for leaf.parent pointing to branch with a Weak<Node>). When we print the counts in leaf ❹, we'll see it will have a strong count of 2 because branch now has a clone of the Rc<Node> of leaf stored in branch.children, but will still have a weak count of 0.

When the inner scope ends ❺, branch goes out of scope and the strong count of the Rc<Node> decreases to 0, so its Node is dropped. The weak count of 1 from leaf.parent has no bearing on whether or not Node is dropped, so we don't get any memory leaks!

If we try to access the parent of leaf after the end of the scope, we'll get None again ❻. At the end of the program ❼, the Rc<Node> in leaf has a strong count of 1 and a weak count of 0 because the variable leaf is now the only reference to the Rc<Node> again.

All of the logic that manages the counts and value dropping is built into Rc<T> and Weak<T> and their implementations of the Drop trait. By specifying that the relationship from a child to its parent should be a Weak<T> reference in the definition of Node, you're able to have parent nodes point to child nodes and vice versa without creating a reference cycle and memory leaks.

Summary

This chapter covered how to use smart pointers to make different guarantees and trade-offs from those Rust makes by default with regular references. The Box<T> type has a known size and points to data allocated on the heap. The Rc<T> type keeps track of the number of references to data on the heap so that data can have multiple owners. The RefCell<T> type with its interior mutability gives us a type that we can use when we need an immutable type but need to change an inner value of that type; it also enforces the borrowing rules at runtime instead of at compile time.

Also discussed were the Deref and Drop traits, which enable a lot of the functionality of smart pointers. We explored reference cycles that can cause memory leaks and how to prevent them using Weak<T>.

If this chapter has piqued your interest and you want to implement your own smart pointers, check out "The Rustonomicon" at *https://doc.rust-lang.org/stable/nomicon* for more useful information.

Next, we'll talk about concurrency in Rust. You'll even learn about a few new smart pointers.

16

FEARLESS CONCURRENCY

Handling concurrent programming safely and efficiently is another of Rust's major goals. *Concurrent programming*, in which different parts of a program execute independently, and *parallel programming*, in which different parts of a program execute at the same time, are becoming increasingly important as more computers take advantage of their multiple processors. Historically, programming in these contexts has been difficult and error prone. Rust hopes to change that.

Initially, the Rust team thought that ensuring memory safety and preventing concurrency problems were two separate challenges to be solved with different methods. Over time, the team discovered that the ownership and type systems are a powerful set of tools to help manage memory safety *and* concurrency problems! By leveraging ownership and type checking, many concurrency errors are compile-time errors in Rust rather than runtime errors. Therefore, rather than making you spend lots of time trying to reproduce the exact circumstances under which a runtime concurrency bug occurs, incorrect code will refuse to compile and present an error explaining the problem. As a result, you can fix your code while you're working on it rather than potentially after it has been shipped to production. We've nicknamed this aspect of Rust *fearless concurrency*. Fearless concurrency allows you to write code that is free of subtle bugs and is easy to refactor without introducing new bugs.

NOTE *For simplicity's sake, we'll refer to many of the problems as* concurrent *rather than being more precise by saying* concurrent and/or parallel. *If this book were about concurrency and/or parallelism, we'd be more specific. For this chapter, please mentally substitute* concurrent and/or parallel *whenever we use* concurrent.

Many languages are dogmatic about the solutions they offer for handling concurrent problems. For example, Erlang has elegant functionality for message-passing concurrency but has only obscure ways to share state between threads. Supporting only a subset of possible solutions is a reasonable strategy for higher-level languages because a higher-level language promises benefits from giving up some control to gain abstractions. However, lower-level languages are expected to provide the solution with the best performance in any given situation and have fewer abstractions over the hardware. Therefore, Rust offers a variety of tools for modeling problems in whatever way is appropriate for your situation and requirements.

Here are the topics we'll cover in this chapter:

- How to create threads to run multiple pieces of code at the same time
- *Message-passing* concurrency, where channels send messages between threads
- *Shared-state* concurrency, where multiple threads have access to some piece of data
- The Sync and Send traits, which extend Rust's concurrency guarantees to user-defined types as well as types provided by the standard library

Using Threads to Run Code Simultaneously

In most current operating systems, an executed program's code is run in a *process*, and the operating system will manage multiple processes at once. Within a program, you can also have independent parts that run simultaneously. The features that run these independent parts are called *threads*. For example, a web server could have multiple threads so that it can respond to more than one request at the same time.

Splitting the computation in your program into multiple threads to run multiple tasks at the same time can improve performance, but it also adds complexity. Because threads can run simultaneously, there's no inherent guarantee about the order in which parts of your code on different threads will run. This can lead to problems, such as:

- Race conditions, in which threads are accessing data or resources in an inconsistent order
- Deadlocks, in which two threads are waiting for each other, preventing both threads from continuing
- Bugs that only happen in certain situations and are hard to reproduce and fix reliably

Rust attempts to mitigate the negative effects of using threads, but programming in a multithreaded context still takes careful thought and requires a code structure that is different from that in programs running in a single thread.

Programming languages implement threads in a few different ways, and many operating systems provide an API the language it can call for creating new threads. The Rust standard library uses a *1:1* model of thread implementation, whereby a program uses one operating system thread per one language thread. There are crates that implement other models of threading that make different trade-offs to the 1:1 model.

Creating a New Thread with spawn

To create a new thread, we call the thread::spawn function and pass it a closure (we talked about closures in Chapter 13) containing the code we want to run in the new thread. The example in Listing 16-1 prints some text from a main thread and other text from a new thread.

src/main.rs
```rust
use std::thread;
use std::time::Duration;

fn main() {
    thread::spawn(|| {
        for i in 1..10 {
            println!("hi number {i} from the spawned thread!");
            thread::sleep(Duration::from_millis(1));
        }
    });

    for i in 1..5 {
        println!("hi number {i} from the main thread!");
        thread::sleep(Duration::from_millis(1));
    }
}
```

Listing 16-1: Creating a new thread to print one thing while the main thread prints something else

Note that when the main thread of a Rust program completes, all spawned threads are shut down, whether or not they have finished running.

The output from this program might be a little different every time, but it will look similar to the following:

```
hi number 1 from the main thread!
hi number 1 from the spawned thread!
hi number 2 from the main thread!
hi number 2 from the spawned thread!
hi number 3 from the main thread!
hi number 3 from the spawned thread!
hi number 4 from the main thread!
hi number 4 from the spawned thread!
hi number 5 from the spawned thread!
```

The calls to thread::sleep force a thread to stop its execution for a short duration, allowing a different thread to run. The threads will probably take turns, but that isn't guaranteed: it depends on how your operating system schedules the threads. In this run, the main thread printed first, even though the print statement from the spawned thread appears first in the code. And even though we told the spawned thread to print until i is 9, it only got to 5 before the main thread shut down.

If you run this code and only see output from the main thread, or don't see any overlap, try increasing the numbers in the ranges to create more opportunities for the operating system to switch between the threads.

Waiting for All Threads to Finish Using join Handles

The code in Listing 16-1 not only stops the spawned thread prematurely most of the time due to the main thread ending, but because there is no guarantee on the order in which threads run, we also can't guarantee that the spawned thread will get to run at all!

We can fix the problem of the spawned thread not running or of it ending prematurely by saving the return value of thread::spawn in a variable. The return type of thread::spawn is JoinHandle<T>. A JoinHandle<T> is an owned value that, when we call the join method on it, will wait for its thread to finish. Listing 16-2 shows how to use the JoinHandle<T> of the thread we created in Listing 16-1 and how to call join to make sure the spawned thread finishes before main exits.

src/main.rs
```
use std::thread;
use std::time::Duration;

fn main() {
    let handle = thread::spawn(|| {
        for i in 1..10 {
            println!("hi number {i} from the spawned thread!");
            thread::sleep(Duration::from_millis(1));
        }
    });

    for i in 1..5 {
        println!("hi number {i} from the main thread!");
```

```
        thread::sleep(Duration::from_millis(1));
    }

    handle.join().unwrap();
}
```

Listing 16-2: Saving a JoinHandle<T> from thread::spawn to guarantee the thread is run to completion

Calling join on the handle blocks the thread currently running until the thread represented by the handle terminates. *Blocking* a thread means that thread is prevented from performing work or exiting. Because we've put the call to join after the main thread's for loop, running Listing 16-2 should produce output similar to this:

```
hi number 1 from the main thread!
hi number 2 from the main thread!
hi number 1 from the spawned thread!
hi number 3 from the main thread!
hi number 2 from the spawned thread!
hi number 4 from the main thread!
hi number 3 from the spawned thread!
hi number 4 from the spawned thread!
hi number 5 from the spawned thread!
hi number 6 from the spawned thread!
hi number 7 from the spawned thread!
hi number 8 from the spawned thread!
hi number 9 from the spawned thread!
```

The two threads continue alternating, but the main thread waits because of the call to handle.join() and does not end until the spawned thread is finished.

But let's see what happens when we instead move handle.join() before the for loop in main, like this:

src/main.rs
```
use std::thread;
use std::time::Duration;

fn main() {
    let handle = thread::spawn(|| {
        for i in 1..10 {
            println!("hi number {i} from the spawned thread!");
            thread::sleep(Duration::from_millis(1));
        }
    });

    handle.join().unwrap();

    for i in 1..5 {
        println!("hi number {i} from the main thread!");
        thread::sleep(Duration::from_millis(1));
    }
}
```

The main thread will wait for the spawned thread to finish and then run its for loop, so the output won't be interleaved anymore, as shown here:

```
hi number 1 from the spawned thread!
hi number 2 from the spawned thread!
hi number 3 from the spawned thread!
hi number 4 from the spawned thread!
hi number 5 from the spawned thread!
hi number 6 from the spawned thread!
hi number 7 from the spawned thread!
hi number 8 from the spawned thread!
hi number 9 from the spawned thread!
hi number 1 from the main thread!
hi number 2 from the main thread!
hi number 3 from the main thread!
hi number 4 from the main thread!
```

Small details, such as where join is called, can affect whether or not your threads run at the same time.

Using move Closures with Threads

We'll often use the move keyword with closures passed to thread::spawn because the closure will then take ownership of the values it uses from the environment, thus transferring ownership of those values from one thread to another. In "Capturing the Environment with Closures" on page 274, we discussed move in the context of closures. Now we'll concentrate more on the interaction between move and thread::spawn.

Notice in Listing 16-1 that the closure we pass to thread::spawn takes no arguments: we're not using any data from the main thread in the spawned thread's code. To use data from the main thread in the spawned thread, the spawned thread's closure must capture the values it needs. Listing 16-3 shows an attempt to create a vector in the main thread and use it in the spawned thread. However, this won't work yet, as you'll see in a moment.

src/main.rs
```
use std::thread;

fn main() {
    let v = vec![1, 2, 3];

    let handle = thread::spawn(|| {
        println!("Here's a vector: {:?}", v);
    });

    handle.join().unwrap();
}
```

Listing 16-3: Attempting to use a vector created by the main thread in another thread

The closure uses v, so it will capture v and make it part of the closure's environment. Because thread::spawn runs this closure in a new thread, we should be able to access v inside that new thread. But when we compile this example, we get the following error:

```
error[E0373]: closure may outlive the current function, but it borrows `v`,
which is owned by the current function
 --> src/main.rs:6:32
  |
6 |     let handle = thread::spawn(|| {
  |                                ^^ may outlive borrowed value `v`
7 |         println!("Here's a vector: {:?}", v);
  |                                           - `v` is borrowed here
  |
note: function requires argument type to outlive `'static`
 --> src/main.rs:6:18
  |
6 |       let handle = thread::spawn(|| {
  |  _____^
7 | |         println!("Here's a vector: {:?}", v);
8 | |     });
  | |_____^
help: to force the closure to take ownership of `v` (and any other referenced
variables), use the `move` keyword
  |
6 |     let handle = thread::spawn(move || {
  |                                ++++
```

Rust *infers* how to capture v, and because println! only needs a reference to v, the closure tries to borrow v. However, there's a problem: Rust can't tell how long the spawned thread will run, so it doesn't know whether the reference to v will always be valid.

Listing 16-4 provides a scenario that's more likely to have a reference to v that won't be valid.

src/main.rs
```
use std::thread;

fn main() {
    let v = vec![1, 2, 3];

    let handle = thread::spawn(|| {
        println!("Here's a vector: {:?}", v);
    });

    drop(v); // oh no!

    handle.join().unwrap();
}
```

Listing 16-4: A thread with a closure that attempts to capture a reference to v from a main thread that drops v

If Rust allowed us to run this code, there's a possibility that the spawned thread would be immediately put in the background without running at all. The spawned thread has a reference to v inside, but the main thread immediately drops v, using the drop function we discussed in Chapter 15. Then, when the spawned thread starts to execute, v is no longer valid, so a reference to it is also invalid. Oh no!

To fix the compiler error in Listing 16-3, we can use the error message's advice:

```
help: to force the closure to take ownership of `v` (and any other referenced
variables), use the `move` keyword
  |
6 |     let handle = thread::spawn(move || {
  |                                ++++
```

By adding the move keyword before the closure, we force the closure to take ownership of the values it's using rather than allowing Rust to infer that it should borrow the values. The modification to Listing 16-3 shown in Listing 16-5 will compile and run as we intend.

src/main.rs
```rust
use std::thread;

fn main() {
    let v = vec![1, 2, 3];

    let handle = thread::spawn(move || {
        println!("Here's a vector: {:?}", v);
    });

    handle.join().unwrap();
}
```

Listing 16-5: Using the move keyword to force a closure to take ownership of the values it uses

We might be tempted to try the same thing to fix the code in Listing 16-4 where the main thread called drop by using a move closure. However, this fix will not work because what Listing 16-4 is trying to do is disallowed for a different reason. If we added move to the closure, we would move v into the closure's environment, and we could no longer call drop on it in the main thread. We would get this compiler error instead:

```
error[E0382]: use of moved value: `v`
  --> src/main.rs:10:10
   |
4  |     let v = vec![1, 2, 3];
   |         - move occurs because `v` has type `Vec<i32>`, which does not
implement the `Copy` trait
5  |
6  |     let handle = thread::spawn(move || {
   |                                ------- value moved into closure here
7  |         println!("Here's a vector: {:?}", v);
   |                                           - variable moved due to use in
closure
...
10 |     drop(v); // oh no!
   |          ^ value used here after move
```

Rust's ownership rules have saved us again! We got an error from the code in Listing 16-3 because Rust was being conservative and only borrowing v for the thread, which meant the main thread could theoretically invalidate the spawned thread's reference. By telling Rust to move ownership of v to the spawned thread, we're guaranteeing to Rust that the main thread won't use v anymore. If we change Listing 16-4 in the same way, we're then violating the ownership rules when we try to use v in the main thread. The move keyword overrides Rust's conservative default of borrowing; it doesn't let us violate the ownership rules.

Now that we've covered what threads are and the methods supplied by the thread API, let's look at some situations in which we can use threads.

Using Message Passing to Transfer Data Between Threads

One increasingly popular approach to ensuring safe concurrency is *message passing*, where threads or actors communicate by sending each other messages containing data. Here's the idea in a slogan from the Go language documentation at *https://golang.org/doc/effective_go.html#concurrency*: "Do not communicate by sharing memory; instead, share memory by communicating."

To accomplish message-sending concurrency, Rust's standard library provides an implementation of channels. A *channel* is a general programming concept by which data is sent from one thread to another.

You can imagine a channel in programming as being like a directional channel of water, such as a stream or a river. If you put something like a rubber duck into a river, it will travel downstream to the end of the waterway.

A channel has two halves: a transmitter and a receiver. The transmitter half is the upstream location where you put the rubber duck into the river, and the receiver half is where the rubber duck ends up downstream. One part of your code calls methods on the transmitter with the data you want to send, and another part checks the receiving end for arriving messages. A channel is said to be *closed* if either the transmitter or receiver half is dropped.

Here, we'll work up to a program that has one thread to generate values and send them down a channel, and another thread that will receive the values and print them out. We'll be sending simple values between threads using a channel to illustrate the feature. Once you're familiar with the technique, you could use channels for any threads that need to communicate with each other, such as a chat system or a system where many threads perform parts of a calculation and send the parts to one thread that aggregates the results.

First, in Listing 16-6, we'll create a channel but not do anything with it. Note that this won't compile yet because Rust can't tell what type of values we want to send over the channel.

src/main.rs
```
use std::sync::mpsc;

fn main() {
    let (tx, rx) = mpsc::channel();
}
```

Listing 16-6: Creating a channel and assigning the two halves to tx and rx

We create a new channel using the `mpsc::channel` function; mpsc stands for *multiple producer, single consumer*. In short, the way Rust's standard library implements channels means a channel can have multiple *sending* ends that produce values but only one *receiving* end that consumes those values. Imagine multiple streams flowing together into one big river: everything sent down any of the streams will end up in one river at the end. We'll start with a single producer for now, but we'll add multiple producers when we get this example working.

The `mpsc::channel` function returns a tuple, the first element of which is the sending end—the transmitter—and the second element of which is the receiving end—the receiver. The abbreviations tx and rx are traditionally used in many fields for *transmitter* and *receiver*, respectively, so we name our variables as such to indicate each end. We're using a let statement with a pattern that destructures the tuples; we'll discuss the use of patterns in let statements and destructuring in Chapter 18. For now, know that using a let statement in this way is a convenient approach to extract the pieces of the tuple returned by `mpsc::channel`.

Let's move the transmitting end into a spawned thread and have it send one string so that the spawned thread is communicating with the main thread, as shown in Listing 16-7. This is like putting a rubber duck in the river upstream or sending a chat message from one thread to another.

src/main.rs
```
use std::sync::mpsc;
use std::thread;

fn main() {
    let (tx, rx) = mpsc::channel();

    thread::spawn(move || {
        let val = String::from("hi");
        tx.send(val).unwrap();
    });
}
```

Listing 16-7: Moving tx to a spawned thread and sending "hi"

Again, we're using `thread::spawn` to create a new thread and then using move to move tx into the closure so that the spawned thread owns tx. The spawned thread needs to own the transmitter to be able to send messages through the channel.

The transmitter has a send method that takes the value we want to send. The send method returns a `Result<T, E>` type, so if the receiver has already been dropped and there's nowhere to send a value, the send operation will return an error. In this example, we're calling unwrap to panic in case of an error. But in a real application, we would handle it properly: return to Chapter 9 to review strategies for proper error handling.

In Listing 16-8, we'll get the value from the receiver in the main thread. This is like retrieving the rubber duck from the water at the end of the river or receiving a chat message.

src/main.rs

```
use std::sync::mpsc;
use std::thread;

fn main() {
    let (tx, rx) = mpsc::channel();

    thread::spawn(move || {
        let val = String::from("hi");
        tx.send(val).unwrap();
    });

    let received = rx.recv().unwrap();
    println!("Got: {received}");
}
```

Listing 16-8: Receiving the value "hi" in the main thread and printing it

The receiver has two useful methods: recv and try_recv. We're using recv, short for *receive*, which will block the main thread's execution and wait until a value is sent down the channel. Once a value is sent, recv will return it in a Result<T, E>. When the transmitter closes, recv will return an error to signal that no more values will be coming.

The try_recv method doesn't block, but will instead return a Result<T, E> immediately: an Ok value holding a message if one is available and an Err value if there aren't any messages this time. Using try_recv is useful if this thread has other work to do while waiting for messages: we could write a loop that calls try_recv every so often, handles a message if one is available, and otherwise does other work for a little while until checking again.

We've used recv in this example for simplicity; we don't have any other work for the main thread to do other than wait for messages, so blocking the main thread is appropriate.

When we run the code in Listing 16-8, we'll see the value printed from the main thread:

```
Got: hi
```

Perfect!

Channels and Ownership Transference

The ownership rules play a vital role in message sending because they help you write safe, concurrent code. Preventing errors in concurrent programming is the advantage of thinking about ownership throughout your Rust programs. Let's do an experiment to show how channels and ownership work together to prevent problems: we'll try to use a val value in the spawned thread *after* we've sent it down the channel. Try compiling the code in Listing 16-9 to see why this code isn't allowed.

src/main.rs
```
use std::sync::mpsc;
use std::thread;
```

```
fn main() {
    let (tx, rx) = mpsc::channel();

    thread::spawn(move || {
        let val = String::from("hi");
        tx.send(val).unwrap();
        println!("val is {val}");
    });

    let received = rx.recv().unwrap();
    println!("Got: {received}");
}
```

Listing 16-9: Attempting to use val after we've sent it down the channel

Here, we try to print val after we've sent it down the channel via tx.send. Allowing this would be a bad idea: once the value has been sent to another thread, that thread could modify or drop it before we try to use the value again. Potentially, the other thread's modifications could cause errors or unexpected results due to inconsistent or nonexistent data. However, Rust gives us an error if we try to compile the code in Listing 16-9:

```
error[E0382]: borrow of moved value: `val`
  --> src/main.rs:10:31
   |
8  |          let val = String::from("hi");
   |              --- move occurs because `val` has type `String`, which does
not implement the `Copy` trait
9  |          tx.send(val).unwrap();
   |                  --- value moved here
10 |          println!("val is {val}");
   |                           ^^^ value borrowed here after move
```

Our concurrency mistake has caused a compile-time error. The send function takes ownership of its parameter, and when the value is moved the receiver takes ownership of it. This stops us from accidentally using the value again after sending it; the ownership system checks that everything is okay.

Sending Multiple Values and Seeing the Receiver Waiting

The code in Listing 16-8 compiled and ran, but it didn't clearly show us that two separate threads were talking to each other over the channel. In Listing 16-10 we've made some modifications that will prove the code in Listing 16-8 is running concurrently: the spawned thread will now send multiple messages and pause for a second between each message.

src/main.rs
```
use std::sync::mpsc;
use std::thread;
use std::time::Duration;

fn main() {
    let (tx, rx) = mpsc::channel();
```

```
thread::spawn(move || {
    let vals = vec![
        String::from("hi"),
        String::from("from"),
        String::from("the"),
        String::from("thread"),
    ];

    for val in vals {
        tx.send(val).unwrap();
        thread::sleep(Duration::from_secs(1));
    }
});

for received in rx {
    println!("Got: {received}");
}
}
```

Listing 16-10: Sending multiple messages and pausing between each one

This time, the spawned thread has a vector of strings that we want to send to the main thread. We iterate over them, sending each individually, and pause between each by calling the thread::sleep function with a Duration value of one second.

In the main thread, we're not calling the recv function explicitly anymore: instead, we're treating rx as an iterator. For each value received, we're printing it. When the channel is closed, iteration will end.

When running the code in Listing 16-10, you should see the following output with a one-second pause in between each line:

```
Got: hi
Got: from
Got: the
Got: thread
```

Because we don't have any code that pauses or delays in the for loop in the main thread, we can tell that the main thread is waiting to receive values from the spawned thread.

Creating Multiple Producers by Cloning the Transmitter

Earlier we mentioned that mpsc was an acronym for *multiple producer, single consumer*. Let's put mpsc to use and expand the code in Listing 16-10 to create multiple threads that all send values to the same receiver. We can do so by cloning the transmitter, as shown in Listing 16-11.

src/main.rs
```
--snip--

let (tx, rx) = mpsc::channel();

let tx1 = tx.clone();
thread::spawn(move || {
```

```
        let vals = vec![
            String::from("hi"),
            String::from("from"),
            String::from("the"),
            String::from("thread"),
        ];

        for val in vals {
            tx1.send(val).unwrap();
            thread::sleep(Duration::from_secs(1));
        }
    });

    thread::spawn(move || {
        let vals = vec![
            String::from("more"),
            String::from("messages"),
            String::from("for"),
            String::from("you"),
        ];

        for val in vals {
            tx.send(val).unwrap();
            thread::sleep(Duration::from_secs(1));
        }
    });

    for received in rx {
        println!("Got: {received}");
    }

    --snip--
```

Listing 16-11: Sending multiple messages from multiple producers

This time, before we create the first spawned thread, we call clone on the transmitter. This will give us a new transmitter we can pass to the first spawned thread. We pass the original transmitter to a second spawned thread. This gives us two threads, each sending different messages to the one receiver.

When you run the code, your output should look something like this:

```
Got: hi
Got: more
Got: from
Got: messages
Got: for
Got: the
Got: thread
Got: you
```

You might see the values in another order, depending on your system. This is what makes concurrency interesting as well as difficult. If you experiment with thread::sleep, giving it various values in the different threads, each run will be more nondeterministic and create different output each time.

Now that we've looked at how channels work, let's look at a different method of concurrency.

Shared-State Concurrency

Message passing is a fine way to handle concurrency, but it's not the only way. Another method would be for multiple threads to access the same shared data. Consider this part of the slogan from the Go language documentation again: "Do not communicate by sharing memory."

What would communicating by sharing memory look like? In addition, why would message-passing enthusiasts caution not to use memory sharing?

In a way, channels in any programming language are similar to single ownership because once you transfer a value down a channel, you should no longer use that value. Shared-memory concurrency is like multiple ownership: multiple threads can access the same memory location at the same time. As you saw in Chapter 15, where smart pointers made multiple ownership possible, multiple ownership can add complexity because these different owners need managing. Rust's type system and ownership rules greatly assist in getting this management correct. For an example, let's look at mutexes, one of the more common concurrency primitives for shared memory.

Using Mutexes to Allow Access to Data from One Thread at a Time

Mutex is an abbreviation for *mutual exclusion*, as in a mutex allows only one thread to access some data at any given time. To access the data in a mutex, a thread must first signal that it wants access by asking to acquire the mutex's lock. The *lock* is a data structure that is part of the mutex that keeps track of who currently has exclusive access to the data. Therefore, the mutex is described as *guarding* the data it holds via the locking system.

Mutexes have a reputation for being difficult to use because you have to remember two rules:

1. You must attempt to acquire the lock before using the data.
2. When you're done with the data that the mutex guards, you must unlock the data so other threads can acquire the lock.

For a real-world metaphor for a mutex, imagine a panel discussion at a conference with only one microphone. Before a panelist can speak, they have to ask or signal that they want to use the microphone. When they get the microphone, they can talk for as long as they want to and then hand the microphone to the next panelist who requests to speak. If a panelist forgets to hand the microphone off when they're finished with it, no one else is able to speak. If management of the shared microphone goes wrong, the panel won't work as planned!

Management of mutexes can be incredibly tricky to get right, which is why so many people are enthusiastic about channels. However, thanks to Rust's type system and ownership rules, you can't get locking and unlocking wrong.

The API of Mutex<T>

As an example of how to use a mutex, let's start by using a mutex in a single-threaded context, as shown in Listing 16-12.

src/main.rs
```
use std::sync::Mutex;

fn main() {
  ❶ let m = Mutex::new(5);

    {
      ❷ let mut num = m.lock().unwrap();
      ❸ *num = 6;
  ❹ }

  ❺ println!("m = {:?}", m);
}
```

Listing 16-12: Exploring the API of Mutex<T> in a single-threaded context for simplicity

As with many types, we create a Mutex<T> using the associated function new ❶. To access the data inside the mutex, we use the lock method to acquire the lock ❷. This call will block the current thread so it can't do any work until it's our turn to have the lock.

The call to lock would fail if another thread holding the lock panicked. In that case, no one would ever be able to get the lock, so we've chosen to unwrap and have this thread panic if we're in that situation.

After we've acquired the lock, we can treat the return value, named num in this case, as a mutable reference to the data inside. The type system ensures that we acquire a lock before using the value in m. The type of m is Mutex<i32>, not i32, so we *must* call lock to be able to use the i32 value. We can't forget; the type system won't let us access the inner i32 otherwise.

As you might suspect, Mutex<T> is a smart pointer. More accurately, the call to lock *returns* a smart pointer called MutexGuard, wrapped in a LockResult that we handled with the call to unwrap. The MutexGuard smart pointer implements Deref to point at our inner data; the smart pointer also has a Drop implementation that releases the lock automatically when a MutexGuard goes out of scope, which happens at the end of the inner scope ❹. As a result, we don't risk forgetting to release the lock and blocking the mutex from being used by other threads because the lock release happens automatically.

After dropping the lock, we can print the mutex value and see that we were able to change the inner i32 to 6 ❺.

Sharing a Mutex<T> Between Multiple Threads

Now let's try to share a value between multiple threads using Mutex<T>. We'll spin up 10 threads and have them each increment a counter value by 1, so the counter goes from 0 to 10. The example in Listing 16-13 will have a compiler error, and we'll use that error to learn more about using Mutex<T> and how Rust helps us use it correctly.

```
src/main.rs    use std::sync::Mutex;
               use std::thread;

               fn main() {
               ❶ let counter = Mutex::new(0);
                   let mut handles = vec![];

               ❷ for _ in 0..10 {
                   ❸ let handle = thread::spawn(move || {
                       ❹ let mut num = counter.lock().unwrap();

                       ❺ *num += 1;
                       });
                   ❻ handles.push(handle);
                   }

                   for handle in handles {
                   ❼ handle.join().unwrap();
                   }

               ❽ println!("Result: {}", *counter.lock().unwrap());
               }
```

Listing 16-13: Ten threads, each incrementing a counter guarded by a Mutex<T>

We create a counter variable to hold an i32 inside a Mutex<T> ❶, as we did in Listing 16-12. Next, we create 10 threads by iterating over a range of numbers ❷. We use thread::spawn and give all the threads the same closure: one that moves the counter into the thread ❸, acquires a lock on the Mutex<T> by calling the lock method ❹, and then adds 1 to the value in the mutex ❺. When a thread finishes running its closure, num will go out of scope and release the lock so another thread can acquire it.

In the main thread, we collect all the join handles ❻. Then, as we did in Listing 16-2, we call join on each handle to make sure all the threads finish ❼. At that point, the main thread will acquire the lock and print the result of this program ❽.

We hinted that this example wouldn't compile. Now let's find out why!

```
error[E0382]: use of moved value: `counter`
  --> src/main.rs:9:36
   |
5  |       let counter = Mutex::new(0);
   |           ------- move occurs because `counter` has type `Mutex<i32>`, which
does not implement the `Copy` trait
...
9  |           let handle = thread::spawn(move || {
   |                                      ^^^^^^^ value moved into closure here,
in previous iteration of loop
10 |               let mut num = counter.lock().unwrap();
   |                             ------- use occurs due to use in closure
```

The error message states that the counter value was moved in the previous iteration of the loop. Rust is telling us that we can't move the ownership of lock counter into multiple threads. Let's fix the compiler error with the multiple-ownership method we discussed in Chapter 15.

Multiple Ownership with Multiple Threads

In Chapter 15, we gave a value to multiple owners by using the smart pointer Rc<T> to create a reference counted value. Let's do the same here and see what happens. We'll wrap the Mutex<T> in Rc<T> in Listing 16-14 and clone the Rc<T> before moving ownership to the thread.

src/main.rs
```
use std::rc::Rc;
use std::sync::Mutex;
use std::thread;

fn main() {
    let counter = Rc::new(Mutex::new(0));
    let mut handles = vec![];

    for _ in 0..10 {
        let counter = Rc::clone(&counter);
        let handle = thread::spawn(move || {
            let mut num = counter.lock().unwrap();

            *num += 1;
        });
        handles.push(handle);
    }

    for handle in handles {
        handle.join().unwrap();
    }

    println!("Result: {}", *counter.lock().unwrap());
}
```

Listing 16-14: Attempting to use Rc<T> to allow multiple threads to own the Mutex<T>

Once again, we compile and get . . . different errors! The compiler is teaching us a lot.

```
error[E0277]: ❶ `Rc<Mutex<i32>>` cannot be sent between threads safely
  --> src/main.rs:11:22
   |
11 |             let handle = thread::spawn(move || {
   |  _____^^^^^^^^^^^^^_-
   | |                           |
   | |                           `Rc<Mutex<i32>>` cannot be sent between threads
safely
12 | |               let mut num = counter.lock().unwrap();
13 | |
14 | |               *num += 1;
15 | |           });
   | |_____- within this `[closure@src/main.rs:11:36: 15:10]`
   |
```

```
  = help: within `[closure@src/main.rs:11:36: 15:10]`,❷the trait `Send` is not
implemented for `Rc<Mutex<i32>>`
    = note: required because it appears within the type
`[closure@src/main.rs:11:36: 15:10]`
note: required by a bound in `spawn`
```

Wow, that error message is very wordy! Here's the important part to focus on: `Rc<Mutex<i32>>` cannot be sent between threads safely ❶. The compiler is also telling us the reason why: the trait `Send` is not implemented for `Rc<Mutex<i32>>` ❷. We'll talk about Send in the next section: it's one of the traits that ensures the types we use with threads are meant for use in concurrent situations.

Unfortunately, Rc<T> is not safe to share across threads. When Rc<T> manages the reference count, it adds to the count for each call to clone and subtracts from the count when each clone is dropped. But it doesn't use any concurrency primitives to make sure that changes to the count can't be interrupted by another thread. This could lead to wrong counts—subtle bugs that could in turn lead to memory leaks or a value being dropped before we're done with it. What we need is a type that is exactly like Rc<T>, but that makes changes to the reference count in a thread-safe way.

Atomic Reference Counting with Arc<T>

Fortunately, Arc<T> *is* a type like Rc<T> that is safe to use in concurrent situations. The *a* stands for *atomic*, meaning it's an *atomically reference-counted* type. Atomics are an additional kind of concurrency primitive that we won't cover in detail here: see the standard library documentation for std::sync::atomic for more details. At this point, you just need to know that atomics work like primitive types but are safe to share across threads.

You might then wonder why all primitive types aren't atomic and why standard library types aren't implemented to use Arc<T> by default. The reason is that thread safety comes with a performance penalty that you only want to pay when you really need to. If you're just performing operations on values within a single thread, your code can run faster if it doesn't have to enforce the guarantees atomics provide.

Let's return to our example: Arc<T> and Rc<T> have the same API, so we fix our program by changing the use line, the call to new, and the call to clone. The code in Listing 16-15 will finally compile and run.

src/main.rs
```
use std::sync::{Arc, Mutex};
use std::thread;

fn main() {
    let counter = Arc::new(Mutex::new(0));
    let mut handles = vec![];

    for _ in 0..10 {
        let counter = Arc::clone(&counter);
        let handle = thread::spawn(move || {
```

```
        let mut num = counter.lock().unwrap();

        *num += 1;
    });
    handles.push(handle);
}

for handle in handles {
    handle.join().unwrap();
}

println!("Result: {}", *counter.lock().unwrap());
}
```

Listing 16-15: Using an `Arc<T>` to wrap the `Mutex<T>` to be able to share ownership across multiple threads

This code will print the following:

```
Result: 10
```

We did it! We counted from 0 to 10, which may not seem very impressive, but it did teach us a lot about `Mutex<T>` and thread safety. You could also use this program's structure to do more complicated operations than just incrementing a counter. Using this strategy, you can divide a calculation into independent parts, split those parts across threads, and then use a `Mutex<T>` to have each thread update the final result with its part.

Note that if you are doing simple numerical operations, there are types simpler than `Mutex<T>` types provided by the `std::sync::atomic` module of the standard library. These types provide safe, concurrent, atomic access to primitive types. We chose to use `Mutex<T>` with a primitive type for this example so we could concentrate on how `Mutex<T>` works.

Similarities Between RefCell<T>/Rc<T> and Mutex<T>/Arc<T>

You might have noticed that `counter` is immutable, but we could get a mutable reference to the value inside it; this means `Mutex<T>` provides interior mutability, as the `Cell` family does. In the same way we used `RefCell<T>` in Chapter 15 to allow us to mutate contents inside an `Rc<T>`, we use `Mutex<T>` to mutate contents inside an `Arc<T>`.

Another detail to note is that Rust can't protect you from all kinds of logic errors when you use `Mutex<T>`. Recall from Chapter 15 that using `Rc<T>` came with the risk of creating reference cycles, where two `Rc<T>` values refer to each other, causing memory leaks. Similarly, `Mutex<T>` comes with the risk of creating *deadlocks*. These occur when an operation needs to lock two resources and two threads have each acquired one of the locks, causing them to wait for each other forever. If you're interested in deadlocks, try creating a Rust program that has a deadlock; then research deadlock mitigation strategies for mutexes in any language and have a go at implementing them in Rust. The standard library API documentation for Mutex<T> and MutexGuard offers useful information.

We'll round out this chapter by talking about the Send and Sync traits and how we can use them with custom types.

Extensible Concurrency with the Send and Sync Traits

Interestingly, the Rust language has *very* few concurrency features. Almost every concurrency feature we've talked about so far in this chapter has been part of the standard library, not the language. Your options for handling concurrency are not limited to the language or the standard library; you can write your own concurrency features or use those written by others.

However, two concurrency concepts are embedded in the language: the std::marker traits Send and Sync.

Allowing Transference of Ownership Between Threads with Send

The Send marker trait indicates that ownership of values of the type implementing Send can be transferred between threads. Almost every Rust type is Send, but there are some exceptions, including Rc<T>: this cannot be Send because if you cloned an Rc<T> value and tried to transfer ownership of the clone to another thread, both threads might update the reference count at the same time. For this reason, Rc<T> is implemented for use in single-threaded situations where you don't want to pay the thread-safe performance penalty.

Therefore, Rust's type system and trait bounds ensure that you can never accidentally send an Rc<T> value across threads unsafely. When we tried to do this in Listing 16-14, we got the error the trait `Send` is not implemented for `Rc<Mutex<i32>>`. When we switched to Arc<T>, which is Send, the code compiled.

Any type composed entirely of Send types is automatically marked as Send as well. Almost all primitive types are Send, aside from raw pointers, which we'll discuss in Chapter 19.

Allowing Access from Multiple Threads with Sync

The Sync marker trait indicates that it is safe for the type implementing Sync to be referenced from multiple threads. In other words, any type T is Sync if &T (an immutable reference to T) is Send, meaning the reference can be sent safely to another thread. Similar to Send, primitive types are Sync, and types composed entirely of types that are Sync are also Sync.

The smart pointer Rc<T> is also not Sync for the same reasons that it's not Send. The RefCell<T> type (which we talked about in Chapter 15) and the family of related Cell<T> types are not Sync. The implementation of borrow checking that RefCell<T> does at runtime is not thread-safe. The smart pointer Mutex<T> is Sync and can be used to share access with multiple threads, as you saw in "Sharing a Mutex<T> Between Multiple Threads" on page 368.

Implementing Send and Sync Manually Is Unsafe

Because types that are made up of Send and Sync traits are automatically also Send and Sync, we don't have to implement those traits manually. As marker traits, they don't even have any methods to implement. They're just useful for enforcing invariants related to concurrency.

Manually implementing these traits involves implementing unsafe Rust code. We'll talk about using unsafe Rust code in Chapter 19; for now, the important information is that building new concurrent types not made up of Send and Sync parts requires careful thought to uphold the safety guarantees. "The Rustonomicon" at *https://doc.rust-lang.org/stable/nomicon* has more information about these guarantees and how to uphold them.

Summary

This isn't the last you'll see of concurrency in this book: the project in Chapter 20 will use the concepts in this chapter in a more realistic situation than the smaller examples discussed here.

As mentioned earlier, because very little of how Rust handles concurrency is part of the language, many concurrency solutions are implemented as crates. These evolve more quickly than the standard library, so be sure to search online for the current, state-of-the-art crates to use in multithreaded situations.

The Rust standard library provides channels for message passing and smart pointer types, such as Mutex<T> and Arc<T>, that are safe to use in concurrent contexts. The type system and the borrow checker ensure that the code using these solutions won't end up with data races or invalid references. Once you get your code to compile, you can rest assured that it will happily run on multiple threads without the kinds of hard-to-track-down bugs common in other languages. Concurrent programming is no longer a concept to be afraid of: go forth and make your programs concurrent, fearlessly!

Next, we'll talk about idiomatic ways to model problems and structure solutions as your Rust programs get bigger. In addition, we'll discuss how Rust's idioms relate to those you might be familiar with from object-oriented programming.

17

OBJECT-ORIENTED PROGRAMMING FEATURES

 Object-oriented programming (OOP) is a way of modeling programs. Objects as a programmatic concept were introduced in the programming language Simula in the 1960s. Those objects influenced Alan Kay's programming architecture in which objects pass messages to each other. To describe this architecture, he coined the term *object-oriented programming* in 1967. Many competing definitions describe what OOP is, and by some of these definitions Rust is object oriented but by others it is not. In this chapter, we'll explore certain characteristics that are commonly considered object oriented and how those characteristics translate to idiomatic Rust. We'll then show you how to implement an object-oriented design pattern in Rust and discuss the trade-offs of doing so versus implementing a solution using some of Rust's strengths instead.

Characteristics of Object-Oriented Languages

There is no consensus in the programming community about what features a language must have to be considered object oriented. Rust is influenced by many programming paradigms, including OOP; for example, we explored the features that came from functional programming in Chapter 13. Arguably, OOP languages share certain common characteristics, namely objects, encapsulation, and inheritance. Let's look at what each of those characteristics means and whether Rust supports it.

Objects Contain Data and Behavior

The book *Design Patterns: Elements of Reusable Object-Oriented Software* by Erich Gamma, Richard Helm, Ralph Johnson, and John Vlissides (Addison-Wesley, 1994), colloquially referred to as *The Gang of Four* book, is a catalog of object-oriented design patterns. It defines OOP in this way:

> Object-oriented programs are made up of objects. An **object** packages both data and the procedures that operate on that data. The procedures are typically called **methods** or **operations**.

Using this definition, Rust is object oriented: structs and enums have data, and impl blocks provide methods on structs and enums. Even though structs and enums with methods aren't *called* objects, they provide the same functionality, according to the Gang of Four's definition of objects.

Encapsulation That Hides Implementation Details

Another aspect commonly associated with OOP is the idea of *encapsulation*, which means that the implementation details of an object aren't accessible to code using that object. Therefore, the only way to interact with an object is through its public API; code using the object shouldn't be able to reach into the object's internals and change data or behavior directly. This enables the programmer to change and refactor an object's internals without needing to change the code that uses the object.

We discussed how to control encapsulation in Chapter 7: we can use the pub keyword to decide which modules, types, functions, and methods in our code should be public, and by default everything else is private. For example, we can define a struct AveragedCollection that has a field containing a vector of i32 values. The struct can also have a field that contains the average of the values in the vector, meaning the average doesn't have to be computed on demand whenever anyone needs it. In other words, AveragedCollection will cache the calculated average for us. Listing 17-1 has the definition of the AveragedCollection struct.

src/lib.rs
```
pub struct AveragedCollection {
    list: Vec<i32>,
    average: f64,
}
```

Listing 17-1: An AveragedCollection struct that maintains a list of integers and the average of the items in the collection

The struct is marked pub so that other code can use it, but the fields within the struct remain private. This is important in this case because we want to ensure that whenever a value is added or removed from the list, the average is also updated. We do this by implementing add, remove, and average methods on the struct, as shown in Listing 17-2.

src/lib.rs
```
impl AveragedCollection {
    pub fn add(&mut self, value: i32) {
        self.list.push(value);
        self.update_average();
    }

    pub fn remove(&mut self) -> Option<i32> {
        let result = self.list.pop();
        match result {
            Some(value) => {
                self.update_average();
                Some(value)
            }
            None => None,
        }
    }

    pub fn average(&self) -> f64 {
        self.average
    }

    fn update_average(&mut self) {
        let total: i32 = self.list.iter().sum();
        self.average = total as f64 / self.list.len() as f64;
    }
}
```

Listing 17-2: Implementations of the public methods add, remove, and average on AveragedCollection

The public methods add, remove, and average are the only ways to access or modify data in an instance of AveragedCollection. When an item is added to list using the add method or removed using the remove method, the implementations of each call the private update_average method that handles updating the average field as well.

We leave the list and average fields private so there is no way for external code to add or remove items to or from the list field directly; otherwise, the average field might become out of sync when the list changes. The average method returns the value in the average field, allowing external code to read the average but not modify it.

Because we've encapsulated the implementation details of the struct AveragedCollection, we can easily change aspects, such as the data structure, in the future. For instance, we could use a HashSet<i32> instead of a Vec<i32> for the list field. As long as the signatures of the add, remove, and average public methods stayed the same, code using AveragedCollection wouldn't need to change. If we made list public instead, this wouldn't necessarily be the case: HashSet<i32> and Vec<i32> have different methods for adding and removing items, so the external code would likely have to change if it were modifying list directly.

If encapsulation is a required aspect for a language to be considered object oriented, then Rust meets that requirement. The option to use pub or not for different parts of code enables encapsulation of implementation details.

Inheritance as a Type System and as Code Sharing

Inheritance is a mechanism whereby an object can inherit elements from another object's definition, thus gaining the parent object's data and behavior without you having to define them again.

If a language must have inheritance to be object oriented, then Rust is not such a language. There is no way to define a struct that inherits the parent struct's fields and method implementations without using a macro.

However, if you're used to having inheritance in your programming toolbox, you can use other solutions in Rust, depending on your reason for reaching for inheritance in the first place.

You would choose inheritance for two main reasons. One is for reuse of code: you can implement particular behavior for one type, and inheritance enables you to reuse that implementation for a different type. You can do this in a limited way in Rust code using default trait method implementations, which you saw in Listing 10-14 when we added a default implementation of the summarize method on the Summary trait. Any type implementing the Summary trait would have the summarize method available on it without any further code. This is similar to a parent class having an implementation of a method and an inheriting child class also having the implementation of the method. We can also override the default implementation of the summarize method when we implement the Summary trait, which is similar to a child class overriding the implementation of a method inherited from a parent class.

The other reason to use inheritance relates to the type system: to enable a child type to be used in the same places as the parent type. This is also called *polymorphism*, which means that you can substitute multiple objects for each other at runtime if they share certain characteristics.

POLYMORPHISM

To many people, polymorphism is synonymous with inheritance. But it's actually a more general concept that refers to code that can work with data of multiple types. For inheritance, those types are generally subclasses.

Rust instead uses generics to abstract over different possible types and trait bounds to impose constraints on what those types must provide. This is sometimes called *bounded parametric polymorphism*.

Inheritance has recently fallen out of favor as a programming design solution in many programming languages because it's often at risk of sharing more code than necessary. Subclasses shouldn't always share all characteristics of their parent class but will do so with inheritance. This can make a program's design less flexible. It also introduces the possibility of calling methods on subclasses that don't make sense or that cause errors because the methods don't apply to the subclass. In addition, some languages will only allow *single inheritance* (meaning a subclass can only inherit from one class), further restricting the flexibility of a program's design.

For these reasons, Rust takes the different approach of using trait objects instead of inheritance. Let's look at how trait objects enable polymorphism in Rust.

Using Trait Objects That Allow for Values of Different Types

In Chapter 8, we mentioned that one limitation of vectors is that they can store elements of only one type. We created a workaround in Listing 8-9 where we defined a SpreadsheetCell enum that had variants to hold integers, floats, and text. This meant we could store different types of data in each cell and still have a vector that represented a row of cells. This is a perfectly good solution when our interchangeable items are a fixed set of types that we know when our code is compiled.

However, sometimes we want our library user to be able to extend the set of types that are valid in a particular situation. To show how we might achieve this, we'll create an example graphical user interface (GUI) tool that iterates through a list of items, calling a draw method on each one to draw it to the screen—a common technique for GUI tools. We'll create a library crate called gui that contains the structure of a GUI library. This crate might include some types for people to use, such as Button or TextField. In addition, gui users will want to create their own types that can be drawn: for instance, one programmer might add an Image and another might add a SelectBox.

We won't implement a full-fledged GUI library for this example but will show how the pieces would fit together. At the time of writing the library, we can't know and define all the types other programmers might want to create. But we do know that gui needs to keep track of many values of different types, and it needs to call a draw method on each of these differently typed values. It doesn't need to know exactly what will happen when we call the draw method, just that the value will have that method available for us to call.

To do this in a language with inheritance, we might define a class named Component that has a method named draw on it. The other classes, such as Button, Image, and SelectBox, would inherit from Component and thus inherit the draw method. They could each override the draw method to define their custom behavior, but the framework could treat all of the types as if they were Component instances and call draw on them. But because Rust doesn't have inheritance, we need another way to structure the gui library to allow users to extend it with new types.

Defining a Trait for Common Behavior

To implement the behavior we want gui to have, we'll define a trait named Draw that will have one method named draw. Then we can define a vector that takes a trait object. A *trait object* points to both an instance of a type implementing our specified trait and a table used to look up trait methods on that type at runtime. We create a trait object by specifying some sort of pointer, such as an & reference or a Box<T> smart pointer, then the dyn keyword, and then specifying the relevant trait. (We'll talk about the reason trait objects must use a pointer in "Dynamically Sized Types and the Sized Trait" on page 444.) We can use trait objects in place of a generic or concrete type. Wherever we use a trait object, Rust's type system will ensure at compile time that any value used in that context will implement the trait object's trait. Consequently, we don't need to know all the possible types at compile time.

We've mentioned that, in Rust, we refrain from calling structs and enums "objects" to distinguish them from other languages' objects. In a struct or enum, the data in the struct fields and the behavior in impl blocks are separated, whereas in other languages, the data and behavior combined into one concept is often labeled an object. However, trait objects *are* more like objects in other languages in the sense that they combine data and behavior. But trait objects differ from traditional objects in that we can't add data to a trait object. Trait objects aren't as generally useful as objects in other languages: their specific purpose is to allow abstraction across common behavior.

Listing 17-3 shows how to define a trait named Draw with one method named draw.

src/lib.rs
```
pub trait Draw {
    fn draw(&self);
}
```

Listing 17-3: Definition of the Draw trait

This syntax should look familiar from our discussions on how to define traits in Chapter 10. Next comes some new syntax: Listing 17-4 defines a struct named Screen that holds a vector named components. This vector is of type Box<dyn Draw>, which is a trait object; it's a stand-in for any type inside a Box that implements the Draw trait.

src/lib.rs
```
pub struct Screen {
    pub components: Vec<Box<dyn Draw>>,
}
```

Listing 17-4: Definition of the Screen struct with a components field holding a vector of trait objects that implement the Draw trait

On the Screen struct, we'll define a method named run that will call the draw method on each of its components, as shown in Listing 17-5.

src/lib.rs
```
impl Screen {
    pub fn run(&self) {
        for component in self.components.iter() {
            component.draw();
```

```
            }
        }
    }
```

Listing 17-5: A run method on Screen that calls the draw method on each component

This works differently from defining a struct that uses a generic type parameter with trait bounds. A generic type parameter can be substituted with only one concrete type at a time, whereas trait objects allow for multiple concrete types to fill in for the trait object at runtime. For example, we could have defined the Screen struct using a generic type and a trait bound, as in Listing 17-6.

src/lib.rs
```
pub struct Screen<T: Draw> {
    pub components: Vec<T>,
}

impl<T> Screen<T>
where
    T: Draw,
{
    pub fn run(&self) {
        for component in self.components.iter() {
            component.draw();
        }
    }
}
```

Listing 17-6: An alternate implementation of the Screen struct and its run method using generics and trait bounds

This restricts us to a Screen instance that has a list of components all of type Button or all of type TextField. If you'll only ever have homogeneous collections, using generics and trait bounds is preferable because the definitions will be monomorphized at compile time to use the concrete types.

On the other hand, with the method using trait objects, one Screen instance can hold a Vec<T> that contains a Box<Button> as well as a Box<TextField>. Let's look at how this works, and then we'll talk about the runtime performance implications.

Implementing the Trait

Now we'll add some types that implement the Draw trait. We'll provide the Button type. Again, actually implementing a GUI library is beyond the scope of this book, so the draw method won't have any useful implementation in its body. To imagine what the implementation might look like, a Button struct might have fields for width, height, and label, as shown in Listing 17-7.

src/lib.rs
```
pub struct Button {
    pub width: u32,
    pub height: u32,
    pub label: String,
}
```

```
impl Draw for Button {
    fn draw(&self) {
        // code to actually draw a button
    }
}
```

Listing 17-7: A Button struct that implements the Draw trait

The width, height, and label fields on Button will differ from the fields on other components; for example, a TextField type might have those same fields plus a placeholder field. Each of the types we want to draw on the screen will implement the Draw trait but will use different code in the draw method to define how to draw that particular type, as Button has here (without the actual GUI code, as mentioned). The Button type, for instance, might have an additional impl block containing methods related to what happens when a user clicks the button. These kinds of methods won't apply to types like TextField.

If someone using our library decides to implement a SelectBox struct that has width, height, and options fields, they would implement the Draw trait on the SelectBox type as well, as shown in Listing 17-8.

src/main.rs
```
use gui::Draw;

struct SelectBox {
    width: u32,
    height: u32,
    options: Vec<String>,
}

impl Draw for SelectBox {
    fn draw(&self) {
        // code to actually draw a select box
    }
}
```

Listing 17-8: Another crate using gui and implementing the Draw trait on a SelectBox struct

Our library's user can now write their main function to create a Screen instance. To the Screen instance, they can add a SelectBox and a Button by putting each in a Box<T> to become a trait object. They can then call the run method on the Screen instance, which will call draw on each of the components. Listing 17-9 shows this implementation.

src/main.rs
```
use gui::{Button, Screen};

fn main() {
    let screen = Screen {
        components: vec![
            Box::new(SelectBox {
                width: 75,
                height: 10,
                options: vec![
```

```
                    String::from("Yes"),
                    String::from("Maybe"),
                    String::from("No"),
                ],
            }),
            Box::new(Button {
                width: 50,
                height: 10,
                label: String::from("OK"),
            }),
        ],
    };

    screen.run();
}
```

Listing 17-9: Using trait objects to store values of different types that implement the same trait

When we wrote the library, we didn't know that someone might add the SelectBox type, but our Screen implementation was able to operate on the new type and draw it because SelectBox implements the Draw trait, which means it implements the draw method.

This concept—of being concerned only with the messages a value responds to rather than the value's concrete type—is similar to the concept of *duck typing* in dynamically typed languages: if it walks like a duck and quacks like a duck, then it must be a duck! In the implementation of run on Screen in Listing 17-5, run doesn't need to know what the concrete type of each component is. It doesn't check whether a component is an instance of a Button or a SelectBox, it just calls the draw method on the component. By specifying Box<dyn Draw> as the type of the values in the components vector, we've defined Screen to need values that we can call the draw method on.

The advantage of using trait objects and Rust's type system to write code similar to code using duck typing is that we never have to check whether a value implements a particular method at runtime or worry about getting errors if a value doesn't implement a method but we call it anyway. Rust won't compile our code if the values don't implement the traits that the trait objects need.

For example, Listing 17-10 shows what happens if we try to create a Screen with a String as a component.

src/main.rs

```
use gui::Screen;

fn main() {
    let screen = Screen {
        components: vec![Box::new(String::from("Hi"))],
    };

    screen.run();
}
```

Listing 17-10: Attempting to use a type that doesn't implement the trait object's trait

We'll get this error because String doesn't implement the Draw trait:

```
error[E0277]: the trait bound `String: Draw` is not satisfied
 --> src/main.rs:5:26
  |
5 |         components: vec![Box::new(String::from("Hi"))],
  |                         ^^^^^^^^^^^^^^^^^^^^^^^^^^^^^^ the trait `Draw` is
not implemented for `String`
  |
  = note: required for the cast to the object type `dyn Draw`
```

This error lets us know that either we're passing something to Screen that we didn't mean to pass and so should pass a different type, or we should implement Draw on String so that Screen is able to call draw on it.

Trait Objects Perform Dynamic Dispatch

Recall in "Performance of Code Using Generics" on page 191 our discussion on the monomorphization process performed by the compiler when we use trait bounds on generics: the compiler generates nongeneric implementations of functions and methods for each concrete type that we use in place of a generic type parameter. The code that results from monomorphization is doing *static dispatch*, which is when the compiler knows what method you're calling at compile time. This is opposed to *dynamic dispatch*, which is when the compiler can't tell at compile time which method you're calling. In dynamic dispatch cases, the compiler emits code that at runtime will figure out which method to call.

When we use trait objects, Rust must use dynamic dispatch. The compiler doesn't know all the types that might be used with the code that's using trait objects, so it doesn't know which method implemented on which type to call. Instead, at runtime, Rust uses the pointers inside the trait object to know which method to call. This lookup incurs a runtime cost that doesn't occur with static dispatch. Dynamic dispatch also prevents the compiler from choosing to inline a method's code, which in turn prevents some optimizations. However, we did get extra flexibility in the code that we wrote in Listing 17-5 and were able to support in Listing 17-9, so it's a trade-off to consider.

Implementing an Object-Oriented Design Pattern

The *state pattern* is an object-oriented design pattern. The crux of the pattern is that we define a set of states a value can have internally. The states are represented by a set of *state objects*, and the value's behavior changes based on its state. We're going to work through an example of a blog post struct that has a field to hold its state, which will be a state object from the set "draft," "review," or "published."

The state objects share functionality: in Rust, of course, we use structs and traits rather than objects and inheritance. Each state object is responsible for its own behavior and for governing when it should change into another state. The value that holds a state object knows nothing about the different behavior of the states or when to transition between states.

The advantage of using the state pattern is that, when the business requirements of the program change, we won't need to change the code of the value holding the state or the code that uses the value. We'll only need to update the code inside one of the state objects to change its rules or perhaps add more state objects.

First we're going to implement the state pattern in a more traditional object-oriented way, then we'll use an approach that's a bit more natural in Rust. Let's dig in to incrementally implement a blog post workflow using the state pattern.

The final functionality will look like this:

1. A blog post starts as an empty draft.
2. When the draft is done, a review of the post is requested.
3. When the post is approved, it gets published.
4. Only published blog posts return content to print, so unapproved posts can't accidentally be published.

Any other changes attempted on a post should have no effect. For example, if we try to approve a draft blog post before we've requested a review, the post should remain an unpublished draft.

Listing 17-11 shows this workflow in code form: this is an example usage of the API we'll implement in a library crate named blog. This won't compile yet because we haven't implemented the blog crate.

src/main.rs
```
use blog::Post;

fn main() {
  ❶ let mut post = Post::new();

  ❷ post.add_text("I ate a salad for lunch today");
  ❸ assert_eq!("", post.content());

  ❹ post.request_review();
  ❺ assert_eq!("", post.content());

  ❻ post.approve();
  ❼ assert_eq!("I ate a salad for lunch today", post.content());
}
```

Listing 17-11: Code that demonstrates the desired behavior we want our blog crate to have

We want to allow the user to create a new draft blog post with Post::new ❶. We want to allow text to be added to the blog post ❷. If we try to get the post's content immediately, before approval, we shouldn't get any text because the post is still a draft. We've added assert_eq! in the code for demonstration purposes ❸. An excellent unit test for this would be to assert that a draft blog post returns an empty string from the content method, but we're not going to write tests for this example.

Next, we want to enable a request for a review of the post ❹, and we want content to return an empty string while waiting for the review ❺. When the post receives approval ❻, it should get published, meaning the text of the post will be returned when content is called ❼.

Notice that the only type we're interacting with from the crate is the Post type. This type will use the state pattern and will hold a value that will be one of three state objects representing the various states a post can be in—draft, review, or published. Changing from one state to another will be managed internally within the Post type. The states change in response to the methods called by our library's users on the Post instance, but they don't have to manage the state changes directly. Also, users can't make a mistake with the states, such as publishing a post before it's reviewed.

Defining Post and Creating a New Instance in the Draft State

Let's get started on the implementation of the library! We know we need a public Post struct that holds some content, so we'll start with the definition of the struct and an associated public new function to create an instance of Post, as shown in Listing 17-12. We'll also make a private State trait that will define the behavior that all state objects for a Post must have.

Then Post will hold a trait object of Box<dyn State> inside an Option<T> in a private field named state to hold the state object. You'll see why the Option<T> is necessary in a bit.

src/lib.rs
```
pub struct Post {
    state: Option<Box<dyn State>>,
    content: String,
}

impl Post {
    pub fn new() -> Post {
        Post {
         ❶ state: Some(Box::new(Draft {})),
         ❷ content: String::new(),
        }
    }
}

trait State {}

struct Draft {}

impl State for Draft {}
```

Listing 17-12: Definition of a Post struct and a new function that creates a new Post instance, a State trait, and a Draft struct

The State trait defines the behavior shared by different post states. The state objects are Draft, PendingReview, and Published, and they will all implement the State trait. For now, the trait doesn't have any methods, and we'll start by defining just the Draft state because that is the state we want a post to start in.

When we create a new Post, we set its state field to a Some value that holds a Box ❶. This Box points to a new instance of the Draft struct. This ensures that whenever we create a new instance of Post, it will start out as a draft. Because the state field of Post is private, there is no way to create a Post in any other state! In the Post::new function, we set the content field to a new, empty String ❷.

Storing the Text of the Post Content

We saw in Listing 17-11 that we want to be able to call a method named add_text and pass it a &str that is then added as the text content of the blog post. We implement this as a method, rather than exposing the content field as pub, so that later we can implement a method that will control how the content field's data is read. The add_text method is pretty straightforward, so let's add the implementation in Listing 17-13 to the impl Post block.

src/lib.rs
```
impl Post {
    --snip--
    pub fn add_text(&mut self, text: &str) {
        self.content.push_str(text);
    }
}
```

Listing 17-13: Implementing the add_text method to add text to a post's content

The add_text method takes a mutable reference to self because we're changing the Post instance that we're calling add_text on. We then call push_str on the String in content and pass the text argument to add to the saved content. This behavior doesn't depend on the state the post is in, so it's not part of the state pattern. The add_text method doesn't interact with the state field at all, but it is part of the behavior we want to support.

Ensuring the Content of a Draft Post Is Empty

Even after we've called add_text and added some content to our post, we still want the content method to return an empty string slice because the post is still in the draft state, as shown at ❸ in Listing 17-11. For now, let's implement the content method with the simplest thing that will fulfill this requirement: always returning an empty string slice. We'll change this later once we implement the ability to change a post's state so it can be published. So far, posts can only be in the draft state, so the post content should always be empty. Listing 17-14 shows this placeholder implementation.

src/lib.rs
```
impl Post {
    --snip--
    pub fn content(&self) -> &str {
        ""
    }
}
```

Listing 17-14: Adding a placeholder implementation for the content method on Post that always returns an empty string slice

With this added content method, everything in Listing 17-11 up to the line at ❸ works as intended.

Requesting a Review Changes the Post's State

Next, we need to add functionality to request a review of a post, which should change its state from Draft to PendingReview. Listing 17-15 shows this code.

src/lib.rs
```
impl Post {
    --snip--
  ❶ pub fn request_review(&mut self) {
      ❷ if let Some(s) = self.state.take() {
          ❸ self.state = Some(s.request_review())
        }
    }
}

trait State {
  ❹ fn request_review(self: Box<Self>) -> Box<dyn State>;
}

struct Draft {}

impl State for Draft {
    fn request_review(self: Box<Self>) -> Box<dyn State> {
      ❺ Box::new(PendingReview {})
    }
}

struct PendingReview {}

impl State for PendingReview {
    fn request_review(self: Box<Self>) -> Box<dyn State> {
      ❻ self
    }
}
```

Listing 17-15: Implementing request_review methods on Post and the State trait

We give Post a public method named request_review that will take a mutable reference to self ❶. Then we call an internal request_review method on the current state of Post ❸, and this second request_review method consumes the current state and returns a new state.

We add the request_review method to the State trait ❹; all types that implement the trait now need to implement the request_review method. Note that rather than having self, &self, or &mut self as the first parameter of the method, we have self: Box<Self>. This syntax means the method is only valid when called on a Box holding the type. This syntax takes ownership of Box<Self>, invalidating the old state so the state value of the Post can transform into a new state.

To consume the old state, the request_review method needs to take ownership of the state value. This is where the Option in the state field of

Post comes in: we call the take method to take the Some value out of the state field and leave a None in its place because Rust doesn't let us have unpopulated fields in structs ❷. This lets us move the state value out of Post rather than borrowing it. Then we'll set the post's state value to the result of this operation.

We need to set state to None temporarily rather than setting it directly with code like self.state = self.state.request_review(); to get ownership of the state value. This ensures Post can't use the old state value after we've transformed it into a new state.

The request_review method on Draft returns a new, boxed instance of a new PendingReview struct ❺, which represents the state when a post is waiting for a review. The PendingReview struct also implements the request_review method but doesn't do any transformations. Rather, it returns itself ❻ because when we request a review on a post already in the PendingReview state, it should stay in the PendingReview state.

Now we can start seeing the advantages of the state pattern: the request_review method on Post is the same no matter its state value. Each state is responsible for its own rules.

We'll leave the content method on Post as is, returning an empty string slice. We can now have a Post in the PendingReview state as well as in the Draft state, but we want the same behavior in the PendingReview state. Listing 17-11 now works up to the line at ❺!

Adding approve to Change the Behavior of content

The approve method will be similar to the request_review method: it will set state to the value that the current state says it should have when that state is approved, as shown in Listing 17-16.

src/lib.rs
```
impl Post {
    --snip--
    pub fn approve(&mut self) {
        if let Some(s) = self.state.take() {
            self.state = Some(s.approve())
        }
    }
}

trait State {
    fn request_review(self: Box<Self>) -> Box<dyn State>;
    fn approve(self: Box<Self>) -> Box<dyn State>;
}

struct Draft {}

impl State for Draft {
    --snip--
    fn approve(self: Box<Self>) -> Box<dyn State> {
      ❶ self
    }
}
```

```
struct PendingReview {}

impl State for PendingReview {
    --snip--
    fn approve(self: Box<Self>) -> Box<dyn State> {
      ❷ Box::new(Published {})
    }
}

struct Published {}

impl State for Published {
    fn request_review(self: Box<Self>) -> Box<dyn State> {
        self
    }

    fn approve(self: Box<Self>) -> Box<dyn State> {
        self
    }
}
```

Listing 17-16: Implementing the approve method on Post and the State trait

We add the approve method to the State trait and add a new struct that implements State, the Published state.

Similar to the way request_review on PendingReview works, if we call the approve method on a Draft, it will have no effect because approve will return self ❶. When we call approve on PendingReview, it returns a new, boxed instance of the Published struct ❷. The Published struct implements the State trait, and for both the request_review method and the approve method, it returns itself because the post should stay in the Published state in those cases.

Now we need to update the content method on Post. We want the value returned from content to depend on the current state of the Post, so we're going to have the Post delegate to a content method defined on its state, as shown in Listing 17-17.

src/lib.rs
```
impl Post {
    --snip--
    pub fn content(&self) -> &str {
        self.state.as_ref().unwrap().content(self)
    }
    --snip--
}
```

Listing 17-17: Updating the content method on Post to delegate to a content method on State

Because the goal is to keep all of these rules inside the structs that implement State, we call a content method on the value in state and pass the post instance (that is, self) as an argument. Then we return the value that's returned from using the content method on the state value.

We call the as_ref method on the Option because we want a reference to the value inside the Option rather than ownership of the value. Because state is an Option<Box<dyn State>>, when we call as_ref, an Option<&Box<dyn State>> is returned. If we didn't call as_ref, we would get an error because we can't move state out of the borrowed &self of the function parameter.

We then call the unwrap method, which we know will never panic because we know the methods on Post ensure that state will always contain a Some value when those methods are done. This is one of the cases we talked about in "Cases in Which You Have More Information Than the Compiler" on page 176 when we know that a None value is never possible, even though the compiler isn't able to understand that.

At this point, when we call content on the &Box<dyn State>, deref coercion will take effect on the & and the Box so the content method will ultimately be called on the type that implements the State trait. That means we need to add content to the State trait definition, and that is where we'll put the logic for what content to return depending on which state we have, as shown in Listing 17-18.

src/lib.rs
```
trait State {
    --snip--
    fn content<'a>(&self, post: &'a Post) -> &'a str {
      ❶ ""
    }
}

--snip--
struct Published {}

impl State for Published {
    --snip--
    fn content<'a>(&self, post: &'a Post) -> &'a str {
      ❷ &post.content
    }
}
```

Listing 17-18: Adding the content method to the State trait

We add a default implementation for the content method that returns an empty string slice ❶. That means we don't need to implement content on the Draft and PendingReview structs. The Published struct will override the content method and return the value in post.content ❷.

Note that we need lifetime annotations on this method, as we discussed in Chapter 10. We're taking a reference to a post as an argument and returning a reference to part of that post, so the lifetime of the returned reference is related to the lifetime of the post argument.

And we're done—all of Listing 17-11 now works! We've implemented the state pattern with the rules of the blog post workflow. The logic related to the rules lives in the state objects rather than being scattered throughout Post.

Trade-offs of the State Pattern

We've shown that Rust is capable of implementing the object-oriented state pattern to encapsulate the different kinds of behavior a post should have in each state. The methods on Post know nothing about the various behaviors. The way we organized the code, we have to look in only one place to know the different ways a published post can behave: the implementation of the State trait on the Published struct.

If we were to create an alternative implementation that didn't use the state pattern, we might instead use match expressions in the methods on Post or even in the main code that checks the state of the post and changes behavior in those places. That would mean we would have to look in several places to understand all the implications of a post being in the published state! This would only increase the more states we added: each of those match expressions would need another arm.

With the state pattern, the Post methods and the places we use Post don't need match expressions, and to add a new state, we would only need to add a new struct and implement the trait methods on that one struct.

The implementation using the state pattern is easy to extend to add more functionality. To see the simplicity of maintaining code that uses the state pattern, try a few of these suggestions:

- Add a reject method that changes the post's state from PendingReview back to Draft.
- Require two calls to approve before the state can be changed to Published.
- Allow users to add text content only when a post is in the Draft state. Hint: have the state object responsible for what might change about the content but not responsible for modifying the Post.

One downside of the state pattern is that, because the states implement the transitions between states, some of the states are coupled to each other. If we add another state between PendingReview and Published, such as Scheduled, we would have to change the code in PendingReview to transition to Scheduled instead. It would be less work if PendingReview didn't need to change with the addition of a new state, but that would mean switching to another design pattern.

Another downside is that we've duplicated some logic. To eliminate some of the duplication, we might try to make default implementations for the request_review and approve methods on the State trait that return self. However, this wouldn't work: when using State as a trait object, the trait doesn't know what the concrete self will be exactly, so the return type isn't known at compile time.

Other duplication includes the similar implementations of the request _review and approve methods on Post. Both methods delegate to the implementation of the same method on the value in the state field of Option and set the new value of the state field to the result. If we had a lot of methods on Post that followed this pattern, we might consider defining a macro to eliminate the repetition (see "Macros" on page 449).

By implementing the state pattern exactly as it's defined for object-oriented languages, we're not taking as full advantage of Rust's strengths as we could. Let's look at some changes we can make to the blog crate that can make invalid states and transitions into compile-time errors.

Encoding States and Behavior as Types

We'll show you how to rethink the state pattern to get a different set of trade-offs. Rather than encapsulating the states and transitions completely so outside code has no knowledge of them, we'll encode the states into different types. Consequently, Rust's type checking system will prevent attempts to use draft posts where only published posts are allowed by issuing a compiler error.

Let's consider the first part of main in Listing 17-11:

src/main.rs
```
fn main() {
    let mut post = Post::new();

    post.add_text("I ate a salad for lunch today");
    assert_eq!("", post.content());
}
```

We still enable the creation of new posts in the draft state using Post::new and the ability to add text to the post's content. But instead of having a content method on a draft post that returns an empty string, we'll make it so draft posts don't have the content method at all. That way, if we try to get a draft post's content, we'll get a compiler error telling us the method doesn't exist. As a result, it will be impossible for us to accidentally display draft post content in production because that code won't even compile. Listing 17-19 shows the definition of a Post struct and a DraftPost struct, as well as methods on each.

src/lib.rs
```
pub struct Post {
    content: String,
}

pub struct DraftPost {
    content: String,
}
```

```
impl Post {
  ❶ pub fn new() -> DraftPost {
        DraftPost {
            content: String::new(),
        }
    }

  ❷ pub fn content(&self) -> &str {
        &self.content
    }
}

impl DraftPost {
  ❸ pub fn add_text(&mut self, text: &str) {
        self.content.push_str(text);
    }
}
```

Listing 17-19: A Post with a content method and a DraftPost without a content method

Both the Post and DraftPost structs have a private content field that stores the blog post text. The structs no longer have the state field because we're moving the encoding of the state to the types of the structs. The Post struct will represent a published post, and it has a content method that returns the content ❷.

We still have a Post::new function, but instead of returning an instance of Post, it returns an instance of DraftPost ❶. Because content is private and there aren't any functions that return Post, it's not possible to create an instance of Post right now.

The DraftPost struct has an add_text method, so we can add text to content as before ❸, but note that DraftPost does not have a content method defined! So now the program ensures all posts start as draft posts, and draft posts don't have their content available for display. Any attempt to get around these constraints will result in a compiler error.

Implementing Transitions as Transformations into Different Types

So how do we get a published post? We want to enforce the rule that a draft post has to be reviewed and approved before it can be published. A post in the pending review state should still not display any content. Let's implement these constraints by adding another struct, PendingReviewPost, defining the request_review method on DraftPost to return a PendingReviewPost and defining an approve method on PendingReviewPost to return a Post, as shown in Listing 17-20.

src/lib.rs
```
impl DraftPost {
    --snip--
    pub fn request_review(self) -> PendingReviewPost {
        PendingReviewPost {
            content: self.content,
        }
    }
}
```

```
pub struct PendingReviewPost {
    content: String,
}

impl PendingReviewPost {
    pub fn approve(self) -> Post {
        Post {
            content: self.content,
        }
    }
}
```

Listing 17-20: A `PendingReviewPost` that gets created by calling `request_review` on `DraftPost` and an `approve` method that turns a `PendingReviewPost` into a published `Post`

The request_review and approve methods take ownership of self, thus consuming the DraftPost and PendingReviewPost instances and transforming them into a PendingReviewPost and a published Post, respectively. This way, we won't have any lingering DraftPost instances after we've called request _review on them, and so forth. The PendingReviewPost struct doesn't have a content method defined on it, so attempting to read its content results in a compiler error, as with DraftPost. Because the only way to get a published Post instance that does have a content method defined is to call the approve method on a PendingReviewPost, and the only way to get a PendingReviewPost is to call the request_review method on a DraftPost, we've now encoded the blog post workflow into the type system.

But we also have to make some small changes to main. The request_review and approve methods return new instances rather than modifying the struct they're called on, so we need to add more let post = shadowing assignments to save the returned instances. We also can't have the assertions about the draft and pending review posts' contents be empty strings, nor do we need them: we can't compile code that tries to use the content of posts in those states any longer. The updated code in main is shown in Listing 17-21.

src/main.rs

```
use blog::Post;

fn main() {
    let mut post = Post::new();

    post.add_text("I ate a salad for lunch today");

    let post = post.request_review();

    let post = post.approve();

    assert_eq!("I ate a salad for lunch today", post.content());
}
```

Listing 17-21: Modifications to main to use the new implementation of the blog post workflow

The changes we needed to make to main to reassign post mean that this implementation doesn't quite follow the object-oriented state pattern anymore: the transformations between the states are no longer encapsulated entirely within the Post implementation. However, our gain is that invalid states are now impossible because of the type system and the type checking that happens at compile time! This ensures that certain bugs, such as display of the content of an unpublished post, will be discovered before they make it to production.

Try the tasks suggested at the start of this section on the blog crate as it is after Listing 17-21 to see what you think about the design of this version of the code. Note that some of the tasks might be completed already in this design.

We've seen that even though Rust is capable of implementing object-oriented design patterns, other patterns, such as encoding state into the type system, are also available in Rust. These patterns have different trade-offs. Although you might be very familiar with object-oriented patterns, rethinking the problem to take advantage of Rust's features can provide benefits, such as preventing some bugs at compile time. Object-oriented patterns won't always be the best solution in Rust due to certain features, like ownership, that object-oriented languages don't have.

Summary

Regardless of whether you think Rust is an object-oriented language after reading this chapter, you now know that you can use trait objects to get some object-oriented features in Rust. Dynamic dispatch can give your code some flexibility in exchange for a bit of runtime performance. You can use this flexibility to implement object-oriented patterns that can help your code's maintainability. Rust also has other features, like ownership, that object-oriented languages don't have. An object-oriented pattern won't always be the best way to take advantage of Rust's strengths, but it is an available option.

Next, we'll look at patterns, which are another of Rust's features that enable lots of flexibility. We've looked at them briefly throughout the book but haven't seen their full capability yet. Let's go!

18

PATTERNS AND MATCHING

Patterns are a special syntax in Rust for matching against the structure of types, both complex and simple. Using patterns in conjunction with `match` expressions and other constructs gives you more control over a program's control flow. A pattern consists of some combination of the following:

- Literals
- Destructured arrays, enums, structs, or tuples
- Variables
- Wildcards
- Placeholders

Some example patterns include x, (a, 3), and Some(Color::Red). In the contexts in which patterns are valid, these components describe the shape of data. Our program then matches values against the patterns to determine whether it has the correct shape of data to continue running a particular piece of code.

To use a pattern, we compare it to some value. If the pattern matches the value, we use the value parts in our code. Recall the match expressions in Chapter 6 that used patterns, such as the coin-sorting machine example. If the value fits the shape of the pattern, we can use the named pieces. If it doesn't, the code associated with the pattern won't run.

This chapter is a reference on all things related to patterns. We'll cover the valid places to use patterns, the difference between refutable and irrefutable patterns, and the different kinds of pattern syntax that you might see. By the end of the chapter, you'll know how to use patterns to express many concepts in a clear way.

All the Places Patterns Can Be Used

Patterns pop up in a number of places in Rust, and you've been using them a lot without realizing it! This section discusses all the places where patterns are valid.

match Arms

As discussed in Chapter 6, we use patterns in the arms of match expressions. Formally, match expressions are defined as the keyword match, a value to match on, and one or more match arms that consist of a pattern and an expression to run if the value matches that arm's pattern, like this:

```
match VALUE {
    PATTERN => EXPRESSION,
    PATTERN => EXPRESSION,
    PATTERN => EXPRESSION,
}
```

For example, here's the match expression from Listing 6-5 that matches on an Option<i32> value in the variable x:

```
match x {
    None => None,
    Some(i) => Some(i + 1),
}
```

The patterns in this match expression are the None and Some(i) to the left of each arrow.

One requirement for match expressions is that they need to be *exhaustive* in the sense that all possibilities for the value in the match expression must be accounted for. One way to ensure you've covered every possibility is to have a catch-all pattern for the last arm: for example, a variable name matching any value can never fail and thus covers every remaining case.

The particular pattern _ will match anything, but it never binds to a variable, so it's often used in the last match arm. The _ pattern can be useful when you want to ignore any value not specified, for example. We'll cover the _ pattern in more detail in "Ignoring Values in a Pattern" on page 411.

Conditional if let Expressions

In Chapter 6, we discussed how to use if let expressions mainly as a shorter way to write the equivalent of a match that only matches one case. Optionally, if let can have a corresponding else containing code to run if the pattern in the if let doesn't match.

Listing 18-1 shows that it's also possible to mix and match if let, else if, and else if let expressions. Doing so gives us more flexibility than a match expression in which we can express only one value to compare with the patterns. Also, Rust doesn't require that the conditions in a series of if let, else if, and else if let arms relate to each other.

The code in Listing 18-1 determines what color to make your background based on a series of checks for several conditions. For this example, we've created variables with hardcoded values that a real program might receive from user input.

src/main.rs

```
fn main() {
    let favorite_color: Option<&str> = None;
    let is_tuesday = false;
    let age: Result<u8, _> = "34".parse();

❶   if let Some(color) = favorite_color {
❷       println!(
            "Using your favorite, {color}, as the background"
        );
❸   } else if is_tuesday {
❹       println!("Tuesday is green day!");
❺   } else if let Ok(age) = age {
❻       if age > 30 {
❼           println!("Using purple as the background color");
        } else {
❽           println!("Using orange as the background color");
        }
❾   } else {
❿       println!("Using blue as the background color");
    }
}
```

Listing 18-1: Mixing if let, else if, else if let, and else

If the user specifies a favorite color ❶, that color is used as the background ❷. If no favorite color is specified and today is Tuesday ❸, the background color is green ❹. Otherwise, if the user specifies their age as a string and we can parse it as a number successfully ❺, the color is either purple ❼ or orange ❽ depending on the value of the number ❻. If none of these conditions apply ❾, the background color is blue ❿.

This conditional structure lets us support complex requirements. With the hardcoded values we have here, this example will print Using purple as the background color.

You can see that if let can also introduce shadowed variables in the same way that match arms can: the line if let Ok(age) = age ❺ introduces a new shadowed age variable that contains the value inside the Ok variant. This means we need to place the if age > 30 condition ❻ within that block: we can't combine these two conditions into if let Ok(age) = age && age > 30. The shadowed age we want to compare to 30 isn't valid until the new scope starts with the curly bracket.

The downside of using if let expressions is that the compiler doesn't check for exhaustiveness, whereas with match expressions it does. If we omitted the last else block ❾ and therefore missed handling some cases, the compiler would not alert us to the possible logic bug.

while let Conditional Loops

Similar in construction to if let, the while let conditional loop allows a while loop to run for as long as a pattern continues to match. In Listing 18-2, we code a while let loop that uses a vector as a stack and prints the values in the vector in the opposite order in which they were pushed.

src/main.rs

```
let mut stack = Vec::new();

stack.push(1);
stack.push(2);
stack.push(3);

while let Some(top) = stack.pop() {
    println!("{top}");
}
```

Listing 18-2: Using a while let loop to print values for as long as stack.pop() returns Some

This example prints 3, 2, and then 1. The pop method takes the last element out of the vector and returns Some(value). If the vector is empty, pop returns None. The while loop continues running the code in its block as long as pop returns Some. When pop returns None, the loop stops. We can use while let to pop every element off our stack.

for Loops

In a for loop, the value that directly follows the keyword for is a pattern. For example, in for x in y, the x is the pattern. Listing 18-3 demonstrates how to use a pattern in a for loop to *destructure*, or break apart, a tuple as part of the for loop.

src/main.rs

```
let v = vec!['a', 'b', 'c'];

for (index, value) in v.iter().enumerate() {
    println!("{value} is at index {index}");
}
```

Listing 18-3: Using a pattern in a for loop to destructure a tuple

The code in Listing 18-3 will print the following:

```
a is at index 0
b is at index 1
c is at index 2
```

We adapt an iterator using the `enumerate` method so it produces a value and the index for that value, placed into a tuple. The first value produced is the tuple (0, 'a'). When this value is matched to the pattern (`index`, `value`), *index* will be 0 and *value* will be 'a', printing the first line of the output.

let Statements

Prior to this chapter, we had only explicitly discussed using patterns with `match` and `if let`, but in fact, we've used patterns in other places as well, including in let statements. For example, consider this straightforward variable assignment with let:

```
let x = 5;
```

Every time you've used a let statement like this you've been using patterns, although you might not have realized it! More formally, a let statement looks like this:

```
let PATTERN = EXPRESSION;
```

In statements like let x = 5; with a variable name in the *PATTERN* slot, the variable name is just a particularly simple form of a pattern. Rust compares the expression against the pattern and assigns any names it finds. So, in the let x = 5; example, x is a pattern that means "bind what matches here to the variable x." Because the name x is the whole pattern, this pattern effectively means "bind everything to the variable x, whatever the value is."

To see the pattern-matching aspect of let more clearly, consider Listing 18-4, which uses a pattern with let to destructure a tuple.

```
let (x, y, z) = (1, 2, 3);
```

Listing 18-4: Using a pattern to destructure a tuple and create three variables at once

Here, we match a tuple against a pattern. Rust compares the value (1, 2, 3) to the pattern (x, y, z) and sees that the value matches the pattern, in that it sees that the number of elements is the same in both, so Rust binds 1 to x, 2 to y, and 3 to z. You can think of this tuple pattern as nesting three individual variable patterns inside it.

If the number of elements in the pattern doesn't match the number of elements in the tuple, the overall type won't match and we'll get a compiler error. For example, Listing 18-5 shows an attempt to destructure a tuple with three elements into two variables, which won't work.

```
let (x, y) = (1, 2, 3);
```

Listing 18-5: Incorrectly constructing a pattern whose variables don't match the number of elements in the tuple

Attempting to compile this code results in this type error:

```
error[E0308]: mismatched types
 --> src/main.rs:2:9
  |
2 |     let (x, y) = (1, 2, 3);
  |         ^^^^^^   --------- this expression has type `({integer}, {integer},
{integer})`
  |         |
  |         expected a tuple with 3 elements, found one with 2 elements
  |
  = note: expected tuple `({integer}, {integer}, {integer})`
             found tuple `(_, _)`
```

To fix the error, we could ignore one or more of the values in the tuple using _ or .., as you'll see in "Ignoring Values in a Pattern" on page 411. If the problem is that we have too many variables in the pattern, the solution is to make the types match by removing variables so the number of variables equals the number of elements in the tuple.

Function Parameters

Function parameters can also be patterns. The code in Listing 18-6, which declares a function named foo that takes one parameter named x of type i32, should by now look familiar.

```rust
fn foo(x: i32) {
    // code goes here
}
```

Listing 18-6: A function signature using patterns in the parameters

The x part is a pattern! As we did with let, we could match a tuple in a function's arguments to the pattern. Listing 18-7 splits the values in a tuple as we pass it to a function.

src/main.rs
```rust
fn print_coordinates(&(x, y): &(i32, i32)) {
    println!("Current location: ({x}, {y})");
}

fn main() {
    let point = (3, 5);
    print_coordinates(&point);
}
```

Listing 18-7: A function with parameters that destructure a tuple

This code prints Current location: (3, 5). The values &(3, 5) match the pattern &(x, y), so x is the value 3 and y is the value 5.

We can also use patterns in closure parameter lists in the same way as in function parameter lists because closures are similar to functions, as discussed in Chapter 13.

At this point, you've seen several ways to use patterns, but patterns don't work the same in every place we can use them. In some places, the patterns must be irrefutable; in other circumstances, they can be refutable. We'll discuss these two concepts next.

Refutability: Whether a Pattern Might Fail to Match

Patterns come in two forms: refutable and irrefutable. Patterns that will match for any possible value passed are *irrefutable*. An example would be x in the statement let x = 5; because x matches anything and therefore cannot fail to match. Patterns that can fail to match for some possible value are *refutable*. An example would be Some(x) in the expression if let Some(x) = a_value because if the value in the a_value variable is None rather than Some, the Some(x) pattern will not match.

Function parameters, let statements, and for loops can only accept irrefutable patterns because the program cannot do anything meaningful when values don't match. The if let and while let expressions accept refutable and irrefutable patterns, but the compiler warns against irrefutable patterns because, by definition, they're intended to handle possible failure: the functionality of a conditional is in its ability to perform differently depending on success or failure.

In general, you shouldn't have to worry about the distinction between refutable and irrefutable patterns; however, you do need to be familiar with the concept of refutability so you can respond when you see it in an error message. In those cases, you'll need to change either the pattern or the construct you're using the pattern with, depending on the intended behavior of the code.

Let's look at an example of what happens when we try to use a refutable pattern where Rust requires an irrefutable pattern and vice versa. Listing 18-8 shows a let statement, but for the pattern, we've specified Some(x), a refutable pattern. As you might expect, this code will not compile.

```
let Some(x) = some_option_value;
```

Listing 18-8: Attempting to use a refutable pattern with let

If some_option_value were a None value, it would fail to match the pattern Some(x), meaning the pattern is refutable. However, the let statement can only accept an irrefutable pattern because there is nothing valid the code can do with a None value. At compile time, Rust will complain that we've tried to use a refutable pattern where an irrefutable pattern is required:

```
error[E0005]: refutable pattern in local binding: `None` not covered
  --> src/main.rs:3:9
   |
3  |     let Some(x) = some_option_value;
   |         ^^^^^^^ pattern `None` not covered
   |
   = note: `let` bindings require an "irrefutable pattern", like a `struct` or
an `enum` with only one variant
```

```
        = note: for more information, visit
https://doc.rust-lang.org/book/ch18-02-refutability.html
        = note: the matched value is of type `Option<i32>`
help: you might want to use `if let` to ignore the variant that isn't matched
        |
3       |       let x = if let Some(x) = some_option_value { x } else { todo!() };
        |               ++++++++++                                    ++++++++++++++++++++++++
```

Because we didn't cover (and couldn't cover!) every valid value with the pattern Some(x), Rust rightfully produces a compiler error.

If we have a refutable pattern where an irrefutable pattern is needed, we can fix it by changing the code that uses the pattern: instead of using let, we can use if let. Then, if the pattern doesn't match, the code will just skip the code in the curly brackets, giving it a way to continue validly. Listing 18-9 shows how to fix the code in Listing 18-8.

```
if let Some(x) = some_option_value {
    println!("{x}");
}
```

Listing 18-9: Using if let and a block with refutable patterns instead of let

We've given the code an out! This code is perfectly valid, although it means we cannot use an irrefutable pattern without receiving an error. If we give if let a pattern that will always match, such as x, as shown in Listing 18-10, the compiler will give a warning.

```
if let x = 5 {
    println!("{x}");
};
```

Listing 18-10: Attempting to use an irrefutable pattern with if let

Rust complains that it doesn't make sense to use if let with an irrefutable pattern:

```
warning: irrefutable `if let` pattern
 --> src/main.rs:2:8
  |
2 |     if let x = 5 {
  |            ^^^^^^^^^
  |
  = note: `#[warn(irrefutable_let_patterns)]` on by default
  = note: this pattern will always match, so the `if let` is
useless
  = help: consider replacing the `if let` with a `let`
```

For this reason, match arms must use refutable patterns, except for the last arm, which should match any remaining values with an irrefutable pattern. Rust allows us to use an irrefutable pattern in a match with only one arm, but this syntax isn't particularly useful and could be replaced with a simpler let statement.

Now that you know where to use patterns and the difference between refutable and irrefutable patterns, let's cover all the syntax we can use to create patterns.

Pattern Syntax

In this section, we gather all the syntax that is valid in patterns and discuss why and when you might want to use each one.

Matching Literals

As you saw in Chapter 6, you can match patterns against literals directly. The following code gives some examples:

src/main.rs
```
let x = 1;

match x {
    1 => println!("one"),
    2 => println!("two"),
    3 => println!("three"),
    _ => println!("anything"),
}
```

This code prints one because the value in x is 1. This syntax is useful when you want your code to take an action if it gets a particular concrete value.

Matching Named Variables

Named variables are irrefutable patterns that match any value, and we've used them many times in this book. However, there is a complication when you use named variables in match expressions. Because match starts a new scope, variables declared as part of a pattern inside the match expression will shadow those with the same name outside the match construct, as is the case with all variables. In Listing 18-11, we declare a variable named x with the value Some(5) and a variable y with the value 10. We then create a match expression on the value x. Look at the patterns in the match arms and println! at the end, and try to figure out what the code will print before running this code or reading further.

src/main.rs
```
fn main() {
  ❶ let x = Some(5);
  ❷ let y = 10;

    match x {
      ❸ Some(50) => println!("Got 50"),
      ❹ Some(y) => println!("Matched, y = {y}"),
      ❺ _ => println!("Default case, x = {:?}", x),
    }

  ❻ println!("at the end: x = {:?}, y = {y}", x);
}
```

Listing 18-11: A match expression with an arm that introduces a shadowed variable y

Let's walk through what happens when the match expression runs. The pattern in the first match arm ❸ doesn't match the defined value of x ❶, so the code continues.

The pattern in the second match arm ❹ introduces a new variable named y that will match any value inside a Some value. Because we're in a new scope inside the match expression, this is a new y variable, not the y we declared at the beginning with the value 10 ❷. This new y binding will match any value inside a Some, which is what we have in x. Therefore, this new y binds to the inner value of the Some in x. That value is 5, so the expression for that arm executes and prints Matched, y = 5.

If x had been a None value instead of Some(5), the patterns in the first two arms wouldn't have matched, so the value would have matched to the underscore ❺. We didn't introduce the x variable in the pattern of the underscore arm, so the x in the expression is still the outer x that hasn't been shadowed. In this hypothetical case, the match would print Default case, x = None.

When the match expression is done, its scope ends, and so does the scope of the inner y. The last println! ❻ produces at the end: x = Some(5), y = 10.

To create a match expression that compares the values of the outer x and y, rather than introducing a shadowed variable, we would need to use a match guard conditional instead. We'll talk about match guards in "Extra Conditionals with Match Guards" on page 415.

Multiple Patterns

In match expressions, you can match multiple patterns using the | syntax, which is the pattern *or* operator. For example, in the following code we match the value of x against the match arms, the first of which has an *or* option, meaning if the value of x matches either of the values in that arm, that arm's code will run:

src/main.rs
```
let x = 1;

match x {
    1 | 2 => println!("one or two"),
    3 => println!("three"),
    _ => println!("anything"),
}
```

This code prints one or two.

Matching Ranges of Values with ..=

The ..= syntax allows us to match to an inclusive range of values. In the following code, when a pattern matches any of the values within the given range, that arm will execute:

src/main.rs
```
let x = 5;

match x {
    1..=5 => println!("one through five"),
```

```
        _ => println!("something else"),
}
```

If x is 1, 2, 3, 4, or 5, the first arm will match. This syntax is more convenient for multiple match values than using the | operator to express the same idea; if we were to use |, we would have to specify 1 | 2 | 3 | 4 | 5. Specifying a range is much shorter, especially if we want to match, say, any number between 1 and 1,000!

The compiler checks that the range isn't empty at compile time, and because the only types for which Rust can tell if a range is empty or not are char and numeric values, ranges are only allowed with numeric or char values.

Here is an example using ranges of char values:

```
let x = 'c';

match x {
    'a'..='j' => println!("early ASCII letter"),
    'k'..='z' => println!("late ASCII letter"),
    _ => println!("something else"),
}
```

Rust can tell that 'c' is within the first pattern's range and prints early ASCII letter.

Destructuring to Break Apart Values

We can also use patterns to destructure structs, enums, and tuples to use different parts of these values. Let's walk through each value.

Destructuring Structs

Listing 18-12 shows a Point struct with two fields, x and y, that we can break apart using a pattern with a let statement.

src/main.rs
```
struct Point {
    x: i32,
    y: i32,
}

fn main() {
    let p = Point { x: 0, y: 7 };

    let Point { x: a, y: b } = p;
    assert_eq!(0, a);
    assert_eq!(7, b);
}
```

Listing 18-12: Destructuring a struct's fields into separate variables

This code creates the variables a and b that match the values of the x and y fields of the p struct. This example shows that the names of the variables in the pattern don't have to match the field names of the struct. However, it's common to match the variable names to the field names

Patterns and Matching   **407**

to make it easier to remember which variables came from which fields. Because of this common usage, and because writing let Point { x: x, y: y } = p; contains a lot of duplication, Rust has a shorthand for patterns that match struct fields: you only need to list the name of the struct field, and the variables created from the pattern will have the same names. Listing 18-13 behaves in the same way as the code in Listing 18-12, but the variables created in the let pattern are x and y instead of a and b.

src/main.rs
```
struct Point {
    x: i32,
    y: i32,
}

fn main() {
    let p = Point { x: 0, y: 7 };

    let Point { x, y } = p;
    assert_eq!(0, x);
    assert_eq!(7, y);
}
```

Listing 18-13: Destructuring struct fields using struct field shorthand

This code creates the variables x and y that match the x and y fields of the p variable. The outcome is that the variables x and y contain the values from the p struct.

We can also destructure with literal values as part of the struct pattern rather than creating variables for all the fields. Doing so allows us to test some of the fields for particular values while creating variables to destructure the other fields.

In Listing 18-14, we have a match expression that separates Point values into three cases: points that lie directly on the x axis (which is true when y = 0), on the y axis (x = 0), or on neither axis.

src/main.rs
```
fn main() {
    let p = Point { x: 0, y: 7 };

    match p {
        Point { x, y: 0 } => println!("On the x axis at {x}"),
        Point { x: 0, y } => println!("On the y axis at {y}"),
        Point { x, y } => {
            println!("On neither axis: ({x}, {y})");
        }
    }
}
```

Listing 18-14: Destructuring and matching literal values in one pattern

The first arm will match any point that lies on the x axis by specifying that the y field matches if its value matches the literal 0. The pattern still creates an x variable that we can use in the code for this arm.

Similarly, the second arm matches any point on the y axis by specifying that the x field matches if its value is 0 and creates a variable y for the value of the y field. The third arm doesn't specify any literals, so it matches any other Point and creates variables for both the x and y fields.

In this example, the value p matches the second arm by virtue of x containing a 0, so this code will print On the y axis at 7.

Remember that a match expression stops checking arms once it has found the first matching pattern, so even though Point { x: 0, y: 0} is on the x axis and the y axis, this code would only print On the x axis at 0.

Destructuring Enums

We've destructured enums in this book (for example, Listing 6-5), but we haven't yet explicitly discussed that the pattern to destructure an enum corresponds to the way the data stored within the enum is defined. As an example, in Listing 18-15 we use the Message enum from Listing 6-2 and write a match with patterns that will destructure each inner value.

```
src/main.rs   enum Message {
                  Quit,
                  Move { x: i32, y: i32 },
                  Write(String),
                  ChangeColor(i32, i32, i32),
              }

              fn main() {
                ❶ let msg = Message::ChangeColor(0, 160, 255);

                  match msg {
                    ❷ Message::Quit => {
                          println!(
                              "The Quit variant has no data to destructure."
                          );
                      }
                    ❸ Message::Move { x, y } => {
                          println!(
                              "Move in the x dir {x}, in the y dir {y}"
                          );
                      }
                    ❹ Message::Write(text) => {
                          println!("Text message: {text}");
                      }
                    ❺ Message::ChangeColor(r, g, b) => println!(
                          "Change color to red {r}, green {g}, and blue {b}"
                      ),
                  }
              }
```

Listing 18-15: Destructuring enum variants that hold different kinds of values

This code will print Change color to red 0, green 160, and blue 255. Try changing the value of msg ❶ to see the code from the other arms run.

For enum variants without any data, like Message::Quit ❷, we can't destructure the value any further. We can only match on the literal Message::Quit value, and no variables are in that pattern.

For struct-like enum variants, such as `Message::Move` ❸, we can use a pattern similar to the pattern we specify to match structs. After the variant name, we place curly brackets and then list the fields with variables so we break apart the pieces to use in the code for this arm. Here we use the shorthand form as we did in Listing 18-13.

For tuple-like enum variants, like `Message::Write` that holds a tuple with one element ❹ and `Message::ChangeColor` that holds a tuple with three elements ❺, the pattern is similar to the pattern we specify to match tuples. The number of variables in the pattern must match the number of elements in the variant we're matching.

Destructuring Nested Structs and Enums

So far, our examples have all been matching structs or enums one level deep, but matching can work on nested items too! For example, we can refactor the code in Listing 18-15 to support RGB and HSV colors in the `ChangeColor` message, as shown in Listing 18-16.

```rust
enum Color {
    Rgb(i32, i32, i32),
    Hsv(i32, i32, i32),
}

enum Message {
    Quit,
    Move { x: i32, y: i32 },
    Write(String),
    ChangeColor(Color),
}

fn main() {
    let msg = Message::ChangeColor(Color::Hsv(0, 160, 255));

    match msg {
        Message::ChangeColor(Color::Rgb(r, g, b)) => println!(
            "Change color to red {r}, green {g}, and blue {b}"
        ),
        Message::ChangeColor(Color::Hsv(h, s, v)) => println!(
            "Change color to hue {h}, saturation {s}, value {v}"
        ),
        _ => (),
    }
}
```
src/main.rs

Listing 18-16: Matching on nested enums

The pattern of the first arm in the `match` expression matches a `Message::ChangeColor` enum variant that contains a `Color::Rgb` variant; then the pattern binds to the three inner i32 values. The pattern of the second arm also matches a `Message::ChangeColor` enum variant, but the inner enum matches `Color::Hsv` instead. We can specify these complex conditions in one `match` expression, even though two enums are involved.

Destructuring Structs and Tuples

We can mix, match, and nest destructuring patterns in even more complex ways. The following example shows a complicated destructure where we nest structs and tuples inside a tuple and destructure all the primitive values out:

```
let ((feet, inches), Point { x, y }) =
    ((3, 10), Point { x: 3, y: -10 });
```

This code lets us break complex types into their component parts so we can use the values we're interested in separately.

Destructuring with patterns is a convenient way to use pieces of values, such as the value from each field in a struct, separately from each other.

Ignoring Values in a Pattern

You've seen that it's sometimes useful to ignore values in a pattern, such as in the last arm of a match, to get a catch-all that doesn't actually do anything but does account for all remaining possible values. There are a few ways to ignore entire values or parts of values in a pattern: using the _ pattern (which you've seen), using the _ pattern within another pattern, using a name that starts with an underscore, or using .. to ignore remaining parts of a value. Let's explore how and why to use each of these patterns.

An Entire Value with _

We've used the underscore as a wildcard pattern that will match any value but not bind to the value. This is especially useful as the last arm in a match expression, but we can also use it in any pattern, including function parameters, as shown in Listing 18-17.

src/main.rs
```
fn foo(_: i32, y: i32) {
    println!("This code only uses the y parameter: {y}");
}

fn main() {
    foo(3, 4);
}
```

Listing 18-17: Using _ in a function signature

This code will completely ignore the value 3 passed as the first argument, and will print This code only uses the y parameter: 4.

In most cases when you no longer need a particular function parameter, you would change the signature so it doesn't include the unused parameter. Ignoring a function parameter can be especially useful in cases when, for example, you're implementing a trait when you need a certain type signature but the function body in your implementation doesn't need one of the parameters. You then avoid getting a compiler warning about unused function parameters, as you would if you used a name instead.

Parts of a Value with a Nested _

We can also use _ inside another pattern to ignore just part of a value, for example, when we want to test for only part of a value but have no use for the other parts in the corresponding code we want to run. Listing 18-18 shows code responsible for managing a setting's value. The business requirements are that the user should not be allowed to overwrite an existing customization of a setting but can unset the setting and give it a value if it is currently unset.

src/main.rs
```
let mut setting_value = Some(5);
let new_setting_value = Some(10);

match (setting_value, new_setting_value) {
    (Some(_), Some(_)) => {
        println!("Can't overwrite an existing customized value");
    }
    _ => {
        setting_value = new_setting_value;
    }
}

println!("setting is {:?}", setting_value);
```

Listing 18-18: Using an underscore within patterns that match Some variants when we don't need to use the value inside the Some

This code will print Can't overwrite an existing customized value and then setting is Some(5). In the first match arm, we don't need to match on or use the values inside either Some variant, but we do need to test for the case when setting_value and new_setting_value are the Some variant. In that case, we print the reason for not changing setting_value, and it doesn't get changed.

In all other cases (if either setting_value or new_setting_value is None) expressed by the _ pattern in the second arm, we want to allow new_setting _value to become setting_value.

We can also use underscores in multiple places within one pattern to ignore particular values. Listing 18-19 shows an example of ignoring the second and fourth values in a tuple of five items.

src/main.rs
```
let numbers = (2, 4, 8, 16, 32);

match numbers {
    (first, _, third, _, fifth) => {
        println!("Some numbers: {first}, {third}, {fifth}");
    }
}
```

Listing 18-19: Ignoring multiple parts of a tuple

This code will print Some numbers: 2, 8, 32, and the values 4 and 16 will be ignored.

An Unused Variable by Starting Its Name with _

If you create a variable but don't use it anywhere, Rust will usually issue a warning because an unused variable could be a bug. However, sometimes it's useful to be able to create a variable you won't use yet, such as when you're prototyping or just starting a project. In this situation, you can tell Rust not to warn you about the unused variable by starting the name of the variable with an underscore. In Listing 18-20, we create two unused variables, but when we compile this code, we should only get a warning about one of them.

src/main.rs
```
fn main() {
    let _x = 5;
    let y = 10;
}
```

Listing 18-20: Starting a variable name with an underscore to avoid getting unused variable warnings

Here, we get a warning about not using the variable y, but we don't get a warning about not using _x.

Note that there is a subtle difference between using only _ and using a name that starts with an underscore. The syntax _x still binds the value to the variable, whereas _ doesn't bind at all. To show a case where this distinction matters, Listing 18-21 will provide us with an error.

src/main.rs
```
let s = Some(String::from("Hello!"));

if let Some(_s) = s {
    println!("found a string");
}

println!("{:?}", s);
```

Listing 18-21: An unused variable starting with an underscore still binds the value, which might take ownership of the value.

We'll receive an error because the s value will still be moved into _s, which prevents us from using s again. However, using the underscore by itself doesn't ever bind to the value. Listing 18-22 will compile without any errors because s doesn't get moved into _.

src/main.rs
```
let s = Some(String::from("Hello!"));

if let Some(_) = s {
    println!("found a string");
}

println!("{:?}", s);
```

Listing 18-22: Using an underscore does not bind the value.

This code works just fine because we never bind s to anything; it isn't moved.

Remaining Parts of a Value with ..

With values that have many parts, we can use the .. syntax to use specific parts and ignore the rest, avoiding the need to list underscores for each ignored value. The .. pattern ignores any parts of a value that we haven't explicitly matched in the rest of the pattern. In Listing 18-23, we have a Point struct that holds a coordinate in three-dimensional space. In the match expression, we want to operate only on the x coordinate and ignore the values in the y and z fields.

src/main.rs
```rust
struct Point {
    x: i32,
    y: i32,
    z: i32,
}

let origin = Point { x: 0, y: 0, z: 0 };

match origin {
    Point { x, .. } => println!("x is {x}"),
}
```

Listing 18-23: Ignoring all fields of a Point except for x by using ..

We list the x value and then just include the .. pattern. This is quicker than having to list y: _ and z: _, particularly when we're working with structs that have lots of fields in situations where only one or two fields are relevant.

The syntax .. will expand to as many values as it needs to be. Listing 18-24 shows how to use .. with a tuple.

src/main.rs
```rust
fn main() {
    let numbers = (2, 4, 8, 16, 32);

    match numbers {
        (first, .., last) => {
            println!("Some numbers: {first}, {last}");
        }
    }
}
```

Listing 18-24: Matching only the first and last values in a tuple and ignoring all other values

In this code, the first and last values are matched with first and last. The .. will match and ignore everything in the middle.

However, using .. must be unambiguous. If it is unclear which values are intended for matching and which should be ignored, Rust will give us an error. Listing 18-25 shows an example of using .. ambiguously, so it will not compile.

src/main.rs
```rust
fn main() {
    let numbers = (2, 4, 8, 16, 32);
```

```
match numbers {
    (.., second, ..) => {
        println!("Some numbers: {second}");
    },
}
```

Listing 18-25: An attempt to use .. in an ambiguous way

When we compile this example, we get this error:

```
error: `..` can only be used once per tuple pattern
 --> src/main.rs:5:22
  |
5 |          (.., second, ..) => {
  |           --              ^^ can only be used once per tuple pattern
  |           |
  |           previously used here
```

It's impossible for Rust to determine how many values in the tuple to ignore before matching a value with second and then how many further values to ignore thereafter. This code could mean that we want to ignore 2, bind second to 4, and then ignore 8, 16, and 32; or that we want to ignore 2 and 4, bind second to 8, and then ignore 16 and 32; and so forth. The variable name second doesn't mean anything special to Rust, so we get a compiler error because using .. in two places like this is ambiguous.

Extra Conditionals with Match Guards

A *match guard* is an additional if condition, specified after the pattern in a match arm, that must also match for that arm to be chosen. Match guards are useful for expressing more complex ideas than a pattern alone allows.

The condition can use variables created in the pattern. Listing 18-26 shows a match where the first arm has the pattern Some(x) and also has a match guard of if x % 2 == 0 (which will be true if the number is even).

src/main.rs
```
let num = Some(4);

match num {
    Some(x) if x % 2 == 0 => println!("The number {x} is even"),
    Some(x) => println!("The number {x} is odd"),
    None => (),
}
```

Listing 18-26: Adding a match guard to a pattern

This example will print The number 4 is even. When num is compared to the pattern in the first arm, it matches because Some(4) matches Some(x). Then the match guard checks whether the remainder of dividing x by 2 is equal to 0, and because it is, the first arm is selected.

If num had been Some(5) instead, the match guard in the first arm would have been false because the remainder of 5 divided by 2 is 1, which is not equal to 0. Rust would then go to the second arm, which would match because the second arm doesn't have a match guard and therefore matches any Some variant.

There is no way to express the if x % 2 == 0 condition within a pattern, so the match guard gives us the ability to express this logic. The downside of this additional expressiveness is that the compiler doesn't try to check for exhaustiveness when match guard expressions are involved.

In Listing 18-11, we mentioned that we could use match guards to solve our pattern-shadowing problem. Recall that we created a new variable inside the pattern in the match expression instead of using the variable outside the match. That new variable meant we couldn't test against the value of the outer variable. Listing 18-27 shows how we can use a match guard to fix this problem.

```rust
src/main.rs   fn main() {
                  let x = Some(5);
                  let y = 10;

                  match x {
                      Some(50) => println!("Got 50"),
                      Some(n) if n == y => println!("Matched, n = {n}"),
                      _ => println!("Default case, x = {:?}", x),
                  }

                  println!("at the end: x = {:?}, y = {y}", x);
              }
```

Listing 18-27: Using a match guard to test for equality with an outer variable

This code will now print Default case, x = Some(5). The pattern in the second match arm doesn't introduce a new variable y that would shadow the outer y, meaning we can use the outer y in the match guard. Instead of specifying the pattern as Some(y), which would have shadowed the outer y, we specify Some(n). This creates a new variable n that doesn't shadow anything because there is no n variable outside the match.

The match guard if n == y is not a pattern and therefore doesn't introduce new variables. This y *is* the outer y rather than a new shadowed y, and we can look for a value that has the same value as the outer y by comparing n to y.

You can also use the *or* operator | in a match guard to specify multiple patterns; the match guard condition will apply to all the patterns. Listing 18-28 shows the precedence when combining a pattern that uses | with a match guard. The important part of this example is that the if y match guard applies to 4, 5, *and* 6, even though it might look like if y only applies to 6.

```rust
src/main.rs   let x = 4;
              let y = false;

              match x {
                  4 | 5 | 6 if y => println!("yes"),
                  _ => println!("no"),
              }
```

Listing 18-28: Combining multiple patterns with a match guard

The match condition states that the arm only matches if the value of x is equal to 4, 5, or 6 *and* if y is true. When this code runs, the pattern of the first arm matches because x is 4, but the match guard if y is false, so the first arm is not chosen. The code moves on to the second arm, which does match, and this program prints no. The reason is that the if condition applies to the whole pattern 4 | 5 | 6, not just to the last value 6. In other words, the precedence of a match guard in relation to a pattern behaves like this:

```
(4 | 5 | 6) if y => ...
```

rather than this:

```
4 | 5 | (6 if y) => ...
```

After running the code, the precedence behavior is evident: if the match guard were applied only to the final value in the list of values specified using the | operator, the arm would have matched and the program would have printed yes.

@ Bindings

The *at* operator @ lets us create a variable that holds a value at the same time we're testing that value for a pattern match. In Listing 18-29, we want to test that a Message::Hello id field is within the range 3..=7. We also want to bind the value to the variable id_variable so we can use it in the code associated with the arm. We could name this variable id, the same as the field, but for this example we'll use a different name.

src/main.rs
```
enum Message {
    Hello { id: i32 },
}

let msg = Message::Hello { id: 5 };

match msg {
    Message::Hello {
        id: id_variable @ 3..=7,
    } => println!("Found an id in range: {id_variable}"),
    Message::Hello { id: 10..=12 } => {
        println!("Found an id in another range")
    }
    Message::Hello { id } => println!("Some other id: {id}"),
}
```

Listing 18-29: Using @ to bind to a value in a pattern while also testing it

This example will print Found an id in range: 5. By specifying id_variable @ before the range 3..=7, we're capturing whatever value matched the range while also testing that the value matched the range pattern.

In the second arm, where we only have a range specified in the pattern, the code associated with the arm doesn't have a variable that contains the actual value of the id field. The id field's value could have been 10, 11, or 12, but the code that goes with that pattern doesn't know which it is. The pattern code isn't able to use the value from the id field because we haven't saved the id value in a variable.

In the last arm, where we've specified a variable without a range, we do have the value available to use in the arm's code in a variable named id. The reason is that we've used the struct field shorthand syntax. But we haven't applied any test to the value in the id field in this arm, as we did with the first two arms: any value would match this pattern.

Using @ lets us test a value and save it in a variable within one pattern.

Summary

Rust's patterns are very useful in distinguishing between different kinds of data. When used in match expressions, Rust ensures your patterns cover every possible value, or your program won't compile. Patterns in let statements and function parameters make those constructs more useful, enabling the destructuring of values into smaller parts and assigning those parts to variables. We can create simple or complex patterns to suit our needs.

Next, for the penultimate chapter of the book, we'll look at some advanced aspects of a variety of Rust's features.

19

ADVANCED FEATURES

By now, you've learned the most commonly used parts of the Rust programming language. Before we do one more project, in Chapter 20, we'll look at a few aspects of the language you might run into every once in a while, but may not use every day. You can use this chapter as a reference for when you encounter any unknowns. The features covered here are useful in very specific situations. Although you might not reach for them often, we want to make sure you have a grasp of all the features Rust has to offer.

In this chapter, we'll cover:

- Unsafe Rust: how to opt out of some of Rust's guarantees and take responsibility for manually upholding those guarantees
- Advanced traits: associated types, default type parameters, fully qualified syntax, supertraits, and the newtype pattern in relation to traits
- Advanced types: more about the newtype pattern, type aliases, the never type, and dynamically sized types
- Advanced functions and closures: function pointers and returning closures
- Macros: ways to define code that defines more code at compile time

It's a panoply of Rust features with something for everyone! Let's dive in!

Unsafe Rust

All the code we've discussed so far has had Rust's memory safety guarantees enforced at compile time. However, Rust has a second language hidden inside it that doesn't enforce these memory safety guarantees: it's called *unsafe Rust* and works just like regular Rust, but gives us extra superpowers.

Unsafe Rust exists because, by nature, static analysis is conservative. When the compiler tries to determine whether or not code upholds the guarantees, it's better for it to reject some valid programs than to accept some invalid programs. Although the code *might* be okay, if the Rust compiler doesn't have enough information to be confident, it will reject the code. In these cases, you can use unsafe code to tell the compiler, "Trust me, I know what I'm doing." Be warned, however, that you use unsafe Rust at your own risk: if you use unsafe code incorrectly, problems can occur due to memory unsafety, such as null pointer dereferencing.

Another reason Rust has an unsafe alter ego is that the underlying computer hardware is inherently unsafe. If Rust didn't let you do unsafe operations, you couldn't do certain tasks. Rust needs to allow you to do low-level systems programming, such as directly interacting with the operating system or even writing your own operating system. Working with low-level systems programming is one of the goals of the language. Let's explore what we can do with unsafe Rust and how to do it.

Unsafe Superpowers

To switch to unsafe Rust, use the unsafe keyword and then start a new block that holds the unsafe code. You can take five actions in unsafe Rust that you can't in safe Rust, which we call *unsafe superpowers*. Those superpowers include the ability to:

1. Dereference a raw pointer
2. Call an unsafe function or method
3. Access or modify a mutable static variable

4. Implement an unsafe trait

5. Access fields of unions

It's important to understand that unsafe doesn't turn off the borrow checker or disable any of Rust's other safety checks: if you use a reference in unsafe code, it will still be checked. The unsafe keyword only gives you access to these five features that are then not checked by the compiler for memory safety. You'll still get some degree of safety inside an unsafe block.

In addition, unsafe does not mean the code inside the block is necessarily dangerous or that it will definitely have memory safety problems: the intent is that as the programmer, you'll ensure the code inside an unsafe block will access memory in a valid way.

People are fallible and mistakes will happen, but by requiring these five unsafe operations to be inside blocks annotated with unsafe, you'll know that any errors related to memory safety must be within an unsafe block. Keep unsafe blocks small; you'll be thankful later when you investigate memory bugs.

To isolate unsafe code as much as possible, it's best to enclose such code within a safe abstraction and provide a safe API, which we'll discuss later in the chapter when we examine unsafe functions and methods. Parts of the standard library are implemented as safe abstractions over unsafe code that has been audited. Wrapping unsafe code in a safe abstraction prevents uses of unsafe from leaking out into all the places that you or your users might want to use the functionality implemented with unsafe code, because using a safe abstraction is safe.

Let's look at each of the five unsafe superpowers in turn. We'll also look at some abstractions that provide a safe interface to unsafe code.

Dereferencing a Raw Pointer

In "Dangling References" on page 75, we mentioned that the compiler ensures references are always valid. Unsafe Rust has two new types called *raw pointers* that are similar to references. As with references, raw pointers can be immutable or mutable and are written as *const T and *mut T, respectively. The asterisk isn't the dereference operator; it's part of the type name. In the context of raw pointers, *immutable* means that the pointer can't be directly assigned to after being dereferenced.

Different from references and smart pointers, raw pointers:

- Are allowed to ignore the borrowing rules by having both immutable and mutable pointers or multiple mutable pointers to the same location

- Aren't guaranteed to point to valid memory

- Are allowed to be null

- Don't implement any automatic cleanup

By opting out of having Rust enforce these guarantees, you can give up guaranteed safety in exchange for greater performance or the ability to interface with another language or hardware where Rust's guarantees don't apply.

Listing 19-1 shows how to create an immutable and a mutable raw pointer from references.

```
let mut num = 5;

let r1 = &num as *const i32;
let r2 = &mut num as *mut i32;
```

Listing 19-1: Creating raw pointers from references

Notice that we don't include the unsafe keyword in this code. We can create raw pointers in safe code; we just can't dereference raw pointers outside an unsafe block, as you'll see in a bit.

We've created raw pointers by using as to cast an immutable and a mutable reference into their corresponding raw pointer types. Because we created them directly from references guaranteed to be valid, we know these particular raw pointers are valid, but we can't make that assumption about just any raw pointer.

To demonstrate this, next we'll create a raw pointer whose validity we can't be so certain of. Listing 19-2 shows how to create a raw pointer to an arbitrary location in memory. Trying to use arbitrary memory is undefined: there might be data at that address or there might not, the compiler might optimize the code so there is no memory access, or the program might terminate with a segmentation fault. Usually, there is no good reason to write code like this, but it is possible.

```
let address = 0x012345usize;
let r = address as *const i32;
```

Listing 19-2: Creating a raw pointer to an arbitrary memory address

Recall that we can create raw pointers in safe code, but we can't *dereference* raw pointers and read the data being pointed to. In Listing 19-3, we use the dereference operator * on a raw pointer that requires an unsafe block.

```
let mut num = 5;

let r1 = &num as *const i32;
let r2 = &mut num as *mut i32;

unsafe {
    println!("r1 is: {}", *r1);
    println!("r2 is: {}", *r2);
}
```

Listing 19-3: Dereferencing raw pointers within an unsafe block

Creating a pointer does no harm; it's only when we try to access the value that it points at that we might end up dealing with an invalid value.

Note also that in Listings 19-1 and 19-3, we created *const i32 and *mut i32 raw pointers that both pointed to the same memory location, where num is stored. If we instead tried to create an immutable and a mutable reference to num, the code would not have compiled because Rust's ownership rules don't allow a mutable reference at the same time as any immutable references. With raw pointers, we can create a mutable pointer and an immutable pointer to the same location and change data through the mutable pointer, potentially creating a data race. Be careful!

With all of these dangers, why would you ever use raw pointers? One major use case is when interfacing with C code, as you'll see in the next section. Another case is when building up safe abstractions that the borrow checker doesn't understand. We'll introduce unsafe functions and then look at an example of a safe abstraction that uses unsafe code.

Calling an Unsafe Function or Method

The second type of operation you can perform in an unsafe block is calling unsafe functions. Unsafe functions and methods look exactly like regular functions and methods, but they have an extra unsafe before the rest of the definition. The unsafe keyword in this context indicates the function has requirements we need to uphold when we call this function, because Rust can't guarantee we've met these requirements. By calling an unsafe function within an unsafe block, we're saying that we've read this function's documentation and we take responsibility for upholding the function's contracts.

Here is an unsafe function named dangerous that doesn't do anything in its body:

```
unsafe fn dangerous() {}

unsafe {
    dangerous();
}
```

We must call the dangerous function within a separate unsafe block. If we try to call dangerous without the unsafe block, we'll get an error:

```
error[E0133]: call to unsafe function is unsafe and requires
unsafe function or block
  --> src/main.rs:4:5
   |
4  |     dangerous();
   |     ^^^^^^^^^^^ call to unsafe function
   |
   = note: consult the function's documentation for information on
how to avoid undefined behavior
```

With the unsafe block, we're asserting to Rust that we've read the function's documentation, we understand how to use it properly, and we've verified that we're fulfilling the contract of the function.

Bodies of unsafe functions are effectively unsafe blocks, so to perform other unsafe operations within an unsafe function, we don't need to add another unsafe block.

Creating a Safe Abstraction over Unsafe Code

Just because a function contains unsafe code doesn't mean we need to mark the entire function as unsafe. In fact, wrapping unsafe code in a safe function is a common abstraction. As an example, let's study the split_at_mut function from the standard library, which requires some unsafe code. We'll explore how we might implement it. This safe method is defined on mutable slices: it takes one slice and makes it two by splitting the slice at the index given as an argument. Listing 19-4 shows how to use split_at_mut.

```
let mut v = vec![1, 2, 3, 4, 5, 6];

let r = &mut v[..];

let (a, b) = r.split_at_mut(3);

assert_eq!(a, &mut [1, 2, 3]);
assert_eq!(b, &mut [4, 5, 6]);
```

Listing 19-4: Using the safe split_at_mut function

We can't implement this function using only safe Rust. An attempt might look something like Listing 19-5, which won't compile. For simplicity, we'll implement split_at_mut as a function rather than a method and only for slices of i32 values rather than for a generic type T.

```
fn split_at_mut(
    values: &mut [i32],
    mid: usize,
) -> (&mut [i32], &mut [i32]) {
    let len = values.len();

    assert!(mid <= len);

    (&mut values[..mid], &mut values[mid..])
}
```

Listing 19-5: An attempted implementation of split_at_mut using only safe Rust

This function first gets the total length of the slice. Then it asserts that the index given as a parameter is within the slice by checking whether it's less than or equal to the length. The assertion means that if we pass an index that is greater than the length to split the slice at, the function will panic before it attempts to use that index.

Then we return two mutable slices in a tuple: one from the start of the original slice to the mid index and another from mid to the end of the slice.

When we try to compile the code in Listing 19-5, we'll get an error:

```
error[E0499]: cannot borrow `*values` as mutable more than once at a time
 --> src/main.rs:9:31
  |
2 |     values: &mut [i32],
  |             - let's call the lifetime of this reference `'1`
```

```
...
9 |    (&mut values[..mid], &mut values[mid..])
  |    -------------------------^^^^^^--------
  |     |     |       |
  |     |     |       second mutable borrow occurs here
  |     |     first mutable borrow occurs here
  |     returning this value requires that `*values` is borrowed for `'1`
```

Rust's borrow checker can't understand that we're borrowing different parts of the slice; it only knows that we're borrowing from the same slice twice. Borrowing different parts of a slice is fundamentally okay because the two slices aren't overlapping, but Rust isn't smart enough to know this. When we know code is okay, but Rust doesn't, it's time to reach for unsafe code.

Listing 19-6 shows how to use an unsafe block, a raw pointer, and some calls to unsafe functions to make the implementation of split_at_mut work.

```
use std::slice;

fn split_at_mut(
    values: &mut [i32],
    mid: usize,
) -> (&mut [i32], &mut [i32]) {
❶ let len = values.len();
❷ let ptr = values.as_mut_ptr();

❸ assert!(mid <= len);

❹ unsafe {
        (
          ❺ slice::from_raw_parts_mut(ptr, mid),
          ❻ slice::from_raw_parts_mut(ptr.add(mid), len - mid),
        )
    }
}
```

Listing 19-6: Using unsafe code in the implementation of the split_at_mut function

Recall from "The Slice Type" on page 77 that a slice is a pointer to some data and the length of the slice. We use the len method to get the length of a slice ❶ and the as_mut_ptr method to access the raw pointer of a slice ❷. In this case, because we have a mutable slice to i32 values, as_mut_ptr returns a raw pointer with the type *mut i32, which we've stored in the variable ptr.

We keep the assertion that the mid index is within the slice ❸. Then we get to the unsafe code ❹: the slice::from_raw_parts_mut function takes a raw pointer and a length, and it creates a slice. We use it to create a slice that starts from ptr and is mid items long ❺. Then we call the add method on ptr with mid as an argument to get a raw pointer that starts at mid, and we create a slice using that pointer and the remaining number of items after mid as the length ❻.

The function slice::from_raw_parts_mut is unsafe because it takes a raw pointer and must trust that this pointer is valid. The add method on raw pointers is also unsafe because it must trust that the offset location is also a valid pointer. Therefore, we had to put an unsafe block around our calls to slice::from_raw_parts_mut and add so we could call them. By looking at the code and by adding the assertion that mid must be less than or equal to len, we can tell that all the raw pointers used within the unsafe block will be valid pointers to data within the slice. This is an acceptable and appropriate use of unsafe.

Note that we don't need to mark the resultant split_at_mut function as unsafe, and we can call this function from safe Rust. We've created a safe abstraction to the unsafe code with an implementation of the function that uses unsafe code in a safe way, because it creates only valid pointers from the data this function has access to.

In contrast, the use of slice::from_raw_parts_mut in Listing 19-7 would likely crash when the slice is used. This code takes an arbitrary memory location and creates a slice 10,000 items long.

```
use std::slice;

let address = 0x01234usize;
let r = address as *mut i32;

let values: &[i32] = unsafe {
    slice::from_raw_parts_mut(r, 10000)
};
```

Listing 19-7: Creating a slice from an arbitrary memory location

We don't own the memory at this arbitrary location, and there is no guarantee that the slice this code creates contains valid i32 values. Attempting to use values as though it's a valid slice results in undefined behavior.

Using extern Functions to Call External Code

Sometimes your Rust code might need to interact with code written in another language. For this, Rust has the keyword extern that facilitates the creation and use of a *Foreign Function Interface (FFI)*, which is a way for a programming language to define functions and enable a different (foreign) programming language to call those functions.

Listing 19-8 demonstrates how to set up an integration with the abs function from the C standard library. Functions declared within extern blocks are always unsafe to call from Rust code. The reason is that other languages don't enforce Rust's rules and guarantees, and Rust can't check them, so responsibility falls on the programmer to ensure safety.

src/main.rs
```
extern "C" {
    fn abs(input: i32) -> i32;
}
```

```
fn main() {
    unsafe {
        println!(
            "Absolute value of -3 according to C: {}",
            abs(-3)
        );
    }
}
```

Listing 19-8: Declaring and calling an extern function defined in another language

Within the extern "C" block, we list the names and signatures of external functions from another language we want to call. The "C" part defines which *application binary interface (ABI)* the external function uses: the ABI defines how to call the function at the assembly level. The "C" ABI is the most common and follows the C programming language's ABI.

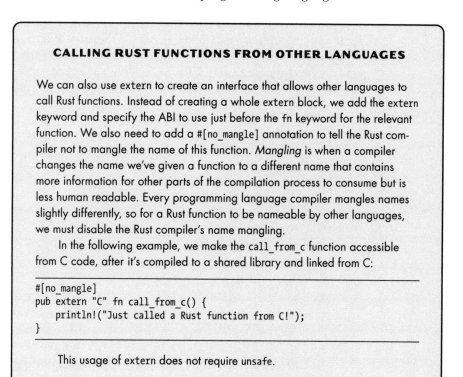

CALLING RUST FUNCTIONS FROM OTHER LANGUAGES

We can also use extern to create an interface that allows other languages to call Rust functions. Instead of creating a whole extern block, we add the extern keyword and specify the ABI to use just before the fn keyword for the relevant function. We also need to add a #[no_mangle] annotation to tell the Rust compiler not to mangle the name of this function. *Mangling* is when a compiler changes the name we've given a function to a different name that contains more information for other parts of the compilation process to consume but is less human readable. Every programming language compiler mangles names slightly differently, so for a Rust function to be nameable by other languages, we must disable the Rust compiler's name mangling.

In the following example, we make the call_from_c function accessible from C code, after it's compiled to a shared library and linked from C:

```
#[no_mangle]
pub extern "C" fn call_from_c() {
    println!("Just called a Rust function from C!");
}
```

This usage of extern does not require unsafe.

Accessing or Modifying a Mutable Static Variable

In this book, we've not yet talked about global variables, which Rust does support but can be problematic with Rust's ownership rules. If two threads are accessing the same mutable global variable, it can cause a data race.

In Rust, global variables are called *static* variables. Listing 19-9 shows an example declaration and use of a static variable with a string slice as a value.

src/main.rs
```
static HELLO_WORLD: &str = "Hello, world!";

fn main() {
    println!("value is: {HELLO_WORLD}");
}
```

Listing 19-9: Defining and using an immutable static variable

Static variables are similar to constants, which we discussed in "Constants" on page 33. The names of static variables are in `SCREAMING_SNAKE_CASE` by convention. Static variables can only store references with the `'static` lifetime, which means the Rust compiler can figure out the lifetime and we aren't required to annotate it explicitly. Accessing an immutable static variable is safe.

A subtle difference between constants and immutable static variables is that values in a static variable have a fixed address in memory. Using the value will always access the same data. Constants, on the other hand, are allowed to duplicate their data whenever they're used. Another difference is that static variables can be mutable. Accessing and modifying mutable static variables is *unsafe*. Listing 19-10 shows how to declare, access, and modify a mutable static variable named `COUNTER`.

src/main.rs
```
static mut COUNTER: u32 = 0;

fn add_to_count(inc: u32) {
    unsafe {
        COUNTER += inc;
    }
}

fn main() {
    add_to_count(3);

    unsafe {
        println!("COUNTER: {COUNTER}");
    }
}
```

Listing 19-10: Reading from or writing to a mutable static variable is unsafe.

As with regular variables, we specify mutability using the `mut` keyword. Any code that reads or writes from `COUNTER` must be within an `unsafe` block. This code compiles and prints `COUNTER: 3` as we would expect because it's single threaded. Having multiple threads access `COUNTER` would likely result in data races.

With mutable data that is globally accessible, it's difficult to ensure there are no data races, which is why Rust considers mutable static variables to be unsafe. Where possible, it's preferable to use the concurrency techniques and thread-safe smart pointers we discussed in Chapter 16 so the compiler checks that data access from different threads is done safely.

Implementing an Unsafe Trait

We can use unsafe to implement an unsafe trait. A trait is unsafe when at least one of its methods has some invariant that the compiler can't verify. We declare that a trait is unsafe by adding the unsafe keyword before trait and marking the implementation of the trait as unsafe too, as shown in Listing 19-11.

```
unsafe trait Foo {
    // methods go here
}

unsafe impl Foo for i32 {
    // method implementations go here
}
```

Listing 19-11: Defining and implementing an unsafe trait

By using unsafe impl, we're promising that we'll uphold the invariants that the compiler can't verify.

As an example, recall the Send and Sync marker traits we discussed in "Extensible Concurrency with the Send and Sync Traits" on page 373: the compiler implements these traits automatically if our types are composed entirely of Send and Sync types. If we implement a type that contains a type that is not Send or Sync, such as raw pointers, and we want to mark that type as Send or Sync, we must use unsafe. Rust can't verify that our type upholds the guarantees that it can be safely sent across threads or accessed from multiple threads; therefore, we need to do those checks manually and indicate as such with unsafe.

Accessing Fields of a Union

The final action that works only with unsafe is accessing fields of a union. A union is similar to a struct, but only one declared field is used in a particular instance at one time. Unions are primarily used to interface with unions in C code. Accessing union fields is unsafe because Rust can't guarantee the type of the data currently being stored in the union instance. You can learn more about unions in the Rust Reference at *https://doc.rust-lang.org/reference/items/unions.html*.

When to Use Unsafe Code

Using unsafe to use one of the five superpowers just discussed isn't wrong or even frowned upon, but it is trickier to get unsafe code correct because the compiler can't help uphold memory safety. When you have a reason to use unsafe code, you can do so, and having the explicit unsafe annotation makes it easier to track down the source of problems when they occur.

Advanced Traits

We first covered traits in "Traits: Defining Shared Behavior" on page 192, but we didn't discuss the more advanced details. Now that you know more about Rust, we can get into the nitty-gritty.

Associated Types

Associated types connect a type placeholder with a trait such that the trait method definitions can use these placeholder types in their signatures. The implementor of a trait will specify the concrete type to be used instead of the placeholder type for the particular implementation. That way, we can define a trait that uses some types without needing to know exactly what those types are until the trait is implemented.

We've described most of the advanced features in this chapter as being rarely needed. Associated types are somewhere in the middle: they're used more rarely than features explained in the rest of the book but more commonly than many of the other features discussed in this chapter.

One example of a trait with an associated type is the Iterator trait that the standard library provides. The associated type is named Item and stands in for the type of the values the type implementing the Iterator trait is iterating over. The definition of the Iterator trait is as shown in Listing 19-12.

```
pub trait Iterator {
    type Item;

    fn next(&mut self) -> Option<Self::Item>;
}
```

Listing 19-12: The definition of the Iterator trait that has an associated type Item

The type Item is a placeholder, and the next method's definition shows that it will return values of type Option<Self::Item>. Implementors of the Iterator trait will specify the concrete type for Item, and the next method will return an Option containing a value of that concrete type.

Associated types might seem like a similar concept to generics, in that the latter allow us to define a function without specifying what types it can handle. To examine the difference between the two concepts, we'll look at an implementation of the Iterator trait on a type named Counter that specifies the Item type is u32:

src/lib.rs
```
impl Iterator for Counter {
    type Item = u32;

    fn next(&mut self) -> Option<Self::Item> {
        --snip--
```

This syntax seems comparable to that of generics. So why not just define the Iterator trait with generics, as shown in Listing 19-13?

```
pub trait Iterator<T> {
    fn next(&mut self) -> Option<T>;
}
```

Listing 19-13: A hypothetical definition of the Iterator trait using generics

The difference is that when using generics, as in Listing 19-13, we must annotate the types in each implementation; because we can also implement Iterator<String> for Counter or any other type, we could have multiple implementations of Iterator for Counter. In other words, when a trait has a generic parameter, it can be implemented for a type multiple times, changing the concrete types of the generic type parameters each time. When we use the next method on Counter, we would have to provide type annotations to indicate which implementation of Iterator we want to use.

With associated types, we don't need to annotate types because we can't implement a trait on a type multiple times. In Listing 19-12 with the definition that uses associated types, we can choose what the type of Item will be only once because there can be only one impl Iterator for Counter. We don't have to specify that we want an iterator of u32 values everywhere we call next on Counter.

Associated types also become part of the trait's contract: implementors of the trait must provide a type to stand in for the associated type placeholder. Associated types often have a name that describes how the type will be used, and documenting the associated type in the API documentation is a good practice.

Default Generic Type Parameters and Operator Overloading

When we use generic type parameters, we can specify a default concrete type for the generic type. This eliminates the need for implementors of the trait to specify a concrete type if the default type works. You specify a default type when declaring a generic type with the *<PlaceholderType=ConcreteType>* syntax.

A great example of a situation where this technique is useful is with *operator overloading*, in which you customize the behavior of an operator (such as +) in particular situations.

Rust doesn't allow you to create your own operators or overload arbitrary operators. But you can overload the operations and corresponding traits listed in std::ops by implementing the traits associated with the operator. For example, in Listing 19-14 we overload the + operator to add two Point instances together. We do this by implementing the Add trait on a Point struct.

src/main.rs   use std::ops::Add;

```
#[derive(Debug, Copy, Clone, PartialEq)]
```

```
struct Point {
    x: i32,
    y: i32,
}

impl Add for Point {
    type Output = Point;

    fn add(self, other: Point) -> Point {
        Point {
            x: self.x + other.x,
            y: self.y + other.y,
        }
    }
}

fn main() {
    assert_eq!(
        Point { x: 1, y: 0 } + Point { x: 2, y: 3 },
        Point { x: 3, y: 3 }
    );
}
```

Listing 19-14: Implementing the Add trait to overload the + operator for Point instances

The add method adds the x values of two Point instances and the y values of two Point instances to create a new Point. The Add trait has an associated type named Output that determines the type returned from the add method.

The default generic type in this code is within the Add trait. Here is its definition:

```
trait Add<Rhs=Self> {
    type Output;

    fn add(self, rhs: Rhs) -> Self::Output;
}
```

This code should look generally familiar: a trait with one method and an associated type. The new part is Rhs=Self: this syntax is called *default type parameters*. The Rhs generic type parameter (short for "right-hand side") defines the type of the rhs parameter in the add method. If we don't specify a concrete type for Rhs when we implement the Add trait, the type of Rhs will default to Self, which will be the type we're implementing Add on.

When we implemented Add for Point, we used the default for Rhs because we wanted to add two Point instances. Let's look at an example of implementing the Add trait where we want to customize the Rhs type rather than using the default.

We have two structs, Millimeters and Meters, holding values in different units. This thin wrapping of an existing type in another struct is known as the *newtype pattern*, which we describe in more detail in "Using the Newtype Pattern to Implement External Traits" on page 439. We want to add values in millimeters to values in meters and have the implementation of Add do the conversion correctly. We can implement Add for Millimeters with Meters as the Rhs, as shown in Listing 19-15.

src/lib.rs
```
use std::ops::Add;

struct Millimeters(u32);
struct Meters(u32);

impl Add<Meters> for Millimeters {
    type Output = Millimeters;

    fn add(self, other: Meters) -> Millimeters {
        Millimeters(self.0 + (other.0 * 1000))
    }
}
```

Listing 19-15: Implementing the Add trait on Millimeters to add Millimeters and Meters

To add Millimeters and Meters, we specify impl Add<Meters> to set the value of the Rhs type parameter instead of using the default of Self.

You'll use default type parameters in two main ways:

1. To extend a type without breaking existing code
2. To allow customization in specific cases most users won't need

The standard library's Add trait is an example of the second purpose: usually, you'll add two like types, but the Add trait provides the ability to customize beyond that. Using a default type parameter in the Add trait definition means you don't have to specify the extra parameter most of the time. In other words, a bit of implementation boilerplate isn't needed, making it easier to use the trait.

The first purpose is similar to the second but in reverse: if you want to add a type parameter to an existing trait, you can give it a default to allow extension of the functionality of the trait without breaking the existing implementation code.

Disambiguating Between Methods with the Same Name

Nothing in Rust prevents a trait from having a method with the same name as another trait's method, nor does Rust prevent you from implementing both traits on one type. It's also possible to implement a method directly on the type with the same name as methods from traits.

When calling methods with the same name, you'll need to tell Rust which one you want to use. Consider the code in Listing 19-16 where we've defined two traits, Pilot and Wizard, that both have a method called fly. We then implement both traits on a type Human that already has a method named fly implemented on it. Each fly method does something different.

src/main.rs
```
trait Pilot {
    fn fly(&self);
}
```

```
trait Wizard {
    fn fly(&self);
}

struct Human;

impl Pilot for Human {
    fn fly(&self) {
        println!("This is your captain speaking.");
    }
}

impl Wizard for Human {
    fn fly(&self) {
        println!("Up!");
    }
}

impl Human {
    fn fly(&self) {
        println!("*waving arms furiously*");
    }
}
```

Listing 19-16: Two traits are defined to have a fly method and are implemented on the Human type, and a fly method is implemented on Human directly.

When we call fly on an instance of Human, the compiler defaults to calling the method that is directly implemented on the type, as shown in Listing 19-17.

src/main.rs
```
fn main() {
    let person = Human;
    person.fly();
}
```

Listing 19-17: Calling fly on an instance of Human

Running this code will print *waving arms furiously*, showing that Rust called the fly method implemented on Human directly.

To call the fly methods from either the Pilot trait or the Wizard trait, we need to use more explicit syntax to specify which fly method we mean. Listing 19-18 demonstrates this syntax.

src/main.rs
```
fn main() {
    let person = Human;
    Pilot::fly(&person);
    Wizard::fly(&person);
    person.fly();
}
```

Listing 19-18: Specifying which trait's fly method we want to call

Specifying the trait name before the method name clarifies to Rust which implementation of fly we want to call. We could also write Human::fly(&person), which is equivalent to the person.fly() that we used in Listing 19-18, but this is a bit longer to write if we don't need to disambiguate.

Running this code prints the following:

```
This is your captain speaking.
Up!
*waving arms furiously*
```

Because the fly method takes a self parameter, if we had two *types* that both implement one *trait*, Rust could figure out which implementation of a trait to use based on the type of self.

However, associated functions that are not methods don't have a self parameter. When there are multiple types or traits that define non-method functions with the same function name, Rust doesn't always know which type you mean unless you use fully qualified syntax. For example, in Listing 19-19 we create a trait for an animal shelter that wants to name all baby dogs Spot. We make an Animal trait with an associated non-method function baby_name. The Animal trait is implemented for the struct Dog, on which we also provide an associated non-method function baby_name directly.

src/main.rs
```
trait Animal {
    fn baby_name() -> String;
}

struct Dog;

impl Dog {
    fn baby_name() -> String {
        String::from("Spot")
    }
}

impl Animal for Dog {
    fn baby_name() -> String {
        String::from("puppy")
    }
}

fn main() {
    println!("A baby dog is called a {}", Dog::baby_name());
}
```

Listing 19-19: A trait with an associated function and a type with an associated function of the same name that also implements the trait

We implement the code for naming all puppies Spot in the baby_name associated function that is defined on Dog. The Dog type also implements the trait Animal, which describes characteristics that all animals have. Baby dogs are called puppies, and that is expressed in the implementation of the Animal trait on Dog in the baby_name function associated with the Animal trait.

In main, we call the Dog::baby_name function, which calls the associated function defined on Dog directly. This code prints the following:

```
A baby dog is called a Spot
```

This output isn't what we wanted. We want to call the baby_name function that is part of the Animal trait that we implemented on Dog so the code prints A baby dog is called a puppy. The technique of specifying the trait name that we used in Listing 19-18 doesn't help here; if we change main to the code in Listing 19-20, we'll get a compilation error.

src/main.rs
```
fn main() {
    println!("A baby dog is called a {}", Animal::baby_name());
}
```

Listing 19-20: Attempting to call the baby_name function from the Animal trait, but Rust doesn't know which implementation to use

Because Animal::baby_name doesn't have a self parameter, and there could be other types that implement the Animal trait, Rust can't figure out which implementation of Animal::baby_name we want. We'll get this compiler error:

```
error[E0283]: type annotations needed
  --> src/main.rs:20:43
   |
20 |     println!("A baby dog is called a {}", Animal::baby_name());
   |                                           ^^^^^^^^^^^^^^^^^^^ cannot infer
type
   |
   = note: cannot satisfy `_: Animal`
```

To disambiguate and tell Rust that we want to use the implementation of Animal for Dog as opposed to the implementation of Animal for some other type, we need to use fully qualified syntax. Listing 19-21 demonstrates how to use fully qualified syntax.

src/main.rs
```
fn main() {
    println!(
        "A baby dog is called a {}",
        <Dog as Animal>::baby_name()
    );
}
```

Listing 19-21: Using fully qualified syntax to specify that we want to call the baby_name function from the Animal trait as implemented on Dog

We're providing Rust with a type annotation within the angle brackets, which indicates we want to call the baby_name method from the Animal trait as implemented on Dog by saying that we want to treat the Dog type as an Animal for this function call. This code will now print what we want:

```
A baby dog is called a puppy
```

In general, fully qualified syntax is defined as follows:

```
<Type as Trait>::function(receiver_if_method, next_arg, ...);
```

For associated functions that aren't methods, there would not be a receiver: there would only be the list of other arguments. You could use fully qualified syntax everywhere that you call functions or methods. However, you're allowed to omit any part of this syntax that Rust can figure out from other information in the program. You only need to use this more verbose syntax in cases where there are multiple implementations that use the same name and Rust needs help to identify which implementation you want to call.

Using Supertraits

Sometimes you might write a trait definition that depends on another trait: for a type to implement the first trait, you want to require that type to also implement the second trait. You would do this so that your trait definition can make use of the associated items of the second trait. The trait your trait definition is relying on is called a *supertrait* of your trait.

For example, let's say we want to make an OutlinePrint trait with an outline _print method that will print a given value formatted so that it's framed in asterisks. That is, given a Point struct that implements the standard library trait Display to result in (x, y), when we call outline_print on a Point instance that has 1 for x and 3 for y, it should print the following:

```
**********
*        *
* (1, 3) *
*        *
**********
```

In the implementation of the outline_print method, we want to use the Display trait's functionality. Therefore, we need to specify that the OutlinePrint trait will work only for types that also implement Display and provide the functionality that OutlinePrint needs. We can do that in the trait definition by specifying OutlinePrint: Display. This technique is similar to adding a trait bound to the trait. Listing 19-22 shows an implementation of the OutlinePrint trait.

src/main.rs

```
use std::fmt;

trait OutlinePrint: fmt::Display {
    fn outline_print(&self) {
        let output = self.to_string();
        let len = output.len();
```

```
        println!("{}", "*".repeat(len + 4));
        println!("*{}*", " ".repeat(len + 2));
        println!("* {} *", output);
        println!("*{}*", " ".repeat(len + 2));
        println!("{}", "*".repeat(len + 4));
    }
}
```

Listing 19-22: Implementing the OutlinePrint trait that requires the functionality from Display

Because we've specified that OutlinePrint requires the Display trait, we can use the to_string function that is automatically implemented for any type that implements Display. If we tried to use to_string without adding a colon and specifying the Display trait after the trait name, we'd get an error saying that no method named to_string was found for the type &Self in the current scope.

Let's see what happens when we try to implement OutlinePrint on a type that doesn't implement Display, such as the Point struct:

src/main.rs
```
struct Point {
    x: i32,
    y: i32,
}

impl OutlinePrint for Point {}
```

We get an error saying that Display is required but not implemented:

```
error[E0277]: `Point` doesn't implement `std::fmt::Display`
  --> src/main.rs:20:6
   |
20 | impl OutlinePrint for Point {}
   |      ^^^^^^^^^^^^ `Point` cannot be formatted with the default formatter
   |
   = help: the trait `std::fmt::Display` is not implemented for `Point`
   = note: in format strings you may be able to use `{:?}` (or {:#?} for
pretty-print) instead
note: required by a bound in `OutlinePrint`
  --> src/main.rs:3:21
   |
3  | trait OutlinePrint: fmt::Display {
   |                     ^^^^^^^^^^^^ required by this bound in `OutlinePrint`
```

To fix this, we implement Display on Point and satisfy the constraint that OutlinePrint requires, like so:

src/main.rs
```
use std::fmt;

impl fmt::Display for Point {
    fn fmt(&self, f: &mut fmt::Formatter) -> fmt::Result {
        write!(f, "({}, {})", self.x, self.y)
    }
}
```

Then, implementing the `OutlinePrint` trait on `Point` will compile successfully, and we can call `outline_print` on a `Point` instance to display it within an outline of asterisks.

Using the Newtype Pattern to Implement External Traits

In "Implementing a Trait on a Type" on page 193, we mentioned the orphan rule that states we're only allowed to implement a trait on a type if either the trait or the type, or both, are local to our crate. It's possible to get around this restriction using the *newtype pattern*, which involves creating a new type in a tuple struct. (We covered tuple structs in "Using Tuple Structs Without Named Fields to Create Different Types" on page 89.) The tuple struct will have one field and be a thin wrapper around the type for which we want to implement a trait. Then the wrapper type is local to our crate, and we can implement the trait on the wrapper. *Newtype* is a term that originates from the Haskell programming language. There is no runtime performance penalty for using this pattern, and the wrapper type is elided at compile time.

As an example, let's say we want to implement `Display` on `Vec<T>`, which the orphan rule prevents us from doing directly because the `Display` trait and the `Vec<T>` type are defined outside our crate. We can make a `Wrapper` struct that holds an instance of `Vec<T>`; then we can implement `Display` on `Wrapper` and use the `Vec<T>` value, as shown in Listing 19-23.

src/main.rs
```
use std::fmt;

struct Wrapper(Vec<String>);

impl fmt::Display for Wrapper {
    fn fmt(&self, f: &mut fmt::Formatter) -> fmt::Result {
        write!(f, "[{}]", self.0.join(", "))
    }
}

fn main() {
    let w = Wrapper(vec![
        String::from("hello"),
        String::from("world"),
    ]);
    println!("w = {w}");
}
```

Listing 19-23: Creating a `Wrapper` type around `Vec<String>` to implement `Display`

The implementation of `Display` uses `self.0` to access the inner `Vec<T>` because `Wrapper` is a tuple struct and `Vec<T>` is the item at index 0 in the tuple. Then we can use the functionality of the `Display` type on `Wrapper`.

The downside of using this technique is that `Wrapper` is a new type, so it doesn't have the methods of the value it's holding. We would have to implement all the methods of `Vec<T>` directly on `Wrapper` such that the methods delegate to `self.0`, which would allow us to treat `Wrapper` exactly like a `Vec<T>`.

If we wanted the new type to have every method the inner type has, implementing the Deref trait on the Wrapper to return the inner type would be a solution (we discussed implementing the Deref trait in "Treating Smart Pointers Like Regular References with Deref" on page 321). If we didn't want the Wrapper type to have all the methods of the inner type—for example, to restrict the Wrapper type's behavior—we would have to implement just the methods we do want manually.

This newtype pattern is also useful even when traits are not involved. Let's switch focus and look at some advanced ways to interact with Rust's type system.

Advanced Types

The Rust type system has some features that we've so far mentioned but haven't yet discussed. We'll start by discussing newtypes in general as we examine why newtypes are useful as types. Then we'll move on to type aliases, a feature similar to newtypes but with slightly different semantics. We'll also discuss the ! type and dynamically sized types.

Using the Newtype Pattern for Type Safety and Abstraction

This section assumes you've read the earlier section "Using the Newtype Pattern to Implement External Traits" on page 439. The newtype pattern is also useful for tasks beyond those we've discussed so far, including statically enforcing that values are never confused and indicating the units of a value. You saw an example of using newtypes to indicate units in Listing 19-15: recall that the Millimeters and Meters structs wrapped u32 values in a newtype. If we wrote a function with a parameter of type Millimeters, we wouldn't be able to compile a program that accidentally tried to call that function with a value of type Meters or a plain u32.

We can also use the newtype pattern to abstract away some implementation details of a type: the new type can expose a public API that is different from the API of the private inner type.

Newtypes can also hide internal implementation. For example, we could provide a People type to wrap a HashMap<i32, String> that stores a person's ID associated with their name. Code using People would only interact with the public API we provide, such as a method to add a name string to the People collection; that code wouldn't need to know that we assign an i32 ID to names internally. The newtype pattern is a lightweight way to achieve encapsulation to hide implementation details, which we discussed in "Encapsulation That Hides Implementation Details" on page 376.

Creating Type Synonyms with Type Aliases

Rust provides the ability to declare a *type alias* to give an existing type another name. For this we use the type keyword. For example, we can create the alias Kilometers to i32 like so:

```
type Kilometers = i32;
```

Now the alias Kilometers is a *synonym* for i32; unlike the Millimeters and Meters types we created in Listing 19-15, Kilometers is not a separate, new type. Values that have the type Kilometers will be treated the same as values of type i32:

```
type Kilometers = i32;

let x: i32 = 5;
let y: Kilometers = 5;

println!("x + y = {}", x + y);
```

Because Kilometers and i32 are the same type, we can add values of both types and we can pass Kilometers values to functions that take i32 parameters. However, using this method, we don't get the type-checking benefits that we get from the newtype pattern discussed earlier. In other words, if we mix up Kilometers and i32 values somewhere, the compiler will not give us an error.

The main use case for type synonyms is to reduce repetition. For example, we might have a lengthy type like this:

```
Box<dyn Fn() + Send + 'static>
```

Writing this lengthy type in function signatures and as type annotations all over the code can be tiresome and error prone. Imagine having a project full of code like that in Listing 19-24.

```
let f: Box<dyn Fn() + Send + 'static> = Box::new(|| {
    println!("hi");
});

fn takes_long_type(f: Box<dyn Fn() + Send + 'static>) {
    --snip--
}

fn returns_long_type() -> Box<dyn Fn() + Send + 'static> {
    --snip--
}
```

Listing 19-24: Using a long type in many places

A type alias makes this code more manageable by reducing the repetition. In Listing 19-25, we've introduced an alias named Thunk for the verbose type and can replace all uses of the type with the shorter alias Thunk.

```
type Thunk = Box<dyn Fn() + Send + 'static>;

let f: Thunk = Box::new(|| println!("hi"));

fn takes_long_type(f: Thunk) {
    --snip--
}
```

```
fn returns_long_type() -> Thunk {
    --snip--
}
```

Listing 19-25: Introducing a type alias, Thunk, to reduce repetition

This code is much easier to read and write! Choosing a meaningful name for a type alias can help communicate your intent as well (*thunk* is a word for code to be evaluated at a later time, so it's an appropriate name for a closure that gets stored).

Type aliases are also commonly used with the Result<T, E> type for reducing repetition. Consider the std::io module in the standard library. I/O operations often return a Result<T, E> to handle situations when operations fail to work. This library has a std::io::Error struct that represents all possible I/O errors. Many of the functions in std::io will be returning Result<T, E> where the E is std::io::Error, such as these functions in the Write trait:

```
use std::fmt;
use std::io::Error;

pub trait Write {
    fn write(&mut self, buf: &[u8]) -> Result<usize, Error>;
    fn flush(&mut self) -> Result<(), Error>;

    fn write_all(&mut self, buf: &[u8]) -> Result<(), Error>;
    fn write_fmt(
        &mut self,
        fmt: fmt::Arguments,
    ) -> Result<(), Error>;
}
```

The Result<..., Error> is repeated a lot. As such, std::io has this type alias declaration:

```
type Result<T> = std::result::Result<T, std::io::Error>;
```

Because this declaration is in the std::io module, we can use the fully qualified alias std::io::Result<T>; that is, a Result<T, E> with the E filled in as std::io::Error. The Write trait function signatures end up looking like this:

```
pub trait Write {
    fn write(&mut self, buf: &[u8]) -> Result<usize>;
    fn flush(&mut self) -> Result<()>;

    fn write_all(&mut self, buf: &[u8]) -> Result<()>;
    fn write_fmt(&mut self, fmt: fmt::Arguments) -> Result<()>;
}
```

The type alias helps in two ways: it makes code easier to write *and* it gives us a consistent interface across all of std::io. Because it's an alias, it's just another Result<T, E>, which means we can use any methods that work on Result<T, E> with it, as well as special syntax like the ? operator.

The Never Type That Never Returns

Rust has a special type named ! that's known in type theory lingo as the *empty type* because it has no values. We prefer to call it the *never type* because it stands in the place of the return type when a function will never return. Here is an example:

```
fn bar() -> ! {
    --snip--
}
```

This code is read as "the function bar returns never." Functions that return never are called *diverging functions*. We can't create values of the type !, so bar can never possibly return.

But what use is a type you can never create values for? Recall the code from Listing 2-5, part of the number-guessing game; we've reproduced a bit of it here in Listing 19-26.

```
let guess: u32 = match guess.trim().parse() {
    Ok(num) => num,
    Err(_) => continue,
};
```

Listing 19-26: A match with an arm that ends in continue

At the time, we skipped over some details in this code. In "The match Control Flow Construct" on page 110, we discussed that match arms must all return the same type. So, for example, the following code doesn't work:

```
let guess = match guess.trim().parse() {
    Ok(_) => 5,
    Err(_) => "hello",
};
```

The type of guess in this code would have to be an integer *and* a string, and Rust requires that guess have only one type. So what does continue return? How were we allowed to return a u32 from one arm and have another arm that ends with continue in Listing 19-26?

As you might have guessed, continue has a ! value. That is, when Rust computes the type of guess, it looks at both match arms, the former with a value of u32 and the latter with a ! value. Because ! can never have a value, Rust decides that the type of guess is u32.

The formal way of describing this behavior is that expressions of type ! can be coerced into any other type. We're allowed to end this match arm with continue because continue doesn't return a value; instead, it moves control back to the top of the loop, so in the Err case, we never assign a value to guess.

The never type is useful with the panic! macro as well. Recall the unwrap function that we call on Option<T> values to produce a value or panic with this definition:

```
impl<T> Option<T> {
    pub fn unwrap(self) -> T {
        match self {
            Some(val) => val,
            None => panic!(
                "called `Option::unwrap()` on a `None` value"
            ),
        }
    }
}
```

In this code, the same thing happens as in the match in Listing 19-26: Rust sees that val has the type T and panic! has the type !, so the result of the overall match expression is T. This code works because panic! doesn't produce a value; it ends the program. In the None case, we won't be returning a value from unwrap, so this code is valid.

One final expression that has the type ! is a loop:

```
print!("forever ");

loop {
    print!("and ever ");
}
```

Here, the loop never ends, so ! is the value of the expression. However, this wouldn't be true if we included a break, because the loop would terminate when it got to the break.

Dynamically Sized Types and the Sized Trait

Rust needs to know certain details about its types, such as how much space to allocate for a value of a particular type. This leaves one corner of its type system a little confusing at first: the concept of *dynamically sized types*. Sometimes referred to as *DSTs* or *unsized types*, these types let us write code using values whose size we can know only at runtime.

Let's dig into the details of a dynamically sized type called str, which we've been using throughout the book. That's right, not &str, but str on its own, is a DST. We can't know how long the string is until runtime, meaning we can't create a variable of type str, nor can we take an argument of type str. Consider the following code, which does not work:

```
let s1: str = "Hello there!";
let s2: str = "How's it going?";
```

Rust needs to know how much memory to allocate for any value of a particular type, and all values of a type must use the same amount of memory. If Rust allowed us to write this code, these two str values would need to take up the same amount of space. But they have different lengths: s1 needs 12 bytes of storage and s2 needs 15. This is why it's not possible to create a variable holding a dynamically sized type.

So what do we do? In this case, you already know the answer: we make the types of s1 and s2 a &str rather than a str. Recall from "String Slices" on page 79 that the slice data structure just stores the starting position and the length of the slice. So, although a &T is a single value that stores the memory address of where the T is located, a &str is *two* values: the address of the str and its length. As such, we can know the size of a &str value at compile time: it's twice the length of a usize. That is, we always know the size of a &str, no matter how long the string it refers to is. In general, this is the way in which dynamically sized types are used in Rust: they have an extra bit of metadata that stores the size of the dynamic information. The golden rule of dynamically sized types is that we must always put values of dynamically sized types behind a pointer of some kind.

We can combine str with all kinds of pointers: for example, Box<str> or Rc<str>. In fact, you've seen this before but with a different dynamically sized type: traits. Every trait is a dynamically sized type we can refer to by using the name of the trait. In "Using Trait Objects That Allow for Values of Different Types" on page 379, we mentioned that to use traits as trait objects, we must put them behind a pointer, such as &dyn Trait or Box<dyn Trait> (Rc<dyn Trait> would work too).

To work with DSTs, Rust provides the Sized trait to determine whether or not a type's size is known at compile time. This trait is automatically implemented for everything whose size is known at compile time. In addition, Rust implicitly adds a bound on Sized to every generic function. That is, a generic function definition like this:

```
fn generic<T>(t: T) {
    --snip--
}
```

is actually treated as though we had written this:

```
fn generic<T: Sized>(t: T) {
    --snip--
}
```

By default, generic functions will work only on types that have a known size at compile time. However, you can use the following special syntax to relax this restriction:

```
fn generic<T: ?Sized>(t: &T) {
    --snip--
}
```

A trait bound on ?Sized means "T may or may not be Sized" and this notation overrides the default that generic types must have a known size at compile time. The ?Trait syntax with this meaning is only available for Sized, not any other traits.

Also note that we switched the type of the t parameter from T to &T. Because the type might not be Sized, we need to use it behind some kind of pointer. In this case, we've chosen a reference.

Next, we'll talk about functions and closures!

Advanced Functions and Closures

This section explores some advanced features related to functions and closures, including function pointers and returning closures.

Function Pointers

We've talked about how to pass closures to functions; you can also pass regular functions to functions! This technique is useful when you want to pass a function you've already defined rather than defining a new closure. Functions coerce to the type fn (with a lowercase *f*), not to be confused with the Fn closure trait. The fn type is called a *function pointer*. Passing functions with function pointers will allow you to use functions as arguments to other functions.

The syntax for specifying that a parameter is a function pointer is similar to that of closures, as shown in Listing 19-27, where we've defined a function add_one that adds 1 to its parameter. The function do_twice takes two parameters: a function pointer to any function that takes an i32 parameter and returns an i32, and one i32 value. The do_twice function calls the function f twice, passing it the arg value, then adds the two function call results together. The main function calls do_twice with the arguments add_one and 5.

src/main.rs
```
fn add_one(x: i32) -> i32 {
    x + 1
}

fn do_twice(f: fn(i32) -> i32, arg: i32) -> i32 {
    f(arg) + f(arg)
}

fn main() {
    let answer = do_twice(add_one, 5);

    println!("The answer is: {answer}");
}
```

Listing 19-27: Using the fn type to accept a function pointer as an argument

This code prints The answer is: 12. We specify that the parameter f in do_twice is an fn that takes one parameter of type i32 and returns an i32. We can then call f in the body of do_twice. In main, we can pass the function name add_one as the first argument to do_twice.

Unlike closures, fn is a type rather than a trait, so we specify fn as the parameter type directly rather than declaring a generic type parameter with one of the Fn traits as a trait bound.

Function pointers implement all three of the closure traits (Fn, FnMut, and FnOnce), meaning you can always pass a function pointer as an argument for a function that expects a closure. It's best to write functions using a generic type and one of the closure traits so your functions can accept either functions or closures.

That said, one example of where you would want to only accept fn and not closures is when interfacing with external code that doesn't have closures: C functions can accept functions as arguments, but C doesn't have closures.

As an example of where you could use either a closure defined inline or a named function, let's look at a use of the map method provided by the Iterator trait in the standard library. To use the map function to turn a vector of numbers into a vector of strings, we could use a closure, like this:

```
let list_of_numbers = vec![1, 2, 3];
let list_of_strings: Vec<String> = list_of_numbers
    .iter()
    .map(|i| i.to_string())
    .collect();
```

Or we could name a function as the argument to map instead of the closure, like this:

```
let list_of_numbers = vec![1, 2, 3];
let list_of_strings: Vec<String> = list_of_numbers
    .iter()
    .map(ToString::to_string)
    .collect();
```

Note that we must use the fully qualified syntax that we talked about in "Advanced Traits" on page 430 because there are multiple functions available named to_string.

Here, we're using the to_string function defined in the ToString trait, which the standard library has implemented for any type that implements Display.

Recall from "Enum Values" on page 104 that the name of each enum variant that we define also becomes an initializer function. We can use these initializer functions as function pointers that implement the closure traits, which means we can specify the initializer functions as arguments for methods that take closures, like so:

```
enum Status {
    Value(u32),
    Stop,
}
```

```
let list_of_statuses: Vec<Status> = (0u32..20)
    .map(Status::Value)
    .collect();
```

Here, we create `Status::Value` instances using each `u32` value in the range that `map` is called on by using the initializer function of `Status::Value`. Some people prefer this style and some people prefer to use closures. They compile to the same code, so use whichever style is clearer to you.

Returning Closures

Closures are represented by traits, which means you can't return closures directly. In most cases where you might want to return a trait, you can instead use the concrete type that implements the trait as the return value of the function. However, you can't do that with closures because they don't have a concrete type that is returnable; you're not allowed to use the function pointer `fn` as a return type, for example.

The following code tries to return a closure directly, but it won't compile:

```
fn returns_closure() -> dyn Fn(i32) -> i32 {
    |x| x + 1
}
```

The compiler error is as follows:

```
error[E0746]: return type cannot have an unboxed trait object
  --> src/lib.rs:1:25
   |
 1 | fn returns_closure() -> dyn Fn(i32) -> i32 {
   |                         ^^^^^^^^^^^^^^^^^^^ doesn't have a size known at
compile-time
   |
   = note: for information on `impl Trait`, see
<https://doc.rust-lang.org/book/ch10-02-traits.html#returning-types-that-
implement-traits>
help: use `impl Fn(i32) -> i32` as the return type, as all return paths are of
type `[closure@src/lib.rs:2:5: 2:14]`, which implements `Fn(i32) -> i32`
   |
 1 | fn returns_closure() -> impl Fn(i32) -> i32 {
   |                         ~~~~~~~~~~~~~~~~~~~
```

The error references the `Sized` trait again! Rust doesn't know how much space it will need to store the closure. We saw a solution to this problem earlier. We can use a trait object:

```
fn returns_closure() -> Box<dyn Fn(i32) -> i32> {
    Box::new(|x| x + 1)
}
```

This code will compile just fine. For more about trait objects, refer to "Using Trait Objects That Allow for Values of Different Types" on page 379. Next, let's look at macros!

Macros

We've used macros like `println!` throughout this book, but we haven't fully explored what a macro is and how it works. The term *macro* refers to a family of features in Rust: *declarative* macros with `macro_rules!` and three kinds of *procedural* macros:

- Custom #[derive] macros that specify code added with the derive attribute used on structs and enums
- Attribute-like macros that define custom attributes usable on any item
- Function-like macros that look like function calls but operate on the tokens specified as their argument

We'll talk about each of these in turn, but first, let's look at why we even need macros when we already have functions.

The Difference Between Macros and Functions

Fundamentally, macros are a way of writing code that writes other code, which is known as *metaprogramming*. In Appendix C, we discuss the derive attribute, which generates an implementation of various traits for you. We've also used the `println!` and `vec!` macros throughout the book. All of these macros *expand* to produce more code than the code you've written manually.

Metaprogramming is useful for reducing the amount of code you have to write and maintain, which is also one of the roles of functions. However, macros have some additional powers that functions don't have.

A function signature must declare the number and type of parameters the function has. Macros, on the other hand, can take a variable number of parameters: we can call `println!("hello")` with one argument or `println! ("hello {}", name)` with two arguments. Also, macros are expanded before the compiler interprets the meaning of the code, so a macro can, for example, implement a trait on a given type. A function can't, because it gets called at runtime and a trait needs to be implemented at compile time.

The downside to implementing a macro instead of a function is that macro definitions are more complex than function definitions because you're writing Rust code that writes Rust code. Due to this indirection, macro definitions are generally more difficult to read, understand, and maintain than function definitions.

Another important difference between macros and functions is that you must define macros or bring them into scope *before* you call them in a file, as opposed to functions you can define anywhere and call anywhere.

Declarative Macros with macro_rules! for General Metaprogramming

The most widely used form of macros in Rust is the *declarative macro*. These are also sometimes referred to as "macros by example," "`macro_rules!` macros," or just plain "macros." At their core, declarative macros allow you to write something similar to a Rust `match` expression. As discussed in Chapter 6, `match` expressions are control structures that take an expression, compare the resultant value of the expression to patterns, and then run the code associated with the matching pattern. Macros also compare a value to patterns that are associated with particular code: in this situation, the value is the literal Rust source code passed to the macro; the patterns are compared with the structure of that source code; and the code associated with each pattern, when matched, replaces the code passed to the macro. This all happens during compilation.

To define a macro, you use the macro_rules! construct. Let's explore how to use macro_rules! by looking at how the vec! macro is defined. Chapter 8 covered how we can use the vec! macro to create a new vector with particular values. For example, the following macro creates a new vector containing three integers:

```
let v: Vec<u32> = vec![1, 2, 3];
```

We could also use the vec! macro to make a vector of two integers or a vector of five string slices. We wouldn't be able to use a function to do the same because we wouldn't know the number or type of values up front.

Listing 19-28 shows a slightly simplified definition of the vec! macro.

src/lib.rs
```
❶ #[macro_export]
❷ macro_rules! vec {
    ❸ ( $( $x:expr ),* ) => {
        {
            let mut temp_vec = Vec::new();
            ❹ $(
                ❺ temp_vec.push(❻$x);
            )*
            ❼ temp_vec
        }
    };
}
```

Listing 19-28: A simplified version of the vec! macro definition

NOTE   *The actual definition of the vec! macro in the standard library includes code to pre-allocate the correct amount of memory up front. That code is an optimization that we don't include here, to make the example simpler.*

The #[macro_export] annotation ❶ indicates that this macro should be made available whenever the crate in which the macro is defined is brought into scope. Without this annotation, the macro can't be brought into scope.

We then start the macro definition with macro_rules! and the name of the macro we're defining *without* the exclamation mark ❷. The name, in this case vec, is followed by curly brackets denoting the body of the macro definition.

The structure in the vec! body is similar to the structure of a match expression. Here we have one arm with the pattern ($($x:expr),*), followed by => and the block of code associated with this pattern ❸. If the pattern matches, the associated block of code will be emitted. Given that this is the only pattern in this macro, there is only one valid way to match; any other pattern will result in an error. More complex macros will have more than one arm.

Valid pattern syntax in macro definitions is different from the pattern syntax covered in Chapter 18 because macro patterns are matched against Rust code structure rather than values. Let's walk through what the pattern pieces in Listing 19-28 mean; for the full macro pattern syntax, see the Rust Reference at *https://doc.rust-lang.org/reference/macros-by-example.html*.

First we use a set of parentheses to encompass the whole pattern. We use a dollar sign ($) to declare a variable in the macro system that will contain the Rust code matching the pattern. The dollar sign makes it clear this is a macro variable as opposed to a regular Rust variable. Next comes a set of parentheses that captures values that match the pattern within the parentheses for use in the replacement code. Within $() is $x:expr, which matches any Rust expression and gives the expression the name $x.

The comma following $() indicates that a literal comma separator character could optionally appear after the code that matches the code in $(). The * specifies that the pattern matches zero or more of whatever precedes the *.

When we call this macro with vec![1, 2, 3];, the $x pattern matches three times with the three expressions 1, 2, and 3.

Now let's look at the pattern in the body of the code associated with this arm: temp_vec.push() ❺ within $()* at ❹ and ❼ is generated for each part that matches $() in the pattern zero or more times depending on how many times the pattern matches. The $x ❻ is replaced with each expression matched. When we call this macro with vec![1, 2, 3];, the code generated that replaces this macro call will be the following:

```
{
    let mut temp_vec = Vec::new();
    temp_vec.push(1);
    temp_vec.push(2);
    temp_vec.push(3);
    temp_vec
}
```

We've defined a macro that can take any number of arguments of any type and can generate code to create a vector containing the specified elements.

To learn more about how to write macros, consult the online documentation or other resources, such as "The Little Book of Rust Macros" at *https://veykril.github.io/tlborm* started by Daniel Keep and continued by Lukas Wirth.

Procedural Macros for Generating Code from Attributes

The second form of macros is the procedural macro, which acts more like a function (and is a type of procedure). *Procedural macros* accept some code as an input, operate on that code, and produce some code as an output rather than matching against patterns and replacing the code with other code as declarative macros do. The three kinds of procedural macros are custom derive, attribute-like, and function-like, and all work in a similar fashion.

When creating procedural macros, the definitions must reside in their own crate with a special crate type. This is for complex technical reasons that we hope to eliminate in the future. In Listing 19-29, we show how to define a procedural macro, where some_attribute is a placeholder for using a specific macro variety.

src/lib.rs
```
use proc_macro::TokenStream;

#[some_attribute]
pub fn some_name(input: TokenStream) -> TokenStream {
}
```

Listing 19-29: An example of defining a procedural macro

The function that defines a procedural macro takes a TokenStream as an input and produces a TokenStream as an output. The TokenStream type is defined by the proc_macro crate that is included with Rust and represents a sequence of tokens. This is the core of the macro: the source code that the macro is operating on makes up the input TokenStream, and the code the macro produces is the output TokenStream. The function also has an attribute attached to it that specifies which kind of procedural macro we're creating. We can have multiple kinds of procedural macros in the same crate.

Let's look at the different kinds of procedural macros. We'll start with a custom derive macro and then explain the small dissimilarities that make the other forms different.

How to Write a Custom derive Macro

Let's create a crate named hello_macro that defines a trait named HelloMacro with one associated function named hello_macro. Rather than making our users implement the HelloMacro trait for each of their types, we'll provide a procedural macro so users can annotate their type with #[derive(HelloMacro)] to get a default implementation of the hello_macro function. The default implementation will print Hello, Macro! My name is *TypeName*! where *TypeName* is the name of the type on which this trait has been defined. In other words, we'll write a crate that enables another programmer to write code like Listing 19-30 using our crate.

src/main.rs
```
use hello_macro::HelloMacro;
use hello_macro_derive::HelloMacro;

#[derive(HelloMacro)]
struct Pancakes;

fn main() {
    Pancakes::hello_macro();
}
```

Listing 19-30: The code a user of our crate will be able to write when using our procedural macro

This code will print Hello, Macro! My name is Pancakes! when we're done. The first step is to make a new library crate, like this:

```
$ cargo new hello_macro --lib
```

Next, we'll define the HelloMacro trait and its associated function:

src/lib.rs
```
pub trait HelloMacro {
    fn hello_macro();
}
```

We have a trait and its function. At this point, our crate user could implement the trait to achieve the desired functionality, like so:

```
use hello_macro::HelloMacro;

struct Pancakes;

impl HelloMacro for Pancakes {
    fn hello_macro() {
        println!("Hello, Macro! My name is Pancakes!");
    }
}

fn main() {
    Pancakes::hello_macro();
}
```

However, they would need to write the implementation block for each type they wanted to use with hello_macro; we want to spare them from having to do this work.

Additionally, we can't yet provide the hello_macro function with default implementation that will print the name of the type the trait is implemented on: Rust doesn't have reflection capabilities, so it can't look up the type's name at runtime. We need a macro to generate code at compile time.

The next step is to define the procedural macro. At the time of this writing, procedural macros need to be in their own crate. Eventually, this restriction might be lifted. The convention for structuring crates and macro crates is as follows: for a crate named *foo*, a custom derive procedural macro crate is called *foo*_derive. Let's start a new crate called hello_macro_derive inside our hello_macro project:

```
$ cargo new hello_macro_derive --lib
```

Our two crates are tightly related, so we create the procedural macro crate within the directory of our hello_macro crate. If we change the trait definition in hello_macro, we'll have to change the implementation of the procedural macro in hello_macro_derive as well. The two crates will need to be published separately, and programmers using these crates will need to add both as dependencies and bring them both into scope. We could instead have the hello_macro crate use hello_macro_derive as a dependency and re-export the procedural macro code. However, the way we've structured the project makes it possible for programmers to use hello_macro even if they don't want the derive functionality.

We need to declare the hello_macro_derive crate as a procedural macro crate. We'll also need functionality from the syn and quote crates, as you'll see in a moment, so we need to add them as dependencies. Add the following to the *Cargo.toml* file for hello_macro_derive:

hello_macro
_derive/
Cargo.toml

```
[lib]
proc-macro = true

[dependencies]
syn = "1.0"
quote = "1.0"
```

To start defining the procedural macro, place the code in Listing 19-31 into your *src/lib.rs* file for the hello_macro_derive crate. Note that this code won't compile until we add a definition for the impl_hello_macro function.

hello_macro
_derive/src/lib.rs

```
use proc_macro::TokenStream;
use quote::quote;
use syn;

#[proc_macro_derive(HelloMacro)]
pub fn hello_macro_derive(input: TokenStream) -> TokenStream {
    // Construct a representation of Rust code as a syntax tree
    // that we can manipulate.
    let ast = syn::parse(input).unwrap();

    // Build the trait implementation.
    impl_hello_macro(&ast)
}
```

Listing 19-31: Code that most procedural macro crates will require in order to process Rust code

Notice that we've split the code into the hello_macro_derive function, which is responsible for parsing the TokenStream, and the impl_hello_macro function, which is responsible for transforming the syntax tree: this makes writing a procedural macro more convenient. The code in the outer function (hello_macro_derive in this case) will be the same for almost every procedural macro crate you see or create. The code you specify in the body of the inner function (impl_hello_macro in this case) will be different depending on your procedural macro's purpose.

We've introduced three new crates: proc_macro, syn (available from *https://crates.io/crates/syn*), and quote (available from *https://crates.io/crates/quote*). The proc_macro crate comes with Rust, so we didn't need to add that to the dependencies in *Cargo.toml*. The proc_macro crate is the compiler's API that allows us to read and manipulate Rust code from our code.

The syn crate parses Rust code from a string into a data structure that we can perform operations on. The quote crate turns syn data structures back into

Rust code. These crates make it much simpler to parse any sort of Rust code we might want to handle: writing a full parser for Rust code is no simple task.

The hello_macro_derive function will be called when a user of our library specifies #[derive(HelloMacro)] on a type. This is possible because we've annotated the hello_macro_derive function here with proc_macro_derive and specified the name HelloMacro, which matches our trait name; this is the convention most procedural macros follow.

The hello_macro_derive function first converts the input from a TokenStream to a data structure that we can then interpret and perform operations on. This is where syn comes into play. The parse function in syn takes a TokenStream and returns a DeriveInput struct representing the parsed Rust code. Listing 19-32 shows the relevant parts of the DeriveInput struct we get from parsing the struct Pancakes; string.

```
DeriveInput {
    --snip--

    ident: Ident {
        ident: "Pancakes",
        span: #0 bytes(95..103)
    },
    data: Struct(
        DataStruct {
            struct_token: Struct,
            fields: Unit,
            semi_token: Some(
                Semi
            )
        }
    )
}
```

Listing 19-32: The DeriveInput instance we get when parsing the code that has the macro's attribute in Listing 19-30

The fields of this struct show that the Rust code we've parsed is a unit struct with the ident (*identifier*, meaning the name) of Pancakes. There are more fields on this struct for describing all sorts of Rust code; check the syn documentation for DeriveInput at *https://docs.rs/syn/1.0/syn/struct.DeriveInput.html* for more information.

Soon we'll define the impl_hello_macro function, which is where we'll build the new Rust code we want to include. But before we do, note that the output for our derive macro is also a TokenStream. The returned TokenStream is added to the code that our crate users write, so when they compile their crate, they'll get the extra functionality that we provide in the modified TokenStream.

You might have noticed that we're calling unwrap to cause the hello _macro_derive function to panic if the call to the syn::parse function fails here. It's necessary for our procedural macro to panic on errors because proc_macro_derive functions must return TokenStream rather than Result to conform to the procedural macro API. We've simplified this example by using unwrap; in production code, you should provide more specific error messages about what went wrong by using panic! or expect.

Now that we have the code to turn the annotated Rust code from a TokenStream into a DeriveInput instance, let's generate the code that implements the HelloMacro trait on the annotated type, as shown in Listing 19-33.

hello_macro
_derive/src/lib.rs

```
fn impl_hello_macro(ast: &syn::DeriveInput) -> TokenStream {
    let name = &ast.ident;
    let gen = quote! {
        impl HelloMacro for #name {
            fn hello_macro() {
                println!(
                    "Hello, Macro! My name is {}!",
                    stringify!(#name)
                );
            }
        }
    };
    gen.into()
}
```

Listing 19-33: Implementing the HelloMacro trait using the parsed Rust code

We get an Ident struct instance containing the name (identifier) of the annotated type using ast.ident. The struct in Listing 19-32 shows that when we run the impl_hello_macro function on the code in Listing 19-30, the ident we get will have the ident field with a value of "Pancakes". Thus the name variable in Listing 19-33 will contain an Ident struct instance that, when printed, will be the string "Pancakes", the name of the struct in Listing 19-30.

The quote! macro lets us define the Rust code that we want to return. The compiler expects something different to the direct result of the quote! macro's execution, so we need to convert it to a TokenStream. We do this by calling the into method, which consumes this intermediate representation and returns a value of the required TokenStream type.

The quote! macro also provides some very cool templating mechanics: we can enter #name, and quote! will replace it with the value in the variable name. You can even do some repetition similar to the way regular macros work. Check out the quote crate's docs at *https://docs.rs/quote* for a thorough introduction.

We want our procedural macro to generate an implementation of our HelloMacro trait for the type the user annotated, which we can get by using #name. The trait implementation has the one function hello_macro, whose body contains the functionality we want to provide: printing Hello, Macro! My name is and then the name of the annotated type.

The stringify! macro used here is built into Rust. It takes a Rust expression, such as 1 + 2, and at compile time turns the expression into a string literal, such as "1 + 2". This is different from format! or println!, macros which evaluate the expression and then turn the result into a String. There is a possibility that the #name input might be an expression to print literally, so we use stringify!. Using stringify! also saves an allocation by converting #name to a string literal at compile time.

At this point, `cargo build` should complete successfully in both `hello_macro` and `hello_macro_derive`. Let's hook up these crates to the code in Listing 19-30 to see the procedural macro in action! Create a new binary project in your *projects* directory using `cargo new pancakes`. We need to add `hello_macro` and `hello_macro_derive` as dependencies in the pancakes crate's *Cargo.toml*. If you're publishing your versions of `hello_macro` and `hello_macro_derive` to *https://crates.io*, they would be regular dependencies; if not, you can specify them as `path` dependencies as follows:

```
[dependencies]
hello_macro = { path = "../hello_macro" }
hello_macro_derive = { path = "../hello_macro/hello_macro_derive" }
```

Put the code in Listing 19-30 into *src/main.rs*, and run `cargo run`: it should print `Hello, Macro! My name is Pancakes!` The implementation of the `HelloMacro` trait from the procedural macro was included without the pancakes crate needing to implement it; the `#[derive(HelloMacro)]` added the trait implementation.

Next, let's explore how the other kinds of procedural macros differ from custom `derive` macros.

Attribute-Like Macros

Attribute-like macros are similar to custom `derive` macros, but instead of generating code for the `derive` attribute, they allow you to create new attributes. They're also more flexible: `derive` only works for structs and enums; attributes can be applied to other items as well, such as functions. Here's an example of using an attribute-like macro. Say you have an attribute named `route` that annotates functions when using a web application framework:

```
#[route(GET, "/")]
fn index() {
```

This `#[route]` attribute would be defined by the framework as a procedural macro. The signature of the macro definition function would look like this:

```
#[proc_macro_attribute]
pub fn route(
    attr: TokenStream,
    item: TokenStream
) -> TokenStream {
```

Here, we have two parameters of type `TokenStream`. The first is for the contents of the attribute: the `GET, "/"` part. The second is the body of the item the attribute is attached to: in this case, `fn index() {}` and the rest of the function's body.

Other than that, attribute-like macros work the same way as custom `derive` macros: you create a crate with the `proc-macro` crate type and implement a function that generates the code you want!

Function-Like Macros

Function-like macros define macros that look like function calls. Similarly to macro_rules! macros, they're more flexible than functions; for example, they can take an unknown number of arguments. However, macro_rules! macros can only be defined using the match-like syntax we discussed in "Declarative Macros with macro_rules! for General Metaprogramming" on page 449. Function-like macros take a TokenStream parameter, and their definition manipulates that TokenStream using Rust code as the other two types of procedural macros do. An example of a function-like macro is an sql! macro that might be called like so:

```
let sql = sql!(SELECT * FROM posts WHERE id=1);
```

This macro would parse the SQL statement inside it and check that it's syntactically correct, which is much more complex processing than a macro _rules! macro can do. The sql! macro would be defined like this:

```
#[proc_macro]
pub fn sql(input: TokenStream) -> TokenStream {
```

This definition is similar to the custom derive macro's signature: we receive the tokens that are inside the parentheses and return the code we wanted to generate.

Summary

Whew! Now you have some Rust features in your toolbox that you likely won't use often, but you'll know they're available in very particular circumstances. We've introduced several complex topics so that when you encounter them in error message suggestions or in other people's code, you'll be able to recognize these concepts and syntax. Use this chapter as a reference to guide you to solutions.

Next, we'll put everything we've discussed throughout the book into practice and do one more project!

20

FINAL PROJECT: BUILDING A MULTITHREADED WEB SERVER

 It's been a long journey, but we've reached the end of the book. In this chapter, we'll build one more project together to demonstrate some of the concepts we covered in the final chapters, as well as recap some earlier lessons.

For our final project, we'll make a web server that says "hello" and looks like Figure 20-1 in a web browser.

Here is our plan for building the web server:

1. Learn a bit about TCP and HTTP.
2. Listen for TCP connections on a socket.
3. Parse a small number of HTTP requests.
4. Create a proper HTTP response.
5. Improve the throughput of our server with a thread pool.

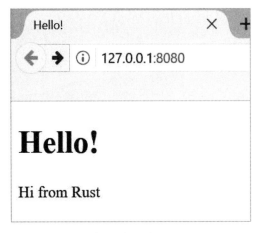

Figure 20-1: Our final shared project

Before we get started, we should mention one detail: the method we'll use won't be the best way to build a web server with Rust. Community members have published a number of production-ready crates available at *https:// crates.io* that provide more complete web server and thread pool implementations than we'll build. However, our intention in this chapter is to help you learn, not to take the easy route. Because Rust is a systems programming language, we can choose the level of abstraction we want to work with and can go to a lower level than is possible or practical in other languages. We'll therefore write the basic HTTP server and thread pool manually so you can learn the general ideas and techniques behind the crates you might use in the future.

Building a Single-Threaded Web Server

We'll start by getting a single-threaded web server working. Before we begin, let's look at a quick overview of the protocols involved in building web servers. The details of these protocols are beyond the scope of this book, but a brief overview will give you the information you need.

The two main protocols involved in web servers are *Hypertext Transfer Protocol (HTTP)* and *Transmission Control Protocol (TCP)*. Both protocols are *request-response* protocols, meaning a *client* initiates requests and a *server* listens to the requests and provides a response to the client. The contents of those requests and responses are defined by the protocols.

TCP is the lower-level protocol that describes the details of how information gets from one server to another but doesn't specify what that information is. HTTP builds on top of TCP by defining the contents of the requests and responses. It's technically possible to use HTTP with other protocols, but in the vast majority of cases, HTTP sends its data over TCP. We'll work with the raw bytes of TCP and HTTP requests and responses.

Listening to the TCP Connection

Our web server needs to listen to a TCP connection, so that's the first part we'll work on. The standard library offers a std::net module that lets us do this. Let's make a new project in the usual fashion:

```
$ cargo new hello
    Created binary (application) `hello` project
$ cd hello
```

Now enter the code in Listing 20-1 in *src/main.rs* to start. This code will listen at the local address 127.0.0.1:7878 for incoming TCP streams. When it gets an incoming stream, it will print Connection established!.

src/main.rs
```
use std::net::TcpListener;

fn main() {
❶ let listener = TcpListener::bind("127.0.0.1:7878").unwrap();

❷ for stream in listener.incoming() {
    ❸ let stream = stream.unwrap();

    ❹ println!("Connection established!");
    }
}
```

Listing 20-1: Listening for incoming streams and printing a message when we receive a stream

Using TcpListener, we can listen for TCP connections at the address 127.0.0.1:7878 ❶. In the address, the section before the colon is an IP address representing your computer (this is the same on every computer and doesn't represent the authors' computer specifically), and 7878 is the port. We've chosen this port for two reasons: HTTP isn't normally accepted on this port, so our server is unlikely to conflict with any other web server you might have running on your machine, and 7878 is *rust* typed on a telephone.

The bind function in this scenario works like the new function in that it will return a new TcpListener instance. The function is called bind because, in networking, connecting to a port to listen to is known as "binding to a port."

The bind function returns a Result<T, E>, which indicates that it's possible for binding to fail. For example, connecting to port 80 requires administrator privileges (non-administrators can listen only on ports higher than 1023), so if we tried to connect to port 80 without being an administrator, binding wouldn't work. Binding also wouldn't work, for example, if we ran two instances of our program and so had two programs listening to the same port. Because we're writing a basic server just for learning purposes, we won't worry about handling these kinds of errors; instead, we use unwrap to stop the program if errors happen.

The incoming method on TcpListener returns an iterator that gives us a sequence of streams ❷ (more specifically, streams of type TcpStream). A single *stream* represents an open connection between the client and the server.

A *connection* is the name for the full request and response process in which a client connects to the server, the server generates a response, and the server closes the connection. As such, we will read from the TcpStream to see what the client sent and then write our response to the stream to send data back to the client. Overall, this for loop will process each connection in turn and produce a series of streams for us to handle.

For now, our handling of the stream consists of calling unwrap to terminate our program if the stream has any errors ❸; if there aren't any errors, the program prints a message ❹. We'll add more functionality for the success case in the next listing. The reason we might receive errors from the incoming method when a client connects to the server is that we're not actually iterating over connections. Instead, we're iterating over *connection attempts*. The connection might not be successful for a number of reasons, many of them operating system specific. For example, many operating systems have a limit to the number of simultaneous open connections they can support; new connection attempts beyond that number will produce an error until some of the open connections are closed.

Let's try running this code! Invoke cargo run in the terminal and then load *127.0.0.1:7878* in a web browser. The browser should show an error message like "Connection reset" because the server isn't currently sending back any data. But when you look at your terminal, you should see several messages that were printed when the browser connected to the server!

```
    Running `target/debug/hello`
Connection established!
Connection established!
Connection established!
```

Sometimes you'll see multiple messages printed for one browser request; the reason might be that the browser is making a request for the page as well as a request for other resources, like the *favicon.ico* icon that appears in the browser tab.

It could also be that the browser is trying to connect to the server multiple times because the server isn't responding with any data. When stream goes out of scope and is dropped at the end of the loop, the connection is closed as part of the drop implementation. Browsers sometimes deal with closed connections by retrying, because the problem might be temporary. The important factor is that we've successfully gotten a handle to a TCP connection!

Remember to stop the program by pressing CTRL-C when you're done running a particular version of the code. Then restart the program by invoking the cargo run command after you've made each set of code changes to make sure you're running the newest code.

Reading the Request

Let's implement the functionality to read the request from the browser! To separate the concerns of first getting a connection and then taking some action with the connection, we'll start a new function for processing connections. In this new `handle_connection` function, we'll read data from the TCP stream and print it so we can see the data being sent from the browser. Change the code to look like Listing 20-2.

src/main.rs ❶
```
use std::{
    io::{prelude::*, BufReader},
    net::{TcpListener, TcpStream},
};

fn main() {
    let listener = TcpListener::bind("127.0.0.1:7878").unwrap();

    for stream in listener.incoming() {
        let stream = stream.unwrap();

      ❷ handle_connection(stream);
    }
}

fn handle_connection(mut stream: TcpStream) {
  ❸ let buf_reader = BufReader::new(&mut stream);
  ❹ let http_request: Vec<_> = buf_reader
      ❺ .lines()
      ❻ .map(|result| result.unwrap())
      ❼ .take_while(|line| !line.is_empty())
        .collect();

  ❽ println!("Request: {:#?}", http_request);
}
```

Listing 20-2: Reading from the TcpStream and printing the data

We bring `std::io::prelude` and `std::io::BufReader` into scope to get access to traits and types that let us read from and write to the stream ❶. In the for loop in the `main` function, instead of printing a message that says we made a connection, we now call the new `handle_connection` function and pass the stream to it ❷.

In the `handle_connection` function, we create a new `BufReader` instance that wraps a mutable reference to the stream ❸. `BufReader` adds buffering by managing calls to the `std::io::Read` trait methods for us.

We create a variable named `http_request` to collect the lines of the request the browser sends to our server. We indicate that we want to collect these lines in a vector by adding the `Vec<_>` type annotation ❹.

`BufReader` implements the `std::io::BufRead` trait, which provides the `lines` method ❺. The `lines` method returns an iterator of `Result<String, std::io::Error>` by splitting the stream of data whenever it sees a newline byte. To get each `String`, we map and unwrap each `Result` ❻. The `Result` might be an error if the data isn't valid UTF-8 or if there was a problem reading from the stream. Again, a production program should handle these errors more gracefully, but we're choosing to stop the program in the error case for simplicity.

The browser signals the end of an HTTP request by sending two newline characters in a row, so to get one request from the stream, we take lines until we get a line that is the empty string ❼. Once we've collected the lines into the vector, we're printing them out using pretty debug formatting ❽ so we can take a look at the instructions the web browser is sending to our server.

Let's try this code! Start the program and make a request in a web browser again. Note that we'll still get an error page in the browser, but our program's output in the terminal will now look similar to this:

```
$ cargo run
   Compiling hello v0.1.0 (file:///projects/hello)
    Finished dev [unoptimized + debuginfo] target(s) in 0.42s
     Running `target/debug/hello`
Request: [
    "GET / HTTP/1.1",
    "Host: 127.0.0.1:7878",
    "User-Agent: Mozilla/5.0 (Macintosh; Intel Mac OS X 10.15; rv:99.0)
Gecko/20100101 Firefox/99.0",
    "Accept:
text/html,application/xhtml+xml,application/xml;q=0.9,image/avif,image/webp,*/*
;q=0.8",
    "Accept-Language: en-US,en;q=0.5",
    "Accept-Encoding: gzip, deflate, br",
    "DNT: 1",
    "Connection: keep-alive",
    "Upgrade-Insecure-Requests: 1",
    "Sec-Fetch-Dest: document",
    "Sec-Fetch-Mode: navigate",
    "Sec-Fetch-Site: none",
    "Sec-Fetch-User: ?1",
    "Cache-Control: max-age=0",
]
```

Depending on your browser, you might get slightly different output. Now that we're printing the request data, we can see why we get multiple connections from one browser request by looking at the path after GET in the first line of the request. If the repeated connections are all requesting /, we know the browser is trying to fetch / repeatedly because it's not getting a response from our program.

Let's break down this request data to understand what the browser is asking of our program.

A Closer Look at an HTTP Request

HTTP is a text-based protocol, and a request takes this format:

```
Method Request-URI HTTP-Version CRLF
headers CRLF
message-body
```

The first line is the *request line* that holds information about what the client is requesting. The first part of the request line indicates the *method* being used, such as GET or POST, which describes how the client is making this request. Our client used a GET request, which means it is asking for information.

The next part of the request line is /, which indicates the *uniform resource identifier (URI)* the client is requesting: a URI is almost, but not quite, the same as a *uniform resource locator (URL)*. The difference between URIs and URLs isn't important for our purposes in this chapter, but the HTTP spec uses the term *URI*, so we can just mentally substitute *URL* for *URI* here.

The last part is the HTTP version the client uses, and then the request line ends in a CRLF sequence. (CRLF stands for *carriage return* and *line feed*, which are terms from the typewriter days!) The CRLF sequence can also be written as \r\n, where \r is a carriage return and \n is a line feed. The *CRLF sequence* separates the request line from the rest of the request data. Note that when the CRLF is printed, we see a new line start rather than \r\n.

Looking at the request line data we received from running our program so far, we see that GET is the method, / is the request URI, and HTTP/1.1 is the version.

After the request line, the remaining lines starting from Host: onward are headers. GET requests have no body.

Try making a request from a different browser or asking for a different address, such as *127.0.0.1:7878/test*, to see how the request data changes.

Now that we know what the browser is asking for, let's send back some data!

Writing a Response

We're going to implement sending data in response to a client request. Responses have the following format:

```
HTTP-Version Status-Code Reason-Phrase CRLF
headers CRLF
message-body
```

The first line is a *status line* that contains the HTTP version used in the response, a numeric status code that summarizes the result of the request, and a reason phrase that provides a text description of the status code. After the CRLF sequence are any headers, another CRLF sequence, and the body of the response.

Here is an example response that uses HTTP version 1.1, and has a status code of 200, an OK reason phrase, no headers, and no body:

```
HTTP/1.1 200 OK\r\n\r\n
```

The status code 200 is the standard success response. The text is a tiny successful HTTP response. Let's write this to the stream as our response to a successful request! From the handle_connection function, remove the println! that was printing the request data and replace it with the code in Listing 20-3.

```
src/main.rs   fn handle_connection(mut stream: TcpStream) {
                  let buf_reader = BufReader::new(&mut stream);
                  let http_request: Vec<_> = buf_reader
                      .lines()
                      .map(|result| result.unwrap())
                      .take_while(|line| !line.is_empty())
                      .collect();

              ❶ let response = "HTTP/1.1 200 OK\r\n\r\n";

              ❷ stream.write_all(response.❸as_bytes()).unwrap();
              }
```

Listing 20-3: Writing a tiny successful HTTP response to the stream

The first new line defines the response variable that holds the success message's data ❶. Then we call as_bytes on our response to convert the string data to bytes ❸. The write_all method on stream takes a &[u8] and sends those bytes directly down the connection ❷. Because the write_all operation could fail, we use unwrap on any error result as before. Again, in a real application you would add error handling here.

With these changes, let's run our code and make a request. We're no longer printing any data to the terminal, so we won't see any output other than the output from Cargo. When you load *127.0.0.1:7878* in a web browser, you should get a blank page instead of an error. You've just handcoded receiving an HTTP request and sending a response!

Returning Real HTML

Let's implement the functionality for returning more than a blank page. Create the new file *hello.html* in the root of your project directory, not in the *src* directory. You can input any HTML you want; Listing 20-4 shows one possibility.

```
hello.html    <!DOCTYPE html>
              <html lang="en">
                <head>
                  <meta charset="utf-8">
                  <title>Hello!</title>
                </head>
                <body>
                  <h1>Hello!</h1>
                  <p>Hi from Rust</p>
                </body>
              </html>
```

Listing 20-4: A sample HTML file to return in a response

This is a minimal HTML5 document with a heading and some text. To return this from the server when a request is received, we'll modify handle_connection as shown in Listing 20-5 to read the HTML file, add it to the response as a body, and send it.

```
src/main.rs    use std::{
               ❶ fs,
                   io::{prelude::*, BufReader},
                   net::{TcpListener, TcpStream},
               };
               --snip--

               fn handle_connection(mut stream: TcpStream) {
                   let buf_reader = BufReader::new(&mut stream);
                   let http_request: Vec<_> = buf_reader
                       .lines()
                       .map(|result| result.unwrap())
                       .take_while(|line| !line.is_empty())
                       .collect();

                   let status_line = "HTTP/1.1 200 OK";
                   let contents = fs::read_to_string("hello.html").unwrap();
                   let length = contents.len();

               ❷ let response = format!(
                       "{status_line}\r\n\
                        Content-Length: {length}\r\n\r\n\
                        {contents}"
                   );

                   stream.write_all(response.as_bytes()).unwrap();
               }
```

Listing 20-5: Sending the contents of hello.html *as the body of the response*

We've added fs to the use statement to bring the standard library's file-system module into scope ❶. The code for reading the contents of a file to a string should look familiar; we used it when we read the contents of a file for our I/O project in Listing 12-4.

Next, we use format! to add the file's contents as the body of the success response ❷. To ensure a valid HTTP response, we add the Content-Length header which is set to the size of our response body, in this case the size of hello.html.

Run this code with cargo run and load *127.0.0.1:7878* in your browser; you should see your HTML rendered!

Currently, we're ignoring the request data in http_request and just sending back the contents of the HTML file unconditionally. That means if you try requesting *127.0.0.1:7878/something-else* in your browser, you'll still get back this same HTML response. At the moment, our server is very limited and does not do what most web servers do. We want to customize our responses depending on the request and only send back the HTML file for a well-formed request to /.

Validating the Request and Selectively Responding

Right now, our web server will return the HTML in the file no matter what the client requested. Let's add functionality to check that the browser is requesting / before returning the HTML file, and return an error if the browser requests anything else. For this we need to modify handle_connection, as shown in Listing 20-6. This new code checks the content of the request received against what we know a request for / looks like and adds if and else blocks to treat requests differently.

```
--snip--

fn handle_connection(mut stream: TcpStream) {
    let buf_reader = BufReader::new(&mut stream);
  ❶ let request_line = buf_reader
        .lines()
        .next()
        .unwrap()
        .unwrap();

  ❷ if request_line == "GET / HTTP/1.1" {
        let status_line = "HTTP/1.1 200 OK";
        let contents = fs::read_to_string("hello.html").unwrap();
        let length = contents.len();

        let response = format!(
            "{status_line}\r\n\
             Content-Length: {length}\r\n\r\n\
             {contents}"
        );

        stream.write_all(response.as_bytes()).unwrap();
  ❸ } else {
        // some other request
    }
}
```

Listing 20-6: Handling requests to / differently from other requests

We're only going to be looking at the first line of the HTTP request, so rather than reading the entire request into a vector, we're calling next to get the first item from the iterator ❶. The first unwrap takes care of the Option and stops the program if the iterator has no items. The second unwrap handles the Result and has the same effect as the unwrap that was in the map added in Listing 20-2.

Next, we check the request_line to see if it equals the request line of a GET request to the / path ❷. If it does, the if block returns the contents of our HTML file.

If the request_line does *not* equal the GET request to the / path, it means we've received some other request. We'll add code to the else block ❸ in a moment to respond to all other requests.

Run this code now and request *127.0.0.1:7878*; you should get the HTML in *hello.html*. If you make any other request, such as *127.0.0.1:7878/ something-else*, you'll get a connection error like those you saw when running the code in Listing 20-1 and Listing 20-2.

Now let's add the code in Listing 20-7 to the else block to return a response with the status code 404, which signals that the content for the request was not found. We'll also return some HTML for a page to render in the browser indicating the response to the end user.

src/main.rs
```
--snip--
} else {
  ❶ let status_line = "HTTP/1.1 404 NOT FOUND";
  ❷ let contents = fs::read_to_string("404.html").unwrap();
    let length = contents.len();

    let response = format!(
        "{status_line}\r\n\
         Content-Length: {length}\r\n\r\n\
         {contents}"
    );

    stream.write_all(response.as_bytes()).unwrap();
}
```

Listing 20-7: Responding with status code 404 and an error page if anything other than / was requested

Here, our response has a status line with status code 404 and the reason phrase NOT FOUND ❶. The body of the response will be the HTML in the file *404.html* ❷. You'll need to create a *404.html* file next to *hello.html* for the error page; again feel free to use any HTML you want, or use the example HTML in Listing 20-8.

404.html
```
<!DOCTYPE html>
<html lang="en">
  <head>
    <meta charset="utf-8">
    <title>Hello!</title>
  </head>
  <body>
    <h1>Oops!</h1>
    <p>Sorry, I don't know what you're asking for.</p>
  </body>
</html>
```

Listing 20-8: Sample content for the page to send back with any 404 response

With these changes, run your server again. Requesting *127.0.0.1:7878* should return the contents of *hello.html*, and any other request, like *127.0.0.1:7878/foo*, should return the error HTML from *404.html*.

A Touch of Refactoring

At the moment, the if and else blocks have a lot of repetition: they're both reading files and writing the contents of the files to the stream. The only differences are the status line and the filename. Let's make the code more concise by pulling out those differences into separate `if` and `else` lines that will assign the values of the status line and the filename to variables; we can then use those variables unconditionally in the code to read the file and write the response. Listing 20-9 shows the resultant code after replacing the large `if` and `else` blocks.

src/main.rs

```
--snip--

fn handle_connection(mut stream: TcpStream) {
    --snip--

    let (status_line, filename) =
        if request_line == "GET / HTTP/1.1" {
            ("HTTP/1.1 200 OK", "hello.html")
        } else {
            ("HTTP/1.1 404 NOT FOUND", "404.html")
        };

    let contents = fs::read_to_string(filename).unwrap();
    let length = contents.len();

    let response = format!(
        "{status_line}\r\n\
        Content-Length: {length}\r\n\r\n\
        {contents}"
    );

    stream.write_all(response.as_bytes()).unwrap();
}
```

Listing 20-9: Refactoring the `if` and `else` blocks to contain only the code that differs between the two cases

Now the `if` and `else` blocks only return the appropriate values for the status line and filename in a tuple; we then use destructuring to assign these two values to `status_line` and `filename` using a pattern in the `let` statement, as discussed in Chapter 18.

The previously duplicated code is now outside the `if` and `else` blocks and uses the `status_line` and `filename` variables. This makes it easier to see the difference between the two cases, and it means we have only one place to update the code if we want to change how the file reading and response writing work. The behavior of the code in Listing 20-9 will be the same as that in Listing 20-8.

Awesome! We now have a simple web server in approximately 40 lines of Rust code that responds to one request with a page of content and responds to all other requests with a 404 response.

Currently, our server runs in a single thread, meaning it can only serve one request at a time. Let's examine how that can be a problem by simulating some slow requests. Then we'll fix it so our server can handle multiple requests at once.

Turning Our Single-Threaded Server into a Multithreaded Server

Right now, the server will process each request in turn, meaning it won't process a second connection until the first is finished processing. If the server received more and more requests, this serial execution would be less and less optimal. If the server receives a request that takes a long time to process, subsequent requests will have to wait until the long request is finished, even if the new requests can be processed quickly. We'll need to fix this, but first we'll look at the problem in action.

Simulating a Slow Request

We'll look at how a slow-processing request can affect other requests made to our current server implementation. Listing 20-10 implements handling a request to */sleep* with a simulated slow response that will cause the server to sleep for five seconds before responding.

src/main.rs
```
use std::{
    fs,
    io::{prelude::*, BufReader},
    net::{TcpListener, TcpStream},
    thread,
    time::Duration,
};
--snip--

fn handle_connection(mut stream: TcpStream) {
    --snip--

    let (status_line, filename) = ❶ match &request_line[..] {
        ❷ "GET / HTTP/1.1" => ("HTTP/1.1 200 OK", "hello.html"),
        ❸ "GET /sleep HTTP/1.1" => {
            thread::sleep(Duration::from_secs(5));
            ("HTTP/1.1 200 OK", "hello.html")
        }
        ❹ _ => ("HTTP/1.1 404 NOT FOUND", "404.html"),
    };

    --snip--
}
```

Listing 20-10: Simulating a slow request by sleeping for five seconds

We switched from if to match now that we have three cases ❶. We need to explicitly match on a slice of request_line to pattern-match against the string literal values; match doesn't do automatic referencing and dereferencing, like the equality method does.

The first arm ❷ is the same as the if block from Listing 20-9. The second arm ❸ matches a request to */sleep*. When that request is received, the server will sleep for five seconds before rendering the successful HTML page. The third arm ❹ is the same as the else block from Listing 20-9.

You can see how primitive our server is: real libraries would handle the recognition of multiple requests in a much less verbose way!

Start the server using cargo run. Then open two browser windows: one for *http://127.0.0.1:7878* and the other for *http://127.0.0.1:7878/sleep*. If you enter the / URI a few times, as before, you'll see it respond quickly. But if you enter */sleep* and then load /, you'll see that / waits until sleep has slept for its full five seconds before loading.

There are multiple techniques we could use to avoid requests backing up behind a slow request; the one we'll implement is a thread pool.

Improving Throughput with a Thread Pool

A *thread pool* is a group of spawned threads that are waiting and ready to handle a task. When the program receives a new task, it assigns one of the threads in the pool to the task, and that thread will process the task. The remaining threads in the pool are available to handle any other tasks that come in while the first thread is processing. When the first thread is done processing its task, it's returned to the pool of idle threads, ready to handle a new task. A thread pool allows you to process connections concurrently, increasing the throughput of your server.

We'll limit the number of threads in the pool to a small number to protect us from DoS attacks; if we had our program create a new thread for each request as it came in, someone making 10 million requests to our server could create havoc by using up all our server's resources and grinding the processing of requests to a halt.

Rather than spawning unlimited threads, then, we'll have a fixed number of threads waiting in the pool. Requests that come in are sent to the pool for processing. The pool will maintain a queue of incoming requests. Each of the threads in the pool will pop off a request from this queue, handle the request, and then ask the queue for another request. With this design, we can process up to *N* requests concurrently, where *N* is the number of threads. If each thread is responding to a long-running request, subsequent requests can still back up in the queue, but we've increased the number of long-running requests we can handle before reaching that point.

This technique is just one of many ways to improve the throughput of a web server. Other options you might explore are the fork/join model, the single-threaded async I/O model, and the multithreaded async I/O model. If you're interested in this topic, you can read more about other solutions and try to implement them; with a low-level language like Rust, all of these options are possible.

Before we begin implementing a thread pool, let's talk about what using the pool should look like. When you're trying to design code, writing the client interface first can help guide your design. Write the API of the code so it's structured in the way you want to call it; then implement the functionality within that structure rather than implementing the functionality and then designing the public API.

Similar to how we used test-driven development in the project in Chapter 12, we'll use compiler-driven development here. We'll write the code that calls the functions we want, and then we'll look at errors from the compiler to determine what we should change next to get the code to work. Before we do that, however, we'll explore the technique we're not going to use as a starting point.

Spawning a Thread for Each Request

First, let's explore how our code might look if it did create a new thread for every connection. As mentioned earlier, this isn't our final plan due to the problems with potentially spawning an unlimited number of threads, but it is a starting point to get a working multithreaded server first. Then we'll add the thread pool as an improvement, and contrasting the two solutions will be easier.

Listing 20-11 shows the changes to make to main to spawn a new thread to handle each stream within the for loop.

src/main.rs
```
fn main() {
    let listener = TcpListener::bind("127.0.0.1:7878").unwrap();

    for stream in listener.incoming() {
        let stream = stream.unwrap();

        thread::spawn(|| {
            handle_connection(stream);
        });
    }
}
```

Listing 20-11: Spawning a new thread for each stream

As you learned in Chapter 16, thread::spawn will create a new thread and then run the code in the closure in the new thread. If you run this code and load */sleep* in your browser, then / in two more browser tabs, you'll indeed see that the requests to / don't have to wait for */sleep* to finish. However, as we mentioned, this will eventually overwhelm the system because you'd be making new threads without any limit.

Creating a Finite Number of Threads

We want our thread pool to work in a similar, familiar way so that switching from threads to a thread pool doesn't require large changes to the code that uses our API. Listing 20-12 shows the hypothetical interface for a ThreadPool struct we want to use instead of thread::spawn.

src/main.rs
```
fn main() {
    let listener = TcpListener::bind("127.0.0.1:7878").unwrap();
  ❶ let pool = ThreadPool::new(4);

    for stream in listener.incoming() {
        let stream = stream.unwrap();
```

```
❷    pool.execute(|| {
         handle_connection(stream);
     });
   }
}
```

Listing 20-12: Our ideal ThreadPool interface

We use ThreadPool::new to create a new thread pool with a configurable number of threads, in this case four ❶. Then, in the for loop, pool.execute has a similar interface as thread::spawn in that it takes a closure the pool should run for each stream ❷. We need to implement pool.execute so it takes the closure and gives it to a thread in the pool to run. This code won't yet compile, but we'll try so that the compiler can guide us in how to fix it.

Building ThreadPool Using Compiler-Driven Development

Make the changes in Listing 20-12 to *src/main.rs*, and then let's use the compiler errors from cargo check to drive our development. Here is the first error we get:

```
$ cargo check
    Checking hello v0.1.0 (file:///projects/hello)
error[E0433]: failed to resolve: use of undeclared type `ThreadPool`
  --> src/main.rs:11:16
   |
11 |     let pool = ThreadPool::new(4);
   |                ^^^^^^^^^^ use of undeclared type `ThreadPool`
```

Great! This error tells us we need a ThreadPool type or module, so we'll build one now. Our ThreadPool implementation will be independent of the kind of work our web server is doing. So let's switch the hello crate from a binary crate to a library crate to hold our ThreadPool implementation. After we change to a library crate, we could also use the separate thread pool library for any work we want to do using a thread pool, not just for serving web requests.

Create a *src/lib.rs* file that contains the following, which is the simplest definition of a ThreadPool struct that we can have for now:

src/lib.rs   `pub struct ThreadPool;`

Then edit the *main.rs* file to bring ThreadPool into scope from the library crate by adding the following code to the top of *src/main.rs*:

src/main.rs   `use hello::ThreadPool;`

This code still won't work, but let's check it again to get the next error that we need to address:

```
$ cargo check
    Checking hello v0.1.0 (file:///projects/hello)
error[E0599]: no function or associated item named `new` found for struct
```

```
`ThreadPool` in the current scope
  --> src/main.rs:12:28
   |
12 |       let pool = ThreadPool::new(4);
   |                              ^^^ function or associated item not found in
`ThreadPool`
```

This error indicates that next we need to create an associated function named new for ThreadPool. We also know that new needs to have one parameter that can accept 4 as an argument and should return a ThreadPool instance. Let's implement the simplest new function that will have those characteristics:

src/lib.rs
```
pub struct ThreadPool;

impl ThreadPool {
    pub fn new(size: usize) -> ThreadPool {
        ThreadPool
    }
}
```

We chose usize as the type of the size parameter because we know that a negative number of threads doesn't make any sense. We also know we'll use this 4 as the number of elements in a collection of threads, which is what the usize type is for, as discussed in "Integer Types" on page 36.

Let's check the code again:

```
$ cargo check
    Checking hello v0.1.0 (file:///projects/hello)
error[E0599]: no method named `execute` found for struct `ThreadPool` in the
current scope
  --> src/main.rs:17:14
   |
17 |           pool.execute(|| {
   |                ^^^^^^^ method not found in `ThreadPool`
```

Now the error occurs because we don't have an execute method on ThreadPool. Recall from "Creating a Finite Number of Threads" on page 473 that we decided our thread pool should have an interface similar to thread::spawn. In addition, we'll implement the execute function so it takes the closure it's given and gives it to an idle thread in the pool to run.

We'll define the execute method on ThreadPool to take a closure as a parameter. Recall from "Moving Captured Values Out of Closures and the Fn Traits" on page 280 that we can take closures as parameters with three different traits: Fn, FnMut, and FnOnce. We need to decide which kind of closure to use here. We know we'll end up doing something similar to the standard library thread::spawn implementation, so we can look at what bounds the signature of thread::spawn has on its parameter. The documentation shows us the following:

```
pub fn spawn<F, T>(f: F) -> JoinHandle<T>
    where
        F: FnOnce() -> T,
```

```
    F: Send + 'static,
    T: Send + 'static,
```

The F type parameter is the one we're concerned with here; the T type parameter is related to the return value, and we're not concerned with that. We can see that spawn uses FnOnce as the trait bound on F. This is probably what we want as well, because we'll eventually pass the argument we get in execute to spawn. We can be further confident that FnOnce is the trait we want to use because the thread for running a request will only execute that request's closure one time, which matches the Once in FnOnce.

The F type parameter also has the trait bound Send and the lifetime bound 'static, which are useful in our situation: we need Send to transfer the closure from one thread to another and 'static because we don't know how long the thread will take to execute. Let's create an execute method on ThreadPool that will take a generic parameter of type F with these bounds:

src/lib.rs
```
impl ThreadPool {
    --snip--
    pub fn execute<F>(&self, f: F)
    where
        F: FnOnce()❶ + Send + 'static,
    {
    }
}
```

We still use the () after FnOnce ❶ because this FnOnce represents a closure that takes no parameters and returns the unit type (). Just like function definitions, the return type can be omitted from the signature, but even if we have no parameters, we still need the parentheses.

Again, this is the simplest implementation of the execute method: it does nothing, but we're only trying to make our code compile. Let's check it again:

```
$ cargo check
    Checking hello v0.1.0 (file:///projects/hello)
    Finished dev [unoptimized + debuginfo] target(s) in 0.24s
```

It compiles! But note that if you try cargo run and make a request in the browser, you'll see the errors in the browser that we saw at the beginning of the chapter. Our library isn't actually calling the closure passed to execute yet!

NOTE *A saying you might hear about languages with strict compilers, such as Haskell and Rust, is "if the code compiles, it works." But this saying is not universally true. Our project compiles, but it does absolutely nothing! If we were building a real, complete project, this would be a good time to start writing unit tests to check that the code compiles and has the behavior we want.*

Validating the Number of Threads in new

We aren't doing anything with the parameters to new and execute. Let's implement the bodies of these functions with the behavior we want. To start, let's think about new. Earlier we chose an unsigned type for the size parameter because a pool with a negative number of threads makes no sense. However, a pool with zero threads also makes no sense, yet zero is a perfectly valid usize. We'll add code to check that size is greater than zero before we return a ThreadPool instance and have the program panic if it receives a zero by using the assert! macro, as shown in Listing 20-13.

src/lib.rs

```
impl ThreadPool {
    /// Create a new ThreadPool.
    ///
    /// The size is the number of threads in the pool.
    ///
❶  /// # Panics
    ///
    /// The `new` function will panic if the size is zero.
    pub fn new(size: usize) -> ThreadPool {
❷      assert!(size > 0);

        ThreadPool
    }

    --snip--
}
```

Listing 20-13: Implementing ThreadPool::new to panic if size is zero

We've also added some documentation for our ThreadPool with doc comments. Note that we followed good documentation practices by adding a section that calls out the situations in which our function can panic ❶, as discussed in Chapter 14. Try running cargo doc --open and clicking the ThreadPool struct to see what the generated docs for new look like!

Instead of adding the assert! macro as we've done here ❷, we could change new into build and return a Result like we did with Config::build in the I/O project in Listing 12-9. But we've decided in this case that trying to create a thread pool without any threads should be an unrecoverable error. If you're feeling ambitious, try to write a function named build with the following signature to compare with the new function:

```
pub fn build(
    size: usize
) -> Result<ThreadPool, PoolCreationError> {
```

Creating Space to Store the Threads

Now that we have a way to know we have a valid number of threads to store in the pool, we can create those threads and store them in the ThreadPool struct before returning the struct. But how do we "store" a thread? Let's take another look at the thread::spawn signature:

```
pub fn spawn<F, T>(f: F) -> JoinHandle<T>
    where
        F: FnOnce() -> T,
        F: Send + 'static,
        T: Send + 'static,
```

The spawn function returns a JoinHandle<T>, where T is the type that the closure returns. Let's try using JoinHandle too and see what happens. In our case, the closures we're passing to the thread pool will handle the connection and not return anything, so T will be the unit type ().

The code in Listing 20-14 will compile but doesn't create any threads yet. We've changed the definition of ThreadPool to hold a vector of thread ::JoinHandle<()> instances, initialized the vector with a capacity of size, set up a for loop that will run some code to create the threads, and returned a ThreadPool instance containing them.

src/lib.rs

```
❶ use std::thread;

pub struct ThreadPool {
  ❷ threads: Vec<thread::JoinHandle<()>>,
}

impl ThreadPool {
    --snip--
    pub fn new(size: usize) -> ThreadPool {
        assert!(size > 0);

      ❸ let mut threads = Vec::with_capacity(size);

        for _ in 0..size {
            // create some threads and store them in the vector
        }

        ThreadPool { threads }
    }
    --snip--
}
```

Listing 20-14: Creating a vector for ThreadPool to hold the threads

We've brought std::thread into scope in the library crate ❶ because we're using thread::JoinHandle as the type of the items in the vector in ThreadPool ❷.

Once a valid size is received, our ThreadPool creates a new vector that can hold size items ❸. The with_capacity function performs the same task as Vec::new but with an important difference: it pre-allocates space in the vector. Because we know we need to store size elements in the vector, doing this allocation up front is slightly more efficient than using Vec::new, which resizes itself as elements are inserted.

When you run cargo check again, it should succeed.

Sending Code from the ThreadPool to a Thread

We left a comment in the for loop in Listing 20-14 regarding the creation of threads. Here, we'll look at how we actually create threads. The standard library provides thread::spawn as a way to create threads, and thread::spawn expects to get some code the thread should run as soon as the thread is created. However, in our case, we want to create the threads and have them *wait* for code that we'll send later. The standard library's implementation of threads doesn't include any way to do that; we have to implement it manually.

We'll implement this behavior by introducing a new data structure between the ThreadPool and the threads that will manage this new behavior. We'll call this data structure *Worker*, which is a common term in pooling implementations. The Worker picks up code that needs to be run and runs the code in its thread.

Think of people working in the kitchen at a restaurant: the workers wait until orders come in from customers, and then they're responsible for taking those orders and filling them.

Instead of storing a vector of JoinHandle<()> instances in the thread pool, we'll store instances of the Worker struct. Each Worker will store a single JoinHandle<()> instance. Then we'll implement a method on Worker that will take a closure of code to run and send it to the already running thread for execution. We'll also give each Worker an id so we can distinguish between the different instances of Worker in the pool when logging or debugging.

Here is the new process that will happen when we create a ThreadPool. We'll implement the code that sends the closure to the thread after we have Worker set up in this way:

1. Define a Worker struct that holds an id and a JoinHandle<()>.

2. Change ThreadPool to hold a vector of Worker instances.

3. Define a Worker::new function that takes an id number and returns a Worker instance that holds the id and a thread spawned with an empty closure.

4. In ThreadPool::new, use the for loop counter to generate an id, create a new Worker with that id, and store the Worker in the vector.

If you're up for a challenge, try implementing these changes on your own before looking at the code in Listing 20-15.

Ready? Here is Listing 20-15 with one way to make the preceding modifications.

src/lib.rs

```rust
use std::thread;

pub struct ThreadPool {
    ❶ workers: Vec<Worker>,
}

impl ThreadPool {
    --snip--
    pub fn new(size: usize) -> ThreadPool {
        assert!(size > 0);

        let mut workers = Vec::with_capacity(size);

        ❷ for id in 0..size {
            ❸ workers.push(Worker::new(id));
        }

        ThreadPool { workers }
    }
```

```
    --snip--
}

❹ struct Worker {
    id: usize,
    thread: thread::JoinHandle<()>,
}

impl Worker {
  ❺ fn new(id: usize) -> Worker {
      ❻ let thread = thread::spawn(|| {});

        Worker {❼ id,❽ thread }
    }
}
```

Listing 20-15: Modifying ThreadPool *to hold* Worker *instances instead of holding threads directly*

We've changed the name of the field on ThreadPool from threads to workers because it's now holding Worker instances instead of JoinHandle<()> instances ❶. We use the counter in the for loop ❷ as an argument to Worker::new, and we store each new Worker in the vector named workers ❸.

External code (like our server in *src/main.rs*) doesn't need to know the implementation details regarding using a Worker struct within ThreadPool, so we make the Worker struct ❹ and its new function ❺ private. The Worker::new function uses the id we give it ❼ and stores a JoinHandle<()> instance ❽ that is created by spawning a new thread using an empty closure ❻.

NOTE *If the operating system can't create a thread because there aren't enough system resources,* thread::spawn *will panic. That will cause our whole server to panic, even though the creation of some threads might succeed. For simplicity's sake, this behavior is fine, but in a production thread pool implementation, you'd likely want to use* std::thread::Builder *and its* spawn *method that returns* Result *instead.*

This code will compile and will store the number of Worker instances we specified as an argument to ThreadPool::new. But we're *still* not processing the closure that we get in execute. Let's look at how to do that next.

Sending Requests to Threads via Channels

The next problem we'll tackle is that the closures given to thread::spawn do absolutely nothing. Currently, we get the closure we want to execute in the execute method. But we need to give thread::spawn a closure to run when we create each Worker during the creation of the ThreadPool.

We want the Worker structs that we just created to fetch the code to run from a queue held in the ThreadPool and send that code to its thread to run.

The channels we learned about in Chapter 16—a simple way to communicate between two threads—would be perfect for this use case. We'll use a channel to function as the queue of jobs, and execute will send a job from the ThreadPool to the Worker instances, which will send the job to its thread. Here is the plan:

1. The ThreadPool will create a channel and hold on to the sender.
2. Each Worker will hold on to the receiver.
3. We'll create a new Job struct that will hold the closures we want to send down the channel.
4. The execute method will send the job it wants to execute through the sender.
5. In its thread, the Worker will loop over its receiver and execute the closures of any jobs it receives.

Let's start by creating a channel in ThreadPool::new and holding the sender in the ThreadPool instance, as shown in Listing 20-16. The Job struct doesn't hold anything for now but will be the type of item we're sending down the channel.

src/lib.rs

```
use std::{sync::mpsc, thread};

pub struct ThreadPool {
    workers: Vec<Worker>,
    sender: mpsc::Sender<Job>,
}

struct Job;

impl ThreadPool {
    --snip--
    pub fn new(size: usize) -> ThreadPool {
        assert!(size > 0);

      ❶ let (sender, receiver) = mpsc::channel();

        let mut workers = Vec::with_capacity(size);

        for id in 0..size {
            workers.push(Worker::new(id));
        }

        ThreadPool { workers, ❷ sender }
    }
    --snip--
}
```

Listing 20-16: Modifying ThreadPool to store the sender of a channel that transmits Job instances

In ThreadPool::new, we create our new channel ❶ and have the pool hold the sender ❷. This will successfully compile.

Let's try passing a receiver of the channel into each Worker as the thread pool creates the channel. We know we want to use the receiver in the thread that the `Worker` instances spawn, so we'll reference the receiver parameter in the closure. The code in Listing 20-17 won't quite compile yet.

src/lib.rs
```
impl ThreadPool {
    --snip--
    pub fn new(size: usize) -> ThreadPool {
        assert!(size > 0);

        let (sender, receiver) = mpsc::channel();

        let mut workers = Vec::with_capacity(size);

        for id in 0..size {
          ❶ workers.push(Worker::new(id, receiver));
        }

        ThreadPool { workers, sender }
    }
    --snip--
}

--snip--

impl Worker {
    fn new(id: usize, receiver: mpsc::Receiver<Job>) -> Worker {
        let thread = thread::spawn(|| {
          ❷ receiver;
        });

        Worker { id, thread }
    }
}
```

Listing 20-17: Passing the receiver to each Worker

We've made some small and straightforward changes: we pass the receiver into `Worker::new` ❶, and then we use it inside the closure ❷.

When we try to check this code, we get this error:

```
$ cargo check
   Checking hello v0.1.0 (file:///projects/hello)
error[E0382]: use of moved value: `receiver`
  --> src/lib.rs:26:42
   |
21 |         let (sender, receiver) = mpsc::channel();
   |                      -------- move occurs because `receiver` has type
`std::sync::mpsc::Receiver<Job>`, which does not implement the `Copy` trait
...
26 |             workers.push(Worker::new(id, receiver));
   |                                          ^^^^^^^^ value moved here, in
previous iteration of loop
```

The code is trying to pass receiver to multiple `Worker` instances. This won't work, as you'll recall from Chapter 16: the channel implementation that Rust provides is multiple *producer*, single *consumer*. This means we can't just clone the consuming end of the channel to fix this code. We also don't want to send a message multiple times to multiple consumers; we want one list of messages with multiple `Worker` instances such that each message gets processed once.

Additionally, taking a job off the channel queue involves mutating the receiver, so the threads need a safe way to share and modify receiver; otherwise, we might get race conditions (as covered in Chapter 16).

Recall the thread-safe smart pointers discussed in Chapter 16: to share ownership across multiple threads and allow the threads to mutate the value, we need to use `Arc<Mutex<T>>`. The `Arc` type will let multiple `Worker` instances own the receiver, and `Mutex` will ensure that only one `Worker` gets a job from the receiver at a time. Listing 20-18 shows the changes we need to make.

src/lib.rs
```
use std::{
    sync::{mpsc, Arc, Mutex},
    thread,
};
--snip--

impl ThreadPool {
    --snip--
    pub fn new(size: usize) -> ThreadPool {
        assert!(size > 0);

        let (sender, receiver) = mpsc::channel();

    ❶ let receiver = Arc::new(Mutex::new(receiver));

        let mut workers = Vec::with_capacity(size);

        for id in 0..size {
            workers.push(
                Worker::new(id, Arc::clone(&❷receiver))
            );
        }

        ThreadPool { workers, sender }
    }

    --snip--
}

--snip--

impl Worker {
    fn new(
        id: usize,
        receiver: Arc<Mutex<mpsc::Receiver<Job>>>,
    ) -> Worker {
        --snip--
    }
}
```

Listing 20-18: Sharing the receiver among the `Worker` instances using `Arc` and `Mutex`

In `ThreadPool::new`, we put the receiver in an `Arc` and a `Mutex` ❶. For each new `Worker`, we clone the `Arc` to bump the reference count so the `Worker` instances can share ownership of the receiver ❷.

With these changes, the code compiles! We're getting there!

Implementing the execute Method

Let's finally implement the execute method on `ThreadPool`. We'll also change `Job` from a struct to a type alias for a trait object that holds the type of closure that execute receives. As discussed in "Creating Type Synonyms with Type Aliases" on page 440, type aliases allow us to make long types shorter for ease of use. Look at Listing 20-19.

src/lib.rs

```
--snip--

type Job = Box<dyn FnOnce() + Send + 'static>;

impl ThreadPool {
    --snip--

    pub fn execute<F>(&self, f: F)
    where
        F: FnOnce() + Send + 'static,
    {
      ❶ let job = Box::new(f);

      ❷ self.sender.send(job).unwrap();
    }
}

--snip--
```

Listing 20-19: Creating a `Job` type alias for a `Box` that holds each closure and then sending the job down the channel

After creating a new `Job` instance using the closure we get in execute ❶, we send that job down the sending end of the channel ❷. We're calling unwrap on send for the case that sending fails. This might happen if, for example, we stop all our threads from executing, meaning the receiving end has stopped receiving new messages. At the moment, we can't stop our threads from executing: our threads continue executing as long as the pool exists. The reason we use unwrap is that we know the failure case won't happen, but the compiler doesn't know that.

But we're not quite done yet! In the `Worker`, our closure being passed to `thread::spawn` still only *references* the receiving end of the channel. Instead, we need the closure to loop forever, asking the receiving end of the channel for a job and running the job when it gets one. Let's make the change shown in Listing 20-20 to `Worker::new`.

src/lib.rs

```
--snip--

impl Worker {
    fn new(
```

```
        id: usize,
        receiver: Arc<Mutex<mpsc::Receiver<Job>>>,
    ) -> Worker {
        let thread = thread::spawn(move || loop {
            let job = receiver
        ❶ .lock()
        ❷ .unwrap()
        ❸ .recv()
        ❹ .unwrap();

            println!("Worker {id} got a job; executing.");

            job();
        });

        Worker { id, thread }
    }
}
```

Listing 20-20: Receiving and executing the jobs in the Worker *instance's thread*

Here, we first call lock on the receiver to acquire the mutex ❶, and then we call unwrap to panic on any errors ❷. Acquiring a lock might fail if the mutex is in a *poisoned* state, which can happen if some other thread panicked while holding the lock rather than releasing the lock. In this situation, calling unwrap to have this thread panic is the correct action to take. Feel free to change this unwrap to an expect with an error message that is meaningful to you.

If we get the lock on the mutex, we call recv to receive a Job from the channel ❸. A final unwrap moves past any errors here as well ❹, which might occur if the thread holding the sender has shut down, similar to how the send method returns Err if the receiver shuts down.

The call to recv blocks, so if there is no job yet, the current thread will wait until a job becomes available. The Mutex<T> ensures that only one Worker thread at a time is trying to request a job.

Our thread pool is now in a working state! Give it a cargo run and make some requests:

```
$ cargo run
   Compiling hello v0.1.0 (file:///projects/hello)
warning: field is never read: `workers`
 --> src/lib.rs:7:5
  |
7 |     workers: Vec<Worker>,
  |     ^^^^^^^^^^^^^^^^^^^^
  |
  = note: `#[warn(dead_code)]` on by default

warning: field is never read: `id`
  --> src/lib.rs:48:5
   |
48 |     id: usize,
   |     ^^^^^^^^^
```

```
warning: field is never read: `thread`
  --> src/lib.rs:49:5
   |
49 |       thread: thread::JoinHandle<()>,
   |       ^^^^^^^^^^^^^^^^^^^^^^^^^^^^^^^

warning: `hello` (lib) generated 3 warnings
    Finished dev [unoptimized + debuginfo] target(s) in 1.40s
     Running `target/debug/hello`
Worker 0 got a job; executing.
Worker 2 got a job; executing.
Worker 1 got a job; executing.
Worker 3 got a job; executing.
Worker 0 got a job; executing.
Worker 2 got a job; executing.
Worker 1 got a job; executing.
Worker 3 got a job; executing.
Worker 0 got a job; executing.
Worker 2 got a job; executing.
```

Success! We now have a thread pool that executes connections asynchronously. There are never more than four threads created, so our system won't get overloaded if the server receives a lot of requests. If we make a request to */sleep*, the server will be able to serve other requests by having another thread run them.

NOTE *If you open /sleep in multiple browser windows simultaneously, they might load one at a time in five-second intervals. Some web browsers execute multiple instances of the same request sequentially for caching reasons. This limitation is not caused by our web server.*

After learning about the while let loop in Chapter 18, you might be wondering why we didn't write the Worker thread code as shown in Listing 20-21.

src/lib.rs
```
--snip--

impl Worker {
    fn new(
        id: usize,
        receiver: Arc<Mutex<mpsc::Receiver<Job>>>,
    ) -> Worker {
        let thread = thread::spawn(move || {
            while let Ok(job) = receiver.lock().unwrap().recv() {
                println!("Worker {id} got a job; executing.");

                job();
            }
        });

        Worker { id, thread }
    }
}
```

Listing 20-21: An alternative implementation of Worker::new using while let

This code compiles and runs but doesn't result in the desired threading behavior: a slow request will still cause other requests to wait to be processed. The reason is somewhat subtle: the `Mutex` struct has no public unlock method because the ownership of the lock is based on the lifetime of the `MutexGuard<T>` within the `LockResult<MutexGuard<T>>` that the lock method returns. At compile time, the borrow checker can then enforce the rule that a resource guarded by a `Mutex` cannot be accessed unless we hold the lock. However, this implementation can also result in the lock being held longer than intended if we aren't mindful of the lifetime of the `MutexGuard<T>`.

The code in Listing 20-20 that uses `let job = receiver.lock().unwrap()` `.recv().unwrap();` works because with `let`, any temporary values used in the expression on the right-hand side of the equal sign are immediately dropped when the `let` statement ends. However, `while let` (and `if let` and `match`) does not drop temporary values until the end of the associated block. In Listing 20-21, the lock remains held for the duration of the call to `job()`, meaning other `Worker` instances cannot receive jobs.

Graceful Shutdown and Cleanup

The code in Listing 20-20 is responding to requests asynchronously through the use of a thread pool, as we intended. We get some warnings about the `workers`, `id`, and `thread` fields that we're not using in a direct way that reminds us we're not cleaning up anything. When we use the less elegant CTRL-C method to halt the main thread, all other threads are stopped immediately as well, even if they're in the middle of serving a request.

Next, then, we'll implement the `Drop` trait to call join on each of the threads in the pool so they can finish the requests they're working on before closing. Then we'll implement a way to tell the threads they should stop accepting new requests and shut down. To see this code in action, we'll modify our server to accept only two requests before gracefully shutting down its thread pool.

Implementing the Drop Trait on ThreadPool

Let's start with implementing `Drop` on our thread pool. When the pool is dropped, our threads should all join to make sure they finish their work. Listing 20-22 shows a first attempt at a `Drop` implementation; this code won't quite work yet.

`src/lib.rs`
```
impl Drop for ThreadPool {
    fn drop(&mut self) {
      ❶ for worker in &mut self.workers {
          ❷ println!("Shutting down worker {}", worker.id);

          ❸ worker.thread.join().unwrap();
        }
    }
}
```

Listing 20-22: Joining each thread when the thread pool goes out of scope

First we loop through each of the thread pool workers ❶. We use &mut for this because self is a mutable reference, and we also need to be able to mutate worker. For each worker, we print a message saying that this particular Worker instance is shutting down ❷, and then we call join on that Worker instance's thread ❸. If the call to join fails, we use unwrap to make Rust panic and go into an ungraceful shutdown.

Here is the error we get when we compile this code:

```
error[E0507]: cannot move out of `worker.thread` which is behind a mutable
reference
  --> src/lib.rs:52:13
   |
52 |             worker.thread.join().unwrap();
   |             ^^^^^^^^^^^^^ ------ `worker.thread` moved due to this
method call
   |             |
   |             move occurs because `worker.thread` has type
`JoinHandle<()>`, which does not implement the `Copy` trait
   |
note: this function takes ownership of the receiver `self`, which moves
`worker.thread`
```

The error tells us we can't call join because we only have a mutable borrow of each worker and join takes ownership of its argument. To solve this issue, we need to move the thread out of the Worker instance that owns thread so join can consume the thread. We did this in Listing 17-15: if Worker holds an Option<thread::JoinHandle<()>> instead, we can call the take method on the Option to move the value out of the Some variant and leave a None variant in its place. In other words, a Worker that is running will have a Some variant in thread, and when we want to clean up a Worker, we'll replace Some with None so the Worker doesn't have a thread to run.

So we know we want to update the definition of Worker like this:

src/lib.rs
```
struct Worker {
    id: usize,
    thread: Option<thread::JoinHandle<()>>,
}
```

Now let's lean on the compiler to find the other places that need to change. Checking this code, we get two errors:

```
error[E0599]: no method named `join` found for enum `Option` in the current
scope
  --> src/lib.rs:52:27
   |
52 |             worker.thread.join().unwrap();
   |                           ^^^^ method not found in
`Option<JoinHandle<()>>`

error[E0308]: mismatched types
  --> src/lib.rs:72:22
```

```
       |
72 |            Worker { id, thread }
       |                        ^^^^^^ expected enum `Option`, found struct
`JoinHandle`
       |
    = note: expected enum `Option<JoinHandle<()>>`
                found struct `JoinHandle<_>`
help: try wrapping the expression in `Some`
       |
72 |            Worker { id, thread: Some(thread) }
       |                        +++++++++++++       +
```

Let's address the second error, which points to the code at the end of Worker::new; we need to wrap the thread value in Some when we create a new Worker. Make the following changes to fix this error:

src/lib.rs
```
impl Worker {
    fn new(
        id: usize,
        receiver: Arc<Mutex<mpsc::Receiver<Job>>>,
    ) -> Worker {
        --snip--

        Worker {
            id,
            thread: Some(thread),
        }
    }
}
```

The first error is in our Drop implementation. We mentioned earlier that we intended to call take on the Option value to move thread out of worker. The following changes will do so:

src/lib.rs
```
impl Drop for ThreadPool {
    fn drop(&mut self) {
        for worker in &mut self.workers {
            println!("Shutting down worker {}", worker.id);

          ❶ if let Some(thread) = worker.thread.take() {
              ❷ thread.join().unwrap();
            }
        }
    }
}
```

As discussed in Chapter 17, the take method on Option takes the Some variant out and leaves None in its place. We're using if let to destructure the Some and get the thread ❶; then we call join on the thread ❷. If a Worker instance's thread is already None, we know that Worker has already had its thread cleaned up, so nothing happens in that case.

Signaling to the Threads to Stop Listening for Jobs

With all the changes we've made, our code compiles without any warnings. However, the bad news is that this code doesn't function the way we want it to yet. The key is the logic in the closures run by the threads of the Worker instances: at the moment, we call join, but that won't shut down the threads, because they loop forever looking for jobs. If we try to drop our ThreadPool with our current implementation of drop, the main thread will block forever, waiting for the first thread to finish.

To fix this problem, we'll need a change in the ThreadPool drop implementation and then a change in the Worker loop.

First we'll change the ThreadPool drop implementation to explicitly drop the sender before waiting for the threads to finish. Listing 20-23 shows the changes to ThreadPool to explicitly drop sender. We use the same Option and take technique as we did with the thread to be able to move sender out of ThreadPool.

src/lib.rs
```
pub struct ThreadPool {
    workers: Vec<Worker>,
    sender: Option<mpsc::Sender<Job>>,
}
--snip--
impl ThreadPool {
    pub fn new(size: usize) -> ThreadPool {
        --snip--

        ThreadPool {
            workers,
            sender: Some(sender),
        }
    }

    pub fn execute<F>(&self, f: F)
    where
        F: FnOnce() + Send + 'static,
    {
        let job = Box::new(f);

        self.sender
            .as_ref()
            .unwrap()
            .send(job)
            .unwrap();
    }
}

impl Drop for ThreadPool {
    fn drop(&mut self) {
        ❶ drop(self.sender.take());
```

```
        for worker in &mut self.workers {
            println!("Shutting down worker {}", worker.id);

            if let Some(thread) = worker.thread.take() {
                thread.join().unwrap();
            }
        }
    }
}
```

Listing 20-23: Explicitly dropping sender before joining the Worker threads

Dropping sender ❶ closes the channel, which indicates no more messages will be sent. When that happens, all the calls to recv that the Worker
instances do in the infinite loop will return an error. In Listing 20-24, we
change the Worker loop to gracefully exit the loop in that case, which means
the threads will finish when the ThreadPool drop implementation calls join
on them.

src/lib.rs
```
impl Worker {
    fn new(
        id: usize,
        receiver: Arc<Mutex<mpsc::Receiver<Job>>>,
    ) -> Worker {
        let thread = thread::spawn(move || loop {
            let message = receiver.lock().unwrap().recv();

            match message {
                Ok(job) => {
                    println!(
                        "Worker {id} got a job; executing."
                    );

                    job();
                }
                Err(_) => {
                    println!(
                        "Worker {id} shutting down."
                    );
                    break;
                }
            }
        });

        Worker {
            id,
            thread: Some(thread),
        }
    }
}
```

Listing 20-24: Explicitly breaking out of the loop when recv returns an error

To see this code in action, let's modify main to accept only two requests before gracefully shutting down the server, as shown in Listing 20-25.

src/main.rs

```
fn main() {
    let listener = TcpListener::bind("127.0.0.1:7878").unwrap();
    let pool = ThreadPool::new(4);

    for stream in listener.incoming().take(2) {
        let stream = stream.unwrap();

        pool.execute(|| {
            handle_connection(stream);
        });
    }

    println!("Shutting down.");
}
```

Listing 20-25: Shutting down the server after serving two requests by exiting the loop

You wouldn't want a real-world web server to shut down after serving only two requests. This code just demonstrates that the graceful shutdown and cleanup is in working order.

The take method is defined in the Iterator trait and limits the iteration to the first two items at most. The ThreadPool will go out of scope at the end of main, and the drop implementation will run.

Start the server with cargo run, and make three requests. The third request should error, and in your terminal you should see output similar to this:

```
$ cargo run
   Compiling hello v0.1.0 (file:///projects/hello)
    Finished dev [unoptimized + debuginfo] target(s) in 1.0s
     Running `target/debug/hello`
Worker 0 got a job; executing.
Shutting down.
Shutting down worker 0
Worker 3 got a job; executing.
Worker 1 disconnected; shutting down.
Worker 2 disconnected; shutting down.
Worker 3 disconnected; shutting down.
Worker 0 disconnected; shutting down.
Shutting down worker 1
Shutting down worker 2
Shutting down worker 3
```

You might see a different ordering of Worker IDs and messages printed. We can see how this code works from the messages: Worker instances 0 and 3 got the first two requests. The server stopped accepting connections after the second connection, and the Drop implementation on ThreadPool starts executing before Worker 3 even starts its job. Dropping the sender disconnects all the Worker instances and tells them to shut down. The Worker instances each print a message when they disconnect, and then the thread pool calls join to wait for each Worker thread to finish.

Notice one interesting aspect of this particular execution: the ThreadPool dropped the sender, and before any Worker received an error, we tried to join Worker 0. Worker 0 had not yet gotten an error from recv, so the main thread blocked, waiting for Worker 0 to finish. In the meantime, Worker 3 received a job and then all threads received an error. When Worker 0 finished, the main thread waited for the rest of the Worker instances to finish. At that point, they had all exited their loops and stopped.

Congrats! We've now completed our project; we have a basic web server that uses a thread pool to respond asynchronously. We're able to perform a graceful shutdown of the server, which cleans up all the threads in the pool. See *https://nostarch.com/rust-programming-language-2nd-edition* to download the full code for this chapter for reference.

We could do more here! If you want to continue enhancing this project, here are some ideas:

- Add more documentation to ThreadPool and its public methods.
- Add tests of the library's functionality.
- Change calls to unwrap to more robust error handling.
- Use ThreadPool to perform some task other than serving web requests.
- Find a thread pool crate on *https://crates.io* and implement a similar web server using the crate instead. Then compare its API and robustness to the thread pool we implemented.

Summary

Well done! You've made it to the end of the book! We want to thank you for joining us on this tour of Rust. You're now ready to implement your own Rust projects and help with other people's projects. Keep in mind that there is a welcoming community of other Rustaceans who would love to help you with any challenges you encounter on your Rust journey.

A

KEYWORDS

The following lists contain keywords that are reserved for current or future use by the Rust language. As such, they cannot be used as identifiers (except as raw identifiers, as we discuss in "Raw Identifiers" on page 497). *Identifiers* are names of functions, variables, parameters, struct fields, modules, crates, constants, macros, static values, attributes, types, traits, or lifetimes.

Keywords Currently in Use

The following is a list of keywords currently in use, with their functionality described.

as   perform primitive casting, disambiguate the specific trait containing an item, or rename items in use statements

async   return a Future instead of blocking the current thread

await   suspend execution until the result of a Future is ready

break   exit a loop immediately

const   define constant items or constant raw pointers

continue   continue to the next loop iteration

crate   in a module path, refers to the crate root

dyn   dynamic dispatch to a trait object

else   fallback for if and if let control flow constructs

enum   define an enumeration

extern   link an external function or variable

false   Boolean false literal

fn   define a function or the function pointer type

for   loop over items from an iterator, implement a trait, or specify a higher-ranked lifetime

if   branch based on the result of a conditional expression

impl   implement inherent or trait functionality

in   part of for loop syntax

let   bind a variable

loop   loop unconditionally

match   match a value to patterns

mod   define a module

move   make a closure take ownership of all its captures

mut   denote mutability in references, raw pointers, or pattern bindings

pub   denote public visibility in struct fields, impl blocks, or modules

ref   bind by reference

return   return from function

Self   a type alias for the type we are defining or implementing

self   method subject or current module

static   global variable or lifetime lasting the entire program execution

struct   define a structure

super   parent module of the current module

trait   define a trait

true   Boolean true literal

type   define a type alias or associated type

union   define a union; is a keyword only when used in a union declaration

unsafe   denote unsafe code, functions, traits, or implementations

use   bring symbols into scope

where   denote clauses that constrain a type

while   loop conditionally based on the result of an expression

Keywords Reserved for Future Use

The following keywords do not yet have any functionality but are reserved by Rust for potential future use:

- abstract
- become
- box
- do
- final
- macro
- override
- priv
- try
- typeof
- unsized
- virtual
- yield

Raw Identifiers

Raw identifiers are the syntax that lets you use keywords where they wouldn't normally be allowed. You use a raw identifier by prefixing a keyword with r#.

For example, match is a keyword. If you try to compile the following function that uses match as its name:

src/main.rs
```
fn match(needle: &str, haystack: &str) -> bool {
    haystack.contains(needle)
}
```

you'll get this error:

```
error: expected identifier, found keyword `match`
 --> src/main.rs:4:4
  |
4 | fn match(needle: &str, haystack: &str) -> bool {
  |    ^^^^^ expected identifier, found keyword
```

The error shows that you can't use the keyword match as the function identifier. To use match as a function name, you need to use the raw identifier syntax, like this:

src/main.rs
```
fn r#match(needle: &str, haystack: &str) -> bool {
    haystack.contains(needle)
}

fn main() {
    assert!(r#match("foo", "foobar"));
}
```

This code will compile without any errors. Note the r# prefix on the function name in its definition as well as where the function is called in main.

Raw identifiers allow you to use any word you choose as an identifier, even if that word happens to be a reserved keyword. This gives us more freedom to choose identifier names, as well as lets us integrate with programs written in a language where these words aren't keywords. In addition, raw identifiers allow you to use libraries written in a different Rust edition than your crate uses. For example, try isn't a keyword in the 2015 edition but is in the 2018 and 2021 editions. If you depend on a library that is written using the 2015 edition and has a try function, you'll need to use the raw identifier syntax, r#try in this case, to call that function from your 2021 edition code. See Appendix E for more information on editions.

B

OPERATORS AND SYMBOLS

 This appendix contains a glossary of Rust's syntax, including operators and other symbols that appear by themselves or in the context of paths, generics, trait bounds, macros, attributes, comments, tuples, and brackets.

Operators

Table B-1 contains the operators in Rust, an example of how the operator would appear in context, a short explanation, and whether that operator is overloadable. If an operator is overloadable, the relevant trait to use to overload that operator is listed.

Table B-1: Operators

Operator	Example	Explanation	Overloadable?
!	ident!(...), ident!{...}, ident![...]	Macro expansion	
!	!expr	Bitwise or logical complement	Not
!=	expr != expr	Nonequality comparison	PartialEq
%	expr % expr	Arithmetic remainder	Rem
%=	var %= expr	Arithmetic remainder and assignment	RemAssign
&	&expr, &mut expr	Borrow	
&	&type, &mut type, &'a type, &'a mut type	Borrowed pointer type	
&	expr & expr	Bitwise AND	BitAnd
&=	var &= expr	Bitwise AND and assignment	BitAndAssign
&&	expr && expr	Short-circuiting logical AND	
*	expr * expr	Arithmetic multiplication	Mul
*=	var *= expr	Arithmetic multiplication and assignment	MulAssign
*	*expr	Dereference	Deref
*	*const type, *mut type	Raw pointer	
+	trait + trait, 'a + trait	Compound type constraint	
+	expr + expr	Arithmetic addition	Add
+=	var += expr	Arithmetic addition and assignment	AddAssign
,	expr, expr	Argument and element separator	
-	- expr	Arithmetic negation	Neg
-	expr - expr	Arithmetic subtraction	Sub
-=	var -= expr	Arithmetic subtraction and assignment	SubAssign
->	fn(...) -> type, |...| -> type	Function and closure return type	
.	expr.ident	Member access	
..	.., expr.., ..expr, expr..expr	Right-exclusive range literal	PartialOrd
..=	..=expr, expr..=expr	Right-inclusive range literal	PartialOrd

Operator	Example	Explanation	Overloadable?
..	..expr	Struct literal update syntax	
..	variant(x, ..), struct_ type { x, .. }	"And the rest" pattern binding	
...	expr...expr	(Deprecated, use ..= instead) In a pattern: inclusive range pattern	
/	expr / expr	Arithmetic division	Div
/=	var /= expr	Arithmetic division and assignment	DivAssign
:	pat: type, ident: type	Constraints	
:	ident: expr	Struct field initializer	
:	'a: loop {...}	Loop label	
;	expr;	Statement and item terminator	
;	[...; len]	Part of fixed-size array syntax	
<<	expr << expr	Left-shift	Shl
<<=	var <<= expr	Left-shift and assignment	ShlAssign
<	expr < expr	Less than comparison	PartialOrd
<=	expr <= expr	Less than or equal to comparison	PartialOrd
=	var = expr, ident = type	Assignment/equivalence	
==	expr == expr	Equality comparison	PartialEq
=>	pat => expr	Part of match arm syntax	
>	expr > expr	Greater than comparison	PartialOrd
>=	expr >= expr	Greater than or equal to comparison	PartialOrd
>>	expr >> expr	Right-shift	Shr
>>=	var >>= expr	Right-shift and assignment	ShrAssign
@	ident @ pat	Pattern binding	
^	expr ^ expr	Bitwise exclusive OR	BitXor
^=	var ^= expr	Bitwise exclusive OR and assignment	BitXorAssign
|	pat | pat	Pattern alternatives	
|	expr | expr	Bitwise OR	BitOr
|=	var |= expr	Bitwise OR and assignment	BitOrAssign
||	expr || expr	Short-circuiting logical OR	
?	expr?	Error propagation	

Non-operator Symbols

The following tables contain all symbols that don't function as operators; that is, they don't behave like a function or method call.

Table B-2 shows symbols that appear on their own and are valid in a variety of locations.

Table B-2: Stand-Alone Syntax

Symbol	Explanation
`'ident`	Named lifetime or loop label
`...u8, ...i32, ...f64, ...usize,` and so on	Numeric literal of specific type
`"..."`	String literal
`r"...", r#"..."#, r##"..."##,` and so on	Raw string literal; escape characters not processed
`b"..."`	Byte string literal; constructs an array of bytes instead of a string
`br"...", br#"..."#, br##"..."##,` and so on	Raw byte string literal; combination of raw and byte string literal
`'...'`	Character literal
`b'...'`	ASCII byte literal
`|...| expr`	Closure
`!`	Always-empty bottom type for diverging functions
`_`	"Ignored" pattern binding; also used to make integer literals readable

Table B-3 shows symbols that appear in the context of a path through the module hierarchy to an item.

Table B-3: Path-Related Syntax

Symbol	Explanation
`ident::ident`	Namespace path
`::path`	Path relative to the crate root (that is, an explicitly absolute path)
`self::path`	Path relative to the current module (that is, an explicitly relative path)
`super::path`	Path relative to the parent of the current module
`type::ident,` `<type as trait>::ident`	Associated constants, functions, and types
`<type>::...`	Associated item for a type that cannot be directly named (for example, `<&T>::...`, `<[T]>::...`, and so on)

Symbol	Explanation
`trait::method(...)`	Disambiguating a method call by naming the trait that defines it
`type::method(...)`	Disambiguating a method call by naming the type for which it's defined
`<type as trait>::method(...)`	Disambiguating a method call by naming the trait and type

Table B-4 shows symbols that appear in the context of using generic type parameters.

Table B-4: Generics

Symbol	Explanation
`path<...>`	Specifies parameters to a generic type in a type (for example, `Vec<u8>`)
`path::<...>, method::<...>`	Specifies parameters to a generic type, function, or method in an expression; often referred to as turbofish (for example, `"42".parse::<i32>()`)
`fn ident<...> ...`	Define generic function
`struct ident<...> ...`	Define generic structure
`enum ident<...> ...`	Define generic enumeration
`impl<...> ...`	Define generic implementation
`for<...> type`	Higher-ranked lifetime bounds
`type<ident=type>`	A generic type where one or more associated types have specific assignments (for example, `Iterator<Item=T>`)

Table B-5 shows symbols that appear in the context of constraining generic type parameters with trait bounds.

Table B-5: Trait Bound Constraints

Symbol	Explanation
`T: U`	Generic parameter T constrained to types that implement U
`T: 'a`	Generic type T must outlive lifetime `'a` (meaning the type cannot transitively contain any references with lifetimes shorter than `'a`)
`T: 'static`	Generic type T contains no borrowed references other than `'static` ones
`'b: 'a`	Generic lifetime `'b` must outlive lifetime `'a`
`T: ?Sized`	Allow generic type parameter to be a dynamically sized type
`'a + trait, trait + trait`	Compound type constraint

Table B-6 shows symbols that appear in the context of calling or defining macros and specifying attributes on an item.

Table B-6: Macros and Attributes

Symbol	Explanation
#[meta]	Outer attribute
#![meta]	Inner attribute
$ident	Macro substitution
$ident:kind	Macro capture
$(...)...	Macro repetition
ident!(...), ident!{...}, ident![...]	Macro invocation

Table B-7 shows symbols that create comments.

Table B-7: Comments

Symbol	Explanation
//	Line comment
//!	Inner line doc comment
///	Outer line doc comment
/*...*/	Block comment
/*!...*/	Inner block doc comment
/**...*/	Outer block doc comment

Table B-8 shows symbols that appear in the context of using tuples.

Table B-8: Tuples

Symbol	Explanation
()	Empty tuple (aka unit), both literal and type
(expr)	Parenthesized expression
(expr,)	Single-element tuple expression
(type,)	Single-element tuple type
(expr, ...)	Tuple expression
(type, ...)	Tuple type
expr(expr, ...)	Function call expression; also used to initialize tuple structs and tuple enum variants
expr.0, expr.1, and so on	Tuple indexing

Table B-9 shows the contexts in which curly brackets are used.

Table B-9: Curly Brackets

Context	Explanation
{...}	Block expression
Type {...}	Struct literal

Table B-10 shows the contexts in which square brackets are used.

Table B-10: Square Brackets

Context	Explanation
[...]	Array literal
[expr; len]	Array literal containing len copies of expr
[type; len]	Array type containing len instances of type
expr[expr]	Collection indexing; overloadable (Index, IndexMut)
expr[..], expr[a..], expr[..b], expr[a..b]	Collection indexing pretending to be collection slicing, using Range, RangeFrom, RangeTo, or RangeFull as the "index"

C

DERIVABLE TRAITS

In various places in the book, we've discussed the derive attribute, which you can apply to a struct or enum definition. The derive attribute generates code that will implement a trait with its own default implementation on the type you've annotated with the derive syntax.

In this appendix, we provide a reference of all the traits in the standard library that you can use with derive. Each section covers:

- What operators and methods deriving this trait will enable
- What the implementation of the trait provided by derive does
- What implementing the trait signifies about the type
- The conditions in which you're allowed or not allowed to implement the trait
- Examples of operations that require the trait

If you want different behavior from that provided by the derive attribute, consult the standard library documentation for each trait for details on how to manually implement them.

The traits listed here are the only ones defined by the standard library that can be implemented on your types using derive. Other traits defined in the standard library don't have sensible default behavior, so it's up to you to implement them in the way that makes sense for what you're trying to accomplish.

An example of a trait that can't be derived is Display, which handles formatting for end users. You should always consider the appropriate way to display a type to an end user. What parts of the type should an end user be allowed to see? What parts would they find relevant? What format of the data would be most relevant to them? The Rust compiler doesn't have this insight, so it can't provide appropriate default behavior for you.

The list of derivable traits provided in this appendix is not comprehensive: libraries can implement derive for their own traits, making the list of traits you can use derive with truly open ended. Implementing derive involves using a procedural macro, which is covered in "Macros" on page 449.

Debug for Programmer Output

The Debug trait enables debug formatting in format strings, which you indicate by adding :? within {} placeholders.

The Debug trait allows you to print instances of a type for debugging purposes, so you and other programmers using your type can inspect an instance at a particular point in a program's execution.

The Debug trait is required, for example, in the use of the assert_eq! macro. This macro prints the values of instances given as arguments if the equality assertion fails so programmers can see why the two instances weren't equal.

PartialEq and Eq for Equality Comparisons

The PartialEq trait allows you to compare instances of a type to check for equality and enables use of the == and != operators.

Deriving PartialEq implements the eq method. When PartialEq is derived on structs, two instances are equal only if *all* fields are equal, and the instances are not equal if *any* fields are not equal. When derived on enums, each variant is equal to itself and not equal to the other variants.

The PartialEq trait is required, for example, with the use of the assert_eq! macro, which needs to be able to compare two instances of a type for equality.

The Eq trait has no methods. Its purpose is to signal that for every value of the annotated type, the value is equal to itself. The Eq trait can only be applied to types that also implement PartialEq, although not all types that implement PartialEq can implement Eq. One example of this is floating-point number types: the implementation of floating-point numbers states that two instances of the not-a-number (NaN) value are not equal to each other.

An example of when `Eq` is required is for keys in a `HashMap<K, V>` so that the `HashMap<K, V>` can tell whether two keys are the same.

PartialOrd and Ord for Ordering Comparisons

The `PartialOrd` trait allows you to compare instances of a type for sorting purposes. A type that implements `PartialOrd` can be used with the `<`, `>`, `<=`, and `>=` operators. You can only apply the `PartialOrd` trait to types that also implement `PartialEq`.

Deriving `PartialOrd` implements the `partial_cmp` method, which returns an `Option<Ordering>` that will be `None` when the values given don't produce an ordering. An example of a value that doesn't produce an ordering, even though most values of that type can be compared, is the `NaN` floating point value. Calling `partial_cmp` with any floating-point number and the `NaN` floating-point value will return `None`.

When derived on structs, `PartialOrd` compares two instances by comparing the value in each field in the order in which the fields appear in the struct definition. When derived on enums, variants of the enum declared earlier in the enum definition are considered less than the variants listed later.

The `PartialOrd` trait is required, for example, for the `gen_range` method from the `rand` crate that generates a random value in the range specified by a range expression.

The `Ord` trait allows you to know that for any two values of the annotated type, a valid ordering will exist. The `Ord` trait implements the `cmp` method, which returns an `Ordering` rather than an `Option<Ordering>` because a valid ordering will always be possible. You can only apply the `Ord` trait to types that also implement `PartialOrd` and `Eq` (and `Eq` requires `PartialEq`). When derived on structs and enums, `cmp` behaves the same way as the derived implementation for `partial_cmp` does with `PartialOrd`.

An example of when `Ord` is required is when storing values in a `BTreeSet<T>`, a data structure that stores data based on the sort order of the values.

Clone and Copy for Duplicating Values

The `Clone` trait allows you to explicitly create a deep copy of a value, and the duplication process might involve running arbitrary code and copying heap data. See "Variables and Data Interacting with Clone" on page 67 for more information on Clone.

Deriving `Clone` implements the `clone` method, which when implemented for the whole type, calls `clone` on each of the parts of the type. This means all the fields or values in the type must also implement `Clone` to derive `Clone`.

An example of when `Clone` is required is when calling the `to_vec` method on a slice. The slice doesn't own the type instances it contains, but the vector returned from `to_vec` will need to own its instances, so `to_vec` calls `clone` on each item. Thus the type stored in the slice must implement `Clone`.

The `Copy` trait allows you to duplicate a value by only copying bits stored on the stack; no arbitrary code is necessary. See "Stack-Only Data: Copy" on page 68 for more information on Copy.

The Copy trait doesn't define any methods to prevent programmers from overloading those methods and violating the assumption that no arbitrary code is being run. That way, all programmers can assume that copying a value will be very fast.

You can derive Copy on any type whose parts all implement Copy. A type that implements Copy must also implement Clone because a type that implements Copy has a trivial implementation of Clone that performs the same task as Copy.

The Copy trait is rarely required; types that implement Copy have optimizations available, meaning you don't have to call clone, which makes the code more concise.

Everything possible with Copy you can also accomplish with Clone, but the code might be slower or have to use clone in places.

Hash for Mapping a Value to a Value of Fixed Size

The Hash trait allows you to take an instance of a type of arbitrary size and map that instance to a value of fixed size using a hash function. Deriving Hash implements the hash method. The derived implementation of the hash method combines the result of calling hash on each of the parts of the type, meaning all fields or values must also implement Hash to derive Hash.

An example of when Hash is required is in storing keys in a HashMap<K, V> to store data efficiently.

Default for Default Values

The Default trait allows you to create a default value for a type. Deriving Default implements the default function. The derived implementation of the default function calls the default function on each part of the type, meaning all fields or values in the type must also implement Default to derive Default.

The Default::default function is commonly used in combination with the struct update syntax discussed in "Creating Instances from Other Instances with Struct Update Syntax" on page 88. You can customize a few fields of a struct and then set and use a default value for the rest of the fields by using ..Default::default().

The Default trait is required when you use the method unwrap_or_default on Option<T> instances, for example. If the Option<T> is None, the method unwrap_or_default will return the result of Default::default for the type T stored in the Option<T>.

D

USEFUL DEVELOPMENT TOOLS

 In this appendix, we talk about some useful development tools that the Rust project provides. We'll look at automatic formatting, quick ways to apply warning fixes, a linter, and integrating with IDEs.

Automatic Formatting with rustfmt

The rustfmt tool reformats your code according to the community code style. Many collaborative projects use rustfmt to prevent arguments about which style to use when writing Rust: everyone formats their code using the tool.

Rust installations include rustfmt by default, so you should already have the programs rustfmt and cargo-fmt on your system. These two commands are analogous to rustc and cargo in that rustfmt allows finer-grained control and cargo-fmt understands conventions of a project that uses Cargo. To format any Cargo project, enter the following:

```
$ cargo fmt
```

Running this command reformats all the Rust code in the current crate. This should only change the code style, not the code semantics. For more information on rustfmt, see its documentation at *https://github.com/rust-lang/rustfmt.*

Fix Your Code with rustfix

The rustfix tool is included with Rust installations and can automatically fix compiler warnings that have a clear way to correct the problem that's likely what you want. You've probably seen compiler warnings before. For example, consider this code:

src/main.rs
```
fn do_something() {}

fn main() {
    for i in 0..100 {
        do_something();
    }
}
```

Here, we're calling the do_something function 100 times, but we never use the variable i in the body of the for loop. Rust warns us about that:

```
$ cargo build
   Compiling myprogram v0.1.0 (file:///projects/myprogram)
warning: unused variable: `i`
 --> src/main.rs:4:9
  |
4 |     for i in 0..100 {
  |         ^ help: consider using `_i` instead
  |
  = note: #[warn(unused_variables)] on by default

   Finished dev [unoptimized + debuginfo] target(s) in 0.50s
```

The warning suggests that we use _i as a name instead: the underscore indicates that we intend for this variable to be unused. We can automatically apply that suggestion using the rustfix tool by running the command cargo fix:

```
$ cargo fix
    Checking myprogram v0.1.0 (file:///projects/myprogram)
      Fixing src/main.rs (1 fix)
    Finished dev [unoptimized + debuginfo] target(s) in 0.59s
```

When we look at *src/main.rs* again, we'll see that cargo fix has changed the code:

src/main.rs
```
fn do_something() {}

fn main() {
    for _i in 0..100 {
```

```
        do_something();
    }
}
```

The for loop variable is now named _i, and the warning no longer appears.

You can also use the cargo fix command to transition your code between different Rust editions. Editions are covered in Appendix E.

More Lints with Clippy

The Clippy tool is a collection of lints to analyze your code so you can catch common mistakes and improve your Rust code. Clippy is included with standard Rust installations.

To run Clippy's lints on any Cargo project, enter the following:

```
$ cargo clippy
```

For example, say you write a program that uses an approximation of a mathematical constant, such as pi, as this program does:

src/main.rs
```
fn main() {
    let x = 3.1415;
    let r = 8.0;
    println!("the area of the circle is {}", x * r * r);
}
```

Running cargo clippy on this project results in this error:

```
error: approximate value of `f{32, 64}::consts::PI` found
  --> src/main.rs:2:13
   |
 2 |     let x = 3.1415;
   |             ^^^^^^
   |
   = note: `#[deny(clippy::approx_constant)]` on by default
   = help: consider using the constant directly
   = help: for further information visit https://rust-lang.github.io/rust-
clippy/master/index.html#approx_constant
```

This error lets you know that Rust already has a more precise PI constant defined, and that your program would be more correct if you used the constant instead. You would then change your code to use the PI constant. The following code doesn't result in any errors or warnings from Clippy:

src/main.rs
```
fn main() {
    let x = std::f64::consts::PI;
    let r = 8.0;
    println!("the area of the circle is {}", x * r * r);
}
```

For more information on Clippy, see its documentation at *https://github .com/rust-lang/rust-clippy*.

IDE Integration Using rust-analyzer

To help with IDE integration, the Rust community recommends using rust-analyzer. This tool is a set of compiler-centric utilities that speak Language Server Protocol, which is a specification for IDEs and programming languages to communicate with each other. Different clients can use rust-analyzer, such as the Rust analyzer plug-in for Visual Studio Code at *https://marketplace.visualstudio.com/items?itemName=rust-lang.rust-analyzer*.

Visit the rust-analyzer project's home page at *https://rust-analyzer.github.io* for installation instructions, then install the language server support in your particular IDE. Your IDE will gain capabilities such as autocompletion, jump to definition, and inline errors.

E

EDITIONS

In Chapter 1, you saw that `cargo new` adds a bit of metadata to your *Cargo.toml* file about an edition. This appendix talks about what that means!

The Rust language and compiler have a six-week release cycle, meaning users get a constant stream of new features. Other programming languages release larger changes less often; Rust releases smaller updates more frequently. After a while, all of these tiny changes add up. But from release to release, it can be difficult to look back and say, "Wow, between Rust 1.10 and Rust 1.31, Rust has changed a lot!"

Every two or three years, the Rust team produces a new Rust *edition*. Each edition brings together the features that have landed into a clear package with fully updated documentation and tooling. New editions ship as part of the usual six-week release process.

Editions serve different purposes for different people:

- For active Rust users, a new edition brings together incremental changes into an easy-to-understand package.
- For non-users, a new edition signals that some major advancements have landed, which might make Rust worth another look.
- For those developing Rust, a new edition provides a rallying point for the project as a whole.

At the time of this writing, three Rust editions are available: Rust 2015, Rust 2018, and Rust 2021. This book is written using Rust 2021 edition idioms.

The edition key in *Cargo.toml* indicates which edition the compiler should use for your code. If the key doesn't exist, Rust uses 2015 as the edition value for backward compatibility reasons.

Each project can opt in to an edition other than the default 2015 edition. Editions can contain incompatible changes, such as including a new keyword that conflicts with identifiers in code. However, unless you opt in to those changes, your code will continue to compile even as you upgrade the Rust compiler version you use.

All Rust compiler versions support any edition that existed prior to that compiler's release, and they can link crates of any supported editions together. Edition changes only affect the way the compiler initially parses code. Therefore, if you're using Rust 2015 and one of your dependencies uses Rust 2018, your project will compile and be able to use that dependency. The opposite situation, where your project uses Rust 2018 and a dependency uses Rust 2015, works as well.

To be clear: most features will be available on all editions. Developers using any Rust edition will continue to see improvements as new stable releases are made. However, in some cases, mainly when new keywords are added, some new features might only be available in later editions. You will need to switch editions if you want to take advantage of such features.

For more details, see *The Edition Guide* at *https://doc.rust-lang.org/stable/ edition-guide.* This is a complete book that enumerates the differences between editions and explains how to automatically upgrade your code to a new edition via cargo fix.

INDEX

API (application programming
    interface), 4, 300–303
application binary interface, 427
Arc<T> type, 370–373, 482–484
arguments, 44
arms
    in if expressions, 50
    in match expressions, 24, 111–112
array data type, 41–43
    accessing elements of, 42
    invalid element access, 42–43
    iterating over elements of, 57–58
    slices of, 83
arrow (->), 47, 500
as_bytes method, 77
as keyword, 135
assert_eq! macro, 222–224
assert! macro, 219–222
assert_ne! macro, 224
associated function, 16, 101
associated types, 430–431
associative array. *See* HashMap<K, V> type
asterisk (*), 500
    dereference operator, 71,
        321–327, 422
    glob operator, 138
    multiplication operator, 39
atomically reference counted, 370–373
at operator (@), 417–418, 501
attribute-like procedural macros, 457
automatic dereferencing, 99
automatic referencing, 99

B

back of house, 123
backtrace, 163–165
backward-compatibility guarantees, xxiii
binary crate, 19, 121, 129, 241, 249
binary literal syntax, 37
binary target, 312
blanket implementations, 200–201
blocking, 357, 363, 368
Boolean data type, 39
borrow checker, 202–209
borrowing, 71–77
Box<T> type, 316–327
break keyword, 28, 54

buffer overread, 163
byte literal syntax, 37, 78, 502

C

Cargo, xxvi, 7–11
    commands
        build, 9–10
        check, 10
        clippy, 513
        doc, 23, 297–299
        fix, 512–513
        fmt, 511–512
        install, 312–313
        login, 304
        new, 8–9, 14, 121, 124
        publish, 297–306
        run, 10, 309
        test, 217–218, 230–236,
            298–299, 311
        update, 21
        yank, 306
    extending with custom
        commands, 313
    workspaces, 307–312
Cargo.lock, 9–10, 21–22, 309–310
Cargo.toml, 8–9, 19–22, 121
    dependencies section, 19–20
    package section, 304–305
    profile section, 296–297
    updating crate versions in, 21
carriage return, 465
cfg (configuration) attribute, 236–237
channels, 361–366, 480–486, 490–493
character data type, 40
checked_* methods, 38
child modules, 125, 127
client, 460
Clippy, 513
clone method
    deep copy creation, 67
    trade-offs of, 251
Clone trait, 509–510
closed channel, 361
closures, 274–284
    capturing the environment with,
        274–276, 278–280, 287–289
    moving ownership into, 279–280

deep copy, 509
Default trait, 510
default type parameters, 431–433
dependencies section in *Cargo.toml*, 9,
 19–20
dependency, 7, 11, 19–22
deref coercion, 150, 325–327
dereference operator, 71, 321–327
DerefMut trait, 326–327
Deref trait, 321–327, 440
derive annotation, 94–96, 452–457,
 507–510
description metadata, 305
destructor, 329
destructuring
 of enums, 409–410
 in patterns, 407–411
 of structs, 407–409, 410–411
 of tuples, 40–41, 411
Dickinson, Emily, 247
dictionary. *See* HashMap<K, V> type
Dijkstra, Edsger W., 215
Display trait, 94, 148, 200–201,
 437–439, 508
division operator (/), 39, 501
doc tests, 298–299
documentation
 comments, 297–299, 477
 offline for Rust, 4
 tests, 298–299
 viewing a crate's, 23
 writing, 297, 299
dot (.), 500
 for method syntax, 97–98
 for struct field access, 86–87
 for tuple element access, 41
double colon (::), 502–503
double free error, 66, 329
double quote ("), 40, 502
Doyle, Sir Arthur Conan, 293
drop function, 64, 329–330
Drop trait, 327–330, 487–493
dynamically sized type (DST), 444–446
dynamic dispatch, 384
dyn keyword, 257, 380

E

editions, xxiii, 9, 498, 513, 515–516
else if expression, 52
else keyword, 50
empty type, 443–444, 502
encapsulation, 119, 123, 376–378
entry method, 157–158
Entry type, 157–158
enumerate method, 78, 401
enums, 103–110
 defining, 103–104
 destructuring, 409–410
 initializer function, 447–448
 instantiating, 104–105
 making public, 131–132
 variants of, 104
environment, 274–276, 278–280, 287–289
environment variables, 265–270
eprintln! macro, 271–272
Eq trait, 508–509
error handling, 161–180
executable file, 6–7, 9
executing code, 6–7, 9
exit status code, 255
expect method, 17–18, 26, 169
expressions, 46–47
extern functions, 426–427

F

fearless concurrency, 354
FFI (Foreign Function Interface), 426
field init shorthand, 87–88
fields, 86
files, 247–248
 naming conventions, 5
 organization, 138–140
filtered-out tests, 233–235
Firefox web browser, xxvi
floating-point data types, 38–39
fn keyword, 15
FnMut trait, 280–281, 447, 475
FnOnce trait, 280–283, 447, 475–476
Fn trait, 280, 447, 475
fn type, 446–448
Foreign Function Interface, 426

for keyword
    loop, 57–58
        patterns in, 400–401
    in trait implementations, 194
format! macro, 150
from function
    on the From trait, 171
    on String, 63, 148
front of house, 123
fully qualified syntax, 433–437, 447
functional programming, 273–274
function-like procedural macros, 458
function pointers, 446–448
functions, 43–49
    arguments to, 44
    bodies, statements and expressions
        in, 46–47
    extern, 426–427
    vs. macros, 449
    making public, 128–129
    with multiple return values using
        a tuple, 70
    parameters of, 44–46
        patterns in, 402
    returning early from, 47
    with return values, 47–49

G

Gallant, Andrew, 244
Gamma, Erich, 376
garbage collector (GC), 59, 63
generics, 181–192, 213–214
    default types for, 431–433
    in enum definitions, 188–189
    in function definitions, 184–187
    in method definitions, 189–191
    performance of, 191–192
    in struct definitions, 187–188
get method
    on HashMap<K, V>, 155
    on Vec<T>, 143–145
getter methods, 99, 179
Git, 8, 11
global variables, 427–428
grapheme clusters, 152–154
grep, 243

guard, 367
guessing game, 13–30

H

hash. *See* HashMap<K, V> type
hasher, 158
hashing function, 158
HashMap<K, V> type, 154–158
    entry method on, 157–158
    get method on, 155
    insert method on, 154–157
    iterating over, 155–156
    new function on, 154–155
    and ownership, 156
    updating, 156–158
hash table. *See* HashMap<K, V> type
Hash trait, 510
heap
    allocating on, 60, 317
    and the stack, 60–61
Hello, World! program, 4–7
Helm, Richard, 376
hexadecimal literal syntax, 37
Hoare, Tony, 108
HTTP (Hypertext Transfer Protocol),
    460, 464–466
hyphen (-)
    for negation, 500
    for subtraction, 39, 500

I

IDE (integrated development
    environment), xxvi, 4, 514
if keyword, 50–54
if let syntax, 116–117
    patterns in, 399–400
ignore attribute, 235–236
immutability. *See* mutability
impl keyword
    for defining associated
        functions, 101
    for defining methods, 97–101
    for implementing traits, 194
impl Trait syntax, 197–200
indexing syntax, 143–145
indirection, 320–321
inheritance, 378–379

module system, 120

module tree, 124–125

monomorphization, 191–192

move keyword, 279–280, 358–361

moving ownership, 64–67

    vs. borrowing, 71–72

    with function calls, 68–69

    with function return values, 69–70

multiple producer, single consumer (mpsc), 362, 365–366

multiple trait bound syntax (+), 198, 500

multiplication, 39

mutability

    of references, 73–75

    of variables, 32–33

Mutex<T> type, 367–373, 482–484, 485–487

mut keyword

    making a reference mutable with, 73–75

    making a variable mutable with, 33

    vs. shadowing, 35–36

*mut T, 421–423, 500

mutual exclusion, 367

N

namespace, 63, 101, 104

never type (!), 443–444, 502

new function

    on HashMap<K, V>, 154–155

    on String, 147–148

    on Vec<T>, 142

new project setup, using Cargo, 14

newtype pattern, 439–440

null, 108–110

numeric operations, 39

O

object. *See* HashMap<K, V> type

object-oriented programming (OOP), 375–396

octal literal syntax, 37

1:1 threading model, 355

open source developers, xxvii

operator overloading, 431–433

operators, 499–501

optimizations, 11

Option<T> enum, 108–110, 113–114

Ordering type, 24

Ord trait, 509

orphan rule, 195, 439

output lifetimes, 210

overflowing_* methods, 38

overflow of integers, 38

ownership, 59–83

    and functions, 68–70

    rules, 61

    of struct data, 90–91

P

package, 121

package registry, 297–306

package section in *Cargo.toml*, 304–305

panicking, 38

panic! macro, 162–165, 226–229

    vs. Result, 175–180

parallel programming, 353–354

parameters, 44

    patterns in, 402

parentheses (()), 504

    for function parameters, 6, 15

    for tuples, 40–41

parent modules, 125, 127

parse method, 26

PartialEq trait, 224, 508–509

PartialOrd trait, 187, 509

paths, 125–130

    absolute, 126

    nested, 137

    relative, 125–126

%PATH% system variable, 3, 312

patterns, 397–418

    binding to values with, 112–113

    destructuring in, 407–411

    in for loops, 400–401

    in function parameters, 402

    in if let syntax, 116–117, 399–400

    ignoring values in, 411–415

    in let statements, 401–402

    in match expressions, 110–116, 398–399

    refutable vs. irrefutable, 403–405

    in while let loops, 400

.pdb file extension, 7

pointer, 60, 315
    dangling, 75
    to data on the heap, 60–61
    raw, 421–423
    smart, 315–351
poisoned mutex, 485
polymorphism, 378–379
PowerShell, 3–4, 6–7, 269–270
prelude, 15, 138
println! macro, 6, 18–19
privacy, 123, 127–129
procedural macros, 451
    attribute-like, 457
    custom derive, 452–457
    function-like, 458
process, 354
proc_macro crate, 452, 454
profiles, 296–297
profile section in *Cargo.toml*, 296–297
propagating errors, 169–175
pub keyword, 122, 127–129
public, 127–129
    API, 129, 300–303
    making items, 128
    making structs and enums, 130
pub use, 135–136, 300–303
push method, 142
push_str method, 63, 149

Q

question mark operator (?), 171–175, 501
quote crate, 454–456

R

race conditions, 74, 355
RAII (Resource Acquisition Is
    Initialization), 64
rand crate, 19–23
random number functionality, 19, 22–23
range syntax, 406–407
Range type, 58
raw identifiers, 497–498
raw pointers, 421–423
Rc<T> type, 330–334, 342–351
read_line method, 17–18
receiver, 361–366

recoverable errors, 161–162, 165–175
recursive type, 317–321
re-export, 135–136, 300–303
RefCell<T> type, 334–351
reference counting, 315, 330–334,
    370–373
reference cycles, 343–351
references
    for accessing data from multiple
        places, 17
    and borrowing, 71–77
    dangling, 75–76
    dereferencing, 71
    mutability of, 73–75
    rules of, 77
refutable patterns, 403–405
registry, 20, 297–306
relative path, 125–126, 130
release mode, 11, 38
release profiles, 296–297
remainder operator (%), 39, 500
request line, 464–465
request-response protocol, 460
Resource Acquisition Is Initialization, 64
Result<T, E> type, 17–18, 165–175
    expect method on, 17–18, 169
    vs. panic!, 175–180
    type aliases for, 442–443
    unwrap method on, 168
    unwrap_or_else method on, 168
return keyword, 47
return values
    of functions, 47–49
    of loops, 55
    multiple using a tuple, 70
rev method, 58
ripgrep, 244, 312–313
RLS (Rust Language Server), xxvi
.rs file extension, 5
running code, 5–7, 9–10
Rustaceans, 3
rust-analyzer, 514
rustc, 3, 5–7
rustfix, 512–513
rustfmt, xxvi, 6, 511–512
Rust Language Server, xxvi
"The Rustonomicon," 145, 351, 374